# Multimedia and Image Management

**Susan E. L. Lake**
Former Technology Education Specialist
Lubbock-Cooper ISD
Lubbock, Texas

**Karen Bean**
Information Management Instructor
Blinn College
Former Teacher
Killeen Independent School District
Killeen, Texas

**THOMSON**

**SOUTH-WESTERN**

Australia · Canada · Mexico · Singapore · Spain · United Kingdom · United States

THOMSON
SOUTH-WESTERN

**Multimedia and Image Management**
Susan Lake and Karen Bean

**Vice President/Executive Publisher:**
Dave Shaut

**Team Leader:**
Karen Schmohe

**Acquisitions Editor:**
Jane Congdon

**Project Manager/Consulting Editor:**
A. W. Kingston

**Executive Marketing Manager:**
Carol Volz

**Marketing Manager:**
Mike Cloran

**Production Editor:**
Todd McCoy

**Production Manager:**
Patricia Matthews Boies

**Manufacturing Coordinator:**
Charlene Taylor

**Compositor:**
Lachina Publishing Services

**Printer:**
Quebecor World
Versailles, Kentucky

**Design Project Manager:**
Stacy Shirley

**Cover and Internal Designer:**
Robb & Associates

**Fee Writers:**
Sharon Massen
Thomas N. Lewis

**Review Coordinator:**
Karen Leahy

**Reviewers:**
Gary L. Schepf
Advanced & Applied Technology
   Studies Educator
The Academy of Irving ISD
Irving, Texas

Linda Mallinson
Business Educator
Orange County Public Schools
Orlando, Florida

For permission to use material from this text or product, contact us by
Tel (800) 730-2214
Fax (800) 730-2215
http://www.thomsonrights.com

For more information
contact South-Western,
5191 Natorp Boulevard,
Mason, Ohio 45040.
Or you can visit our Internet site at:
http://www.swlearning.com

# Enhance Learning with

# Multimedia and Image Management
## ACTIVITIES

There's no better way for students to gain an understanding of the material in a textbook than to have hands-on experience. ***Multimedia and Image Management Activities*** is a software-specific text/CD package that allows students to practice what they've learned, using commercial application programs. The CD included with each book contains data files necessary to complete the exercises.

Designed to follow the sequence of the ***Multimedia and Image Management*** textbook, the ***Activities*** book can be used in any class where multimedia software is being taught. To help students keep pace and to organize class time, each unit in ***Multimedia and Image Management Activities*** is divided into parts, with each part containing activities and mini-projects.

A sample part is located on page 346 of this text.

ISBN 0-538-43464-3

THOMSON
SOUTH-WESTERN

**Join us on the Internet at www.swlearning.com**

# Contents

# SPECIAL FEATURES IN MULTIMEDIA AND IMAGE MANAGEMENT

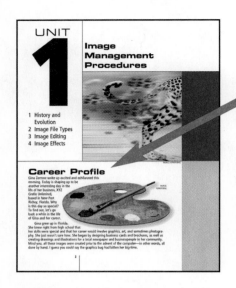

A **Career Profile** introduces each unit opener and demonstrates real-life applications of multimedia skills to be learned.

**Objectives**, listed at the beginning of each chapter, summarize what students will learn throughout the chapter.

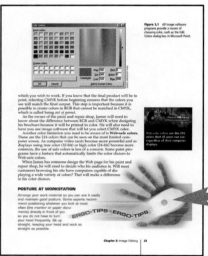

An **Ethics** feature in each chapter gives examples of particular rights and moral issues pertaining to the chapter topic.

**Ergo-Tips** offers posture reminders and keying drills to help students develop and sustain good work habits.

**Key Terms** in the margins throughout the chapter assist students in learning new terminology.

**Good Business** sections offer tips on business practices and skills.

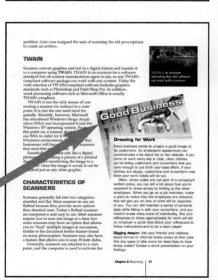

# SPECIAL FEATURES IN MULTIMEDIA AND IMAGE MANAGEMENT

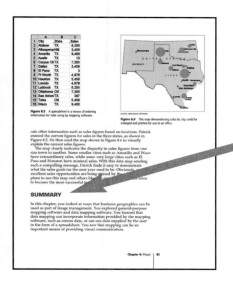

**Review** provides a full list of questions and activities for the student to complete at the end of each chapter.

A **Summary** at the end of each chapter gives a recap of what has been covered.

**Discussion** section at the end of the chapter provides essay questions pertaining to what students have learned.

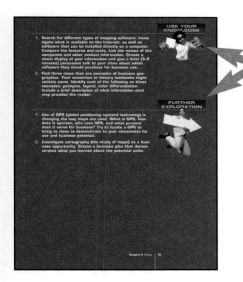

**Use Your Knowledge** and **Further Exploration** provide additional hands-on activities for students to complete.

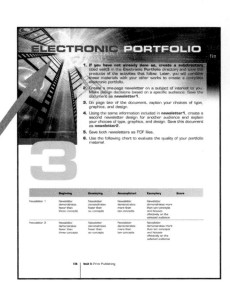

An ongoing **Electronic Portfolio** is featured throughout the text. At the end of each unit, students add to the portfolio as new skills are learned.

# Preface

## TO THE TEACHER

Long ago educators had certain expectations. We knew what concepts students had to master to succeed in the career of their choice. We used textbooks that reinforced the knowledge we already had.

Then our lives changed. Computers took over. We had to teach new things for which we had no preparation. So, we used books that taught the topics we did not know. The books provided us with a way to teach skills such as how to open and save a file, how to change a font, how to insert an image, and how to mail merge a series of addresses.

The books we used looked more like cookbooks than textbooks. One could almost imagine the list of ingredients, followed by the steps, and then the instructions to bake at 350 degrees for 45 minutes for a perfect newsletter. The skills our students acquired with these recipes made it possible for them to learn to use a computer and specific software. We were satisfied that we were meeting the needs of our students.

However, along the way we lost something. We lost the idea that we should teach concepts and not just skills. We lost this idea because we were so inundated with the need to learn new and unfamiliar skills that we had no time to worry about concepts. We did what we had to do.

But the world has changed again. We now know how to make text bold, how to add a table to a document, and how to create a bulleted list. Our cookbooks are still useful, but they should no longer be our only instructional choice.

In today's world, we must teach students a whole new set of concepts. For example, in a business multimedia class, we must address the qualities of a good digital photograph not just how to take a digital photograph. We must discuss what constitutes a professional PowerPoint design not just how to add images to a slide show. We must address issues such as what typography can do for a sales proposal instead of limiting our instruction to ways of changing fonts.

As a result, our task has become even more challenging. Instead of relying on cookbook textbooks alone, now we must choose books and materials that respond to this new set of needs. So, as you are previewing this textbook, look for the concepts. You will notice that this book is not a series of recipes. Instead, it is designed to prepare your students for all the changes they are to encounter in their careers. With this book, once again we can begin to feel that we are meeting all of the needs of our students.

## TO THE STUDENT

Multimedia and image management is not about learning everything there is to know about creating graphics, Web pages, and PowerPoint presentations. Each of these tasks alone would be enough to fill at least a semester or more. Instead this textbook is about learning what concepts drive this field. So, when you enter the world of business, you can understand the jargon, know what expectations are reasonable, and direct in a knowledgeable manner those who do create complex image management tasks.

The course material consists of two resources: the student text and the activities manual. These two resources may be used together, or they may be used independently of one another. The textbook is software independent and is designed to last through many changes of software. The separate activities manual is software specific focusing primarily on products from Microsoft, Jasc, Macromedia, and Adobe.

In the text, you will learn about such things as what a rollover is and what it should be able to do. You will learn what happens when large graphic files are added to a print document. You will understand the difference between a CMYK format and an RGB one. You will also fully explore what features are available in PowerPoint. In addition, you will develop a keen sense of what is appropriate in a business-oriented desktop published document. All these concepts, as well as many others, are addressed in the student textbook.

The activities manual is designed to lead you through a series of tasks to help you understand and apply the concepts developed in the textbook. In the activities book, you will build simple rollovers, measure graphic file sizes, and experiment with CMYK and RGB graphics. You will build basic web pages and desktop-published documents. You will explore the options to be found in PowerPoint. The activities will not replace a text devoted to a single piece of software. Instead, it will help you become familiar with the basic functions of a number of software applications and their potential use in the business world. The intention of the activities manual is not for you to become an "expert" in any of the software programs. Other courses will meet that need.

If you should decide to pursue a career focusing on one or more fields related to image management, you should find that this course has provided a good foundation. You will have acquired both the concepts and the skills that will make it easier for you to pursue an in-depth study of your area of interest.

## HOW TO USE THIS BOOK

There are a number of ways that the student text and the activity book can be used in a classroom. One way to is teach a single chapter from the student text, then have students study one of the relevant software programs from the activities manual. If you only have limited software, you might want to complete all four chapters of a given unit and then move on to one of the software packages that you do have The electronic portfolio at the end of each unit is designed to reinforce and integrate everything the student has learned in both the text and the activities book, so it should be completed after both have been studied.

The student text contains a number of features designed to meet your instructional needs. Each unit opens with a career profile of an actual person engaged in multimedia work. Each chapter contains clear objectives and an estimated time of completion. Within each chapter there are two features—one on good business and one on business ethics. Some chapters include an additional feature called Ergo-Tips. Chapters contain call outs of the terms discussed within the body of the text. The end of chapter materials include short answer review questions, open-ended discussion questions, use-your-knowledge activities, and further exploration material to engage students. The end-of-unit material includes a unit summary and a compilation of terms. As a culminating unit activity, there is an electronic portfolio assignment designed to provide material for an end-of-course portfolio.

In addition to the student text and the activities manual, the complete instructional program includes two CDs: one for the Instructor and one for the student. The Instructor's Resource CD (IRCD) includes a number of resources such as reviews and quizzes to accompany the student text and solutions to the activities in the activities manual. The student CD contains such things as electronic versions of the reviews and quizzes and templates for the various activities in the activity manual.

## FROM THE AUTHORS

We are delighted that you are using our book. We have labored long and hard to make it interesting, complete, and useful. If we succeed in our goal of introducing students to the delight of multimedia, our task will be complete.

## ABOUT THE AUTHORS

**Susan Lake** conducts professional development workshops for educators who want to increase their use of multimedia technology in the classroom. She has taught a range of students from junior high through adults, with 23 years of experience at the high school level in Lubbock, Texas. Susan has shared her experiences at local, state, and national educational conferences. She is the author of several South-Western titles, including *Windows Multimedia Tools, E-Mail in 10 Hours, Desktop Publishing,* and *Getting Organized with Outlook.*

**Karen Bean** is an instructor in the Information Management Department at Blinn College, Brenham, Texas. She has taught Business Education at the high school and community college levels for 27 years. Ms. Bean earned her Bachelor of Business Education degree from the University of Mary Hardin-Baylor in Belton, Texas. She has presented at numerous conferences and has written four curriculum frameworks for Texas high schools. She is a current adviser for Students in Free Enterprise (SIFE) and a past Future Business Leaders of America adviser (FBLA).

# Multimedia
## and Image
# Management

# UNIT 1

# Image Management Procedures

SOURCE: ©PHOTODISC

## Career Profile

Gina Zornow woke up excited and exhilarated this morning. Today is shaping up to be another interesting day in the life of her business, XYZ Grafix Unlimited, based in New Port Richey, Florida. Why is this day so special? To find out, let's go back a while in the life of Gina and her career.

SOURCE: ©PHOTODISC

Gina grew up in Florida. She knew right from high school that her skills were special and that her career would involve graphics, art, and sometimes photography. She just wasn't sure how. She began by designing business cards and brochures, as well as creating drawings and illustrations for a local newspaper and businesspeople in her community. Mind you, all these images were created prior to the advent of the computer—in other words, all done by hand. I guess you could say the graphics bug had bitten her big-time.

(continued)

Gina then attended a technical school and earned a bachelor's degree in technical illustration. GTE discovered her talents and hired her as part of its team of drafters, designers, and artists. While working at GTE, she discovered the computer and all the wonderful things it could do for her. Twenty-seven years later, she retired. Gina now has her own computer-based commercial art, graphics, and design business. She specializes in digital graphics and illustration and uses many software programs—Adobe Photoshop, CorelDraw, Bryce, Poser, Kai's Power Tools, and Corel Photo-Paint, to name a few. Gina has become an expert in all these applications, primarily using Bryce (for real-world imaging) and Poser (for creating people and other creatures). A word she uses daily is *morphing*, a way of manipulating images of objects and people to suit the idea and theme of the concept she is trying to market.

All these programs can become your friends just as they are Gina's. So, why is today a special day for Gina? She is working on an exciting project for yet another company. Her computer is on, it's whizzing and clicking, and the graphics are beginning to come to life. You, too, can do the same as Gina. All these concepts will be yours after you have completed this course in multimedia. ■

Note: Gina Zornow is a real person and her business, XYZ Grafix Unlimited, based in New Port Richey, Florida, is a real business.

ESTIMATED TIME

**2**

H O U R S

# Chapter 1
# History and Evolution

SOURCE: ©PHOTODISC

## Objectives

- *You will understand the changes in the evolution of image management.*
- *You will identify the changes in production techniques for image management.*
- *You will know the terms related to the history of image management.*

## INTRODUCTION

Multimedia and image management is a new field that has emerged in the last few years as a direct result of the growth of computer use in the business world. These new powerful technology tools provide businesses with a means to communicate in ways they could never have done in an earlier age. Congratulations—you are at the forefront of a growing, exciting field of study that promises to provide you with opportunities we can hardly imagine today. Before beginning the study of this new area, it is important for you to understand the three basic concepts of multimedia, image management, and graphics.

**Multimedia** is a broad term that applies to the integration of text, graphics, sound, video, and animation into a document such as a letter, brochure, newsletter, Web page, or presentation. It is not necessary for a document to contain all forms of media in order to be considered multimedia. Use of text and graphics in a flyer is multimedia, as is a Web page that contains all five forms. As soon as you add an image to a text page, you have begun to create multimedia.

**Image management** is a more narrow term that applies to the use of graphics in documents. It encompasses every aspect of graphics from the creation to the final product whether in print or in some other medium. Image management requires you to make decisions such as the size of files, the number and type of colors used, and what format is most appropriate.

**Graphics** can be defined as everything on the page that is not actual textual content from simple line drawings to fully active images found on Web (World Wide Web [WWW]) pages. Graphics can also include elements such as the appearance of the type, including its size, shape, and appearance.

Multimedia and image management choices communicate a message, and the success of a business often depends on the effectiveness of this message. Your task in this course is to learn how to select, create, and use these choices in a way that sends the message you want, and the place to start learning is at the beginning. During the last 20 years, multimedia has changed dramatically, moving from static print to interactive media. A look at two scenes makes these changes clear.

# IMAGE MANAGEMENT YESTERDAY AND TODAY

Imagine you are the owner of a small business selling handmade wreaths at Christmas. You want to expand from a seasonal to a year-round business, so you design a flyer to mail to your current customers. To create your flyer, you must draw your ideas crudely on paper and take it to a printer who will create your ad. The first draft requires two weeks to complete, and you must return several times to check for accuracy and approve the artwork. Each change requires another week to complete and when the product is ready, the cost is several thousand dollars. If you decide to do

## Career Advancement

Students are often so focused on getting that first "real job" that they forget to think clearly about their future employment. What kind of job do you want in five years? Ten years? Successful workers rarely stay in the same job their entire careers. It is therefore important to have a career goal in mind and move toward it. Take classes and employment that will help you gain the skills you will need in the future. Jobs can be like stepping stones, each one leading to the final prize.

The skills you learn in entry-level jobs can serve as a foundation as you advance your career. The more you know about (and appreciate) the "less glamorous" jobs, the better able you will be to function in higher-level positions. For example, an effective art director must schedule tasks so that all the work can be done in a timely manner. If that director has firsthand experience scanning photos or preparing a design layout, he or she will be able to prepare more accurate schedules.

**Digging Deeper:** Use the library or the Internet to trace a career path to your ultimate job goal. Which jobs and tasks will you need to master as you advance in your career? (For example, graphic designers often begin their careers as production artists.) Create a chart or graph that illustrates this career path.

a second version, the time and cost are nearly as much as the original. You want to expand your Christmas trade to other parts of the country, but it is cost-prohibitive. Your only choices are direct mailings and newspaper, radio, or television ads in each market area. None of these are possible for your small business.

In 1980, that was the scene.

Imagine today. You create a flyer on a personal computer in an hour by using as artwork actual photographs of your new wreaths. You print your proof copy in color and make any changes in seconds. You create two versions: one for current customers and one for customers you hope to attract. This information appears the same day on your Web page for access across the world. In addition, you use the information to create a PowerPoint presentation for use by the chamber of commerce. The cost for all three types of documents is minimal. Sales begin to increase immediately.

## THE **ETHICS** OF COPYRIGHT

With the movement to desktop publishing and Web pages, the issue of copyright has become a greater problem for businesses. Images created by others are easily obtainable for use on documents of every type. In the past, the use of these graphics was limited to "cutouts" from other sources, but that is no longer the case. Fine-quality work can be integrated easily, making copyright violations more frequent. It is important for businesses today to be aware of these issues and to guard against such infringements on the rights of others.

SOURCE: ©PHOTODISC

## DESKTOP PUBLISHING

This story of change began even before the introduction of the personal computer. It began with the IBM Selectric (1961) and its "golf ball" print head (see Figures 1.1 and 1.2) that allowed users for the first time to change with ease the type style of their text. Before the Selectric, typewriters were of two types: elite (12 characters per inch) and pica (10 characters per inch). Whatever style your typewriter came with was the style in which you created text. Adding graphics to a document required gluing the image onto an already typed page.

With the advent of the Apple Macintosh computer and the ImageWriter printer in 1984 (see Figures 1.3 and 1.4), suddenly it was possible to choose not only font style but also size and attribute. Graphics could be added digitally to a document. Printing in landscape or portrait became an easy option. With MacPaint and MacDraw, artwork could be created and modified with ease. An early scanner that

**Figure 1.1**  The IBM Selectric typewriter introduced the era of desktop publishing.

**Figure 1.2**  The design of the Selectric "golf ball" element provided options in font sizes and styles.

**Figure 1.3**  The introduction of the Macintosh computer and its graphical user interface and graphical software opened the way to a whole new world of image management.

**Figure 1.4**  The Apple ImageWriter printer made it possible to print more than just text.

replaced the ribbon in the ImageWriter even made it possible to transfer an image directly to the computer.

The next step in image management came with the introduction of Aldus PageMaker (1985), which made possible desktop publishing as we know it today. This software made it simple to move text and graphics around on a page and even to create columns with justified text.

## PRINTING

The first printers attached to personal computers were **dot matrix** printers, also called impact printers. The impact of the print head on the ink ribbon created a series of "dots" that formed letters, as shown

Dot matrix is a means of printing by placing a series of dots close together so that they give the appearance of printed letters.

PostScript **is a programming language that describes the appearance of images or text on the printed page.**

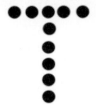

**Figure 1.5** Dot matrix printers use a series of dots to reproduce letters and images on a page.

**Figure 1.6** Laser printing uses toner much as a photocopier does to produce copies, which results in a smooth line.

in Figure 1.5. These printers were slow and noisy, and the quality of the printout was often not professional enough for use by businesses.

With the introduction of the Apple LaserWriter printer (1985) and Adobe PostScript, desktop publishing became a reality. **PostScript** removed the "jaggies" seen in dot matrix printouts. Now a professional-looking document could be printed on the LaserWriter quickly, quietly, and in business quality. Figure 1.6 provides an example of laser printing.

Although laser printers provided excellent black-and-white printouts, they lacked the ability to print in color. The movement to color ink-jet printers such as the Hewlett-Packard DeskJet (1991) made color printouts affordable and attractive. Recently, the drop in prices for color laser printers has begun to make changes even in this area.

## GRAPHICS

Early graphics software applications such as MacPaint and MacDraw were quickly replaced with products such as CorelDraw (1989) and Adobe Photoshop (1990). These newer software programs increased the user's ability to fine-tune artwork and to create renderings that had never been possible in the world of paint and pen.

Graphic development has not been limited to the personal computer user. The development of digital imaging software and technology was begun primarily by the U.S. Department of Defense in the use of spy satellites. In the world of moviemaking, companies such as Industrial Light & Magic have taken graphics technology to even higher standards, using it to create astonishingly vivid images and special effects. Photoshop itself came about partly because of the movie *Star Wars*.

# HARDWARE ADVANCEMENTS

Another step in image management was the introduction of affordable flatbed scanners such as the Hewlett-Packard ScanJet (1991). Scanners like the modern one shown in Figure 1.7 helped bring these advancements within reach of businesses. As **OCR** (optical character recognition) improved, it became possible with scanners to transfer previously typed text to a computer with enough accuracy to eliminate the need to rekey text.

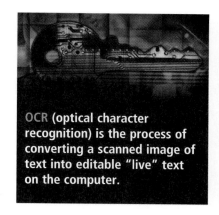

OCR (optical character recognition) is the process of converting a scanned image of text into editable "live" text on the computer.

A major barrier to desktop publishing was limited computer storage space and the need to transfer large files to other computers. Text files fit easily on a floppy disk, but files with graphics and extensive formatting soon became too large to transfer using the previous medium. The Iomega Zip drive (1995) provided one answer (see Figure 1.8). As hard drives have continued to increase in storage capacity and become less expensive, and with the addition of writable CD-ROM drives (as well as writable DVD drives), the storage problem has become less of an issue.

Digital cameras such as the Sony Mavica (1997) shown in Figure 1.9 moved graphics choices from clip art to actual photographs. Early digital cameras were expensive and limited in resolution, but newer digital cameras are quickly reaching the point of providing the equivalent of 35-mm quality. Video camera improvements were just as dramatic, and with the increase in Internet speeds, more video is appearing on Web pages.

SOURCE: ©KPS PHOTOGRAPH

**Figure 1.7**  Scanners transfer printed images into digital images by using light technology.

**Figure 1.8**  The Iomega Zip drive provided a medium to transfer large files from one computer to another.

# WEB PAGES

The addition of *modems,* which allow one computer to communicate to another, made the Internet a significant business tool requiring extensive knowledge of image management. An external modem is pictured in Figure 1.10. Later, **Web browsers** such as Mosaic

**Figure 1.9**  Digital cameras opened the world of photography, making it possible to create images directly without having to begin with a print copy.

**Figure 1.10**  A modem allows one computer to talk with another, creating a network.

A **Web browser** is a software program that allows you to view Web pages created for the Internet.

**Figure 1.11** A good-quality projector is an essential part of the presentation process.

(1992) and Netscape (1994) made it easy for anyone to view the Internet, thus creating a global market accessible to many. As users moved to faster dial-up connections and to broadband, the advertising and information potential moved with it. The Web equivalent of desktop publishing initially required use of *HTML* (Hypertext Markup Language) code. The introduction of software programs such as Netscape Communicator made it possible to manage text, graphics, and sound with ease. In addition, programs such as Macromedia Flash added animation to static pages.

# PRESENTATIONS

Running parallel to the growth of Web pages has been the development of presentation software. Programs such as Microsoft PowerPoint (1987) made it possible to create business documents that provide information in a colorful, interactive, and dramatic format. With the drop in price for projectors such as the one shown in Figure 1.11 and the improvement in light technology such as *DLP* (digital light processing), presentation software continues to grow as an affordable means of conveying information using images and multimedia. DLP is a means of projection developed by Texas Instruments that uses a series of tiny mirrors to reflect an image on a screen.

The following timeline gives an overview of the events and changes in image management over the last four decades. Other events will continue to affect the world of image management. The chapters that follow will provide you with the skills you will need to be an important part of the process.

# SUMMARY

In this chapter, you have seen the evolution of image management, which included the areas of desktop publishing, printing, graphics, hardware advancements, Web pages, and presentation. You have seen a variety of terms explained, such as *graphics, dot matrix, PostScript, optical character recognition, modem,* and *DLP.* With this knowledge, you are ready to move on to learning about images themselves.

**1961** IBM Selectric typewriter and interchangeable typeface

**1981** Hayes 300 bps modem

**1984** Apple Macintosh computer and ImageWriter printer
Apple MacPaint and MacDraw

**1985** Aldus PageMaker
Apple LaserWriter printer and Adobe PostScript

**1987** Microsoft PowerPoint

**1989** CorelDraw

**1990** Adobe Photoshop

**1991** Hewlett-Packard color DeskJet printer
Hewlett-Packard ScanJet printer

**1993** NCSA Mosaic

**1994** Netscape Navigator

**1995** Iomega Zip drive

**1997** Sony Mavica digital camera

Answer the following questions on your own computer.

1. What are graphics?
2. What is image management?
3. In 1980, what problems did small businesses face in the creation of ads?
4. What invention allowed the user for the first time to change the typestyle of text?
5. How were graphics added to a document before the introduction of the personal computer?
6. In what year did it become possible to add graphics digitally to a document, and what computer made it happen?
7. What were the two earliest graphics programs?
8. What program first made it simple to move text and graphics around on a page?
9. What printer and software removed jagged edges and created professional-looking documents?
10. What company introduced an early color printer?
11. What two programs first offered advanced graphics options that allowed the fine-tuning of artwork?
12. What does OCR let the user do, and why is it useful?
13. What problems did desktop publishing documents create for computer users?
14. Give an example of an early digital camera.
15. Name two early Web browsers and explain how they affected businesses.

**DISCUSSION**

1. Discuss the process that made advertising cost-prohibitive at one time.
2. What was the impact of scanners on document editing and storage?
3. How have modems affected business today.

## USE YOUR KNOWLEDGE

1. Select one event from the timeline given in the chapter (make sure each event is selected by someone in the class). Research the event and then list details not included in the text. Include appropriate images to support the details. Present each event to the class in the order in which it occurred. Create a visual timeline in your class by using the materials your class has prepared.

2. Visit http://lcweb.loc.gov/copyright/ to find information on the Digital Millennium Copyright Act. List the details that are important for multimedia and image management. As a class, compile the details and add this event to the class timeline project.

## FURTHER EXPLORATION

Writing history is a complicated process that requires one to make a series of decisions based upon criteria established by the author. The criteria may not be apparent to the reader of the history and that same reader may not be aware that many events will be deleted from the history because they failed to meet the requirements established by the author.

1. Imagine that you are author of this chapter on the evolution of multimedia and image management. What criteria would you establish in your choice of events to include?

2. Using one or more of the sites provided by your instructor or ones you locate yourself, decide which events would you include if you were writing this chapter. Use your criteria to make the selections.

3. Use your choices to create your own timeline.

# **Chapter 2**
## Image File Types

ESTIMATED TIME

**3**

H O U R S

SOURCE: ©PHOTODISC

## INTRODUCTION

Whether a finished project is in a visual or printed format, its impact is only as good as the image it produces. Many factors go into determining how best to produce the image you need. In this chapter, you will explore some of these factors and learn to make decisions that will help you in selecting the best possible image format for your projects.

This knowledge is essential for Amelia Sandefer, who must be able to make file format decisions in her job as an insurance investigator. She visits homes that have been damaged or destroyed by accidents and uses a digital camera to record what she finds. She must also create simple drawings of her findings to attach to her reports for others to read. Since she only has a modem rather than a high-speed Internet connection, she must keep her file sizes small to speed transmission.

## Objectives

- *You will become familiar with terms related to image file types.*
- *You will understand the difference between painting and drawing programs.*
- *You will understand the difference among file types.*
- *You will identify advantages and disadvantages of file types.*

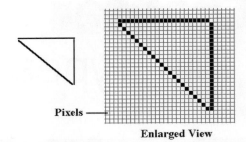

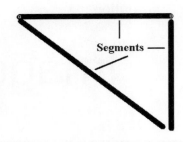

**Figure 2.1** Bitmap images are the most common file format used in image management.

**Figure 2.2** Vector images are smoother than bitmaps and print without jagged edges.

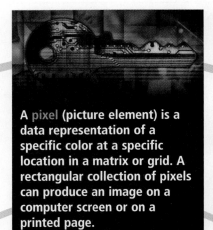

A pixel (picture element) is a data representation of a specific color at a specific location in a matrix or grid. A rectangular collection of pixels can produce an image on a computer screen or on a printed page.

# PAINTING VERSUS DRAWING

Many software programs are available for creating and managing images. Programs often used by businesses are Microsoft Paint, Adobe Photoshop, Macromedia Fireworks, Jasc Paint Shop Pro, Adobe Illustrator, and Macromedia FreeHand.

Image management programs are of two types: painting and drawing. Paint programs create images by using **pixels** (picture elements). Pixels are small squares (usually) with each pixel assigned a color (see Figure 2.1). Drawing programs create images by using mathematically defined lines and curves that are treated as individual objects within the images (see Figure 2.2).

Although paint programs are often easier to use, drawing programs give higher-quality results. Some image management programs such as Photoshop and Paint Shop Pro combine both painting and drawing options within a single program.

# IMAGE FORMATS OR FILE TYPES

Image programs save graphics with specific extensions indicating the file format. The extension is shown by two to four letters following the dot in the name of a file. For example, if a document is named **picture.jpg,** "picture" is the name of the file and ".jpg" is the extension indicating the file format.

You may not be able to see the extension name unless you have

## THE **ETHICS** OF GIF LICENSE

In 1994, CompuServe Inc., and Unisys Corporation, the developers of the GIF file format, announced their intention to require that all commercial software companies using GIF compression in their programs pay licensing fees. This announcement caused a considerable stir and resulted in the development of PNG file formats that were royalty-free. The average business user is unaware that a licensing fee is required because it is paid by the software company. It is a good reminder, however, that not only are software programs protected by copyright but so are the products created using those programs.

enabled this option in the Folder View. Go to My Computer and open the C: drive. Choose View/Tools (depending on your operating system), Folder Options and click the View tab > as shown in Figure 2.3. Remove the check from Hide file extensions for known file types check box. (It is also possible to show or hide file extensions in Mac OS X.)

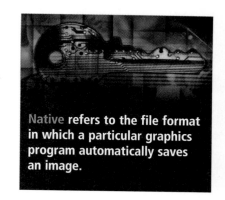

**Native** refers to the file format in which a particular graphics program automatically saves an image.

Each image management program has a file format specific to that program, called its **native** or default format. For instance, Paint Shop Pro automatically saves images as .psp. Adobe Photoshop saves images as .psd. Generally, an image should be saved in its original or native format to use as an archive or backup of that image. By doing this, you can open, edit, and then save the image in a different format without losing any quality. This is an important step in the creation of an image.

Once a copy of the image has been saved in its native format, you can change to another file format by using the drop-down arrow next to the Format or Save as type box, as shown in Figure 2.4. From the list that appears, you can then choose the appropriate file format.

Different file formats are appropriate for different situations, so it is important to understand the distinctions between the various file formats. For example, some programs can only import graphics with specific file formats. Some images look better saved as one format over another, and some images need to be small in order to load quickly on the Internet. Knowledge of file formats enables you to make the best choice.

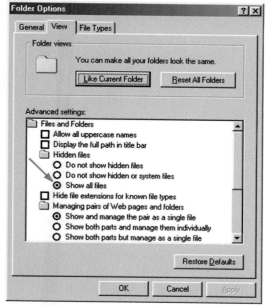

SOURCE: ©MICROSOFT WINDOWS 98

**Figure 2.3**  To see extensions, click on the radio button box indicated by the arrow.

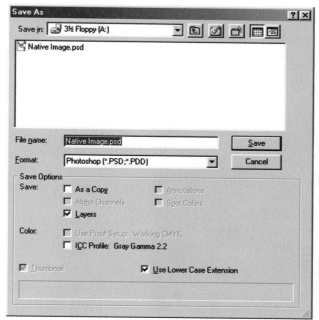

SOURCE: ©MICROSOFT WINDOWS 98

**Figure 2.4**  Once an image has been saved in native format, choose Save as and click on the drop-down arrow to select another format.

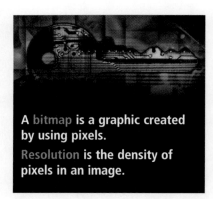

A bitmap is a graphic created by using pixels.

Resolution is the density of pixels in an image.

# PAINTING PROGRAMS

Painting programs (or paint programs) create **bitmap** images made of pixels. Each pixel has a defined color, size, and place in the image. The sharpness of the image is determined by the density of the pixels, and this density determines the **resolution.** *Resolution* is defined as dots per inch (dpi) or by the numbers of pixels in rows and columns (640 × 480). The higher the resolution, the better your image will appear or print out but the larger the file will be.

Amelia has learned that sometimes it is important to save her digital images in the highest possible resolution if she knows that others will want to print a large color version. She also knows that often all that is necessary is an image that can be printed on a black-and-white laser printer. For example, recently she needed an overall picture of a home that had been hit by a careless driver. She knew that a quick low-resolution shot of the damaged brick wall would serve her purpose. At the same time, though, she needed a detailed picture of the interior damage.

One of the most common types of bitmapped images is a *BMP* (Bitmap) file. A BMP image is usually used in word processing documents. BMP file sizes are often quite large, even though they are usually limited to 256 colors because they are not compressed as some other formats are. BMP files work well in programs that require the Microsoft Windows operating system.

A bitmap file type that works well in all environments is *TIF* or *TIFF* (Tagged Image File Format). Like BMP files, these files are quite large and are often used in print documents. TIFF files are not compressed and can show 16 million colors. Many scanners produce images as TIFF files, and some digital cameras can save photographs in TIFF format as well.

The file formats most often used for Web pages are *GIF* (Graphics Interchange Format) and *JPG* or *JPEG* (Joint Photographic Experts Group). GIF, pronounced with either a hard or soft "G," is an image file format developed by CompuServe. Because GIFs use only 256 colors, the file sizes are quite small. GIFs are used to create line drawings, images with transparent backgrounds, and animated figures. Because photographs require greater color depth, they lose much of their quality if they are saved as GIFs.

The time it takes to download a graphic on the Internet depends on the size of the file. To improve download speed, several *algorithms* (sequences of steps to perform a function) have been written to reduce or compress the size of the file. The two types of **compression** are lossless and lossy. **Lossless** compression reduces the file size without losing any pixel information. **Lossy** compression changes some pixels while making the file size smaller. The main drawback of a lossy algorithm is that the greater the compression, the poorer the quality of the image. In business image management, it becomes important to balance quality with file size.

GIF compression is lossless using the *LZW* (Lempel-Ziv-Welch) formula, named for the developers. The two versions are 87a and 89a. Most users find 89a to be the best choice because it allows transparency.

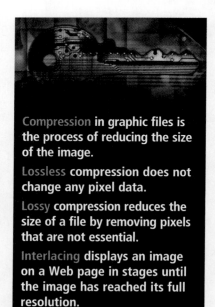

Compression in graphic files is the process of reducing the size of the image.

Lossless compression does not change any pixel data.

Lossy compression reduces the size of a file by removing pixels that are not essential.

Interlacing displays an image on a Web page in stages until the image has reached its full resolution.

Noninterlacing renders an image from top to bottom until the image is complete.

A second consideration when choosing a GIF is **interlaced** or **noninterlaced**. Interlaced images load onto a Web page in stages, with the first image appearing at a minimal resolution, so the viewer can begin to see part of the picture even before it is completely loaded. At intervals, the picture reloads until the maximum resolution is reached. Noninterlaced images build from the top down until a complete image appears. Interlacing slightly increases file size, so it should be limited to large images that take a long time to download. Both Photoshop and Paint Shop Pro provide version options and interlacing choices.

JPG or JPEG (pronounced "jay-peg") is another file type. Using up to 16 million colors, JPG images reproduce the quality, color, and detail found in photographs or graphics using blends and gradients. Most digital cameras save photographs as JPGs to conserve memory space on the camera's storage device.

The JPG compression formula allows you to choose the amount of compression you want, so you can decide at what point the image quality matches your needs. It also allows you to choose between standard and progressive encoding, much as with interlacing for GIFs.

A third choice for use on the Internet is the *PNG* (Portable Network Graphics) format. It retains all 16 million colors and has some valuable features, but it is not supported by all Web browsers.

Amelia has learned to save her images in TIFF format and then to convert them to the format that best serves her purpose. This way she knows that she can always return to the original and create a copy in a different format without losing quality. This came in quite handy last week when she was asked to submit a picture she had taken of a tornado-destroyed home. The corporate office wanted to use her picture in their publication and needed the highest quality possible. Her TIFF version met their needs and she was pleased to see her picture featured the following month.

# DRAWING PROGRAMS

Drawing programs create images made of mathematically defined lines and curves, or **vectors.** An advantage of vector graphics over bitmap images is that regardless of how much the image is enlarged or reduced (called

## Job Search Skills

The first step in finding the job that's right for you is to target specific jobs and careers. Decide what you want—not just now but five or ten years into the future. Have a career plan. One way to know what you want is to try out a wide range of jobs through part-time work, volunteering, and so forth. Then research potential employers that can offer you the kind of job or career you seek.

Perhaps the most important part of the job search involves simply talking with people. Tell everyone you meet you're in the job market; you might make an important contact. Develop a network of people who work in your field of interest. By critiquing your résumé and asking you questions about yourself and your goals, your contacts can help you sharpen your résumé and interviewing skills—key components in a successful job search. Be sure to send acknowledgment letters to everyone you talk with; this builds your credibility and sends the message that you're a professional who is serious about your career. Above all, be persistent!

**Digging Deeper:** Research some local multimedia-related companies and develop a list of people within the companies you might approach for a brief informational interview. Arrange and follow through with an interview. Discuss your impressions in class.

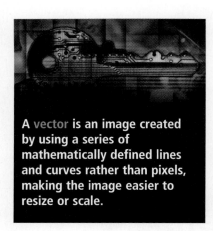

A **vector** is an image created by using a series of mathematically defined lines and curves rather than pixels, making the image easier to resize or scale.

*scaling*), the quality remains the same. A vector graphic is smoother than a bitmap graphic because the image is mathematically derived for each output device.

Once a vector graphic is completed, it can be converted to a bitmap image. (Another name for a bitmap is *raster*, so this process is called *rasterizing*.) Vector graphics are converted to bitmap images for use on the Internet. Shockwave Flash images and animations are vector graphics. Vector graphics are smaller in size than bitmaps, but they are limited because they cannot show gradations of colors as bitmaps can.

The most common native vector file formats are CDR for Corel-Draw, AI for Adobe Illustrator, FH for Macromedia FreeHand, SWF for Shockwave Flash, and WMF for Windows Metafile. *EPS* (Encapsulated PostScript) is a general-purpose vector file format that has both the vector image data and a screen preview in the same file. It is most commonly used for printing purposes.

Amelia finds drawing programs very helpful in her work. She uses a vector program to create sketches of the details that might be necessary to supplement her reports. She likes the fact that she can modify length and width of lines even after completing a drawing. In her last report, Amelia added a drawing showing the path of the automobile from the street to the wall of the home that was struck. She added details such as specific measurements and estimated speed of travel. These kinds of details have made her information well respected by her employer.

## SUMMARY

In this chapter, you have learned about file formats and their purposes as shown in the chart below. Image file types can be divided into two groups: painting programs and drawing programs. Extensions for the most common painting file formats are .bmp, .tif, .gif, .jpg, and .png. Extensions for the file formats used for the Web are .gif, .jpg, and .png. Extensions for the most common drawing file formats are .cdr, .ai, .fh, .swf, and .wmf. The EPS file format, with the extension .eps, is a general-purpose vector file with a bitmapped preview. It is important that you understand the difference between file formats so that you can decide which ones will best meet your needs.

| File Format | Acronym Stands for | Extension | Type of Program |
|---|---|---|---|
| BMP | Bitmap | .bmp | Painting |
| TIFF or TIF | Tagged Image File Format | .tif | Painting |
| GIF | Graphics Interchange Format | .gif | Painting |
| JPG or JPEG | Joint Photographic Experts Group | .jpg | Painting |
| PNG | Portable Network Graphics | .png | Painting |
| PSD | Photoshop Document | .psd | Painting |
| JASC | Jasc Paintshop Pro | .psp | Painting |
| CDR | CorelDraw | .cdr | Drawing |
| AI | Adobe Illustrator | .ai | Drawing |
| FH | Macromedia FreeHand | .fh | Drawing |
| SWF | Shockwave Flash | .swf | Drawing |
| WMF | Windows Metafile | .wmf | Drawing |
| EPS | Encapsulated PostScript | .eps | Drawing |

Answer the following questions on your own computer.

1. What does a file extension look like?
2. What image management programs are often used by businesses?
3. What are the two types of image management programs, and how are they different?
4. What is a native format?
5. What is a bitmap image?
6. List four types of bitmap images.
7. Why are images compressed?
8. What is the difference between lossy and lossless compression?
9. What is an interlaced image?
10. Why might you want to use an interlaced image?
11. In what format do most digital cameras save images?
12. Why is the **PNG** format not used more often?
13. What is the advantage of using a vector graphic?
14. Name three native vector file formats and one general-purpose file format.
15. What company developed the **GIF** format, and what did the developer require beginning in 1994?

DISCUSSION

1. Explain the difference between a vector and a bitmap.
2. Which file format is the most versatile? Why?
3. Why are photographs saved in **JPEG** format if they are to be used on the Internet?
4. Why is it important to understand file extensions?
5. Was CompuServe correct in its decision to charge a licensing fee? Why or why not?

1. Use the table function in a word processing document to create a chart listing the advantages, disadvantages, and uses of all the file formats discussed in this chapter (see the chart that follows the summary).

2. Use a painting program to create a rectangle filled with color. Save the image in at least six different file formats (such as native, BMP, TIF, JPEG, GIF, and PNG). Look at the properties of each file and record, in the table you created in question 1, the size of each file.

3. Use a drawing program to create an image. The image should be a filled rectangle similar to the one created in step 2. Save the image in at least three different file formats (e.g., native, EPS). Look at the properties of each file and record in the table the size of each file.

4. Keeping in mind the advantages, disadvantages, and uses of each file format, choose one file format and write a slogan advertising the file format and its usefulness. Keep the slogan to eight words or fewer.

## FURTHER EXPLORATION

1. Survey your favorite Web sites (at least ten) to determine what file formats the sites are using for their images. To determine the type of file format, right-click on the image and choose Save Picture As. The Save as type box will indicate the extension.

2. Create a chart showing the address of each site and the number of each type of image file used on each site. Observe and record which were interlaced and which were noninterlaced.

3. Do you disagree with the sites' choices of file formats? How long did it take for pages to load? What can you suggest they do to increase the speed at which their pages appear? Write an explanation summarizing your comments.

# Chapter 3
# Image Editing

ESTIMATED TIME

**3**

H O U R S

SOURCE: ©DIGITAL VISION

## INTRODUCTION

Businesses do not have to be involved in the graphic design industry to find knowledge of image management procedures useful. For example, James Billups, the owner of an automobile paint and repair shop, wants you to create a brochure to give customers an idea of the services he provides. He plans to use this information both in print and on the Web.

James has before-and-after digital photographs of cars he has worked on, but he wants you to change the color of one particular car in several ways. In addition, the photograph he wants to use contains some elements he wants removed. James also wants you to delete the license plate number, which is visible in the image.

James wants you to scan and use a photograph of the front of his shop. The manufacturer of the automobile paint he uses

## Objectives

- *You will understand the use of color in images.*
- *You will understand the use of layers in images.*
- *You will learn the tools available in image editing software.*
- *You will understand the difference between the production of bitmap and vector graphics.*

has given permission to include a graphic of its logo, which he copied from its Web site.

All these steps require James to have knowledge of image management procedures.

## IMAGE PROGRAMS

An essential step in managing images is to understand how to use the paint program available to you, whether it is a simple one such as Microsoft Paint provided as part of the Windows operating system or a more complex, stand-alone program such as Adobe Photoshop. Although every program functions in a slightly different way, they all have some features in common. In this chapter, you will learn about these features and then explore them using your own software.

## COLORS

Understanding the use of color is a good place to begin. Your choices of color formats fall into four categories:

1. Two colors (black and white)
2. Grayscale (variations of black)
3. RGB (**r**ed-**g**reen-**b**lue)—the best choice for Web pages or computer screens
4. CMYK (**c**yan-**m**agenta-**y**ellow-bla**ck**)—the best choice for print documents

RGB colors are based on a scale ranging from 0 to 255, with the higher number representing the purest color. For example, if red and green are set to 0 and blue is set to 255, the result will be a pure blue as shown in Figure 3.1. Changing the red and green numbers will dilute the blue.

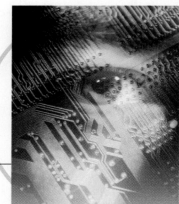

## THE **ETHICS** OF CLASSROOM VS. BUSINESS RULES

In a classroom, it's not unusual to experiment with well-known images such as Disney characters in order to perfect your image management skills. It's both fun and instructive to "morph" a mouse and an elephant so that one grows into the other. In a non-publication environment such activities are harmless. In the business world, however, this is not the case. Keep in mind that creators of copyrighted images are very protective of their rights. What looks like good fun to you might not be seen by others in the same way. Such actions could place your business in legal jeopardy. It's important to be aware that what is done in a classroom as a learning tool cannot always be done in the business world.

Another way to define color is to use hue-saturation-luminescence (HSL). *Hue* represents the base color, such as blue. *Saturation,* or intensity, represents the depth of the base color. *Luminescence,* or light or brightness, determines the amount of white or black added to the base color. Changing any of these amounts also changes the RGB numbers.

All paint programs allow you to work in RGB, but *high-end programs* (more complex or expensive software) such as Photoshop allow you to choose the mode in

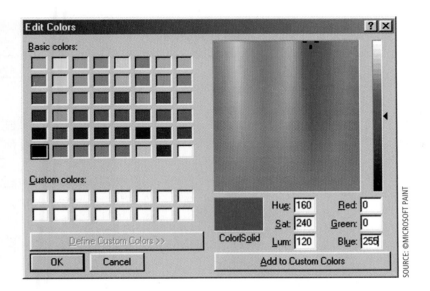

**Figure 3.1** All image software programs provide a means of choosing color, such as the Edit Colors dialog box in Microsoft Paint.

SOURCE: ©MICROSOFT PAINT

which you wish to work. If you know that the final product will be in print, selecting CMYK before beginning ensures that the colors you see will match the final output. This step is important because it is possible to create colors in RGB that cannot be matched in CMYK, which is called being *out of gamut.*

As the owner of the paint and repair shop, James will need to know about the difference between RGB and CMYK when designing his brochure because it will be printed in color. He will also need to have you use image software that will let you select CMYK color.

Another color limitation you need to be aware of is **Web-safe colors.** These are the 216 colors that can be seen on the most limited computer screen. As computer video cards become more powerful and as displays using true color (32-bit) or high color (24-bit) become more common, the use of safe colors is less of a concern. Some paint programs have a feature that automatically limits the color choices to Web-safe colors.

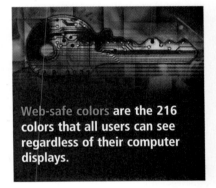

Web-safe colors **are the 216 colors that all users can see regardless of their computer displays.**

When James has someone design the Web page for his paint and repair shop, he will need to decide who his audience is. Will most customers browsing his site have computers capable of displaying a wide variety of colors? That will make a difference in his color choices.

## POSTURE AT WORKSTATION

Arrange your work material so you can see it easily and maintain good posture. Some experts recommend positioning whatever you look at most often (the monitor or paper documents) directly in front of you so you do not have to turn your head frequently. Sit up straight, keeping your head and neck as straight as possible.

*ERGO-TIPS ERGO-TIPS*

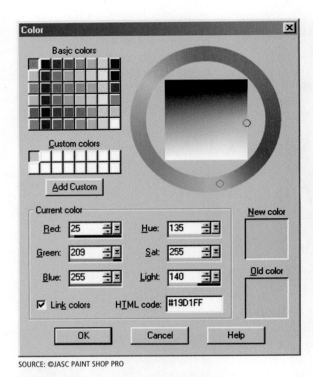

**Figure 3.2** Paint Shop Pro provides a ring of color to use as one means of picking color.

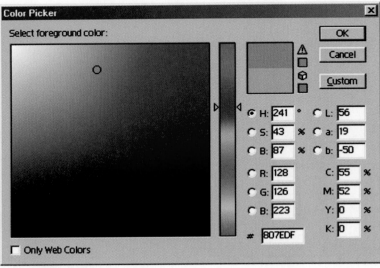

**Figure 3.3** The Adobe Photoshop Color Picker provides four means of selecting color by number: HSB, RGB, LAB, and CMYK.

## COLOR SELECTION

Paint programs always provide two working color choices: foreground and background. The *foreground color* is the color that appears when working with tools such as a paintbrush. The *background color* acts as a "layer" color beneath the original image. If an area is selected and deleted, the background color appears. It's easy to alternate between the two colors by using the right mouse button or the switching arrow, depending on the software.

Colors are selected by clicking on the color box or the foreground/background indicator box. A color selection box, like those shown in Figures 3.1, 3.2, and 3.3, gives you options. You can enter the exact RGB or HSL numbers, you can choose from the basic colors, or you can pick one from the color wheel or box.

If you want to use a specific color on a Web page, some paint programs convert the color to a hexadecimal HTML code for use on the Web.

## COLOR PRINTING

One of the problems that makes it difficult to move from a digital to a print medium is the difference in the way color appears on a computer screen and on paper. You may have encountered a situation where a product that you ordered from a Web page did not appear exactly the way you anticipated. The same is true when moving from the desktop to the printer. The red in one environment will not be the same in another.

There are actually two ways that color is added to a printed page: process color and spot color. *Process color* uses four colors of ink in different proportions (CMYK) to produce the desired image. This mixing of these four colors approximates the color you want. *Spot color* actually uses a single ink in the color you want and applies it to the "spot" you have selected. If you need a color to look exactly the way you anticipate, spot color is the solution. Use of spot color is a separate printing step that can increase the cost of production, so it is generally only used when no other color is present.

For such situations, the *Pantone Matching System* (PMS) has been developed. PMS is a printed chart or series of cards similar to the one shown in Figure 3.4 that allows you to choose a color by name or number. When you designate a specific color based on a Pantone color chart, the printer uses a single ink that matches that color. This means that if your company logo uses a specific Pantone blue, it will always appear the same.

Even though a Pantone ink must be used to produce a Pantone color, often software allows you to indicate your choice of Pantone color so that the CMYK mix will produce the closest possible color. This same Pantone color can also be used for Web pages, but if you are using Web-safe colors the color may not match exactly.

James uses a Pantone chart number to select what color he wants each car to be so there will be no surprises when the brochure is completed. He gives you the Pantone color to use whenever you create documents for him, which makes it easier for you to be productive. He even discusses with you whether he should find out what the Pantone colors are for the logo he has been given permission to use.

### Interviewing Skills

A job interview is often the first time an employer meets a job candidate. The employer uses a job interview to assess potential employees—in particular, their communication skills, punctuality, and professional appearance. Job interviews also give employers a chance to ask questions and explain the specific job to candidates. If you perform well in an interview, you greatly increase your chances of being offered the job.

A successful job interview depends in large measure on preparation. Try to anticipate the questions you are likely to be asked and practice responses in advance, before the actual interview. You should also have a good knowledge of the business and be able to tell about your own job experiences and skills and how they relate directly to the position you are seeking. A proper, professional appearance is also extremely important. The interview is also an opportunity for you to ask the prospective employer about the job. Sell yourself and show that you can contribute to the success of the business.

**Digging Deeper:** Use the Internet to compile a list of commonly asked job interview questions. Pair off with a classmate and, in turn, ask each other the questions you've gathered. Then talk about your responses and discuss ways you might have answered the questions more effectively.

**Figure 3.4** Pantone charts or sample cards allow you to select an exact color for use by a printer.

**Figure 3.5** The first layer of an image is often called the background.

**Figure 3.6** Using layers is a convenient way to let you make changes without affecting other parts of the image.

# LAYERS

Understanding the concept of layers is the next step in working with image management. The following steps will give you an idea of how layers can be used to build an image that appears to be a single picture when it is actually a series of pictures stacked on top of each other.

Imagine that you have a set of four transparent pages.

1. You color one page a graduated shade of blue, as shown in Figure 3.5.
2. On another, you add a picture of three cars and place this page over the blue one.
   Because the layer with the cars is transparent, the color from the background layer shows through (see Figure 3.6).
3. On the third layer, you paint a series of leaves.
4. On the fourth, you type in text and then place the third and fourth pages over the page with the cars (see Figures 3.7 and 3.8). Your layered images now appear to be a single picture.

Layering gives you some convenient choices. Image programs with layering options allow you to turn each layer on or off to see what the image will look like without that information visible. You can also delete one or more layers or add one or more new ones as you need them. It's helpful to use a different layer for each element that might need to be changed and to label each layer as you create it. Labeling makes it easy to know on which layer you are working.

You can move layers up and down. In the steps you followed earlier, the leaves appeared "on top of" the cars because that page was placed on the image after the car layer. Moving the layer down made the leaves appear under the cars.

Because each layer is separate, you can change one element without "overdrawing" the others. This means that if you want to change the blue background page to another color, you can. In the example, the text appears on top of the leaves but they are distracting, so you go to the leaves layer and delete just the portion "under" the text. The result of the changes are seen in Figure 3.9.

## EDITING BITMAP IMAGES

Image management does not often require you to create your own work, but it does require you to know how to edit the work of others. Bitmap images from digital cameras, scans, Web pages, or hand drawings can be modified in numerous ways. Editing allows you to retouch or repair a photograph, remove flaws from the original, or create a different image by using the components from an original.

Image software provides a variety of standard tools to edit graphics:

- Cropping—to remove data from one or more sides of an image
- Rotating—to change the orientation on the page of the entire image or a selected portion
- Erasing—to remove an area or change the color
- Resizing—to change the size of the entire image or a selected portion
- Adding text—to add words
- Painting—to add brush marks, pencil marks, or lines
- Adding figures—to add predesigned figures such as rectangles
- Merging—to add images from other sources
- Matching colors—to match exactly the specific color used in an image
- Cloning—to duplicate part of an image onto another part of the image
- Selecting—to highlight a portion of an image prior to modification
- Using the magic tool—to select all the colors in an area that are alike
- Magnifying—to change the viewing size, making it easier to see pixels

A feature found in many high-end bitmap software programs is an **anti-aliasing** option. Because bitmaps are produced by using pixels, drawing smooth curves or diagonal lines is difficult (see Figure 3.10). Turning on the anti-aliasing option creates a smoother line by altering the edges, making them slightly fuzzy and giving a less jagged line.

**Figure 3.7**  If you decide later that one layer needs to be placed above another, it's easy to move them.

**Figure 3.8**  Each object should be a different layer.

**Figure 3.9**  Using layers made it quick and easy to create this ad for an automobile paint shop.

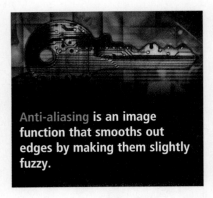

Anti-aliasing **is an image function that smooths out edges by making them slightly fuzzy.**

**Figure 3.10** Pixels can show up in an image as jagged edges.

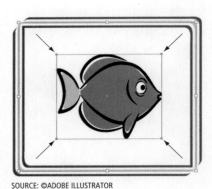

SOURCE: ©ADOBE ILLUSTRATOR

**Figure 3.11** Vector graphic points (see arrows) allow you to change the shape of an image quickly.

# EDITING VECTOR IMAGES

Vector software provides many of the same editing features found in bitmap software with the exception of erasing and cloning, as each of these functions requires pixels to be used. An advantage of a vector image over a bitmap is that it is possible to change the drawing later by readjusting the points of the drawing. See Figure 3.11 for an example of points. In addition, features such as figures and text do not have to be anti-aliased to remove the jaggies, because vectors are mathematically drawn.

Images that were created in a bitmap format cannot be converted to a vector format, but vector graphics can be converted to bitmaps. In vector software, if you save as a bitmap file, the software will automatically convert it for you, which is particularly useful if you want to use a vector image on a Web page.

James is a good customer to work with because he understands image management terms such as *anti-aliasing*. He can make good decisions about the use of vector and bitmap images because he is aware of the limitations and strengths of both.

## SUMMARY

In this chapter, you learned ways in which color is handled, such as the difference between CMYK and RGB. You explored ways in which layers can be used effectively, and you learned ways to edit both bitmap and vector graphics. You saw how knowledge of Pantone color can ensure that the color you choose is the one printed.

Answer the following questions on your own computer.

1. What are your four color format choices?
2. What does the acronym RGB stand for?
3. What does the acronym CMYK stand for?
4. Which color choices are best for print and the Web?
5. What is another way to describe color?
6. How many Web-safe colors are there?
7. What are the two working color choices?
8. Explain at least three options available to you when using layers.
9. What does the cropping tool do?
10. What happens when you merge a file?
11. What does cloning do?
12. What is a magic tool?
13. What editing features does vector software not allow you to use, and why?
14. How can you use a vector graphic on a Web page?

DISCUSSION

1. Which would you rather use—vector or bitmap image software? Explain in detail.
2. Describe the advantages of using layers in image software.
3. Should you be concerned about selecting only Web-safe colors if you are creating an image for use on the Internet? How would you make your decision?

# USE YOUR KNOWLEDGE

1. Find an advertisement from a magazine or one printed from the Internet. Cut apart each element, such as people, backgrounds, and text. Observe the pieces to decide how you would have created this ad and how many layers you would have used. Should you have cut apart pieces of a single image, such as the bow off a package?

2. Look at the colors in the ad and see if you can match them to the color chart in your software. Record the RGB values, the CMYK values, and the HSL values.

3. Decide whether any of these images might have been created with vector software. Write a brief essay in which you explain your findings. Number each cutout according to the layer on which you would have placed it. Attach the cutouts to the essay.

4. Make a list of the tools available to you in your image software. If descriptions of the tools appear on screen, include these descriptions. Make a list of the palettes available to you. Record these tools and palettes in a word processing document.

# FURTHER EXPLORATION

1. Visit or call a local printing facility and ask how it processes images that are produced digitally. Find out what software the company uses and what software its clients use. Ask about the difference between CMYK and RGB. Record the information provided, which may be quite complex, and then provide that information to your class in print or in an oral presentation. If you cannot contact the printer, see if this information is available on the company's Web site.

2. Search the Internet for information on Web-safe colors. Your instructor has a list of several sites that might be helpful. Read the discussions about Web-safe colors, whether they are needed, and just how many are truly Web-safe. Give an overview of your discoveries to your class.

# Chapter 4
# Image Effects

ESTIMATED TIME

3

HOURS

SOURCE: ©DIGITAL VISION

## INTRODUCTION

One of the most enjoyable aspects of using image management software is the ability to modify graphics quickly and easily. Each software program comes with its own special abilities, but some common functions are found in all. Experimenting with your software will reveal many exciting options. Only your imagination limits what special effects you can create using your image management software.

A good example of a business that finds special effects useful is a florist who is a member of a national organization that facilitates the sending of flowers out of town. One service provided by the national agency is to supply images for use in local ads. Yolanda Gomez is a florist who wants to personalize the artwork she uses to reflect community interests. Special effects found in image management software make that possible.

SOURCE: ©ADOBE PHOTOSHOP

**Figure 4.1** Transparent backgrounds enable you to integrate an image onto a page by making it blend in.

It is important to be aware that special effects must be used with care. It's easy to let the fun of the changes cloud good business judgment. Generally, special effects should be used sparingly and only when they communicate a message. They should not be used just to show off your image management skills or to make a splash.

## TRANSPARENCY

One of the simplest image effects is a transparent background for images saved as GIF files. This option removes the background color of an image and allows the background of a Web page to appear in its place, thus making the GIF image appear to "float" on the page. Figure 4.1 makes it easy to see the difference between an image with a transparent background and one without. Notice how the white background separates the image from the page on which it appears. Both the background of the Web page and the transparent background of the original GIF must be a single color for this to be possible.

Yolanda uses this tool to modify the image of the national logo that she uses on her business's Web site so that it appears to be part of her page.

## FILTERS

One of the most spectacular features that is available to you in image management software is filters. Filters enable you to make an instant change to an image. Once an area or an entire image is selected, applying a filter can make subtle as well as dramatic changes. The choices can be simple ones such as blurring an edge or enhancing the entire image by sharpening the edges. More complex choices might include creating a topological map, weaving a pattern of the image, or even liquefying the picture.

Because each software package has different options, you will have to experiment to see what yours provides. For example, Paint Shop Pro provides an Effect Browser that makes it very quick and easy to see what changes the effect will make. Other software allows you to preview changes as you make a selection.

It's easy to get carried away with all the filter options, and you are not limited to just those that come with your software package. Special **plug-ins** can be downloaded from the Web or purchased from *third-party companies* such as Eye Candy. Third-party companies offer additional

### THE **ETHICS** OF MODIFIED IMAGES

The use of filters on images created by others is a very ticklish copyright issue. The law states that you are not allowed to make destructive changes to someone else's work. Even if you have copyright permission to use an image, you must get permission to make the changes, particularly those modifications that might be seen by the owner as defacing the work. While you might not view the use of a blurred filter as harming the image, the owner of the copyright might not agree with you. For any business use of a protected image, it is a good idea to get permission before printing or publishing a modified image.

**Figure 4.2** *(a)* Image software enables you to use the same image in several ways. *(b)* Use of the rough pastel filter converts a photograph into an art object.

Plug-ins **are additional computer instructions that add functionality to a program.**

functions for a software package created by another company. These can be added to your software and used just like the ones that were part of the original software installation.

Yolanda decides to use a filter to create an artistic effect to recognize a widely attended local art event. Using the image of a rose provided by the national organization, she quickly changes the crisp outlines of the flower to make the flower appear as if it were a painted image. Compare the two images shown in Figure 4.2.

## TUBES

Paint Shop Pro has a special-effects feature called *tubes* that provides a series of images that can be dropped onto a page at random spots. Each time you click on a new spot, a different version of the image appears. You can even make your own tubes and save them for your own use. Figure 4.3 shows some random spring flowers Yolanda might use. Notice that both the type of flower and the rotation are different.

SOURCE: ©JASC PAINT SHOP PRO

**Figure 4.3** Paint Shop Pro tubes provide many predrawn figures, making it easy to create an attractive image.

## TEXTURES

Paint Shop Pro also provides an assortment of texture options for painting backgrounds and figures. For example, if you select a pale yellow and a swirling texture, you can fill a page with a series of yellow swirls. Basically, textures enable you to create filters for the colors you use. Figure 4.4 shows a few textures available to you. Yolanda may decide to add a soft paper texture to match one of the pale yellows in the rose to use as a background for the image.

SOURCE: ©PHOTODISC

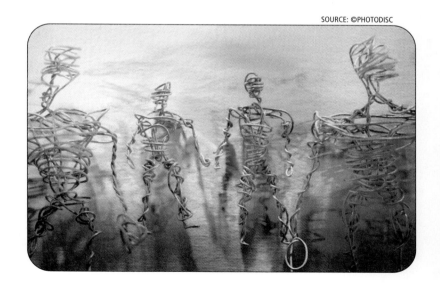

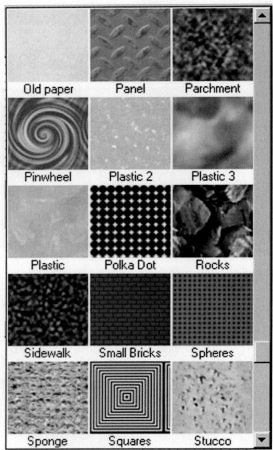

SOURCE: ©JASC PAINT SHOP PRO

**Figure 4.4** The textures available in Paint Shop Pro make for interesting backgrounds.

## GRADIENTS

Gradients enable you to stretch an array of values of one color from one side of an image to another. Paint Shop Pro provides gradients as a color option; Photoshop includes gradients on the basic toolbar. Gradients can be a series of slight changes from one shade or color to another or can be more dramatic, moving from a light shade to a very dark one. It makes for an interesting special effect. Figure 4.5 demonstrates a gradient that spreads from the upper left to the lower right corner.

## FEATHERING

One of the nicest features, feathering slightly blurs the edges of an image to create an attractive effect. Yolanda uses this technique to add a special quality to some images. For a May ad campaign designed to attract June brides, she uses a picture of a bride surrounded by feathered edges, as seen in Figure 4.6.

## CHANNELS

Another option in high-end image software is channels. Channels enable you to separate an image into its basic colors. An image in RGB can be separated into three channels: red, green, and blue. An image in CMYK can be separated into four channels: cyan, magenta, yellow, and black. Once the image is split into channels, you can then modify just the

**Figure 4.5** Gradients can be used in many ways to add interest to your images.

**Figure 4.6** Feathering of the oval around the bride enhances the quality of the image.

single channel. Use of channels is a sophisticated technique reserved for those with considerable knowledge of *color theory,* or the rules that apply to the makeup of color. Channels are also used to create masks, however, which do not require the same level of knowledge of color theory.

## MASKING

A specialized channel called the **alpha channel** is used to create and store masks, which are a means of modifying an image without actually changing the original. Masks are areas that are selected much as you would use a lasso tool, but this process provides far more control of your image. With a mask, you can select an area and then go back and add to or subtract from the selection area because the mask is saved to the alpha channel rather than on the actual image. Your original image is left untouched as you adjust the mask to meet your needs.

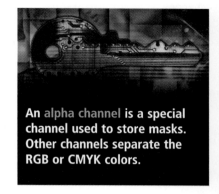

An alpha channel is a special channel used to store masks. Other channels separate the RGB or CMYK colors.

Once the mask is complete and saved to the alpha channel, you can then apply it to a layer to select a specific area. Once you have loaded a selection onto the original layer or channel, you can use it to make a number of changes by applying a single action to the selected area. For example, a mask could be used to blur a selected area or change its contrast. One of the nice benefits of using a mask is that even after you have saved the mask to the alpha channel, if you realize that the selection is not quite right, you can return again to the alpha channel and make further modifications.

Masks fall into two categories: quick and alpha. *Quick* masks give you the same control that an alpha channel does, but they do not save the channel information for another use.

To make it easier to see the mask area, a red tint covers the image, as shown in Figure 4.7. When you are working in the alpha channel, you remove the red tint with a white paintbrush to unmask the painted area. To add a mask, you paint with a black paintbrush. It takes a little practice to become proficient with masks, but it is an image management skill that will serve you well.

Working with the rose she used previously, Yolanda decides to simplify the image for another ad. She experiments with the masking

### Good Business

### Keeping a Positive Attitude

Employees who have a good attitude about their work are more efficient and productive than those who don't. If you enjoy what you do on the job, that enjoyment will be apparent in the quality of the work you produce. Having a good attitude on the job means accepting assignments with a minimum of complaining. It means being pleasant to co-workers. It means focusing on what you have, rather than on what you **don't** have.

Of course, no one expects you to walk around with a smile on your face all the time. And difficulties are a part of every job. It's how you handle the difficulties that makes the difference. When things get rough, remember all the successes you've had. Avoid telling yourself you're no good at your job; the person who hired you obviously didn't think so! If you need to, talk things out with a friend. But don't let the occasional rough spots ruin your overall perspective on your job (and yourself).

**Digging Deeper:** Using the skills and software of your choice, create a "positive thinking" poster to display in your classroom or room at home.

**Figure 4.7** Masks make it easy to select an area of an image in order to apply filters or make other changes.

option to remove a few of the outer leaves by selecting an oval mask for the rose similar to the one shown in Figure 4.7. Applying this oval mask to her image and choosing the inverse option means that everything outside the oval is selected. Once she is satisfied that she has exactly the area she wants, she deletes the outside selection, leaving only the simpler rose on the page. It takes several tries to get the look she is trying to achieve, but she is very satisfied with the result. Masking made it possible for her to try several different oval sizes without disturbing the original image. An added benefit was that she could see her original rose under the alpha channel layer, making it easy to know what adjustments would be needed.

**LIMBER UP!**

Key each of these lines twice to exercise your fingers and to improve your keying techniques. The sentences were constructed to give you practice in all letters of the alphabet.

ERGO-TIPS ERGO-TIPS

1. Zack and our equipment manager will exchange jobs for seven days.
2. Next week Zelda Jacks will become a night supervisor for quality.
3. A man in the park saw a fat lizard quickly devour six juicy bugs.

# UNSHARP MASK

One of the most frequent problems with an image is fuzziness. An easy way to improve a slightly fuzzy image is to use the unsharp mask feature, a name that does not sound as if it would create the desired effect. Unsharp mask automatically sharpens the details of an image and does not require you to create your own mask. Yolanda has learned to apply this mask as a first step before working with JPG images because they often have a few spare pixels called **artifacts** that are not obvious but that detract from the quality of the image.

# COLOR ADJUSTMENT

One special effect you will find useful is adjusting the color of an image that is too dark or too light. You can do this in several ways, but the two most common are to adjust the levels or the curves. Basically, color levels fall into three categories: highlights, shadows, and midtones. *Highlights* represent the lightest part of the image; *shadows,* the darkest; and *midtones,* the middle range. Adjusting the levels of any of these three basic areas can dramatically improve a picture that is too dark or too light.

You can use the adjust levels feature to change the three levels, or you can use the curves option. Curves represent the three levels of color using a graph. Moving the line on the graph in one direction or another can adjust the overall levels. Grabbing the midpoint, as shown in Figure 4.8, and moving it toward the light or toward the dark will automatically adjust your image.

# SUMMARY

In this chapter, you have discovered the exciting possibilities of special effects available in image software. You have explored transparent GIFs, filters, feathering, channels, masking, and color adjustment. It is now time to use all your image management tools by completing the projects in your activity manual.

Artifacts are "spare" pixels that scanners and digital cameras often include in an image, usually caused by lossy compression algorithms. They are not readily seen, but they detract from the sharpness of an image.

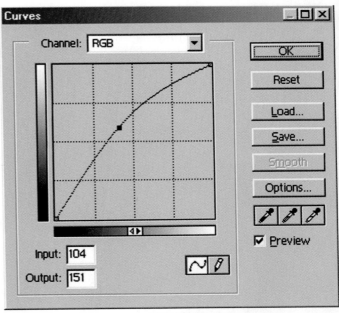

SOURCE: ©ADOBE PHOTOSHOP

**Figure 4.8** You can adjust the levels of an image in several ways. Using the curves function is one of the best.

## REVIEW

**Answer the following questions on your own computer.**

1. What is the danger in using special effects?
2. What effect does transparency have on a GIF?
3. What do filters do to an image?
4. How does a tube function?
5. What does a texture do?
6. What options do gradients give you?
7. What kind of effect does feathering create?
8. In what ways do channels divide colors?
9. What purpose does an alpha channel serve?
10. When would you use a mask?
11. Name two kinds of masks and explain the difference.
12. In a mask, what purpose does the red tint serve?
13. What tools are used to add or remove a mask?
14. Why would you use an unsharp mask?
15. What three levels does the curves feature allow you to adjust?

## DISCUSSION

1. Why would overuse of special effects have a negative impact on a business document?
2. Which filters seem the most useful? Why?
3. Why do feathered images appeal to the senses?
4. When would a business use tubes?
5. What businesses would find special effects most useful?

1. Look in print ads from magazines, brochures, or flyers to find five examples of images that appear to have been created with special effects such as filters, gradients, or feathering. Your counselor's office may have some materials you can use.

2. Evaluate the effectiveness of these special effects. Do they enhance the messages or distract from them? Write a memo to the designer of each ad in which you explain your findings and conclusions. Attach the ad to the memo.

3. From your graphics software, make a list of the filter options available and describe what each does. Add a list of textures and tubes (if you have Paint Shop Pro) that are also available.

**FURTHER
EXPLORATION**

1. If Paint Shop Pro is available, find instructions on the Internet to create your own tubes or find additional tubes that can be added to your software.

2. Find at least three third-party add-on filters for your image software. Make a list of these options and indicate the cost.

3. Share your findings with the class.

# Unit 1: Summary

## Key Concepts

### Chapter 1: History and Evolution

1. With the Apple Macintosh computer and the dot matrix ImageWriter printer, for the first time graphics could be added digitally to a document.
2. With MacPaint and MacDraw, artwork could be created and modified with ease.
3. The introduction of Aldus PageMaker made possible desktop publishing as we know it today.
4. The Apple LaserWriter printer and Adobe PostScript removed the "jaggies" seen in dot matrix printouts.

### Chapter 2: Image File Types

1. Image management programs are of two types: painting and drawing.
2. Painting programs create bitmap images made of pixels.
3. Drawing programs create images made of mathematically defined lines and curves (vectors) that are treated as individual objects within an image.
4. Each image management program has a file format specific to that program called its native or default format.

### Chapter 3: Image Editing

1. Bitmap images from digital cameras, scans, Web pages, or hand drawings can be modified by using painting programs.
2. Vector software provides many of the same editing features found in bitmap software with the exception of erasing and cloning, as each of these functions requires the use of pixels.
3. Painting programs always provide two working color choices: foreground and background.
4. Color choices fall into four categories: black and white, grayscale, RGB (for the Web), and CMYK (for print).
5. Layers allow you to change one element on a page without "overdrawing" other elements.

### Chapter 4: Image Effects

1. A transparent GIF allows the background color of an image to disappear and the background of a Web page to appear in its place, thus making the image seem to "float" on the page.
2. Filters enable you to make an instant change to any image; textures enable you to create filters for the colors you use.
3. Gradients enable you to stretch an array of color from one side of an image or selection to another. Feathering slightly blurs the edges to create an attractive effect.
4. Channels enable you to separate the colors used to create an image.
5. Using a mask saved to the alpha channel, you can select an area to be modified and then add or subtract from the selection area without affecting the original image.
6. Unsharp mask automatically sharpens the details of an image and does not require you to create your own mask.
7. Color levels fall into three categories: highlights, shadows, and midtones. Adjusting the levels of any of these areas can improve a picture.

# Terms

**alpha channel** a special channel used to store masks

**anti-aliasing** an image function that smooths out edges by making them slightly fuzzy

**artifact** "spare" pixels that scanners and digital cameras often include in an image, usually caused by lossy compression algorithms

**bitmap** a graphic created by using pixels

**channel** a graphics option that separates an image into its basic colors

**CMYK** cyan-magenta-yellow-black; the basic colors that are the best choice for print documents

**compression** the process of reducing the size of a graphics image

**desktop publishing** the process of adding both text and graphics to a page to enhance the message

**dot matrix** a means of printing by placing a series of dots close together so that they give the appearance of printed letters

**drawing** a general term for graphics software that uses mathematically defined lines and curves to create an image

**feathering** a graphics technique that slightly blurs the edges of an image

**filter** an image management technique that enables you to make an instant change to an image, such as making the image appear to be painted rather than photographed

**gradient** a graphics technique that stretches an array of values of one color from one side of an image to another

**interlacing** a process that displays an image on a Web page in stages until the image has reached its full resolution

**layering** the process of building an image that appears to be a single picture when it is actually a series of pictures stacked on top of each other

**lossless** a compression formula that does not change any pixel data

**lossy** a compression formula that reduces the size of a file by removing certain pixels

**masking** a means of modifying an image without actually changing the original

**native** describes the file format in which a particular graphics program automatically saves an image

**noninterlacing** a process that displays an image on a Web page by rendering it from top to bottom until the image is complete

**OCR** optical character recognition; the process of converting a scanned image of text into editable "live" text on the computer

**painting** a general term for graphics software that uses pixels to create an image

**pixel** a data representation of a specific color at a specific location in a matrix or grid; a rectangular collection of pixels can produce an image on a computer screen or on a printed page

**plug-ins** additional computer instructions that add functionality to a program

**PostScript** a programming language that describes the appearance of images or text on the printed page

**resolution** the density of pixels in an image

**RGB** red-green-blue; the basic colors that are the best choice for Web pages or computer screens

**texture** a Paint Shop Pro option for painting backgrounds and figures

**transparency** a GIF option that removes the background color of an image

**tube** a Paint Shop Pro option that provides a series of images that can be dropped onto a page of random spots; each time you click on a new spot, a different version of the image appears

**vector** an image created by using a series of mathematically defined lines and curves rather than pixels, making the image easier to rescale

**Web browser** a software program that allows you to view Web pages created for the Internet

**Web-safe colors** the 216 colors that all users can see regardless of their computer displays

# ELECTRONIC PORTFOLIO

**Artists have always carried portfolios of their "works" with** them to interviews. This technique has carried over in today's world to all areas of business but with a significant change. It is becoming the cutting edge of technology to create this portfolio in an electronic format. A portfolio should be considered an extension of your résumé. It serves as a reference to what you say you can accomplish on your résumé.

Beginning with this unit, you will create a portfolio to demonstrate your image management skills and add to it during subsequent units. You goal will be to provide for your instructor, your classmates, and future employers proof of your abilities.

1. Gather information about electronic portfolios:
   - Research electronic portfolios on the Internet.
   - Invite guest speakers with firsthand knowledge and possibly examples of electronic portfolios.
   - Read a book on creating electronic portfolios. A possible resource is *Electronic Portfolios* by Linda E. Ash (SkyLight Professional Development; ISBN: 1-57517-281-X).

2. Prepare a written report and an oral report on your findings about electronic portfolios. The written report should be a minimum of two pages long; the oral report should be a minimum of three minutes and a maximum of five minutes. Each report should emphasize at least five important tips on creating electronic portfolios.

3. Create a folder titled **Electronic Portfolio**. Within this folder create a series of subdirectories titled **unit1**, **unit2**, **unit3**, **unit4**, **unit5**, and **unit6**. Later, you will combine these materials with your other works to create a complete electronic portfolio.

4. Create at least two images using either a vector or a bitmap graphics program. Save them in the **unit1** subdirectory in native format and also as JPG or GIF. Name your documents **image1** and **image2**. While these images do not have to be "works of art," they should demonstrate your knowledge of a wide variety of image management tools.

5. Insert these images into a word processing document and explain how you created them. Save this document as **created_graphics.doc** in the **unit1** subdirectory.

**6.** Use the following table to evaluate the quality of your portfolio material.

| | Beginning | Developing | Accomplished | Exemplary | Score |
|---|---|---|---|---|---|
| Scanned or photographed **image1** | Simple image with few image techniques used | More complex image with at least two techniques used | Complex image with several techniques used | Complex image demonstrating unusual or creative use of techniques | |
| Scanned or photographed **image2** | Simple image with few image techniques used | More complex image with at least two techniques used | Complex image with several techniques used | Complex image demonstrating unusual or creative use of techniques | |
| Graphic explanation | One image inserted with minimal explanation | Both images inserted with adequate explanation | Both images inserted with extensive explanation | Both images inserted with insightful explanation | |

# UNIT 2

# Professional Visual Communication Skills

5 Digital Photography
6 Scanning
7 Charts and Graphs
8 Maps

# Career Profile

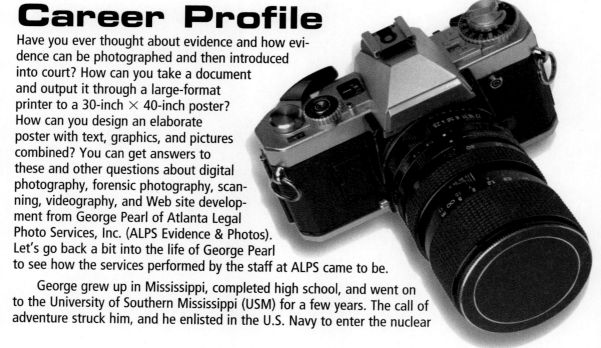

Have you ever thought about evidence and how evidence can be photographed and then introduced into court? How can you take a document and output it through a large-format printer to a 30-inch × 40-inch poster? How can you design an elaborate poster with text, graphics, and pictures combined? You can get answers to these and other questions about digital photography, forensic photography, scanning, videography, and Web site development from George Pearl of Atlanta Legal Photo Services, Inc. (ALPS Evidence & Photos). Let's go back a bit into the life of George Pearl to see how the services performed by the staff at ALPS came to be.

George grew up in Mississippi, completed high school, and went on to the University of Southern Mississippi (USM) for a few years. The call of adventure struck him, and he enlisted in the U.S. Navy to enter the nuclear

44

(continued)

program. As luck would have it, instead he was assigned to aviation electronics school in Tennessee and later to work repairing electronics systems onboard fighter jets. After his stint in the Navy, George worked for the Army Corps of Engineers for a time, but school was on his mind. He went back to USM for a bachelor's degree in radio, TV, and film, with minors in marketing and sales. He took all the photo courses available in the photojournalism department and then went on to advanced TV production workshops as well. George credits his continuous dean's list college grades to his philosophy of education: (1) Sit in the front of the class; (2) Ask questions; and (3) Do what the teacher tells you to do . . . exactly. "Do these three things, and you will excel in school," says George.

His career took him to the University Medical Center in Jackson, Mississippi, where he was the assistant director of medical photography. Knowing that life was calling him to work in another direction with a business of his own, George chose Atlanta as the place in which to set his ideas into motion. By then he knew he wanted to do evidence photography such as forensic and technical photography, primarily for attorneys to use for evidence in civil cases. Before opening his business, George needed to get properly settled in Atlanta. Working for the Georgia Department of Archives and History, he coordinated a photographic project called Vanishing Georgia to photograph and record data of historical importance in Georgia as evidenced by historical pictures. He set up the camera system and proceeded to drive around and rephotograph historical photographs that people would bring to his specialized team. The copy negatives of the historic images were kept in the Georgia Archives for use by future generations, and the original photos were returned to the patrons. This now-finished project provides a visual history of Georgia through photography. Today, with digital cameras the same project could be done less expensively and much more quickly.

From its simple beginnings in his apartment in 1978, the business has grown to occupy five thousand square feet of office space. It houses two labs, a studio for shooting pictures of injured people and other physical evidence, a model building shop, an art finishing room, a video production room, and a computer art and production room (which the company has already outgrown).

How does George use his skills? Digital cameras are a large part of his work, but as he stated, "Students must learn the equipment to know which camera you need for what is being photographed. One camera won't do it all. You have to get the correct tool for each job."

George uses a digital camera for production work such as incorporating pictures when he is trying to make a big court diagram—say, of a roadway. All the details are usually measured at the site, but suppose a curve can't be measured on location because of traffic. The blueprint from the Department of Transportation (DOT) shows the curve, so the trick is to get it into the computer so that the precise curve can be incorporated into the rest of the diagram. He photographs the original large DOT engineering blueprint of the roadway with a digital camera, and then that image goes into the artist's computer. The files on the computer can then have colors, lanes, grass, buildings, titles, and other required elements added over the image to complete the diagram.

Digital cameras are especially valuable when you need a photograph taken correctly, such as is the case with evidence photographs. You may never be able to go back to the scene and find it

exactly as it was when the first evidence photo was taken, so it has to be taken right the first time. Using a digital camera, George can take the photo on location, look at the display, and take a preview look at the photo. He has saved time, trouble, and worry, especially in evidence work.

George isn't just a terrific evidence photographer; he is also a Board Certified Evidence Photographer under the Evidence Photographers International Council. In addition, he is a Board Certified Questioned Document Examiner & Handwriting Expert. In 1986, George was a founding member of the Association of Forensic Document Examiners and even designed the logo for the organization. But that is another story in the life of George Pearl!

As you go into the next units in this text, think back to the topics you have studied and try to imagine yourself in the shoes of the people you have met and will meet in this text. You can be a top-notch worker in the field of multimedia and image management too. Take your skills to the next level—become an expert in a career you love! ■

Note: George Pearl is a real person and his business, Atlanta Legal Photo Services, Inc., based in Atlanta, Georgia, is a real business.

# Chapter 5
# Digital Photography

ESTIMATED TIME

**3**

H O U R S

SOURCE: ©PHOTODISC

## INTRODUCTION

If a picture is worth a thousand words, then its power to communicate is indeed great. Digital photography and photo editing software make it easy to use this power. Although many large corporations and businesses have professional photographers who provide photographs for ads and other uses, small business professionals must often rely on their own photographic skills to produce the pictures they need. One example is the independent real estate agent who must provide shots of a client's home to use for Web listings of houses for sale or for newspaper coverage.

However, even businesspeople who are not responsible for taking their own photographs need to know what constitutes a good photograph and what digital editing options are available to modify photographs they are given. This chapter will provide you with these skills.

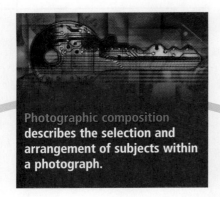

## STEPS TO GOOD COMPOSITION

Knowing how to use a digital camera to take satisfactory photographs is an essential communication skill. The first step in learning how to communicate with others through your camera is understanding the design principles of **photographic composition.** Composition is the selection and arrangement of subjects within the picture area. Your choices of what to include and where to locate your subject in the photograph make the difference between a picture that conveys a message and one that merely captures the random moment.

Photographic composition **describes the selection and arrangement of subjects within a photograph.**

### FOCUS

When beginning to consider your shot, ask yourself what you are taking a picture of. This is not as obvious as it sounds. For example, David Waterman is a real estate agent trying to capture the essence of his client's living room. He must decide what is the most attractive feature. Is it the lovely mantel over the fireplace, or is it the impressive arched windows? A single photograph can tell only one story. Although the mantel and the windows may both be spectacular, David can't effectively give both of these features center stage in a single picture.

Generally, the brightest, lightest, and most colorful object attracts the most attention. If David decides to focus on the mantel but the windows are the brightest objects in his viewfinder, the mantel will lose impact. Moving the camera just a few inches can make the difference between effective and ineffective composition. Take the time to walk around a subject, looking for the most successful angle.

## THE **ETHICS** OF DIGITAL MODIFICATION

In an earlier era, a photograph was a permanent record of an event or moment in a person's life. It was difficult to change the picture once the image was imprinted on film. This is no longer the case. Today's digital technology, which includes scanning and software, makes it possible to edit any photograph and change the image in ways that will not be apparent. Thus, it is possible to alter what once was considered a permanent record. A lawn that was dead and brown becomes green. A person who "intrudes" on the perfect shot can be removed. Even a person missing from the event can be added to the final print.

This ability to change an image and a record has created discussion in the photographic community over what is ethical. If David uses software to give a homeowner's lawn a lovely shade of green, has he violated the image? If you remove someone from a photograph, does that alter the validity of your print? Are you obligated to tell your viewer that the visual record has been edited? You must answer these questions for yourself.

### CENTERING THE SUBJECT

The most frequent mistake amateur photographers make is placing the object of attention in the center of the photograph. Although the mantel should be given prominence in David's picture, it should not be dead center. Psychologically, the human brain prefers to "wander" around a photograph, deciding for itself what is important. Centering removes this satisfying movement. Place the focus point in such a way that the eye can move about the picture.

### RULE OF THIRDS

The **rule of thirds** is an important consideration when choosing

**Figure 5.1** The rock arrangement fills the bottom two-thirds of the image using the rule of thirds to balance the photograph.

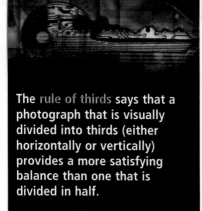

The rule of thirds says that a photograph that is visually divided into thirds (either horizontally or vertically) provides a more satisfying balance than one that is divided in half.

composition. Dividing the photograph horizontally or vertically into thirds provides a satisfying balance that allows many composition options. Notice in Figure 5.1 that the rocks appear in the bottom two-thirds of the picture rather than in the center of the photograph.

## BACKGROUND

Pay close attention to the background information your photograph includes. You may see it as nonessential "clutter"; your viewer will give it more attention. Make sure it adds to your photographic story rather than detracts from it. The horizon is an important background to consider in outdoor shots. It should be straight, and its prominence in a photograph should be gauged. Horizons that are low in the photograph give importance to the sky, as shown in Figure 5.2. One background you may want to look for is one that will frame your picture in some way. Framing is effective in giving the viewer a sense of location and distance.

## UNIFYING ELEMENTS

One way to help the eye "wander" around a photograph is to use lines within a photograph, as shown in Figure 5.3. The lines might be diagonal, S-shaped, or curved. These lines pull the eye along in the direction you intend. Lines can also tie together objects within a photograph, thus reducing the jumble of objects in a photograph.

SOURCE:
©PHOTODISC

**Figure 5.2** Notice how prominent the sky is, dwarfing the house below.

**Figure 5.3** The lines of the fence move your eye from the center of the picture into a lazy curve.

## SPECIAL EFFECTS

The choice of distance from which you photograph an object can turn an ordinary picture into a distinctive photograph. Close-ups or different angles give viewers a perspective they might not have considered, such as the roof shown in Figure 5.4. Shooting up or down rather than straight on is an effective means of getting your viewer's attention by giving the eye something unusual to see. The light you choose and the angle from which it comes is another effect to consider. David may notice that light streaming through a window is distracting, but the same light from another angle may make the room appear light and airy.

**Figure 5.4** The angle and irregular placement of the wood beams adds interest to this photograph.

## ACTION

With a digital camera, it is now much easier to capture action shots, freezing the movement of a sports figure or even a child in a swing, than it was with a traditional camera. In the past, special film speeds were used to produce the effects that are common in today's digital cameras. Because movement was difficult to capture, amateur photographers tended to capture only posed pictures with people facing into the lens. That is no longer necessary or desirable. Just as viewers want to move the eye through the elements of a photograph, those same viewers prefer to feel that they are seeing a moment captured as it happened, not as it was posed. Learn to capture and include motion in your photographs to communicate the message that the photograph is recording the event as it happened. Avoid the staged photograph with people standing in a row.

# DIGITAL CAMERAS

## DIGITAL VERSUS FILM CAMERAS

Digital cameras have advantages over traditional film cameras that make them perfect for today's business. They require no film but instead use standard floppy disks, CD-ROM disks, or internal memory cards. Not having to print first from film means that selection of the perfect photograph is cheaper and quicker, with no time or expense required to develop film. The savings in both time and money can be significant.

One side benefit often overlooked is that with digital media, many more shots can be taken, thus increasing the chances of the perfect picture. Special effects such as different angles or lighting can be tried with no additional expense. Digital cameras can take close-ups with ease, and the camera itself can impose special effects such as sepia tones to give a feeling of antiquity to a modern scene.

## CAMERA FEATURES

Each brand of digital camera has its own features, so you must investigate yours to determine what they are. Some features are common to all. These include a power switch, an option to view a picture already taken, flash choices, zoom options, battery location, and a

## Good Business

### Maintaining Perspective

Once you've been working for a while, you may begin to notice a few things about the job that rub you the wrong way. Maybe you think some of the work rules are unnecessary, or perhaps you don't like the way a job assignment has been delegated. Few workplaces are perfect. Some of your grievances may be legitimate. But not every "problem" is truly serious or a cause for complaint. Don't become the type of employee who finds fault with every little thing.

Always maintain perspective. One good way to do this is to find out if you're the only one who thinks a situation is a real problem. Discuss the matter with more experienced co-workers whom you respect. Does the situation really prevent you from doing your job well? Don't overreact. Your employer and co-workers will appreciate your relaxed attitude, and you will be less likely to suffer from on-the-job stress or burnout.

**Digging deeper:** What are some common challenges faced by people who work in multimedia-related fields (such as tight deadlines or changing technology)? Which of these would you classify as serious problems? Which are simply minor annoyances? Discuss in class.

means of saving photographs and sending them to a computer. Reading your owner's manual or finding information about your camera on the Web will reveal its special features, such as the ability to modify a picture by using software built in to the camera. One popular camera allows the user to choose whether the photograph is a fast-moving action shot or a long shot such as that of a mountain.

An important consideration when selecting a digital camera is the number of pixels it can record. The greater the number of pixels, the better the quality of the photograph. The use of more pixels, however, creates larger file sizes. Depending on the purpose of the photograph, you may not need to use the maximum number of pixels. Photographs to be used on Web pages can be saved as JPG files with a resolution of $640 \times 480$, making them load quickly because of their small file size.

### CARE OF THE CAMERA

Digital cameras are sturdy, but they are carefully designed technology and should be treated with care, just as you would traditional cameras. Follow these rules to keep your camera in good working order:

- Keep the lens area clean by using a soft cloth designed especially for camera lenses.
- Keep the lens cap on when not using the camera.
- Beware of dropping the camera even from a short distance such as onto a counter.
- Never force a disk or memory card in or pull it out if there is resistance.
- Never force an uncooperative switch; instead, find out why the latch or door does not function.

## SOFTWARE

Just as you learned in the previous chapters that you can modify graphics, you can modify digital photographs once they have been saved to a computer. The most frequent modification is removal of the red eye in a subject (which is the reflection of the flash on the retina of the eye). Red eye removal is sometimes an automatic feature of software packaged with your camera, but it can be done manually by selecting the area and replacing the red with a more natural color. Other features allow you to change the amount of contrast or brightness in a photograph or to readjust the color.

### CROPPING

**Cropping** is a tool often used to modify a photograph that doesn't quite communicate the message you want. Cropping tools are standard features in all graphics software. Learning to crop well is an important skill because it allows you to refocus a photograph by using the rules of composition. Cropping can turn a muddled photograph with no point of focus into a photograph that exactly conveys the message you are trying to tell. For example, our real estate agent,

**Figure 5.5a** This photograph has no focus and no sense of movement.

**Figure 5.5b** Cropping the previous photograph to focus on the automobile converts an unappealing image into one that has an impact.

David, who has the perfect photo except for the distracting lamp to one side, can crop the lamp with ease. Notice in Figure 5.5a that the photograph has no focus. Taking that same image and cropping it to create a focus on the car dramatically changes the impact of the photograph, as seen in Figure 5.5b.

Cropping is the cutting away of one or more "sides" of a picture to remove unwanted areas and to increase the focus.

## VIRTUAL REALITY

One of today's most interesting software packages makes it possible to turn a series of photographs taken at different angles and positions into one three-dimensional photograph. Such a photograph allows a viewer to see an object or scene as if the viewer were moving through the room or around the object. This technique requires a series of carefully selected photographs to be *stitched* together by means of special editing software to match the points at which the photographs meet. The process is somewhat tedious and time-consuming, but it can produce astonishing effects. David could use this technique to create a virtual tour of a home, allowing the viewer to move from room to room as if actually present.

## SUMMARY

In this chapter, you learned how to create good digital photographs by using the rules of composition. This included learning about focus, the rule of thirds, backgrounds, and special effects. You looked at the differences between digital and film cameras and read about how to care for your digital camera. You even looked at ways to create a virtual reality by using a digital photograph.

Answer the following questions on your own computer.

1. What is composition?
2. What gets the most attention in a photograph?
3. What is the most frequent mistake amateur photographers make?
4. What is the rule of thirds?
5. Why wouldn't you want to always center an object in a photograph?
6. What purpose does framing serve?
7. How can lines in a photograph influence its message?
8. What special effects can be used to enhance a photograph?
9. Why is action important in a photograph?
10. What are some advantages of digital cameras over traditional film cameras?
11. What features does your digital camera have?
12. Explain how to care for a digital camera.
13. What is red eye?
14. What purpose does cropping serve?
15. What effect does stitching a series of photos produce?

DISCUSSION

Figure 5.6

Figure 5.7

Figure 5.8

Figure 5.9

Using Figures 5.6 through 5.9, discuss the following questions either as a class or as a written assignment.

1. What story does each picture tell?
2. What is the focus in each picture?

3. Which photograph has the best focus and why?
4. How does the rule of thirds apply to the photographs?
5. Which photograph has a frame, and what impact does it have?
6. What unifying elements are present?
7. What special effects are used in these photographs?
8. Which photograph do you like the most and why?
9. How could you use each photograph in an ad?
10. For what other business purposes could you use these images?

USE YOUR KNOWLEDGE

1. Using images from the Internet, from magazines, or supplied by your instructor, choose photographs to demonstrate each of the following rules of composition: (a) rule of thirds, (b) off-center composition, (c) special effects, (d) unifying elements, (e) framing, and (f) cluttered background. Choose one of the photographs and use a pen or marker to crop it to improve its effectiveness. Choose one of the images and identify its strong and weak points. Use your examples to create an instructional brochure that demonstrates digital photography information.

2. Use the Internet or other sources such as newspaper advertisements to determine the prices of at least five digital cameras. Create a comparison chart that shows the brand of camera, the model, the price, the number of pixels, and one other feature such as type of lens. Highlight which camera you would buy.

FURTHER EXPLORATION

Digital cameras have changed photography in significant ways. Many people who are used to using film cameras think that they are better. People who have moved to digital cameras believe they are better. Which side would you choose?

1. Search for a comparison of digital and print photography using the Internet or other sources.

2. Do you think digital photography is better than film? Why? Develop a short persuasive argument for the side you believe is more convincing. Include issues such as cost, quality, longevity of printed image, and convenience.

ESTIMATED TIME
2 HOURS

# Chapter 6
# Scanning

SOURCE: ©DIGITALVISION

## Objectives

- *You will learn the importance of TWAIN in scanning.*
- *You will learn how to activate a scanner.*
- *You will learn how to use scanner and OCR software.*

## INTRODUCTION

One of the most valuable business imaging tools available that uses today's technology is a scanner. Scanners make it possible for you to convert a photograph or other printed graphic to a digital format for use on a computer. Scanners also allow you to convert the printed page to text that can be edited on your computer. A printed document does not have to be rekeyed and so saves considerable time and money. Many businesses are attempting to reduce the amount of paper stored in filing cabinets by moving toward a "paperless" office. Scanners are being used to make this possible.

Goro Mitsui works as a technician for a retail pharmacy. In the past, the pharmacy has stored all the paper copies of prescriptions that it has received, but the storage has become a problem. Goro was assigned the task of scanning the old prescriptions to create an archive.

# TWAIN

Scanners convert graphics and text to a digital format and transfer it to a computer using **TWAIN.** TWAIN is an acronym for a software standard that all scanner manufacturers agree to use, so any TWAIN-compliant software package can work with any scanner. Today the wide selection of TWAIN-compliant software includes graphics standards such as Photoshop and Paint Shop Pro. In addition, word processing software such as Microsoft Office is usually TWAIN compliant.

TWAIN **is an acronym indicating that the software can work with a scanner.**

TWAIN is not the only means of connecting a scanner (or camera) to a computer; it is just the one used most frequently. Recently, however, Microsoft has introduced Windows Image Acquisition (WIA) and incorporated it into the Windows XP operating system. From this point on, a scanner must be able to use WIA in order for it to operate in a Windows environment. This means that businesses will have to purchase scanners that meet this requirement.

Essentially, a scanner acts like a digital photocopier by taking a picture of a printed document and transferring the image to a computer. Once the image is saved, it can be modified just as any other graphic.

# CHARACTERISTICS OF SCANNERS

Scanners generally fall into two categories: sheetfed and flat. Most scanners in use are flatbed because they provide more options than sheetfed ones. Today's flatbed scanners are inexpensive and easy to use. Most scanners require you to scan one image at a time, but some scanners may have an option that allows you to "feed" multiple images in succession, similar to the document feeder feature found on many photocopiers. Scanners may also have a feature that allows you to scan 35-mm slides.

Generally, scanners are attached to a computer, and the computer is used to activate the

## Good Business

### Dressing for Work

Every business wants to project a good image to its customers. An employee's appearance can communicate a lot about his or her attitude. If you come to work every day in neat, clean clothes, you're telling customers and co-workers that you care enough to put forth your best effort. If your clothes are sloppy, customers and co-workers may think your work habits will be too.

Often, dress codes are not part of a company's written policy; you can tell a lot about how you're expected to dress simply by looking at the other employees. When you go on a job interview, make a point to notice how the employees are dressed; this will give you an idea of what will be expected of you. You can still maintain a sense of personal style while fitting in with your co-workers, and you needn't erase every trace of individuality. But your willingness to dress appropriately for work will tell an employer a great deal about your willingness to follow instructions and to be a team player.

**Digging deeper:** Ask your friends and relatives about formal or informal dress codes at their jobs. Are any types of jobs more (or less) likely to have dress codes? Create a short presentation on your findings.

scanner's functions. However, "freestanding" scanners allow you to scan an image and save it to a disk. Once the image is stored on the disk, you must then modify the scanned image on a separate computer using image management software.

The difference in scanner prices is related to the number and quality of pixels the scanner can capture, as well as to the speed at which the scanning occurs. A scanner's capabilities are given in two sets of numbers—bit depth and DPI (dots per inch)—so a scanner might be described as 48-bit color, 1200 × 4800 dpi. The higher each of these numbers, the better the scanner.

## IMAGE QUALITY

**Bit depth** is a measurement to indicate how much information is gathered about the red, green, and blue components of a pixel.

**DPI** is a measurement used with printers and scanners to indicate how many points of ink or pixels are contained in an inch. The greater the number of pixels and dots on a page, the better the output or picture.

DPI and bit depth determine the quality of an image. **Bit depth** describes how much RGB (red, green, blue) information the scanner measures about each pixel. For example, a scanner with 48-bit depth gathers 12 bits of information (48 divided by 3) for the red, green, and blue in each pixel. This actually results in billions of colors being captured.

**DPI** indicates the size of the pixels being captured. If a one-inch-square image is scanned at 16 DPI (similar to Figure 6.1), each pixel would be quite large. If that same square were scanned at 64 DPI, each pixel would be half the size of those in the original scan. Since each pixel can record a single color, it is better to have many small pixels rather than fewer large ones. The more pixels the scanner captures, the more detailed the image.

The issue becomes file size. The more pixels you have, the better your image; however, the increase in the number of pixels will also increase the size of your image file. It becomes necessary to consider your *output device* at this point. An output device is the means you

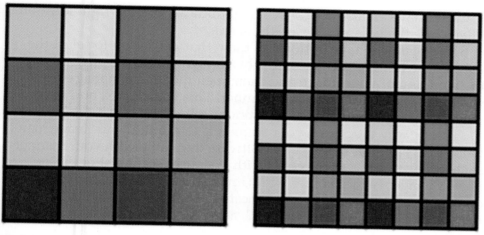

**Figure 6.1** One square is scanned at 16 DPI and the other at 64 DPI. The second square will be a larger file but a more accurate image.

are going to use to produce the image such as a printer or a display screen. If your printer can only print at 300 DPI, then an image scanned at 2400 DPI has more pixels than the printer can use.

Display screens use a different set of rules because the resolution of the image determines the size of the image that is displayed on the screen. For example, an image that is scanned at 300 DPI will be considerably larger than one scanned at 150 DPI. The actual size will be determined by the resolution that the monitor is set to display. If the monitor is set to 800 × 600 the image will be larger than if the monitor is set at 1280 × 1024.

You can find quite involved discussions over the question of what resolution size to use to scan images. As a general rule (which may not always apply), scanning images at 75–150 DPI for use on a computer screen and 300–600 DPI for use on a printer will meet most of your needs. You will have to experiment, however, to determine what works best for your situation.

Goro knows that the prescriptions do not have to be scanned at a high resolution because they are in black-and-white. He uses a low resolution that reduces the size of the scanned files, allowing many more prescriptions to be saved in the same storage device.

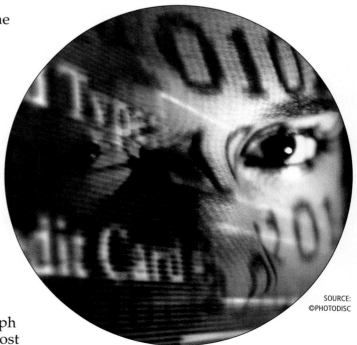

## ACTIVATION OF A SCANNER

To use a flatbed scanner, first place your photograph or document on the glass under the scanner lid. Most

scanners have an arrow at one edge to indicate the top right location. Then close the lid and activate the scanner.

Some scanners have buttons on them that allow you to select the scanning activity. Pressing such a button will automatically activate the scanning of your image and then open the image management software that comes with your scanner. This is the quick and easy way, but you do not have many options when you select this method.

A better way to activate your scanner is to acquire your image manually. One option is to select the software that came with your scanner such as PaperPort (which comes with Visioneer scanners) or Presto Page Manager (which comes with Umax scanners). Once you have opened your software, you must locate the function that will activate the scanner. As shown in Figure 6.2, a TWAIN button on the toolbar in PaperPort acquires your image.

Another option is to use TWAIN-compliant software such as Photoshop, Paint Shop Pro, or Word to acquire the scan.

In Paint Shop Pro (as shown in Figure 6.3), you activate the scan process by selecting File > Import > TWAIN > Acquire. You may have to select your scanner source (the name of your scanner) the first time you use the scanner.

In Photoshop, you activate the scanner by selecting File > Import > [Name of the scanner]. In Microsoft Word, you select Insert > Picture > From Scanner or Camera > Select the Scanner > Custom Insert button.

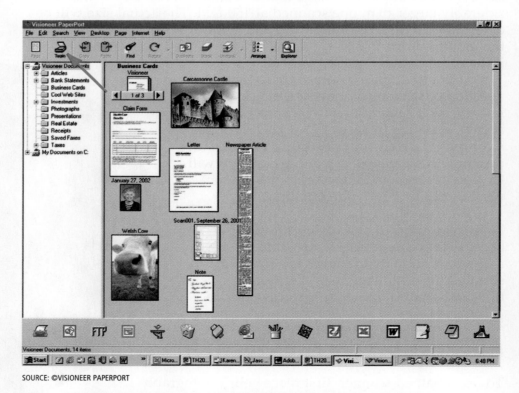

SOURCE: ©VISIONEER PAPERPORT

**Figure 6.2** The TWAIN feature may be activated by a button or a menu command.

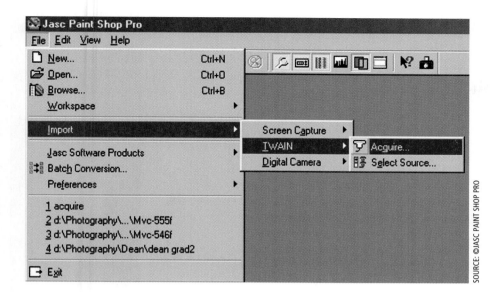

SOURCE: ©JASC PAINT SHOP PRO

**Figure 6.3** The menu command to import a scan may use the word *acquire*.

# SCANNER SOFTWARE

Once you have activated the scanner, your scanner software appears on the computer screen. This software lets you select the image size, type, and resolution before the scan begins. The Visioneer Scan Manager is shown in Figure 6.4. Another image management software package is Vista Scan for the Umax scanner. The interface is different for each software package, but the options are all similar.

Image management software allows you to preview the image before the actual scan occurs. The preview lets you select the area to scan by drawing a box around the area, as shown by the arrow in Figure 6.4.

The software also allows you to set the type of image (black-and-white or color) and the resolution. Be careful when choosing resolution. Remember, scanning at a high resolution creates a very large file size without always improving the quality of the image. In this case, more is not always better. Generally, your choice should be about 150–300 DPI.

Once you have made your selections, choosing Scan produces your image in the original software with which you activated the scanner. Once the scan is completed, you can edit the image in a variety of ways such as cropping and changing the contrast or brightness.

Goro's pharmacy has a flatbed scanner without a sheetfeeder on it, so he has learned to place several prescriptions at once on the glass and then scan them. It has taken some experimentation, but now that he knows exactly how large an area to scan, he no longer

SOURCE: ©PHOTODISC

**Figure 6.4** Scanners allow you to preview the scan and then select the area to scan.

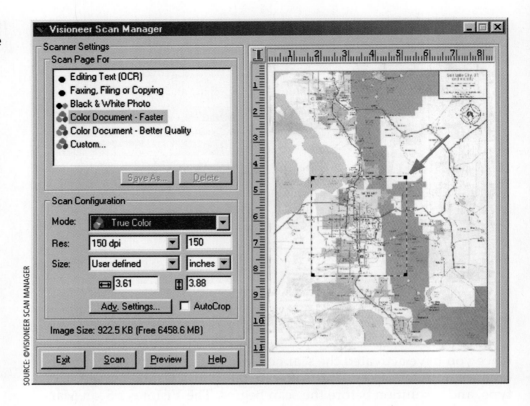

must do a preview scan before beginning the process. He has also set the contrast and brightness to a level that works well with most of the prescriptions. Once the scan is complete, he then uses image management software to "cut" them apart and save the prescriptions as separate documents. A process that was originally quite time-consuming became easier once his skills were developed.

## ARRANGING YOUR WORKSTATION

Image management is a creative use of your computer. Do not extend that creativity to your workstation arrangement. Proper workstation arrangement is vital. Your keyboard should be at elbow height and even with the front edge of your desk. Your monitor should be positioned to avoid glare and situated at least an arm's length away. Your chair should have a good backrest, and your back should be touching the backrest at all times. Keep your feet flat on the floor (or use a footrest). Low levels of light are recommended if you are working on the computer; turn up the lights if you are examining paper documents.

ERGO-TIPS ERGO-TIPS

# OPTICAL CHARACTER RECOGNITION

To convert text to a digital format requires two steps. The first is to create a scanned image of the document to be processed. The second is to then use OCR (optical character recognition) software to read and convert the image of the letters into working text. OCR software is generally packaged with the scanner, just as the image editing software is.

You can access TWAIN scanning from within the actual OCR software package, or you can do a conversion from within the editing software that comes with your scanner.

If you use PaperPort, the conversion to OCR occurs automatically when you drag the image of the document to the icon for your word processing software (as shown in Figure 6.5). Once the conversion is completed, your new text document appears in a word processing window that can be edited just like any other text.

If you use actual OCR software such as TextBridge Pro, you have more conversion options such as choosing the type or quality of the original document. With specialized OCR software, you can "teach" the software to read your text more efficiently. This allows you to do a conversion of other documents with more accuracy. You can also proofread the converted document because questionable words are highlighted for your convenience. Once the conversion is completed, you must save your new file as a word processing document. You can then open and edit the document just as you would any other text.

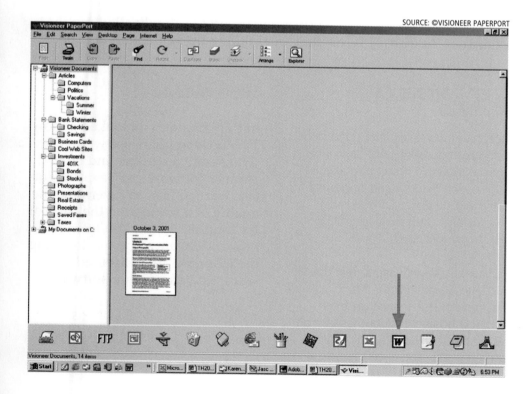

**Figure 6.5** Converting a scan to a text document is called OCR.

**Figure 6.6** Windows XP provides built in OCR capabilities.

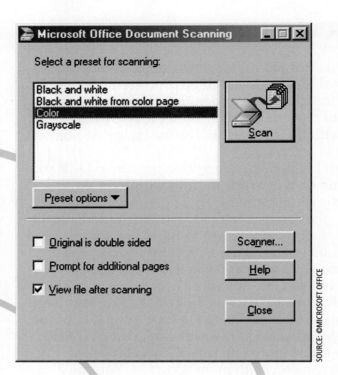

Windows XP includes a version of OCR software (Figure 6.6). With this option, you can scan using only the Windows software and import text directly into a word processing document.

Goro knows that the OCR on his scanner will not convert the hand-written text found on prescriptions to editable text, but he has used it often to convert typed notes that were in the pharmacy's files. His employer is very pleased because the process is slowly allowing the pharmacy to discard boxes that were taking up valuable retail space.

## THE **ETHICS** OF SCANNING

The ability to scan a photograph, graphical work, or text document creates an ethical dilemma. Just because you can scan someone else's work and use it on your computer doesn't mean you should. Laws on copyright and ownership still apply. You should seriously consider these issues before scanning documents. Of particular concern is the issue of scanning a work and then modifying it to make it appear to be your own work. Copyright laws clearly address this issue.

Student use of some works in school is allowed under fair use guidelines. Businesses do not have these same rights. It's important to keep this in mind when making the transition from school to the world of business. Creating business documents from scanned material must be done with care to avoid placing your business in jeopardy of copyright infringement, for which financial penalties can be assessed.

## SUMMARY

In this chapter, you looked at how TWAIN-compliant software works with a scanner and how scanner software can be used. You also learned how to determine the quality of a scanner on the basis of DPI and bit depth. You learned how to activate a scanner by using the manufacturer-provided software, as well as other software.

Answer the following questions on your own computer.

1. What two purposes do scanners serve?
2. What does the term **TWAIN** indicate?
3. How does a scanner work?
4. What two numbers indicate the capabilities of a scanner?
5. Explain two ways in which you can activate a scanner.
6. Once scanner software appears, what options do you have?
7. What is the difference between a scan preview and a scan?
8. What is usually the best choice in **DPI** selection?
9. To convert a scanned printed document, what is required?
10. Why would you want to teach your **OCR** software?

1. Is a paperless office a possibility in the future? Why? What would keep it from happening? Why would it be advantageous?
2. What actions should you take if you are scanning a work created by someone else?
3. What is the difference between using scanned work in school and in business?

## USE YOUR KNOWLEDGE

1. Use the Internet or other sources such as newspaper advertisements to determine the prices of at least three brands of scanners. Create a comparison chart that shows the brand of each scanner, the model, the price, the resolution and bit depth, and one other feature such as the type of software bundled with the scanner. Highlight the scanner you believe is the best choice.

2. Use the Internet or other sources to find three types of **OCR** software available. Write a memo that recommends one type of software over another and that gives the strengths and weaknesses of each, as well as the reasons for your final decision.

## FURTHER EXPLORATION

1. Unlike most computer acronyms, **TWAIN** does not have terms for each letter in the word. There are at least two sets of words often used to indicate what **TWAIN** stands for. Research the term to discover what the acronym may stand for. Share this with your class.

2. Make up your own set of terms for the **TWAIN** acronym. Create a poster for your terms and include at least one image in the poster.

3. Do research, using the Internet, to find other means of connecting scanners (and cameras) to a computer.

# Chapter 7
# Charts and Graphs

**ESTIMATED TIME**

**2**

**H O U R S**

SOURCE: ©PHOTODISC

## INTRODUCTION

Turning numbers into a picture is one of the most challenging aspects of visual communication. Conveying statistical information in a way that is interesting yet accurate is easy with the technology tools available today, but it's not as simple as it may look. The ease is a trap waiting for you. You may ask yourself why this is a trap. It can be a trap because businesspeople rely on charts and graphs to help them make sense of the reams of data that come to them, such as sales figures, inventory, costs, reports of losses or gains, and figures such as miles traveled. The person designing the image that depicts these figures must be able to sort through the statistics first and then choose the figures that are important. The task is not just one of image management; it is one of critical thinking.

## Objectives

- *You will learn how to select an appropriate chart or graph.*
- *You will learn to how to create an effective informational graphic.*
- *You will learn what details to include in a chart or graph.*

A chart with too much information is confusing. A chart type that doesn't fit the type of information being displayed is inaccurate. And a chart that does not include significant figures is misleading. At each point, decisions must be made by the chart designer—decisions that require significant thinking. There are no automatic answers. You must know what you are trying to convey and the best means of doing that. It is a significant image management activity.

## INFORMATIONAL GRAPHICS

Statistics are converted from numbers to informational graphics using charts. The easiest way to create informational graphics is to use the charting/graphing tools available in spreadsheet software such as Microsoft Excel or Lotus 1-2-3, but specialized charting programs with more options are also available. All these tools make it possible to record data and then to experiment with the resulting chart or graph until your visual information needs are met. Often, the exact best way to convey your information will not be apparent to you until you have tried several different approaches. Don't choose too quickly. Give yourself the opportunity to look at several different ways to present your information.

## CHART TYPES

When making a decision about what type chart to use, you can choose from a wide variety of chart types. Figure 7.1 lists the choices available in the Microsoft Chart Wizard. This list includes column, bar, line, pie scatter, area, doughnut, radar, surface, bubble, and stock, as well as cylinder, cone, and pyramid, which are not shown.

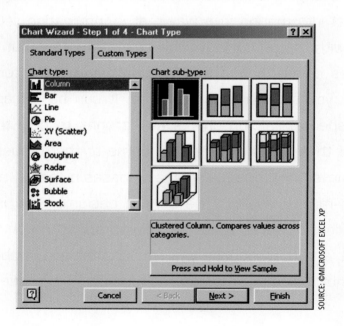

**Figure 7.1** The Microsoft chart wizard takes you through a series of steps making it easy to create an effective chart.

However, most charts fall into four basic types: bar, pie, line, and area. For example, a column chart is merely a vertical bar chart. The difference between one type of chart and another is the use for which it is designed. Vertical column charts generally are used to compare categories, while horizontal bar charts show value.

In addition, within each type, such as an area chart, are multiple subtypes designed to let you choose the most effective way to display information. One of the options available is the decision about dimensions. Most charts can be either two- or three-dimensional, so a column chart can be a series of flat rectangles or a series of boxes that appear to stand out from the background. Notice in Figure 7.1 that there are seven different ways to display columns; three are two-dimensional choices, and four are three-dimensional.

The following guidelines can be used as a general rule to help you make effective choices in the selection of a chart type:

- Column charts compare categories such as changes over time.
- Bar graphs display values rather than trends.
- Pie charts compare parts to the whole.
- Line graphs show trends.
- Area charts show both trends and contributions to the whole.

## CHART DESIGN

Once you have chosen the type of chart, you must now add the significant details. When you are designing a chart, one of the first issues you must be aware of is the purpose of the horizontal and vertical **axis,** for this is where your data will be plotted. Generally, the horizontal axis ($x$) shows categories, while the vertical axis ($y$) shows values. Reversing this standard can be confusing for your audience, so keep these conventions in mind.

Chart design uses a series of standard identification features that include axis labels, legends, and titles. A title provides the reader with information about the overall content. The title should be concise yet clear. A title is not a "throwaway" feature. Often the title conveys as much information as the chart itself. For example, a chart titled

### Maintain High Ethical Standards

**Business** and **ethics** are not mutually exclusive terms. Most businesses work hard to maintain high ethical standards and to present a good public image. A few, regrettably, do not. The temptation to skirt the law regarding multimedia applications can be particularly strong. For example, many graphic images are copyrighted and require permission (and fees paid to the owner) before they can be used in brochures or other documents. Sound files are often illegally pirated and used. It is easy to assume that nobody will find out about such activities.

The bottom line is this: You don't have to do something unethical just because your employer tells you to. Maintain your integrity. If your employer repeatedly asks you to act unethically, you're in the wrong place. Your next employer will likely highly value your honesty.

**Digging deeper:** Suppose your supervisor asks you to create a series of graphs using financial data you know has been falsified. A co-worker was fired last month for refusing to do this. What will you do? Discuss in class.

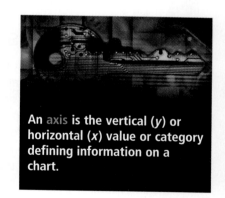

An **axis** is the vertical ($y$) or horizontal ($x$) value or category defining information on a chart.

"Income" is not as helpful as one titled "Income Comparison." Sometimes chart titles can reduce the need for additional information such as axis labels.

Axis labels identify the data type. This is often in the form of dates and dollars, which are easily identified. Some axis labels, however, may not be so easily identified, such as sales figures by type. Don't assume that your audience will be able to tell what each axis is measuring.

A **legend** identifies the numerical data category. Legends can be boxed with color or shade keys to identify the category, or the categories can be identified directly on the chart. As the designer of the informational graphic, you must decide the best way to visually communicate the information supplied by the chart.

Even though the nature of charts is their simplicity, don't leave out significant details such as the date of the information provided and the conditions under which the information was gathered. Footnotes or addendums providing this information can give credibility to your statistical image.

All these features are important image management tools because they make your chart readable and informative. It's easy to forget, as a chart designer, that what was obvious to you when you created the chart is not necessarily obvious to your audience. Including features such as a legend makes it easier to create a useful chart. Don't leave these out unless you are absolutely sure that the information is completely clear. It is better to include them unnecessarily than to risk confusing your reader.

The most important feature to keep in mind when designing an informational graphic is to keep your chart simple and easy to read, avoiding too many technical details that might be confusing. Visual communication skills require you to understand your audience and to know what level of knowledge they bring to your chart. If a chart contains information that your audience cannot

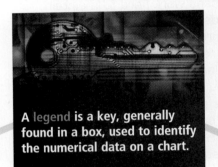

A **legend** is a key, generally found in a box, used to identify the numerical data on a chart.

## THE **ETHICS** OF STATISTICS

It's always tempting to make numbers say what we want. Using charts and graphs in a way that reveals only the information we want others to see is enticing because the very nature of these tools requires us to select a limited amount of information. For example, if a business wants to send the message that its sales are increasing, it could create a graph that shows sales of a particular product but ignores the negative information about other products. It's important to consider the ethics of such decisions. Don't let the need to focus on a limited amount of information distort the actual picture.

understand or that they might misunderstand, then no matter how accurate or complete it may be, you have failed to communicate. And communication is the absolute test of your chart.

To design effective informational graphics, keep in mind the following guidelines:

- Choose the graphic format based on the type of information to be displayed.
- Avoid being overly technical or overly simple.
- Have a specific goal in mind rather than just providing a compilation of information.
- Make sure the information is current.
- Indicate any special conditions under which information was gathered.
- Include a title, axis labels, and legends as appropriate.
- In a pie chart, limit the pieces to no more than five.
- In a line graph, use no more than three lines.

SOURCE: ©PHOTODISC

## CHARTS IN BUSINESS

Yuki Takada is an example of someone who has learned to design successful informational graphics. A group of dentists compiled a set of statistics based on information gathered over the last five years. The dentists hired Yuki Takada as a consultant to create a document for them to use at their monthly meeting to help them better understand the information they have received. The information falls into the following categories:

- Number of patients served
- Location of patients in the city
- How often patients sought services
- Average bill each year
- Average payment received from each patient
- Length of time for insurance payments to be received
- Average payment received from insurance

Rather than create an average of the total combined data, Yuki decides to use charting tools to turn the information into a visual to help the dentists see more clearly what the numbers actually mean. An average number in a table can be deceiving because it smooths out the highs and lows.

Beginning with a spreadsheet containing the essential data as shown in Figure 7.2, Yuki selects the fee information and creates a chart. From the wide variety available to her, she determines that her choices are a bar chart, a line chart, and a pie chart, but these types contain many variations, including three-dimensional options (see Figure 7.3).

| | A | B | C | D | E | F |
|---|---|---|---|---|---|---|
| 1 | | **1998** | **1999** | **2000** | **2001** | **2002** |
| 2 | **number of patients** | 2345 | 2365 | 2325 | 2354 | 2350 |
| 3 | **insurance payment per claim** | $10.00 | $57.00 | $88.00 | $72.00 | $91.00 |
| 4 | **patient payment** | $75.00 | $34.00 | $24.00 | $29.00 | $34.00 |
| 5 | **bill** | $85.00 | $91.00 | $112.00 | $101.00 | $125.00 |
| 6 | **length of wait for insurance (in days)** | 36 | 48 | 44 | 37 | 64 |
| 7 | **visits per year** | 1.2 | 2.1 | 1.8 | 1.5 | 2.1 |
| 8 | | | | | | |
| 9 | | | | | | |
| 10 | Witcherville | 287 | 287 | 288 | 285 | 281 |
| 11 | Riverbridge | 265 | 266 | 265 | 260 | 260 |
| 12 | Stonehenge | 280 | 279 | 270 | 345 | 348 |
| 13 | Brookstone | 225 | 252 | 345 | 330 | 335 |
| 14 | Hollowbrook | 288 | 275 | 240 | 265 | 260 |
| 15 | Madison | 1000 | 1006 | 917 | 869 | 866 |
| 16 | | 0 | 0 | 0 | 0 | 0 |
| 17 | | | | | | |

**Figure 7.2** Charts and graphs begin with spreadsheet information.

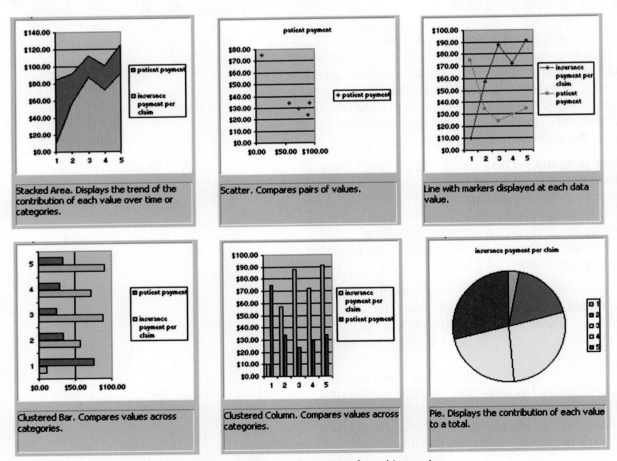

Stacked Area. Displays the trend of the contribution of each value over time or categories.

Scatter. Compares pairs of values.

Line with markers displayed at each data value.

Clustered Bar. Compares values across categories.

Clustered Column. Compares values across categories.

Pie. Displays the contribution of each value to a total.

**Figure 7.3** Microsoft charting software provides a wide variety of graphing options.

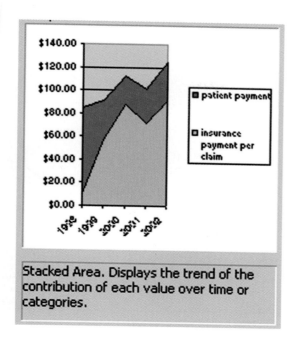

$140.00
$120.00
$100.00
$80.00
$60.00
$40.00
$20.00
$0.00

□ patient payment

□ insurance payment per claim

Stacked Area. Displays the trend of the contribution of each value over time or categories.

**Figure 7.4** Designers of informational graphics have to use critical thinking skills to choose the best means of delivering information.

Using critical thinking skills, Yuki realizes that the pie and line charts do not convey the substance of the information, but the bar graph does. Her choices are horizontal or vertical, but a better one stacks the information to show the overall payment and the impact of each type on the total, as shown in Figure 7.4. Looking again at her choices, Yuki realizes that using the continuous line shown in the area chart gives the best image.

With this decision, Yuki has begun the process of converting the numerical data into a professional visual communication device.

She moves on to the next step by adding identifying features. For the dental group, Yuki titles the chart "Patient Fees."

The legend indicates the area of patient payment and the area of insurance. The term *per claim* found on the spreadsheet isn't necessary and can be eliminated. Yuki could have added a separate legend to show the payment designations, but it would have distracted from the effect of the visual without adding more clarity.

Because the axis information clearly indicates year and payments, no additional designations are needed. The payments include no cents, so the zeroes after the decimals seen on the spreadsheet can be eliminated.

Color is an important consideration when creating graphs. Yuki's use of the white text to identify each payment type makes it easier to see the text and draws attention to the information. Yuki didn't let her ability to use color, three dimensions, and font choices overpower the message she wanted to send.

Figure 7.5 shows the informational graphic Yuki created to display the fee information. With this graphic, the dentists were able to see their numerical information more clearly. Yuki made her decisions based upon the need to convey information quickly and clearly.

**Figure 7.5** The patient fees chart is simple and clear.

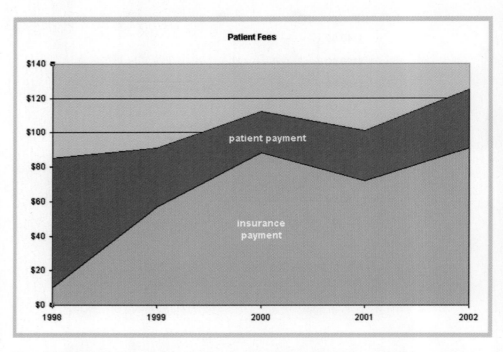

For the remainder of the information, she will make a different set of choices.

## SUMMARY

In this chapter, you learned how to create an effective chart or graph by converting numerical information into an informational graphic. You learned how to select an appropriate graph or chart and what details to include to make it effective in transmitting information. You saw that charting can be an important means of communicating visually.

Answer the following questions on your own computer.

1. What is the most important skill in creating charts and graphs?
2. How are averages in tables deceptive?
3. What are three basic chart types?
4. List three things to keep in mind when designing a chart.
5. What information should be used for the x-axis and the y-axis?
6. What software is most often used to create charts?
7. What should be included in a chart?
8. What is the rule for a title?
9. How can you overpower your chart's message?
10. What additional information should you indicate on a chart?

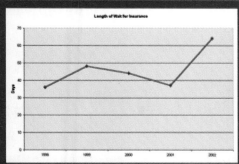

**Figure 7.6** Chart A

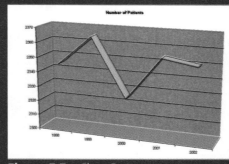

**Figure 7.7** Chart B

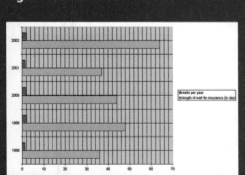

**Figure 7.8** Chart B

Using Figures 7.6 through 7.8, discuss the following questions either as a class or as a written assignment.

1. Which chart is clearest and which is most confusing? Why?
2. Which chart distorts information? How is the information distorted?
3. Which chart needs a legend and which does not? Why?
4. Which chart overpowers the information? How?
5. Choose one of the charts and explain how you would improve it.

## USE YOUR KNOWLEDGE

1. **Locate at least one example of each of the following charts or graphs: pie, bar, line. Business magazines and newspapers are good sources. Write a report in which you explain what each represents and why the author chose that particular charting or graphing form.**

2. **Using the Internet or other resources, find three specialized charting/graphing programs. Create a table in which you compare the cost to other features, such as a free trial download and advertised tools. Create a proposal explaining why specialized software would be a better choice than Microsoft Excel charting software.**

3. **Using Yahoo! Finance or another Internet stock chart, look up a stock in the various charts available. What is the difference? Do any of the charts distort the information? Print copies of at least three different charts to use on a poster that demonstrates your conclusions.**

## FURTHER EXPLORATION

1. **Survey students and faculty to determine how often they use charts/graphs to understand numerical data, which sources they use for this information, and what they find most difficult about using them.**

2. **Use this survey information to create an informational guide for your class to help them produce more easily readable charts/graphs.**

# Chapter 8
## Maps

ESTIMATED TIME

2

HOURS

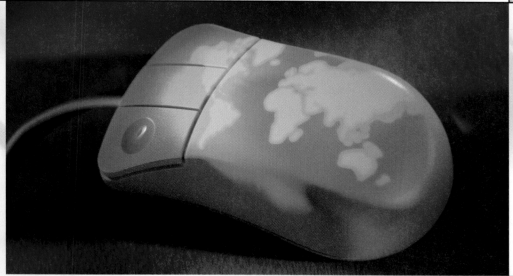

SOURCE: ©PHOTODISC

## INTRODUCTION

**Business geographics,** the use of maps for business purposes, is becoming a vital visual communication skill requiring workers in many careers to know how to use and create maps. Maps today provide visual information about business details such as sales figures and frequency of customer responses. Maps can tell you who your customers are and where they live. They can help you identify new customers. Maps can tell you whether other geographic areas have the same potential. They can tell you what your competitor is doing and where you might place business sites to meet that competition. Being able to use mapping software effectively is an image management tool required in today's world.

## Objectives

- *You will learn what tools are available in mapping software.*
- *You will explore what purpose a data map can serve.*
- *You will discover how to create data maps by using spreadsheet information.*

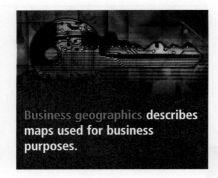

Business geographics describes maps used for business purposes.

Many software mapping programs are available for business purposes. These include general-purpose programs such as Microsoft Expedia Streets & Trips, DeLorme Map'n'Go, and Yahoo! MapQuest and specialized data mapping software such as Microsoft MapPoint and Tactician MapScape.

A good example of someone who effectively uses business geographics is the sales manager for a distributor of a recently improved product. The product has a high sales potential but little brand recognition. Up until now sales have spread by word of mouth. To improve sales, the manager, Patrick Mullin, is given permission to hire six new sales representatives to cover a three-state region: Texas, Oklahoma, and New Mexico. Patrick believes that a focused sales plan can improve the sales record of this product. Part of his planning requires him to complete several mapping tasks, including the following:

a. divide the sales force among the states,
b. locate the sites that are already selling the product, and
c. determine new sites to approach about retailing the product.

Patrick begins by using a general mapping program to consider the possibilities and challenges he faces in his sales area. This software provides a map showing the relative sizes of cities and locations of major roads.

## MAPPING TOOLS

Mapping software, whether it is general-purpose or specialized, has several standard mapping tools:

- Pushpins
- Panning
- Zooming
- Measuring tool
- Legend
- Ability to add colored lines
- Selection area tool
- Direction instructions

## THE **ETHICS** OF MAP PROTECTION

Maps developed by using software such as Yahoo! MapQuest and Microsoft MapPoint are protected by copyright just as if they were text. Maps such as these can be used for information purposes within your business but not for publication unless you have permission from the company that created the maps. Consider how you would go about seeking permission to use a map you need for an outside purpose.

Each tool is designed to be easy to work with and to make it easy to understand the maps available within the software. Learning how to use them with ease is an important visual communication skill that will be valuable regardless of the career you choose.

Pushpins locate specific sites. They can appear in a variety of forms, as shown in Figure 8.1. These pin selections are available in Microsoft MapPoint, but other

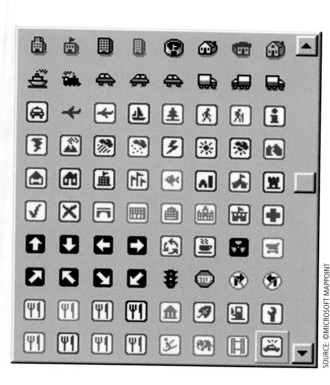

SOURCE: ©MICROSOFT MAPPOINT

**Figure 8.1** Pushpins can be designed using a wide variety of figures—not just the standard image of a tack.

mapping software provides multiple choices also. Pushpins are useful for indicating points of interest or destinations. Using different-style pins makes it easy to identify quickly what information the audience is seeing. For example, Patrick might use one type of pushpin for the town in which the sales representative lives and another type for major accounts.

The ability to zoom in on a particular site or area on a map is essential in mapping software. Both panning and zooming allow this. *Zooming in* enlarges and *zooming out* reduces the area visible on the screen. Details that are not visible on a map at one size often appear when you zoom in. This is one of the advantages of using computerized maps. Details can be omitted at different resolutions to reduce the visual clutter. A selection tool is also usually included, that enables you to select the specific area that you want to zoom in to and then precisely perform the function in one step.

Once you have zoomed in to the area you want to see, you may need to move small distances to adjust the visual area. **Panning** moves across an area by means of a "hand" to guide the user. A panning hand allows you to easily direct your motion with more control than you would get with just standard vertical or horizontal scroll bars.

Knowing the distance from one point to another is one of the most frequently used purposes of a map. Paper maps include the distances from one town to another, requiring you to add the mileage together to determine the distance between towns that might be separated by many miles and many towns along the way. Computerized mapping software simplifies that process using a measuring tool. The measuring tool provides distance information from any location or point to another without requiring you to do the computation. Patrick finds

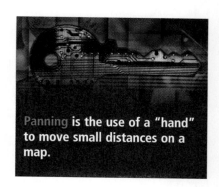

Panning **is the use of a "hand" to move small distances on a map.**

this mapping tool very useful when considering how to set up the territories because he can quickly determine how far his representatives will have to drive to reach each of their customers.

The legend identifies the parts of the map and color codes. Colors help differentiate between areas of information. Just as in the creation of charts in Chapter 7, legends provide helpful information for those using the map. Legends are particularly important because they help your audience understand details that might be missed. Patrick makes sure his legends are clear before he sends maps to his representatives or his employer because he knows that such attention to detail is an essential communication tool.

Many general-purpose and specialized programs provide written direction instructions to guide the user from one destination to another. These directions often include points of interest along the way, road conditions such as construction delays, distances, time to complete the trip, and even the cost of the trip.

Figure 8.2 is an example of a map that Patrick used to begin his decision-making process. He used colored lines to separate the

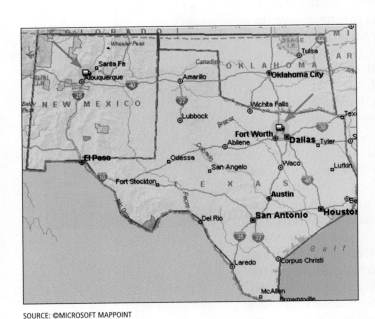

**Figure 8.2** Maps have always been useful, but with image management they have become even more so.

sales territory from surrounding states to make it easier to see. He used pushpins to designate the locations of the warehouses shown by the arrows. The mapping program he used came with large city designations and federal highways, which made identifying trade routes easier. He could also measure the approximate distance that his representatives traveled to help him decide which towns to assign to each area. He even printed out direction instructions to include in information packages for his new sales representatives, and he planned to encourage his sales force to add their own as new accounts were added. This way when a new sales rep took over the territory, that person would not have to waste time learning the routes.

## DATA MAPS

The map in Figure 8.2 was created with general-purpose mapping software, but other programs can provide specialized information called **data mapping.** With data mapping software, it is easy to create a map that contains numerical data in map form. You can create a data map by using either your own spreadsheet data or data provided by the mapping program.

Several data mapping programs are available for use by businesses. Earlier versions of Office contained a data mapping component for use in both Word and Excel. The maps provided in Office were limited to states and countries, so data designations were rather broad. This applet has been replaced with MapPoint, a full-featured program.

Microsoft MapPoint is a complex data mapping program. It makes possible the design of maps that convey visual images of population densities, ages, and income levels based on census data. These maps can show areas within a state or region and even zip codes.

Tactician MapScape, a program used through the Internet, also uses census data and can provide area or region mapping. The advantage of MapScape is that you can access the information from any computer connected to the Internet, which means that you do not have to have specialized software on the computer you are using.

### Following Directions

Employers frequently complain about new workers who will not follow directions or do what they're told. Because of poor communication skills, an employee may sometimes not understand what is being requested. More often, though, an employee simply refuses to do what an employer has asked. This behavior is unacceptable and unprofessional. Your boss is, after all, your boss. Unless you're being asked to do something unethical or something **completely** other than what you were hired for (for example, you were hired as a Web editor but your boss wants you to wash the windows!), you have an obligation to perform the tasks you are assigned. In the workplace, your employer **can** "tell you what to do."

Your willingness to follow directions will help you work well in teams. It will also lead to better, more challenging projects. Employees who will not carry out their assigned tasks will have trouble holding on to their jobs, much less receiving promotions. You will not be able to advance your career if you cannot (or will not) do what your employer asks.

**Digging deeper:** How well can you follow directions? To find out, take the online quiz at http://www.justriddlesandmore.com/direct.html (or search for your own—there are many similar quizzes online).

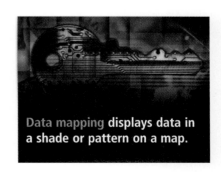

**Data mapping** displays data in a shade or pattern on a map.

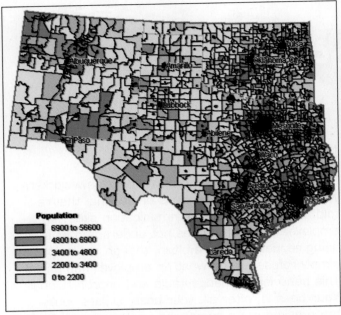

**Figure 8.3** Population maps use colors to demonstrate the density of one area over another.

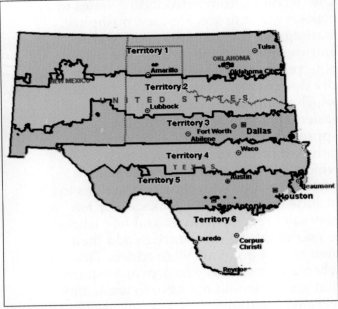

**Figure 8.4** Datamaps can be used as a management tool such as this one showing a possible division of territories.

Figure 8.3 shows the result of using data mapping software based on census information. A series of graduated colors indicates the population density of the three-state area as shown in the legend. With such information, businesspeople such as Patrick can make more informed decisions.

Patrick used the data map shown to consider the territory makeup. Originally, he had planned to create six "square" territories to cut down on the driving distances for the representatives, but that plan did not take into consideration the population density of the areas. Density of population, which means there may be more customers, can cause equal geographic territories to be unequal in sales potential. Patrick viewed the populations of the various territories to even out the possible sales. As shown in Figure 8.3, the greatest population is in a vertical corridor along the east side of the map where the colors are the darkest.

With this information, Patrick considered another possibility—to run territorial lines in horizontal swaths (similar to the map shown in Figure 8.4) so that some high-population areas and some lower-population areas were included in each territory. Patrick used county populations for his map, but he could have also chosen another designation such as a zip code or a state.

## OTHER DATA MAPS

Maps are not just used to indicate locations of cities, distances, or even population densities. They are also used to visually communi-

| | A | B | C |
|---|---|---|---|
| 1 | City | State | Sales |
| 2 | Abilene | TX | 6,200 |
| 3 | Albuquerqu | NM | 3,456 |
| 4 | Amarillo | TX | 9,400 |
| 5 | Austin | TX | 10 |
| 6 | Corpus Ch | TX | 7,300 |
| 7 | Dallas | TX | 3,456 |
| 8 | El Paso | TX | 3 |
| 9 | Ft Worth | TX | 4,678 |
| 10 | Houston | TX | 5,456 |
| 11 | Laredo | TX | 4,678 |
| 12 | Lubbock | TX | 6,200 |
| 13 | Oklahoma | OK | 7,300 |
| 14 | San Antoni | TX | 367 |
| 15 | Tulsa | OK | 5,456 |
| 16 | Waco | TX | 9,400 |

**Figure 8.5** A spreadsheet is a means of entering information for later using by mapping software.

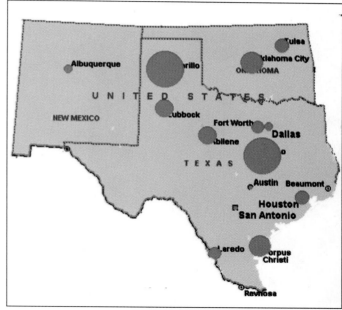

SOURCE: ©MICROSOFT MAPPOINT

**Figure 8.6** This map demonstrating sales by city could be enlarged and printed for use in an office.

cate other information such as sales figures based on locations. Patrick entered the current figures for sales in the three states, as shown in Figure 8.5. He then used the map shown in Figure 8.6 to visually explain the current sales figures.

The map clearly indicates the disparity in sales figures from one size town to another. Some smaller cities such as Amarillo and Waco have extraordinary sales, while some very large cities such as El Paso and Houston have minimal sales. With this data map sending such a compelling message, Patrick finds it easy to demonstrate what the sales goals for the next year need to be. Obviously, some excellent sales opportunities are being missed by the sales force. He plans to use this map and others like it to encourage his sales force to become the most successful team in the nation.

## SUMMARY

In this chapter, you looked at ways that business geographics can be used as part of image management. You explored general-purpose mapping software and data mapping software. You learned that data mapping can incorporate information provided by the mapping software, such as census data, or can use data supplied by the user in the form of a spreadsheet. You saw that mapping can be an important means of providing visual communication.

Answer the following questions on your own computer.

1. What is business geographics?
2. How can business geographics be useful?
3. What is the purpose of pushpins?
4. What is the name of the mapping tool that uses a "hand" moving across the area to guide the user?
5. What is the name of the mapping tool that enlarges or reduces the area visible on the screen?
6. What are the two functions of a legend?
7. How can you differentiate between areas of information?
8. What mapping tool is used to focus on a specific area when zooming in?
9. What is data mapping?
10. Where does the information come from that is used in a data mapping program?

## DISCUSSION

1. How would other mapping features such as the geography of an area affect a business decision?
2. Observe the maps shown in Figures 8.2, 8.3, 8.4, and 8.6. With this combination of information, how would you divide the territories to make them equitable?
3. What other business geographics uses can you see for mapping software?
4. Which is more useful—mapping software stored on a computer or software accessed from the Internet?
5. How can you know that the data mapping information supplied by the software is accurate?

1. Search for different types of mapping software. Investigate what is available on the Internet, as well as software that can be installed directly on a computer. Compare the features and costs. List the names of the companies and other contact information. Create a visual display of your information and give a brief (3–5 minutes) persuasive talk to your class about which software they should purchase for business use.

2. Find three maps that are examples of business geographics. Your economics or history textbooks might contain some. Identify each of the following on these examples: pushpins, legend, color differentiation. Include a brief description of what information each map provides the reader.

**FURTHER EXPLORATION**

1. Use of **GPS** (global positioning system) technology is changing the way maps are used. What is **GPS**, how does it operate, who uses **GPS**, and what purpose does it serve for business? Try to locate a **GPS** to bring to class to demonstrate to your classmates its use and business potential.

2. Investigate cartography (the study of maps) as a business opportunity. Create a business plan that demonstrates what you learned about the potential sales.

# Unit 2: Summary

## Key Concepts

### Chapter 5: Digital Photography

1. Generally, the brightest, lightest, and most colorful object in a photograph attracts the most attention.
2. The focus point of a photograph should be chosen so that the eye can move about the picture.
3. Dividing a photograph horizontally or vertically into thirds provides a satisfying balance.
4. Viewers prefer to feel that they are seeing a moment captured as it happened, not as it was posed.
5. Digital cameras have advantages over traditional film cameras: They save both time and money.
6. Some features are common to all digital cameras, including a power switch, an option to view a picture already taken, flash choices, zoom options, battery location, and a means of saving photographs and sending them to a computer.
7. Cropping is a tool often used to modify a photograph that doesn't quite communicate the message you want.
8. One of today's most interesting software packages makes it possible to turn a series of photographs taken at different angles and positions into one three-dimensional photograph.

### Chapter 6: Scanning

1. Scanners convert graphics and text to a digital format using TWAIN.
2. The difference in scanner prices is related to the number and quality of pixels the scanner can capture, as well as to the speed at which the scanning occurs.
3. Scanner software lets you select the image size, type, and resolution before the scan begins.
4. Scanning at a high resolution creates a very large file size without always improving the quality of the image.
5. To convert text to a digital format requires two steps: (a) scanning an image of the document and then (b) using OCR software to convert the image of the letters into working text.

### Chapter 7: Charts and Graphs

1. The easiest way to create informational graphics is to use the charting/graphing tools available in spreadsheet software such as Microsoft Excel or Lotus 1-2-3.
2. You must sort through the statistics first and then choose the figures that are important.
3. Using charts and graphs is not just an image management skill; it is a critical-thinking skill.
4. When using charts or graphs, you should have a specific purpose in mind rather than just compiling information.
5. The graph or chart format you choose should be based on the type of information to be displayed.
6. The chart or graph should include a title, axis labels, and legends as appropriate.
7. The title should be concise yet clear.
8. Color is an important consideration when creating graphs.

# Chapter 8: Maps

1. Business geographics is becoming a vital communication skill requiring workers in many careers to know how to use and create maps.
2. Maps that provide visual information about details such as sales figures and frequency of customer responses help businesspeople make better-informed decisions.
3. Mapping software has several standard tools: pushpins, panning, zooming, measuring tool, legend, ability to add colored lines, selection area tool, and directions.
4. Data mapping software makes it possible to create a map that contains numerical data.

## Terms

**axis** the vertical ($y$) or horizontal ($x$) value or category defining information on a chart

**bit depth** a measurement to indicate how much information is gathered about the red, green, and blue components of a pixel

**business geographics** maps used for business purposes

**cropping** the cutting away of one or more "sides" of a picture to remove unwanted areas and to increase the focus

**data mapping** data displayed in a shade or pattern on a map

**DPI** dots per inch; a measurement used with printers and scanners to indicate how many points of ink or pixels are contained in an inch

**legend** a key, generally found in a box, used to identify the numerical data on a chart

**panning** the use of a "hand" to move small distances on a map

**photographic composition** the selection and arrangement of subjects within a photograph

**rule of thirds** visually dividing a photograph into thirds (either horizontally or vertically) to provide a satisfying balance

**TWAIN** an acronym indicating that the software can work with a scanner

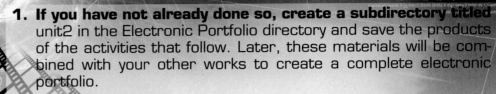

# ELECTRONIC PORTFOLIO

1. **If you have not already done so, create a subdirectory titled** unit2 in the Electronic Portfolio directory and save the products of the activities that follow. Later, these materials will be combined with your other works to create a complete electronic portfolio.

2. With a digital camera, take photographs that demonstrate each of the following:
   a. rule of thirds
   b. off-center composition
   c. special effects
   d. unifying elements
   e. framing
   f. cluttered background

   Rename and save each photograph to identify the effect that it demonstrates such as **thirds.jpg**, **offcenter.jpg**, **special.jpg**, **unifying.jpg**, **framing.jpg**, and **cluttered.jpg**. (If you do not have a digital camera, scan print photographs instead.)

3. Scan this page (or one provided by your instructor) and convert it to text using OCR software. Save it as **ocr.doc**.

4. Survey 20 of your classmates to determine their choice of careers after graduation and where they would like to live. Divide their career choices into five logical categories. Create a chart or graph that most effectively demonstrates the outcome of the survey. Save the chart or graph as a new sheet called **careers.xls**.

5. Use general-purpose mapping software to pinpoint the location choices of the five most popular sites to live after graduation. Save the map as **popularsites**.

6. Use data mapping software to demonstrate where all 20 respondents would most like to live and save it as **allsites**.

**7.** Use the following chart to evaluate the quality of your portfolio material.

| | Beginning | Developing | Accomplished | Exemplary | Score |
|---|---|---|---|---|---|
| Rule-of-thirds image | Image marginally demonstrates concept | Image demonstrates knowledge of concept | Image fully demonstrates concept | Interesting composition fully demonstrating concept | |
| Off-center composition | Image marginally demonstrates concept | Image demonstrates knowledge of concept | Image fully demonstrates concept | Interesting composition fully demonstrating concept | |
| Special effects | Image marginally demonstrates concept | Image demonstrates knowledge of concept | Image fully demonstrates concept | Interesting composition fully demonstrating concept | |
| Unifying elements | Image marginally demonstrates concept | Image demonstrates knowledge of concept | Image fully demonstrates concept | Interesting composition fully demonstrating concept | |
| Framing | Image marginally demonstrates concept | Image demonstrates knowledge of concept | Image fully demonstrates concept | Interesting composition fully demonstrating concept | |
| Cluttered background | Image marginally demonstrates concept | Image demonstrates knowledge of concept | Image fully demonstrates concept | Interesting composition fully demonstrating concept | |
| OCR sample | Sample scanned with many inaccuracies | Sample scanned with some inaccuracies | Sample accurately scanned and corrected | Original choice of sample fully converted to OCR | |
| Career chart | Fewer than 20 survey responses with minimal chart information | 20 survey responses with minimal chart information | 20 survey responses with adequate chart information | 20 or more survey responses with original categories and chart information | |
| Popular sites map | Map contains fewer than five sites with minimal information | Map contains five sites with adequate information | Map contains five sites with complete details | Map contains five sites with fully explained information and clear focus | |
| Allsites datamap | Map contains fewer than 20 sites with minimal information | Map contains 20 sites with adequate information | Map contains 20 sites with complete details | Map contains 20 sites with fully explained information and clear focus | |

# UNIT

# 3

# Print Publishing

SOURCE: ©PHOTODISC

# Career Profile

Roush Hardware is a 50-year-old hometown company that offers a lot of service and a lot of products. Roush has expanded over the years to include the Westerville and Dublin, Ohio, stores, as well as the Worthington shop, which focuses on sales and service.

Some may think that working for almost 20 years at a local hardware store would be boring. But it's not! Just ask Lisa DiNinno, vice-president and general manager. Lisa knows what makes a hardware store a thrill in the lives of its customers—products they need, customer service they want, and friendship with focus on the target market.

Roush Hardware owes much of the growth that Lisa has seen over the years to its customer attitude—and to its quality products and can-do philosophy.

SOURCE: ©PHOTODISC

(continued)

Lisa has seen its advertising and promotional materials change from being mostly hand-done to being mostly outsourced to large wholesalers and printers.

In reflecting on how customers have changed, Lisa said, "Today, they don't want to read a lot of material; the information must attract attention and pop"; customers can get information in so many ways that Lisa must consider the promotional value of each piece she approves for distribution.

Roush advertises in several ways—monthly flyers and seasonal promotions are sent by direct mail. Coupon magazines carry promotional coupons that Lisa must inspect with care; after all, having coupons go out without an expiration date or the Roush name could cost the company business. Lisa must work with suburban newspapers that carry the store's advertisements to be sure the items projected in the papers show their quality and encourage customers to shop for those items. So, the advertisements must be technically correct and the type size, colors, and fonts must be attractive. The same is true for all the mailings and the Yellow Pages insert. Even grocery stores may display large informational posters advertising Roush Hardware products.

Most of the flyers and mass mailings are now outsourced to large wholesalers who design the entire creative item and then present it to Lisa for approval and/or changes. She can select any number of pages from the creative piece but must select at least eight pages to meet press requirements.

Seasonal issues are often done in-house at Roush. Lisa uses Microsoft Publisher and Adobe Photoshop to design an advertising piece. She then adds the written message, selects appropriate black-and-white ad slicks, and creates each issue. After a thorough review, it is printed and photocopied right in the store for mailing. Lisa is responsible for the accuracy of the information, the design of the piece, and the distribution.

Another advertising element that falls under Lisa's domain is the copy for the Yellow Pages insert. Imagine how important it is for the correct information to be placed in a telephone directory that will be used for at least a year.

How did Lisa learn to work with these items and with printers, suppliers, and designers? Her education at Otterbein College gave her a good background in psychology, but she gained expertise through experience and, of course, trial and error. In addition, Lisa attends seminars, reads trade publications, and listens to feedback from colleagues and customers. Lisa must keep up to date on building and equipment changes and how they affect the products the hardware store must stock for its customers.

She is constantly aware of how technology is changing the business environment in which she works. Knowing how to access information and to find specifications through technology is critical to the success of a hardware store. ■

Note: Lisa DiNinno is a real person and Roush Hardware, based in Westerville and Dublin, Ohio, is a real business.

ESTIMATED TIME
3
HOURS

# **Chapter** 9
## Print Type

## Objectives

- *You will learn the importance of typography in print publishing.*
- *You will learn the spacing options available for print type.*
- *You will learn the punctuation of desktop publishing.*

## INTRODUCTION

Image management goes well beyond cropping photographs or creating images with Photoshop. It extends into every aspect of communication from print to presentation and onto the Web. Any time you must make decisions about the appearance of a printed page, a visual presentation, or a Web page, you are making image management choices. In this unit you will explore image management issues that relate to print publications to learn how to make good choices that will communicate effectively.

# DESKTOP PUBLISHING

Print publishing in today's computer driven world is generally referred to as **desktop publishing.** *Desktop publishing* is a term that came into use with the introduction of Aldus PageMaker. Until that time, publishing was in the hands of professionals who used typesetters, light tables, and proof sheets to create print publications. With personal computers and specialized software, nonprofessionals could begin to produce documents at their desks. Although this capability made it possible to create brochures, newsletters, and flyers on a personal computer, it also meant that "amateurs" were required to acquire skills that professionals once spent years of training to perfect. Some of the skills needed to produce quality desktop-published works include an understanding of typography, graphics, layout, and business expectations.

Fortunately, it is now easier to move from unskilled to skilled by using textbooks such as this one. Although in this course you will not likely develop the skills of a professional, you will be able to make good decisions that will give your print publications a professional look. You will be able to do this whether you are using word processing software, a simple desktop publishing program such as Microsoft Publisher, or specialized desktop publishing software such as Adobe PageMaker (which was purchased from Aldus in 1994), QuarkXPress, or a new product such as Adobe InDesign.

Although not every business professional will be proficient in all aspects of image management, without a doubt everyone will need knowledge of desktop publishing even if his or her skills are limited to the creation of a simple ad. Herman Jacobson, as the owner of a local fast-food restaurant, discovers this quickly as he plans for his first newspaper ad to be run in the local thrift paper and asks you to create it.

# TYPOGRAPHY

Desktop publishing requires you to mix the printed word with graphics in such a way that each enhances the message of the other. In this

Desktop publishing is the use of word processing software or specialized desktop publishing software on a personal computer to create a document in which graphics and text enhance the message.

## Flexibility

The fast pace of business requires employees to adjust to new circumstances quickly. Procedures that were effective two or three years ago may be outmoded today. Employers highly value workers who can be flexible and adapt as the need arises.

Although it can sometimes be frustrating to change procedures or to start a project over from scratch, when plans change on the job, learn to roll with it. Don't get stuck in a rut. When someone suggests a new idea, don't automatically resist it. Look at it as an opportunity to learn something new, something that could make you more productive. You should also look for ways to anticipate and initiate change, rather than merely respond to it. The ability to learn and the willingness to add to what you already know will be crucial in your development as a flexible, adaptable employee. The more you know, the easier it will be for you to deal with change.

**Digging deeper:** How has multimedia software (such as Photoshop, QuarkXPress, and Power-Point) changed the way people do business? What advantages do businesses with employees fluent with multimedia software have over businesses without such workers? Discuss in class.

## CORRECT KEYBOARDING TECHNIQUE

Desktop publishing can require extensive keying of text. When you key, keep your fingers curved and upright over the home row keys. Keep your wrists low, but not touching the keyboard.

Lightly tap each key with the tip of your finger, snapping the fingertip toward the palm of your hand. Your hands and arms won't be as tired at the end of the day if you follow these simple techniques.

Typography is the study of all elements of type including the shape, size, and spacing of the characters.

A typeface is the design of the letters, numbers, and symbols that make up a font.

The definition of font originally included typeface, style, and size, but the term now is interchangeable with *typeface*.

Serif describes a typeface with extensions at the ends of the main strokes that define each letter; these extensions are called serifs.

Sans serif described a typeface without serifs.

chapter, you will learn the ins and outs of type. In the next chapter, you will move on to graphics.

Type is not just letters on a page. It is also the shape and size of the letters, the spacing of the type, and the choice of design. All these elements are included in the study of type called **typography.** Basic knowledge of typography means you will understand such things as why you might not want to use grunge type in Herman's weekly ad.

## TYPE FONTS

Type can be identified in three ways: typeface, style, and size. **Typeface** is the shape of letter such as Times Roman or Arial. Originally, type was set with sets of small metal letters called **fonts** that combined all three aspects of type. For example, one font might be identified as 14-point Times Roman Bold. Another font might be identified as 12-point Times Roman. The typeface, style, and size together determined the font.

With the introduction of computer type, the term *font* came to be identified only with the typeface name, such as Times Roman. The size and style were identified separately. As a result, today the terms *font* and *typeface* are used interchangeably.

Typefaces fall into two basic categories: **serif** and **sans serif.** Serif typefaces (or fonts) have small decorative strokes or "feet" at the ends of the main strokes that define each letter. Notice the serif feet in Figure 9.1. Sans serif typefaces (*sans* means "without") have no such strokes and are simpler in appearance.

This font has serifs or strokes.

This font is without strokes (sans serif).

**Figure 9.1** Serif fonts are viewed as more formal; sans serif fonts are seen as casual.

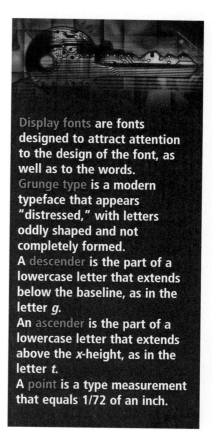

Figure 9.2  Display fonts are interesting but may blur your message because they are so unusual.

The generally accepted rule is that serif typefaces make better text because they are easier to read and that sans serif typefaces make better headings because they slow down the reader. Recent research, however, seems to indicate no difference in reading speed. The most commonly used typefaces are Times New Roman (serif) and Arial (sans serif), shown in Figure 9.1. On Macintosh computers, Times/New York (serif) and Helvetica/Geneva (sans serif) are most commonly used.

Falling into either category are specialized fonts designed to attract attention. One of the most common groups is script typefaces, in which the letters are connected as in handwriting. Other typefaces called **display fonts** are designed to draw attention to the text; they appear to be hand drawn rather than typeset, because of such techniques as adding a circle instead of a dot over the letter *i*. A more recent addition to font choices is **grunge type,** designed to appear "beaten up," with parts of the characters missing or misshapen. Examples of some of these fonts are shown in Figure 9.2.

You first consider using a grunge type to grab the reader's attention in Mr. Jacobson's ad, but after thinking about it, you realize that you are not sure how well it will appear in newsprint. You show Herman several choices to see which he thinks will best represent his restaurant and both of you decide on a different display font.

## TYPE SIZE

Type is measured on the characters that have ascenders and descenders. A **descender** is the part of a lowercase letter that extends below the baseline (the lower red line in Figure 9.3), as in the letter *y;* an **ascender** is the part that extends above the *x*-height (the upper red line), as in the letter *f*. The distance between the top of the highest ascender and the bottom of the lowest descender (shown in blue) determines the size of the font. This size is measured in **points** (a point is approximately 1/72 of an inch).

It's important to realize that the height of the typeface, rather than its width, is measured. This means that if you select another typeface,

Display fonts **are fonts designed to attract attention to the design of the font, as well as to the words.**
Grunge type **is a modern typeface that appears "distressed," with letters oddly shaped and not completely formed.**
A descender **is the part of a lowercase letter that extends below the baseline, as in the letter** *g*.
An ascender **is the part of a lowercase letter that extends above the *x*-height, as in the letter** *t*.
A point **is a type measurement that equals 1/72 of an inch.**

**Figure 9.3** Font measurement is performed with a special point ruler.

even of the same point size, your text length may change, and the content that had fit perfectly on a single page now runs over or under what you intended.

When you experiment with display fonts for Herman's ad, this difference in measurement becomes very apparent. In one font, the headline words all fit on one line; in another font, they run over to the second line and thus change the appearance of the ad.

## TYPESTYLES

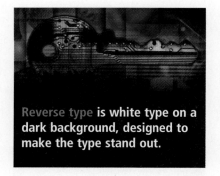

Reverse type **is white type on a dark background, designed to make the type stand out.**

Computerized fonts allow you to create interesting effects with text. These include the standard styles such as bold and italic, but also options such as embossing, engraving, outlining, and shadowing. **Reverse type** is a common style used because the image of white text on a dark background is quite striking (see Figure 9.4). Some desktop programs make this easy, but in word processing programs you may have to use white text with a black box behind it.

One type style that is important for a desktop publisher to consider is italic. When all text was typed on a typewriter, it was not possible to create italicized words. Rules of punctuation required that the names of book titles be italicized, so underlining was used to indicate italic for the typesetter. With the movement to computerized type, it is now possible to italicize titles; underlining is no longer necessary. Use italic instead.

**Figure 9.4** Reverse type is sometimes difficult to print because the dark background may not print as a solid color.

```
Courier is a monospace font.

Times New Roman is a proportional font.

Arial is also a proportional font.
```

**Figure 9.5** A monospace font is generally used only to convey the impression that the text was created with a typewriter.

## SPACING

Another consideration when choosing type is spacing. In the days of typewriters, each letter was assigned the same width so that a "skinny" letter *i* and a "fat" letter *m* were spaced exactly the same; this is called *monospacing*. Computer type has made monospacing no longer necessary; space is now allocated proportionally on the basis of letter width. The Courier font, found in many computer systems, is an example of a **monospace font,** as shown in Figure 9.5. All three examples are 26 points high, but the first example is a monospace font, the second is Times, and the third is Arial.

The use of proportional fonts is the reason you cannot match the spacing of one line of text with another by using the spacebar. Because each letter is given just the space it needs, a line with ten characters may be slightly shorter or longer than another line with ten characters. To line up text, use the tab marker instead to ensure that each line starts at the same place. You discover this concept when you try to line up some information in Herman's ad.

## THE **ETHICS** OF FONT PROTECTION

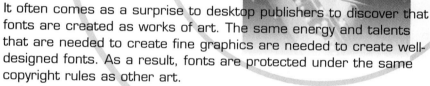

It often comes as a surprise to desktop publishers to discover that fonts are created as works of art. The same energy and talents that are needed to create fine graphics are needed to create well-designed fonts. As a result, fonts are protected under the same copyright rules as other art.

Most fonts are acquired when you purchase other software such as a desktop publishing program that comes with its own set of fonts to enhance the look of your work. Because of the nature of fonts, it is easy to share them with others, but that violates copyright law.

Many fonts are available free on the Web. Unfortunately, often these have not been created by the person providing them for free. Beware of such free fonts when using them in a business environment. Businesses that use specialized fonts in ads or publicly distributed documents must be sure they have a legal right to use them.

## TRACKING

Proportional fonts are not limited to a set amount of spacing between letters. They can be adjusted to "open up" or close the amount of white space, or blank area, between characters. This is called **tracking** or character spacing. In Figure 9.6, the first example is the default, or original, spacing. The second example is expanded; the third is condensed. Even

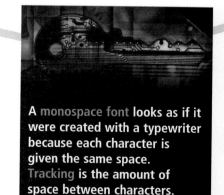

A monospace font looks as if it were created with a typewriter because each character is given the same space. Tracking is the amount of space between characters.

Proportional fonts let you choose the spacing between characters.

Proportional fonts let you choose the spacing between characters.

Proportional fonts let you choose the spacing between characters.

**Figure 9.6**   Changing the character spacing is useful if you need to "squeeze" a little more text on a line.

if the spacing is expanded, however, the distance between letters remains proportional. For some readers, it's easier to read the expanded version; for others, the extra space is a distraction.

## KERNING

Another spacing decision is **kerning**. Some letters "tuck" into the next to make them visually more appealing. Notice in the first example in Figure 9.7 that the letters *T* and *y* are proportionally the same distance apart. If they are kerned, the letter *y* tucks in under the *T*, as shown in the second example. Kerning is particularly important when using larger font sizes for banners and ads. A **ligature,** or the tying together of two letters to form a single unit such as *fi*, is similar to kerning but is usually determined by the font designer rather than by the desktop publisher.

## LEADING

Spacing is not limited to the area between characters. The spacing between lines, called **leading** (pronounced "ledding"), is also a function of typography. In the typewriter world, this spacing was limited to single, double, or perhaps 1.5 spaces. In desktop publishing, the spacing can be whatever you want. Leading is measured in points, with 24 points equaling a double space.

In earlier times, the spacing between paragraphs was the same as the spacing between lines of text; an indent was used to provide a visual cue that a new paragraph was starting. Today, with desktop publishing options easily available, designers often use customized spacing between paragraphs as a cue, instead of indents.

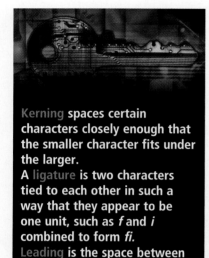

**Kerning** spaces certain characters closely enough that the smaller character fits under the larger.
A **ligature** is two characters tied to each other in such a way that they appear to be one unit, such as *f* and *i* combined to form *fi.*
**Leading** is the space between lines of text or between paragraphs.

# Typeface
# Typeface

**Figure 9.7**   Kerning the fonts used in an ad gives the ad a more professional look.

This line is aligned flush left.

This line is aligned flush right.

This line is aligned centered.

This line is justified. Extra spaces are built into the line to "even" out the words.

**Figure 9.8** Justified text is used in newspapers.

## ALIGNMENT

Another spacing consideration is the placement of text on the line. **Alignment** can be left, right, centered, or justified. Justified text is spread across the line so that text lines up evenly on both the right and left margins, as shown in Figure 9.8.

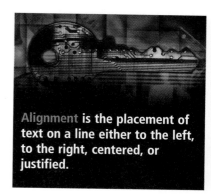

**Alignment** is the placement of text on a line either to the left, to the right, centered, or justified.

## PUNCTUATION

One last type consideration is punctuation. In the typewriter world, students were taught to use two spaces after each end punctuation mark such as a period, question mark, or exclamation point. With the use of computer-generated type, the rules have changed for desktop publishing. It is now considered standard practice to use only one space because proportional type builds in additional space after end punctuation.

SOURCE: ©PHOTODISC

**Jacob's Ladder**

And shakes in town

to the best fries

Climb up

special this week

free drink with

an order of jumbo burger

and curly fries

2698 Wilshire Road          555-3456

**Figure 9.9**  Although the ad is only text, the spacing gives it a graphical feel.

## CAPITALS

Rules of capitalization, such as using capitals at the beginning of proper nouns and at the beginning of sentences, have been in place for generations. In the last few years, some designers have begun to ignore these rules by using no capitals at all or by placing capitals in the middle of words. As a result, the computer world is full of names such as *PageDesign* and *PageWorks*.

The most frequent design decisions for capitals are in headlines, headings, and titles. Your typographic choices for these are as follows:

- No capitals at all
- Up style, in which the first letter of each word is capitalized
- Down style, in which only the first word on the line is capitalized
- All capitals

One of the great temptations when creating a document is to use the all capitals option for titles. Resist this urge because use of all capitals makes your text appear to be shouting. If you must use all capitals, consider using the small caps font option.

As you consider all your options when designing the ad for Herman's restaurant, you decide that only the first and last lines will have capitals, as shown in Figure 9.9.

## EM AND EN DASHES

In the study of punctuation, there are hyphens and there are dashes. A hyphen may indicate a compound word or a break in a word at the end of a line. A dash is used to indicate a sudden break in thought or as a "super comma."

In the typewriter world, a dash as punctuation was typed as two hyphens; if the typed text was converted to print, the typographer converted the two hyphens to an actual dash. With the advent of computerized type, that process has changed. It is now possible to indicate "real" dashes. Professional typographers actually use two kinds of dashes: an "en" dash (to connect ranges of numbers, letters, or dates), and an "em" dash (as a super comma). The **en dash** (–) is the width of the capital letter *N* in whatever font and point size are being used; the **em dash** (—) is the width of the capital letter *M* in whatever font and point size are being used. These dashes are keyed by inserting them as symbols or by using special keyboard shortcuts, depending on the software being used.

There are also **em** and **en spaces,** which can be inserted as if they were white "objects" to separate words the same distances as the dashes; however, with the character spacing and kerning options, it's not as necessary to use these spacing options.

## SUMMARY

In this chapter, you have explored the text side of print included in desktop publishing. You have learned the importance of typography, why the terms *typeface* and *font* are used interchangeably, and how serif and sans serif fonts are different. You have looked at display types, such as grunge fonts and script fonts. You have learned how font size is measured and when to use certain font styles.

You have also looked at spacing issues, including monospace fonts, tracking, kerning, and leading. You have considered how punctuation such as capitals, em and en dashes, and spacing affect desktop publishing decisions.

You are now ready for the next step in print image management: incorporating graphics into your text document.

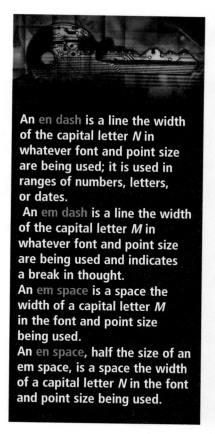

An en dash is a line the width of the capital letter *N* in whatever font and point size are being used; it is used in ranges of numbers, letters, or dates.

An em dash is a line the width of the capital letter *M* in whatever font and point size are being used and indicates a break in thought.

An em space is a space the width of a capital letter *M* in the font and point size being used.

An en space, half the size of an em space, is a space the width of a capital letter *N* in the font and point size being used.

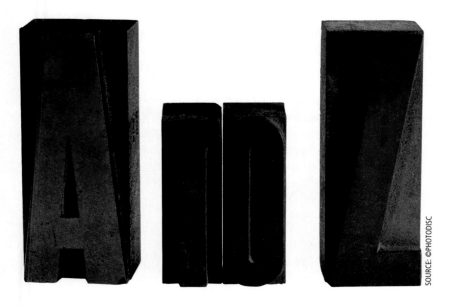

SOURCE: ©PHOTODISC

Answer the following questions on your own computer.

1. When did publishing move to the desktop, and what problems did that move create?
2. What are three programs you can use for desktop publishing?
3. Define desktop publishing in your own words.
4. What is typography, and what three elements of type are included in it?
5. Explain the difference between a typeface and a font.
6. What is a serif, and how does it affect the readability of text?
7. What are display fonts, and why would you use them?
8. How is type measured?
9. Why should you not underline the titles of books?
10. What problems does use of proportional fonts create for the desktop publisher?
11. What is the difference between tracking and kerning?
12. In the typewriter world, what was used instead of leading?
13. What does it mean to justify text?
14. How many spaces should you use after end punctuation such as a period?
15. Why shouldn't you use all capitals, and what could you use instead?

## DISCUSSION

Discuss the following questions either as a class or as a written assignment.

1. What problems will a businessperson have when trying to create a desktop publishing document?
2. How do display fonts such as grunge type affect a business's image?
3. How does adding spacing either to characters by using tracking or to lines by using leading affect the way readers respond to print?
4. Should desktop publishers adhere to old rules of punctuation such as use of capitals, or should they feel free to choose the look they want?
5. Should fonts be covered under copyright laws as works of art? Why or why not?

1. From magazines or newspapers cut out examples of three serif fonts, three sans serif fonts, and three display fonts. Look for examples of grunge type and monospace fonts.

2. Cut out examples of different typestyles such as bold, italic, and reverse type. Locate examples of flush right, flush left, centered, and justified type.

3. If your instructor has a ruler to measure type, use it to determine the type size of several fonts.

4. Locate examples of nonstandard use of capital or lowercase letters.

5. Find an example of letters that appear kerned. Look for an example of a ligature. Find three examples of em dashes, en dashes, and hyphens. Label them.

6. Use all these examples to create a neatly designed poster on which you identify your examples.

1. Search the Internet for free fonts. If your instructor allows it, download some of the more interesting and create a page to demonstrate them to others. Be sure to include the Web site location so that others can access them, too. Consider what effect the "look" of the font gives. Write an explanation of these effects and suggest some types of businesses or uses of these particular fonts.

2. Use the Web to explore the question of copyright and fonts. Create a handout explaining the issues.

# Chapter 10
## Print Graphics

SOURCE: ©DIGITAL VISION

## Objectives

- *You will learn about the use of images in desktop publishing.*
- *You will learn about the drawing tools available in print publications.*
- *You will learn about special effects that can enhance your documents.*

## INTRODUCTION

Text is only one ingredient of desktop publishing. Graphics are the other. Unlike Web and presentation systems, print publications rely on graphics as their multimedia component, since other aspects such as sound and motion are not possible. It is important to understand how to integrate these two elements in order to communicate effectively. The first thing to consider is what exactly constitutes a graphic.

Thomas Silverman has been struggling with this issue for some time. He has been in business for many years and always relied on his straightforward memos to get his point across. Words alone seemed sufficient, but he realizes that is no longer the case. He wants you to help him find a way to use graphics to make his communications more effective.

# GRAPHICS

Anything that is not text can be considered a graphic, although as you saw in the previous chapter even the appearance of text can be graphical in nature. Some of the things graphics can be are as follows:

- Clip art
- Digital photographs from digital cameras or scanned images from prints
- Original artwork created in image management software such as Paint or Photoshop
- Line art such as rules, boxes, or borders created by tools provided in desktop publishing programs
- Charts, graphs, or maps imported from other programs

## PLACEMENT OF IMAGES

All desktop publishing software has the ability to import graphics. The process may be called importing, inserting, or placing. Regardless of the term, the actions are the same: A graphic created in another program is inserted on the page anywhere you want. Graphics may float over the page or be placed inline. Floating graphics are independent of the text; inline graphics are attached to the text and move with it. If you want to make sure a graphic and a particular line of text remain "connected," then you will need to choose the inline option, as shown in Figure 10.1. Most often, you will want to allow a graphic to "float" to give more control over its placement.

Thomas is pleased when you show him how he can insert a chart into a memo that he wants to send to members of a committee on which he is serving. Previously, he would have tried to put into words the statistics that the chart quickly summarizes. By floating the chart rather than making it inline, he is able to put it in a position on the page in which it is most effective.

Here is a line of text with a graphic placed  inline. Notice that it sits on the text line as if it were text itself.

**Figure 10.1** An inline image stays "attached" to text but doesn't offer as many placement options.

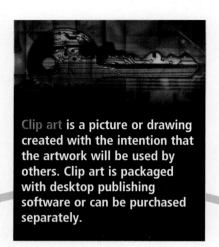

Clip art is a picture or drawing created with the intention that the artwork will be used by others. Clip art is packaged with desktop publishing software or can be purchased separately.

## CLIP ART

**Clip art** is artwork supplied by the publisher of your desktop publishing software or purchased from a third-party vendor for use in a variety of programs. In an earlier time, graphics such as these were provided in books from which you could cut out the images and paste them onto a typed page. Those graphics were generally in black and white and simple in nature. Today's clip art is generally in color and can be intricate works of art.

Clip art has some drawbacks:

- Clip art provides a temptation to use the images as "decoration" instead of to meet a specific need.
- Clip art provided as part of a package such as Microsoft Word may have been seen by readers so often that it loses its effectiveness.
- Clip art provided as part of a desktop publishing package may have copyright restrictions for use by businesses.

With these limitations in mind, clip art offers a way to add an effective component to your desktop-published document. After you showed him how to insert images, Thomas discovered the clip art that came with his word processing software. Unfortunately, it quickly became too much of a good thing. He was adding images every time he was creating a memo. It didn't take him long to realize that clip art for the sake of clip art was not adding to his message.

## FILE TYPES AND SIZES

Web documents limit you to certain file types. Print documents do not place that same restriction on you. Most print documents allow you to use any standard vector and bitmap image. Because these files are not being transmitted over the Internet, file size is not as big a consideration. One concern, however, is printing bottlenecks. Very large graphics-intensive files may not print if the printer does not have enough memory to handle the file size. Also, it is often important to be able to transfer your document to another computer. You need to be aware of the size of the file to determine what medium you must use. Only small desktop publishing documents will fit on a floppy disk. Zip cartridges, CD-ROM disks, or other media must be used for larger files. If you have a network connection, it is possible to transmit files in that way, too.

One way to reduce the file size of a print document is to

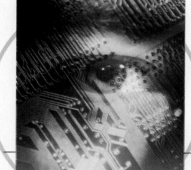

## THE **ETHICS** OF
### CLIP ART RESTRICTIONS

Clip art is a useful tool to add interest to a print document. The problem is that you may become so comfortable with it that you forget about any copyright limitations on its use. Once you move from school to the business world, you need to be aware of these limitations. Not all clip art can be used in print publications distributed to the public without permission from the copyright holder.

You need to investigate the restrictions that come with your software, which is sometimes called *a shrink wrap license* because of the plastic that covers the software package when you purchase it. If you cannot find out the restrictions, you must contact the publisher to verify that you have permission to use the artwork or to gain permission.

reduce the size of the graphics you use. You need to be aware, however, that reducing the physical size of a graphic on a page may not reduce the actual size of the file. It is better to reduce the size of the graphic in its original program, save it there, and then import it into your document. Some desktop publishing programs save incremental versions of your document, which also increases the file size. Using the Save As feature generally eliminates this additional file information, so it's a good idea to save as a new name as your last step.

## TEXT WRAP

One way in which text and graphics can be combined is to wrap the text around the image. **Text wrapping** is a standard feature of desktop publishing offering two options:

1. Text may be wrapped by maintaining a rectangular border between the text and the graphic.
2. Text may be wrapped so that the text and the graphic merge, as shown in Figure 10.2.

The area between a graphic and the text is called the *standoff*. The standoff can be set wide or narrow and is usually measured in points. The width of the standoff becomes an image management decision that you must make. Wider standoffs give more importance to the image, but narrow ones create a smoother flow.

Avoid placing a graphic in the center of text. Instead, place the image along either the right or left margin of the text, matching the margin of the image with the margin of the text. If you are working with two columns of text, you can place a graphic between the two columns so that it breaks into both columns.

Once Thomas began to make deliberate choices of his images, he then became interested in the best way to incorporate them into his memos. You showed him how he could wrap text around them and add to the space separating them from the surrounding text. You also showed him that images shouldn't be placed so text wraps on all sides because it splits up the text and reduces readability.

## Punctuality

One of the biggest complaints employers have about new employees is their lack of punctuality. Sometimes workers don't show up for work on time—or at all—and don't even call in with an explanation. These workers are telling their employers that they don't care about their jobs. Needless to say, such employees don't keep their jobs for very long.

Being punctual doesn't just mean coming to work on time, though. It means being *ready* to work as well. It means waiting on customers promptly, being on time for meetings, and completing your work when it's due. Punctuality builds trust: Your co-workers will learn that they can depend on you to do your own work on time and that they'll rarely need to "fill in" for you. As your reputation for reliability grows, so will the importance of your assignments. So avoid the temptation to hit the snooze bar on the alarm clock and get into the punctuality habit!

**Digging deeper:** Imagine that you are creating a presentation for an important client. A co-worker is responsible for providing you with the sound files for the presentation. The files were due to you this morning, but you haven't received them yet. The presentation needs to be finished by the end of the day. What will you do? Discuss in class.

Text wrapping moves text away from a graphic so that it flows around the image.

> Here is an example of text that is wrapped so that both the image and the text are merged. Notice that the text lines change to accommodate the lines of the graphic.

**Figure 10.2** Wrapped text should always be placed along a margin, rather than in the center of text.

## CAPTIONS

A caption is a brief description of an image or a chart. A caption has more impact than you might expect. It is the third-most-looked-at portion of a print document (after headlines and graphics). A caption can be used in these ways:

- To explain a point made in the text of your document
- To summarize a point
- To add information not provided in the text
- To make an illustration clearer

Photographic captions often include the names of people. Captions are also a way to indicate the source of an image, such as the name of the photographer or the software package from which clip art was taken.

Some desktop publishing software provides options to create captions, but others anticipate that you will merely place a text box below the image. Regardless of the means you use to create a caption, make sure it is separated from the actual body text by using spacing, contrast, or lines.

Keep the caption short, and if the image is wide, consider breaking the caption into two columns. Do not create captions that merely restate the obvious, such as "This is a picture of our bread." Instead, make the caption active and instructive, such as "Our bread contains freshly ground wheat and organic ingredients."

Notice the captions used in the illustrations in this text. They attempt to provide additional information not always found in the body of the text. Thomas picked up quickly on the importance of captions and began to use them with his figures. He discovered that often a caption made his essential point even if his audience didn't read the entire memo.

# DRAWING TOOLS

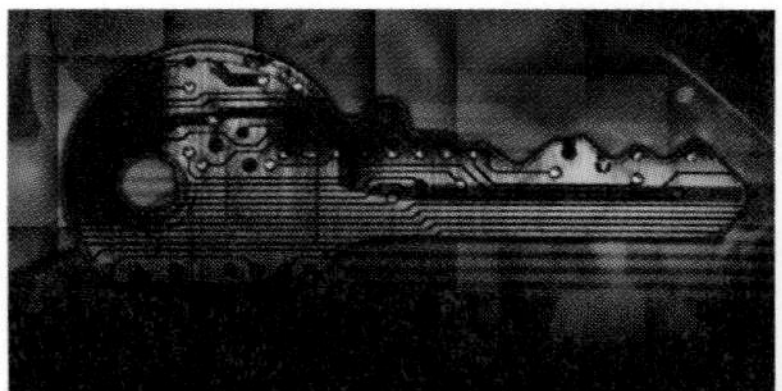

The drawing tools provided by desktop publishing software are generally limited to a few basic actions such as drawing lines and polygons. Some programs may offer a variety of shapes such as arrows or stars. The lines, often called **rules,** can be different colors and thicknesses or weights (measured in points) and may offer an arrow option. Rules are useful for separating text or for adding emphasis to a body of text. Polygon lines can be different colors and sizes. The interior of a polygon can be filled with color, a texture, or a shade of gray. Some software enables you to create a three-dimensional effect. Once you have drawn a rule or polygon, you can change its size, shape, or location.

One use for the drawing tools is to create a pull quote. A **pull quote** (sometimes known as a callout) is an excerpt from the text of a document that is usually a significant statement designed to attract the reader (see Figure 10.3). It is often set off by a pair of rules above and below the quote or in a shaded rectangle. Pull quotes should be placed on the page a distance from the original statement and should be no more than five lines long.

Thomas didn't need pull quotes, but he did find that the arrows in the drawing tools were invaluable as a means of drawing attention to a particular point. He even occasionally used some of the drawing figures instead of clip art.

A rule is a horizontal or vertical line.
A pull quote is a short text or article extract set off by rules or in a box.

---

The drawing tools provided by desktop publishing software are generally limited to a few basic actions such as drawing lines and polygons. Some programs may offer a variety of shapes such as arrows or stars. The lines, often called **rules,** can be different colors and weights.

> **A pull quote is an excerpt from the text of a document designed to attract the reader.**

Rules are useful for separating text or for adding emphasis to a body of text. Polygon lines can be different colors and sizes. The interior of a polygon can be filled with color, a texture, or a shade of gray. Once you have drawn a rule or polygon, you can change its size, shape, or location.

One use for the drawing tools is to create a pull quote. A **pull quote** (sometimes known as a callout) is an excerpt from the text of a document that is usually a significant statement designed to attract the reader. It is often set off by a pair of rules above and below the quote or in a shaded rectangle. Pull quotes should be placed on the page a distance from the original statement and should be no more than five lines long.

Thomas didn't need pull quotes, but he did find that the arrows in the drawing tools were invaluable.

**Figure 10.3**   A pull quote can be set off in a box or by rules above and below it.

# SPECIAL EFFECTS

Two very different graphic special effects are words used as artwork and watermarks.

## WORDS AS ART

Some desktop publishing programs allow you to create artwork from actual text by converting words to images that curve, have a three-dimensional effect, or are in multiple colors. The best known of these options is **WordArt,** provided in Microsoft products such as Word or Publisher as shown in Figure 10.4. Novice desktop publishers often mistakenly rely on WordArt or a similar product to create titles and names when standard text would be more appropriate. WordArt has a strong element of novelty. It's important to remember that what is novel the first time loses its impact when seen the next time. To avoid this problem, use special features such as WordArt only when you know that the novelty will make the impression you want. Most of the time changes in font, size, or style can be more effective.

## WATERMARKS

**Watermarks** have a long history and were originally images or words impressed into paper to identify the manufacturer of the paper. They were also used as security devices to indicate authenticity. While actual watermarks are still in use, desktop publishing programs also use the concept of watermarks. Instead of being embedded in the paper, desktop publishing watermarks are pale images placed on a page as a background layer. In this way logos or words are often used to subtly identify a company or organization. Watermarks are also used to identify special considerations for a document such as confidentiality, as shown in Figure 10.5.

Some desktop publishing software has specific watermark options (as does some image management software), but most require you to create them yourselves. To do that, you must modify the image by eliminating all color and converting the black to the palest shade of gray that will still print. Once you have converted the image, you

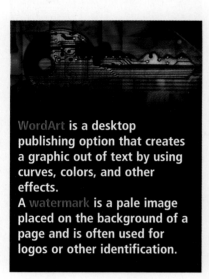

**WordArt** is a desktop publishing option that creates a graphic out of text by using curves, colors, and other effects.

A **watermark** is a pale image placed on the background of a page and is often used for logos or other identification.

A caption is a brief description of an image or a chart. A caption has more impact than you might expect. It is the third most looked at portion of a print document (after headlines and graphics).

Photographic captions often include the names of people. Captions are also a way to indicate the source of an image such as the name of the photographer or the software package from which clip art was taken.

Some desktop publishing software provides options to create captions, but others anticipate that you will merely place a text box below the image.

**Figure 10.4** Word graphics make an interesting effect but need to be used sparingly.

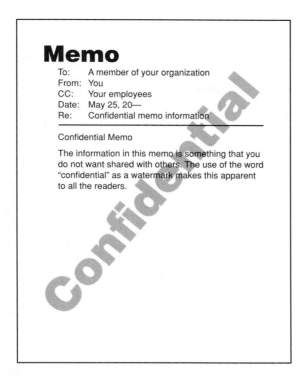

**Figure 10.5** Watermarks are gray images placed on a page but designed to be unobtrusive yet informative.

place the image on the page and send it to the lowest level possible so that all text and graphics appear on top of it.

The concept of watermarks has extended into image management, with digital watermarks being added to images to indicate ownership and to protect them from unauthorized use. Digital watermarks may be hidden code, but more often they are identifying pixels embedded into the image to discourage others from using the picture without permission. When the image is purchased, a watermark-free picture is then provided.

Thomas liked being able to add a confidential watermark when he sent out memos that he did not want shared with others. Using this tool and all the others you were able to share with him, he now believes that his memos are easier to read and more informative. He is convinced that using image management tools is making him a more effective manager.

## SUMMARY

In this chapter, you have learned the difference between inline and floating graphics, when to use clip art, how to wrap text, and why to use captions. You have investigated the drawing tools available in desktop publishing programs and have looked at two special effects: watermarks and words as artwork. You are now ready to see how to combine text and graphics into an effective design.

**Answer the following questions on your own computer.**

1. What is the difference between an inline graphic and a floating graphic?
2. Why would you want to use an inline graphic?
3. What are the problems associated with using clip art?
4. What graphic file types can you use in print documents?
5. What must you consider when trying to print a graphics-intensive document?
6. How can you make the file size of a desktop publishing document smaller?
7. What does text wrapping do?
8. What are the two options for text wrapping?
9. Why is a caption important?
10. What purpose does a caption serve?
11. What makes an effective caption?
12. What is another name for a line?
13. What is a pull quote?
14. What is one use for a watermark?
15. What should you often use instead of WordArt?

## DISCUSSION

**Discuss the following questions either as a class or as a written assignment.**

1. How can clip art be used effectively?
2. How do you react when you see a document that contains clip art with which you are already familiar?
3. What happens if a graphic is "wrapped" in the middle of a body of text?
4. Why are captions the third-most-read part of a document?
5. What makes pull quotes interesting?

1. Find magazine articles with graphics (at least five) containing examples of each of the following:

   text wrap—a minimum of three examples
   captions
   rules
   rectangle
   pull quote
   clip art

   *Extra Credit:* WordArt or watermark

2. Neatly glue each article to a blank piece of paper and then label the items you found. Include a reference number for each item labeled for use in the report.

   *Optional:* If you have a scanner, copy the pages and import them into your word processing software. Use text boxes to identify the items you found. (You can use this later as part of your electronic portfolio.)

3. Write a report of at least one page in which you explain the following:

   - Which text wrap examples were most effective?
   - What was included in the caption(s)? How effective was the caption?
   - What kind of information did the pull quote include?
   - Was the clip art effective? Why or why not?
   - What purposes did the rules and rectangles serve?
   - If you found a watermark or example of WordArt, what impact did it have?

4. Gather the report and the examples into a bound document.

1. Locate and read the shrink wrap license that came with your word processing software and/or your desktop publishing software. What limitations did you find on the use of the clip art provided in that package? If you do not have the original license, use the Internet to locate the information on the publisher's site. You may have to write to the publisher to find out what the restrictions are.

2. When you have finished your search, distribute to the class a one-page document explaining your findings.

# Chapter 11
## Print Design

SOURCE: ©DIGITAL VISION

## Objectives

- *You will learn what techniques are used to create satisfying designs.*
- *You will learn about focus in print design.*
- *You will learn about elements that make a satisfying design.*
- *You will learn about design techniques used in desktop publishing.*

## INTRODUCTION

Dropping clip art randomly onto a page is not desktop publishing. Good desktop publishing skills require you to know where to drop images and what effect the placement will have on your page. You have seen in the previous two chapters how to work with text and graphics. In this chapter, you will begin to integrate these skills artfully to create a quality desktop-published document. The place to begin in this process is to understand what your readers will see when they first glance at your page.

Marian Jamison works for a local community college that is having a series of tours for prospective students and their families. As a public relations tool, each department will use a digital camera to photograph each student during his or her exploration of the campus. These photographs are then added to a

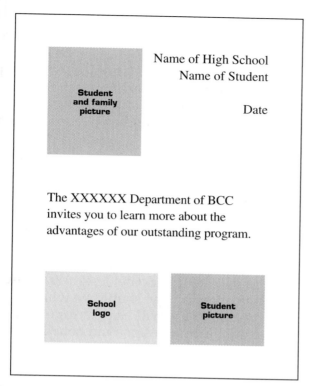

**Figure 11.1** This layout is a good example of a page that needs to be refocused.

prepared page and printed in color to be given to the student as a memento of the visit similar to the one shown in Figure 11.1. It is a popular recruitment tool, but Marian thinks the design needs to be changed. She uses her design skills to make improvements.

# FOCUS PLAN

Text alone on a page is read from the upper left corner, to the right, and then down to the left in a figure Z pattern. When you add graphics to a page, you can alter this pattern. This means that you as the page designer can decide the direction in which a reader gathers the information on a page. To do that, you must understand where the eye will land at first glance and where the eye will move next. With that information, you can then decide (1) where to place items, (2) how large to make them, and (3) what impact they will have. These three elements make up a **focus plan.**

As a general rule, if there are graphics on a page along with text, the eye is drawn to the largest, boldest, and most colorful item on a page rather than beginning in the upper left corner. Once the eye focuses on the first element, it is then drawn to the next most attractive element. After each eye jump, the inclination is to return to the standard Z pattern. Your task is to decide whether you want the reader to return to a standard Z pattern or if you want the reader to see graphic or text elements on the page in a different order.

A focus plan determines the path the eye will follow on a page.

**Figure 11.2** Good design requires knowing where the eye will focus first.

In Figure 11.2, what attracts you first and then next? What path does your eye follow? Did you start at the bottom of the page and then work up? Why?

Marian realizes that the first problem with the page is that there is no focus. The largest text box is in the middle of the page drawing the eye, but the student pictures are also attracting the eye. The eye wanders over the page without direction.

## WHITE SPACE

Strange as it may seem, the areas in which text or graphics do *not* appear have as much importance as the areas in which they do appear. This area is called **white space** (or sometimes *negative space*), and it acts as a design element of its own. A block of white space can be used as a means of guiding the eye, as well as of resting it. Some designers believe that as much as 50 percent of a page should be white space. The percentage you decide to use will be determined by the type of publication, but most publication designs can benefit from an increase in white space.

You can add white space to a page in ways other than just leaving areas empty. Here are some of your choices:

- Wide **gutters** (The term is usually used for the area between columns, but it may also be an extra-wide inside margin used to provide binding space)
- Extra leading (spacing) between paragraphs or lines of text
- Ragged text rather than justified text, so that space is open at the end or beginning of the text line
- Wider top or side margins
- Choice of type
- Wider *standoffs* (the space separating graphics and text)

White space can pose two problems: trapped white space and rivers of white. *Trapped white space* is just what it sounds like—white space surrounded on all sides by text or graphics. Trapped white space is not nearly as effective a design element as open white space. When designing a page, look for trapped white space that can be "freed." You will not reduce the content of the page, but you will increase its readability and interest.

Marian sees that there is significant white space but it is not used as a design element. She sees that it could be better used if it were used as a focus instead of a way to spread apart the other elements.

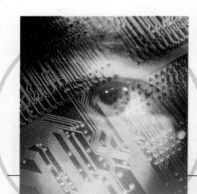

## THE **ETHICS** OF PAGE DESIGN RESTRICTIONS

Up to now, the ethical discussions have been about restrictions on a business's use of graphics, type, and other copyright-protected elements. Page design, however, does not have such restrictions. If you see a design layout that meets your business needs, you are free to duplicate that design in your own work. You cannot use any of the elements such as images or text, but you can adapt an existing design arrangement and incorporate it into your own publication. For example, if you see a poster with an unusual way of attaching elements, you can use that idea in your own handouts. Learn to watch for effective design as a way to enhance your own work.

*Rivers of white* are found most often when text is justified because the extra space inserted in a line can be duplicated on the line above and below. The eye is drawn to the river of white space instead of to the text. What did your eye do when it encountered the white space in Figure 11.1?

## LAYOUT

Once you have an idea about how you want a page to appear, it is a good idea to sketch out on paper the **layout** before actually beginning work in a desktop publishing program. In this way, you can create the focus plan that works best without being distracted by the actual content on which you are working. You can also decide whether to use landscape or portrait orientation.

Often, page designers use a grid or frames as a layout tool. Some desktop publishing software allows you to build a series of frames in which to place text and graphics. These frames make it easy to design a page before you have to consider content.

One of the ways professionals design pages with text blocks without actually including the words that will appear on the page is to use **greeking** (see Figure 11.3). Greeking is nonsensical text that often begins with the words *Lorem ipsum dolor sit amet* that is used as placeholder in a design page. The actual words are not essential. You can just as easily type in nonsense words of your own and then copy and paste to fill in the space you need, but greeking is the accepted means of doing this. There is even a Web site that will produce up to 50 greeked paragraphs for you to use in your document.

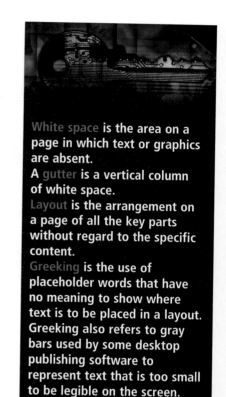

**White space** is the area on a page in which text or graphics are absent.
A **gutter** is a vertical column of white space.
**Layout** is the arrangement on a page of all the key parts without regard to the specific content.
**Greeking** is the use of placeholder words that have no meaning to show where text is to be placed in a layout. Greeking also refers to gray bars used by some desktop publishing software to represent text that is too small to be legible on the screen.

Lorem ipsum dolor sit amet, consectetuer adipiscing elit, sed diam nonummy nibh euismod tincidunt ut laoreet dolore magna aliquam erat volputate. Ut wisi enim ad minim veniam, quis nostrud exerci tation ullamcorper suscipit lobortis nisl ut aliquip ex ea commodo consequat. Duis autem vel eum iriure dolor in hendrerit in vulputate velit esse molestie consequat, vel illum dolore eu feugiat nulla facilisis at vero eros et accumsan et iusto odio dignissim qui blandit praesent luptatum zzril delenit augue duis dolore te feugait facilisi.

SOURCE: ©ADOBE PAGEMAKER

**Figure 11.3** Greeking (nonsense words) acts as a text placeholder during the design process.

## CARPAL TUNNEL SYNDROME

Repetitive stress injury (RSI) results from repeated movement of a particular part of the body. For example, graphic artists use their "mouse hand" more than some other workers do. People who work at a computer are at risk for developing a form of RSI called carpal tunnel syndrome (CTS). CTS is a painful inflammatory disease that affects the wrists, hands, and forearms. Symptoms include numb or tingling hands and wrists; pain in the forearm, elbow, or shoulder; and difficulty in gripping objects. Practicing the ERGO-TIPS in your textbook can reduce your risk for CTS.

Greeking is also used in desktop publishing programs such as PageMaker to preview pages in which text would be too small to see legibly on the screen. Gray bars are used to show where the small type exists in the layout. The use of greeked text also improves the speed at which the display can be drawn, which can be important if you are using a less powerful computer.

Some desktop publishing programs provide you with *thumbnail* images (small pictures) of templates from which to choose a layout, as shown in Figure 11.4. Because the thumbnails are small, you are not

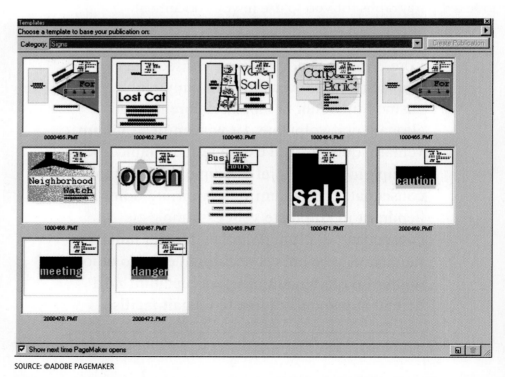

SOURCE: ©ADOBE PAGEMAKER

**Figure 11.4** Often, businesses are pressed for time. Templates simplify the quick creation of well-designed documents.

distracted by content. From these images, it becomes possible to decide on a layout based on a focus plan. If you do not want to design your own layout, thumbnail templates are a good choice because professional designers created these templates. Even when using a template created by someone else, however, it is important to understand the focus plan that was used to create the layout.

Marian already has a layout page with little content, since her copy of the promotional page is designed to be added to after the student pictures are taken. This makes it easier for her to look at her design without concern for the actual photographs. However, the center text box is specific. She may want to change it to greeked text. Marian also looked at some professional template designs of newsletters and flyers to see if there were any that met her needs. She found a couple of ideas that she plans to use, but there were none that specifically met the requirements of this particular type of document.

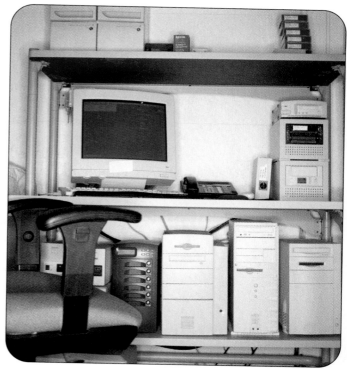

## SATISFYING DESIGN

Regardless of the focus plan you choose, you will want your page to have a satisfying design. Without this, the elements will appear to be placed randomly and your message will be ineffective. Several concepts can be used in creating satisfying pages.

### RULE OF THIRDS

One way to create a satisfying page is to use the rule of thirds, as discussed in the chapter on photography. Just as in a photograph, dividing the printed page into thirds either vertically or horizontally makes for an attractive design. The use of uneven columns, with one column wide and the other narrow, is often a way to use the rule of thirds. Notice in Figure 11.5 that the page is split into halves. Compare Figure 11.5 with Figure 11.2. Which is more appealing?

### ALIGNMENT

The human brain tends to try to make things "fit." For this reason, if an image on a page is just slightly out of alignment, the brain will try to push it into place. This mental effort to make things fit can create a design that is not satisfying. To avoid this problem, align elements so that they either fit well or don't fit at all. This means that if you move an image off

**555-2512**
1014 Barrel Road
Forrester Plaza

Hours:
Monday–Saturday 9:00–5:00

Vintage Fountain Pens
Bottled Ink–all colors
Hand Crafted Nibs

Custom
Designed
Fountain Pens

**The Ink Bottle**

**Figure 11.5** Dividing a page into halves is not as pleasing to the eye as dividing it into thirds.

center or away from its expected place, move it far enough so that the eye clearly perceives that you intended its placement there.

## REPETITION

Another important design tool is the use of repetition and consistency to give a page a sense of unity. You can create repetition by using details such as the same font, the same rules, or even the same images in different sizes. White space can be effective when used repetitively. A page filled with information can create visual overload. Use of repetition and similar elements helps soothe that overload. It also makes for a satisfying design.

One feature that some software provides is a choice of *themes* to unify the pages included in a document. Themes include complementary colors, font styles, and rules. They are useful as design shortcuts to provide a consistent appearance. Look at the design of your textbook. Can you find themes or repetition?

## SYMMETRY

Although repetition is useful, symmetrical pages are not always the way to create it. Placing elements so that everything on the page is "even" often creates a boring design. Centering text on a page is a form of symmetry that gives a formal tone to a page. *Asymmetrical*, or uneven, arrangements of elements, is more interesting. Compare the two examples in Figures 11.6 and 11.7. Everything in the first example is symmetrical. In the second example, some elements are asymmetrical. Which example do you prefer?

**Figure 11.6** Symmetry creates a formal look that may lack interest.

**Figure 11.7** Pages designed with some asymmetrical elements are often more interesting than those without.

## BALANCE

Balance and symmetry are related but different. A balanced page is far more satisfying to the mind than a symmetrical one. Balance uses different kinds of elements to "even out" a page, whereas symmetry uses the same kinds of elements. A graphic may be balanced by a block of white space; text may be balanced with other text or with a graphic. Balance is not as obvious as symmetry and often requires a trained eye to see. Not every item on a page needs balance—just enough to give the page a sense of completeness. Consider Figure 11.5. Notice how the white space opposite each text box helps balance the page.

## ATTACHED ELEMENTS

One last design tool requires you to see text and graphics as "floating" on a page of white. You don't want these elements to float off, so one good design technique is to attach them to the page in some way. Letting one element touch another, thus linking the pieces until they are tied to the border of the page, is one way to do that. You will notice that graphics often **bleed** off a page—that is, they come to the very edge of the page—in professional publications as a means of tying all the elements to the page. Unfortunately, most personal printers cannot print to the edge of a page. You can use borders or colored backgrounds, however, to help enclose all the elements on a page. Notice in Figure 11.8 that the lines bleed off the page, thus tying all the pieces together.

Marian used the techniques that are helpful in creating a satisfying design and changed the focus and arrangement of the page. She decided that she would move the large student and family picture to the upper right and use the name of the student and date as a caption, eliminating the name of the high school (see Figure 11.9). This left a large block of white space that forced the eye to the picture, which then moved the eye to the center information block.

She added the school's Web address to the center block and placed the logo so it touched the address. She moved the smaller picture to the lower left and then placed a thin rule border around the outside to attach the pieces. Her focus plan means that now the eye starts in the upper right, moves to the program information, down to the

### Taking Initiative at Work

Probably the best way you can advance your career is to take initiative at work. Don't ever just stand around looking for something to do. If you complete an assignment, go to your supervisor and request something else to do. Don't wait to be given a new task—ask for more work and responsibility. Supervisors notice and respond favorably to employees who do so. One good way to take initiative at work is to find small ways to improve the way a job is done. Or consider doing a job in a slightly different way.

Taking initiative on the job can be a bit tricky, though. Employers aren't looking for workers to come in and start "running the show." Taking initiative doesn't mean insisting that things be done your way. It means determining what your employer wants and needs and then doing it the best way possible.

**Digging deeper:** Think about the processes involved in creating a Web page. Brainstorm in class to develop alternative—and more efficient—procedures.

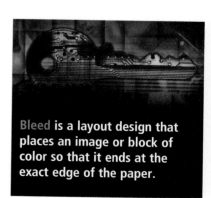

Bleed is a layout design that places an image or block of color so that it ends at the exact edge of the paper.

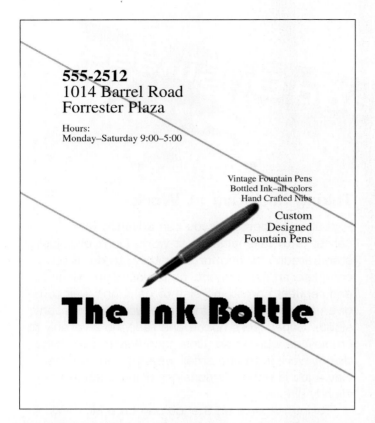
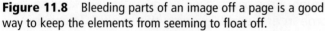

**Figure 11.8** Bleeding parts of an image off a page is a good way to keep the elements from seeming to float off.

**Figure 11.9** A few changes to the school's page changes the focus, directing the reader as the designer wants.

school's logo and over the picture. Which design do you believe is better? Are there changes or choices you would make to improve this design?

## SUMMARY

In this chapter, you have learned to look for the focus on a page, how to enhance your message by using white space, and what elements make for a satisfying design. You have learned to identify techniques such as the rule of thirds, alignment, repetition, symmetry, balance, and bleeds.

Answer the following questions on your own computer.

1. Explain the Z pattern.
2. What does the human eye look at first on a page?
3. What is white space?
4. How can white space be added to a page?
5. What is trapped white space?
6. Where are rivers of white most often found?
7. What is the best way to create a layout plan?
8. Why would you want to use a thumbnail image before making a design decision?
9. What is one way to use the rule of thirds on a page?
10. What happens if you place an object on a page so that it is only slightly misaligned?
11. What are two ways to give unity to a page?
12. What is the difference between symmetry and balance?
13. How can you keep elements from floating off a page?
14. What is a bleed?
15. Why can it be difficult to create a bleed in desktop publishing?

Discuss the following questions either as a class or as a written assignment.

1. When are you aware of using the Z pattern in your reading? How often do you think others are aware of the pattern?
2. What problems would a designer encounter who wanted to reserve 50 percent of a page for white space?
3. Why would the rule of thirds apply to photographs as well as to desktop-published documents?
4. Do you prefer symmetrical or asymmetrical pages? Why?
5. If a printer is unable to print to the edge of a page, what could you do to create a bleed?

## USE YOUR KNOWLEDGE

1. On the covers of five magazines, draw lines on each to indicate the focus plan. Label the first point #1, the second #2, and so on until all major elements are included.

2. Label significant examples of white space.

3. Label any trapped white space or rivers of white.

4. Find examples of the rule of thirds, symmetrical alignment, asymmetrical alignment, repetition, balance, and a bleed. Label each one.

5. Write a review of each of the layouts, indicating its strengths and weaknesses.

## FURTHER EXPLORATION

1. It is not actually correct to say that all languages are read from left to right. Some languages are read from right to left, others from bottom to top. Research the different patterns of reading and create different designs that might be more effective in other languages.

2. Research the history of greeking. See if you can find out what the words actually mean. Why were these particular words used?

# Chapter 12
## Print Standards

**ESTIMATED TIME**

**3**

**H O U R S**

SOURCE: ©PHOTODISC

## INTRODUCTION

The standards that businesses use in their desktop-published documents are more rigorous than those that are used in a classroom. In a classroom, you are free to experiment and explore all the possibilities the software offers. Once you are producing documents for the business world or overseeing the production of such documents, however, you need to be aware that your audience has changed. No longer is flashier better than quiet. No longer should every feature be used to demonstrate your skills. Business publications adhere to a more formal set of rules.

## Objectives

- *You will learn to apply business standards in print publications.*
- *You will learn to consider readability in print documents.*
- *You will learn to use the question of audience to determine your choices in print design.*
- *You will learn how Adobe Acrobat can be used as a business tool.*

# GENERAL RULES

A number of general rules apply in business situations. While none of these rules are "engraved in stone," they will give you guidelines to help you make good business decisions and to ensure that your desktop-published document will be given the attention it deserves. Keep each of these guidelines in mind as you design print publications, and ignore them only when you know that your publication will be enhanced by breaking the rule.

## THE **ETHICS** OF SELLING OUT

Is it "selling out" to use one set of print standards for one audience and a different set for another audience? No, not if communication is your goal. Although each of us wants to produce work that reflects our own personalities, it is more important in the business world to reach the intended audience. If your style offends the audience or confuses them, then you have failed to communicate. This possibility means that at times you will have to make choices that you would not make if you were creating a document just for yourself. You are not selling out; you are using good judgment.

## FONTS

Limit the number of fonts in a document to no more than three. Often, a single font with different attributes and sizes can serve better than multiple fonts. Use of a single font provides your design with the elements of repetition and consistency.

If you do mix fonts, make sure the font choices are very different from each other. Generally, a serif font is used for body text and a sans serif font is used for headings and titles. Two similar fonts, regardless of the type, make it appear that you have inadvertently chosen the wrong font. A serif font and a sans serif font should be distinctively different to avoid this. Your audience needs to be aware that your choice was intentional.

## INFORMATION

Incorporate essential information into print documents. This includes the physical address of the business, including city and state, phone number with area code, and Web address. It is easy to forget that your document may be read by someone in a different city or state who may not know about your business. If you are publishing a newsletter, be sure to include a *masthead* with information such as staff names, contributors, subscription information, addresses, and logo.

When designing your document, group together related information, rather than spread it throughout the page. Your message will be clearer as a result. The mind tends to absorb information in "chunks," so you want to make this easy by visually joining information that you want connected in the mind of your audience. In Figure 12.1, compare the two business cards. Which one does a better job of conveying the message?

## SPACING

The human eye finds it difficult to read across an entire page of text. Shorter passages speed up reading and increase comprehension.

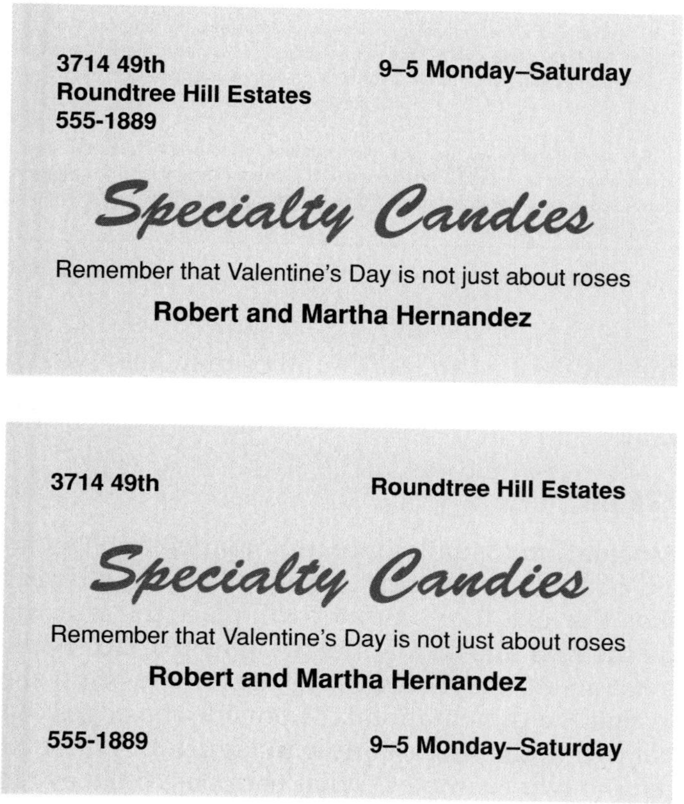

**3714 49th**
**Roundtree Hill Estates**
**555-1889**

**9–5 Monday–Saturday**

*Specialty Candies*

Remember that Valentine's Day is not just about roses
**Robert and Martha Hernandez**

---

**3714 49th**

**Roundtree Hill Estates**

*Specialty Candies*

Remember that Valentine's Day is not just about roses
**Robert and Martha Hernandez**

**555-1889**

**9–5 Monday–Saturday**

**Figure 12.1** Although it may appear attractive to separate information on a page, the reader will appreciate your grouping similar information.

When designing your pages, check to see that long lines of body text do not run across your page. Break text into columns to make the lines easier to read. In Figure 12.2, compare the two paragraphs. Which one is easier to read?

In an earlier time, business documents were indented using a tab key that moved five spaces, a standard dictated by the limitations of a typewriter. This is no longer necessary or appropriate. Instead, desktop publishing rules encourage you to indent paragraphs an

Specialty Candies, a popular choice for all occasions, is offering a Valentine's Day basket that is the perfect choice for your sweetheart. It's a heart-shaped basket filled with chocolates including the all-time favorite, hand-dipped strawberries. You can't go wrong if you choose this gift for that special person.

Specialty Candies, a four-year-old company established by Robert and Martha Hernandez, can be found in the Roundtree Hill Estates shopping center. Shopping hours are 9–5 Monday through Saturday. Come by and visit. You'll be sure to find the perfect choice for your Valentine.

**Figure 12.2** Lines that flow across a page are tedious to read. Columns make the text more interesting.

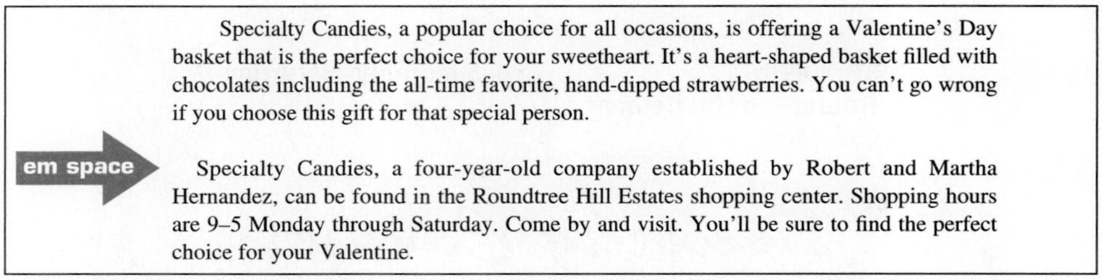

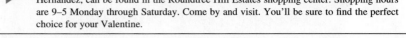

Specialty Candies, a popular choice for all occasions, is offering a Valentine's Day basket that is the perfect choice for your sweetheart. It's a heart-shaped basket filled with chocolates including the all-time favorite, hand-dipped strawberries. You can't go wrong if you choose this gift for that special person.

**em space** ➤ Specialty Candies, a four-year-old company established by Robert and Martha Hernandez, can be found in the Roundtree Hill Estates shopping center. Shopping hours are 9–5 Monday through Saturday. Come by and visit. You'll be sure to find the perfect choice for your Valentine.

**Figure 12.3** In an earlier time, typists were taught to indent a paragraph with five spaces.

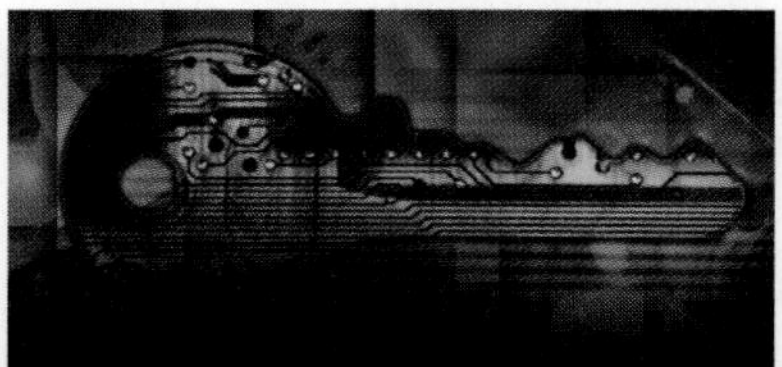

em space (the width of a capital *M*), rather than key five spaces. See Figure 12.3 to compare the two choices. What is distracting about the first paragraph?

## PUNCTUATION

**Hanging punctuation** (usually quotation marks) appears at the beginning and end of a paragraph that is generally set in a large type size. When you key the text, the computer will place the punctuation marks inside the first line so that the margins line up. While this is logical, it is not an attractive design. Instead, the margin should be realigned so that the punctuation falls outside the edges of the text margin, as shown in the first example in Figure 12.4. Notice the difference between the two examples. What happens to the eye in the second example?

In the era of typewritten business documents, the only choice for indicating quotation marks were the same keys used to indicate inches and feet (called tick marks). This is no longer the case. Today you should use **curly quotes** for quotation marks in place of the straight marks. Use of straight marks indicates a novice desktop publisher. Notice the difference in the two quotes in Figure 12.5.

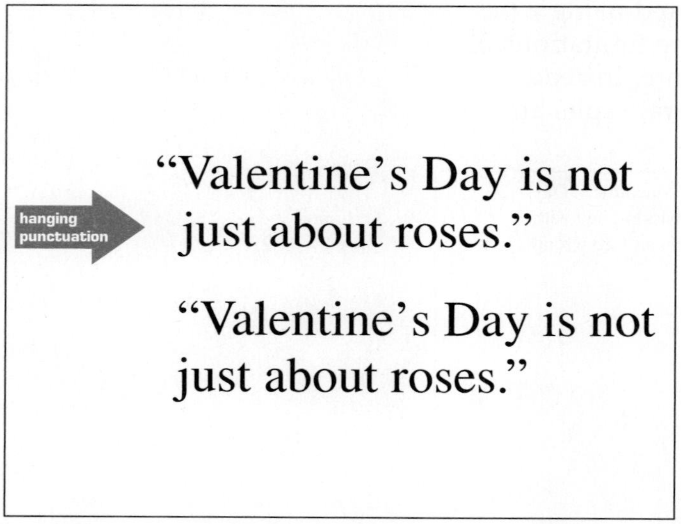

**Hanging punctuation is** punctuation such as quotation marks that needs to "hang" outside a paragraph rather than line up with the text below.
**Curly quotes** are rounded marks used for quotation marks and apostrophes.

**hanging punctuation** ➤

"Valentine's Day is not just about roses."

"Valentine's Day is not just about roses."

**Figure 12.4** Hanging punctuation should be visually separate from the line.

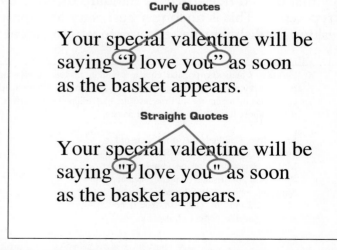

Curly Quotes

Your special valentine will be saying "I love you" as soon as the basket appears.

Straight Quotes

Your special valentine will be saying "I love you" as soon as the basket appears.

**Figure 12.5** Curly quotes should always be used as quotation marks.

## DROP CAP

A **drop cap** is the first letter of a paragraph that has been enhanced to give it emphasis. The letter may be larger or more ornate to create this effect. Use this technique judiciously. Drop caps (Figure 12.6) create a formal look that might not always be appropriate for every document. When you do use drop caps, place them "above the fold," meaning the top half of the page. They should never be used for every paragraph on a page.

## WIDOWS/ORPHANS

A **widow** is the first sentence of a paragraph that is separated from the rest of its paragraph. The widow line appears at the bottom of the column or page, and the rest of the paragraph is on the next column or page. An **orphan** is a single line of text (often only a word or two) that appears at the top of a column or a page; the rest of the paragraph appears at the bottom of the previous column or page.

Both of these situations make it awkward to read the paragraph smoothly. Avoid widows, such as those shown in Figure 12.7, and orphans. Their use is a sign of a poorly constructed design. You should also avoid placing a subhead at the bottom of a column for the same reason that you avoid widows and orphans.

## TOMBSTONE

A **tombstone** is created when two headings are placed across from each other on a page that is designed with columns. Notice in Figure 12.8 the tombstoning of "Valentine Baskets" and "Location." Headings placed in this position can confuse a reader who might read them as a single heading.

Avoid this kind of distraction by careful placement of all headings. An image or photograph placed at the top of one of the columns is a good way to separate information that may appear side by side. For

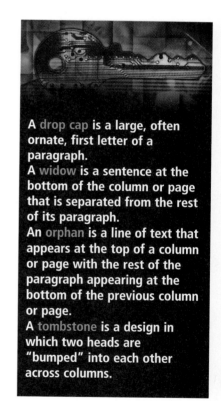

Specialty Candies, a popular choice for all occasions, is offering a Valentine's Day basket that is the perfect choice for your sweetheart. It's a heart-shaped basket filled with chocolates including the all-time favorite, hand-dipped strawberries. You can't go wrong if you choose this gift for that special person.

**Figure 12.6** A drop cap adds a touch of elegance to text.

A drop cap is a large, often ornate, first letter of a paragraph.
A widow is a sentence at the bottom of the column or page that is separated from the rest of its paragraph.
An orphan is a line of text that appears at the top of a column or page with the rest of the paragraph appearing at the bottom of the previous column or page.
A tombstone is a design in which two heads are "bumped" into each other across columns.

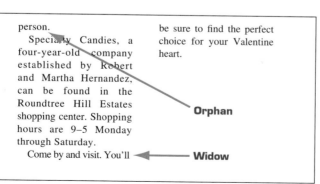

Specialty Candies, a popular choice for all occasions, is offering a Valentine's Day basket that is the perfect choice for your sweetheart. It's a heart-shaped basket filled with chocolates including the all-time favorite, hand-dipped strawberries. You can't go wrong if you choose this gift for that special

person.
Specialty Candies, a four-year-old company established by Robert and Martha Hernandez, can be found in the Roundtree Hill Estates shopping center. Shopping hours are 9–5 Monday through Saturday.
Come by and visit. You'll

be sure to find the perfect choice for your Valentine heart.

**Orphan**

**Widow**

**Figure 12.7** Widows and orphans sit on lines by themselves.

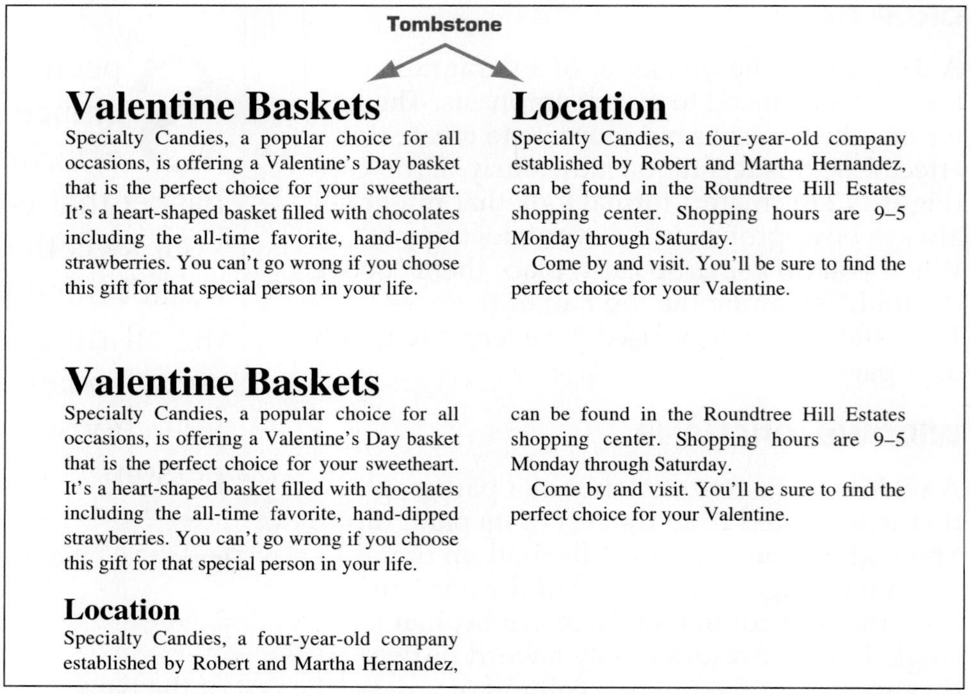

**Tombstone**

## Valentine Baskets

Specialty Candies, a popular choice for all occasions, is offering a Valentine's Day basket that is the perfect choice for your sweetheart. It's a heart-shaped basket filled with chocolates including the all-time favorite, hand-dipped strawberries. You can't go wrong if you choose this gift for that special person in your life.

## Location

Specialty Candies, a four-year-old company established by Robert and Martha Hernandez, can be found in the Roundtree Hill Estates shopping center. Shopping hours are 9–5 Monday through Saturday.

Come by and visit. You'll be sure to find the perfect choice for your Valentine.

## Valentine Baskets

Specialty Candies, a popular choice for all occasions, is offering a Valentine's Day basket that is the perfect choice for your sweetheart. It's a heart-shaped basket filled with chocolates including the all-time favorite, hand-dipped strawberries. You can't go wrong if you choose this gift for that special person in your life.

can be found in the Roundtree Hill Estates shopping center. Shopping hours are 9–5 Monday through Saturday.

Come by and visit. You'll be sure to find the perfect choice for your Valentine.

## Location

Specialty Candies, a four-year-old company established by Robert and Martha Hernandez,

**Figure 12.8**  Tombstone heading may confuse your readers.

example, in Figure 12.8, a map could be placed above the "Location" heading to eliminate the problem.

# AUDIENCE CONSIDERATIONS

Although some standards apply to all designs, other rules depend on your audience. Keep these rules in mind as you decide who will be reading your page and how you want them to respond to it. Are you trying to attract new customers in a 15- to 19-year-old age bracket? Are you providing important information for your employees? Each of these audiences provides a different set of challenges. For one, you may want your page to appear light and youthful. For the other, you may want the page to be seriously professional.

Design decisions such as the following help send the message you want:

- Base your font choice decisions on the audience. Display fonts are interesting and attract attention. Standard fonts create a more serious impression. Know your intentions when choosing fonts.
- Consider your reading audience when choosing font size of body text. An audience that is quite young or one that is quite old may find small text difficult to read.
- Consider the production process as well. Depending on the printing process used, reverse type and shades of gray may not

3714 49th
Roundtree Hill Estates
555-1889

9–5 Monday–Saturday

*Specialty Candies*

Remember that Valentine's Day is not just about roses

**Robert and Martha Hernandez**

♥ ♥ ♥

**Figure 12.9** Dingbats can be used as bullets or decorative text.

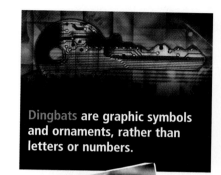

Dingbats are graphic symbols and ornaments, rather than letters or numbers.

print as expected. If you must photocopy a document, the blacks and grays may appear washed out.

- Determine how busy a page needs to be. Overly busy pages appeal to younger readers, who expect more activity on a page layout. Older readers find busy pages distracting.
- Use borders appropriately. A border can add interest to an informal page, but it may appear "fluffy" in a formal document. If you must use a border in a formal document, it should be simple lines rather than images.
- Vary your choice of bullets. Bullets are always helpful to draw the eye to a list. For a formal look, use the standard "dot." Less formal documents can contain decorative bullets called **dingbats.** The hearts in Figure 12.9 are dingbats. Many dingbat fonts are available. They may be called dingbats, symbols, wingdings, or some other name. Regardless of the name, a dingbat is a symbol.

# ADOBE ACROBAT

A technology tool that can be particularly useful as a business standard is Adobe Acrobat. With this software you can take a document that has been created using virtually any software program such as Excel or PageMaker and

## Good Business

### Organizational Skills

Today's workers are asked to do a lot, and you can quickly become overwhelmed if you don't organize your work properly. Good organizational skills help you stay focused, allow you to be more productive, and prevent you from wasting time. Little things can make a big difference. For example, keep supplies and materials in the same place (so you know where they are the next time you need them). Give your electronic files and folders descriptive names so that you can find them easily. Avoid unnecessary complication.

Break down large tasks into smaller pieces. You can't build a Web site, for example, in one fell swoop; you have to do it in parts: create a design, find appropriate artwork, register a domain name, find a Web host, and so forth. Create a to-do list to help keep you focused; delete items as you complete them. Keep working methodically and steadily, and you'll soon find that you've finished the large task by taking care of the components.

**Digging deeper:** Create an electronic to-do list or task planner you can access from your computer. Begin using it immediately to improve your organizational skills.

encode it in Portable Document Format (**PDF**). As you might expect, PDF files are identified by the file extension .pdf. PDF files can be read using Acrobat Reader on any platform (Macintosh or PC) and with any computer without having the original software installed on that computer. Acrobat Reader is becoming commonplace on most computers and can be downloaded free of charge. PDF files can be distributed on floppy disk, CD-ROM, or other media. They can also be incorporated into Web pages providing access to them through the Internet.

While Acrobat Reader is free for all users, to create PDF files requires additional Acrobat software that must be purchased just as you would any other software. The package contains two software products: a distiller and editing software. The Acrobat **distiller** software converts any document, such as one created in Microsoft Word, into a PDF document. You distill a document by printing to Acrobat Distiller instead of to a standard printer. This action creates the PDF file from the original document. Adobe software such as PageMaker also allows you to distill documents directly from within an open PageMaker file.

With the editing component of the software, you can protect the PDF file in many ways. You can prevent changes and you can select an option that disables the printing or saving functions. In addition, you can require a password to open the file. You can use the editing software to check spelling, setup navigation guides, and make other improvements from the original file. You can set up form options that allow the reader to enter information into specific fields, making the document into a form.

SOURCE: ©PHOTODISC

# SUMMARY

In this chapter, you have learned what standards apply to documents created in a business environment using the following list. These include font choices, punctuation, paragraph endings, and audience. You have learned to consider the readability of a long line and how print choices will affect your final product. You have learned to think about standards other than those you have previously encountered in school. You also learned how to create PDF files to share across platforms.

## PROFESSIONAL DESIGN CONSIDERATIONS

- Limit the number of fonts in a document to no more than three.
- When mixing fonts, make sure the font choices are very different from each other.
- Base your font choice decisions on the audience.
- Consider your reading audience when choosing font size of body text.
- Incorporate essential information such as physical address including city and state, phone number with area code, and Web address.
- Group together related information, rather than spread it throughout the page.
- Check that long lines of body text do not run across a page.
- Indent paragraphs an em space (the width of a capital *M*).
- Place hanging punctuation outside the edges of type on both the right and left sides of the paragraph.
- Use curly quotes for quotation marks.
- Use drop caps judiciously.
- Use borders appropriately.
- Vary your choice of bullets.
- Avoid widows and orphans.
- Avoid placing a subhead at the bottom of a column.
- Avoid tombstone headings.
- Consider the production process.
- Determine how busy a page needs to be.

SOURCE: ©PHOTODISC

**Answer the following questions on your own computer.**

1. What is the suggested limit to the number of different kinds of fonts used in a single document?
2. Why is it important to include information such as area code in business documents?
3. Why should information on a page be grouped?
4. Why should lines of text not be run across a page?
5. How much should you indent a paragraph?
6. What is hanging punctuation?
7. Why haven't curly quotes always been used before in businesses?
8. Where are widows and orphans found?
9. Why should you avoid tombstone headings?
10. What consideration do you have to make when choosing font size?
11. When is use of reverse text a problem?
12. What effect does an overly busy page have on older readers?
13. What kinds of borders are appropriate for business documents?
14. What is a drop cap?
15. What is one use of a dingbat?
16. On what platforms can you use Adobe Acrobat Reader?
17. If a computer does not have Acrobat Reader, what can you do?
18. What is required if you wish to create **PDF** documents?
19. What is a distiller?
20. What can you do if you want do distribute a **PDF** file that you do not want printed or copied?

## DISCUSSION

**Discuss the following questions either as a class or as a written assignment.**

1. Why are multiple font choices discouraged?
2. Why does grouping information improve your message?
3. Why would you only want to indent an em space rather than five keyed spaces?
4. What happens when punctuation is set "inside" the paragraph?
5. Why is a bullet helpful when including a list?
6. Do you have Adobe Acrobat Reader installed on your computer?
7. How often do you use it or encounter situations where you needed it?
8. What limitations do you see with it? What advantages?

1. In magazines or other print documents, find examples of the following:

   a. More than three font selections on a page
   b. Dingbats
   c. Hanging punctuation
   d. Curly quotes
   e. Widows or orphans
   f. Tombstones
   g. Drop caps

2. Who is the audience for each of the examples you selected?

3. Why did the designer of the page make these choices? Was it lack of knowledge or intentional? Would the document have been more successful or less if different choices had been made? Write a brief (one-page) report in which you explain your conclusions. Attach your examples to the report.

1. Locate an example of a page that could be considered "busy" and one that is "quiet." Survey students and adults to see what their responses are to each of them (including the age and gender of each respondent). Which do they find easier to read? Which do they like better? Why? Create a chart that demonstrates your conclusions.

2. Find a magazine or newspaper that was printed at least 30 years ago. Look at the design elements. Can you see any difference between the way the pages were designed then and the way pages are today? Is it immediately apparent to you that this is an older design? What makes the difference? Are there any features that you would want to use today? Write a brief report explaining your findings.

# Unit 3: Summary

## Key Concepts

### Chapter 9: Print Type

1. With personal computers and specialized software such as Microsoft Publisher, Adobe PageMaker, or QuarkXPress, nonprofessionals can create brochures, newsletters, and flyers at their desktops.
2. Type can be identified in three ways: typeface, style, and size.
3. Typefaces fall into two basic categories: serif and sans serif.
4. Type is measured on the ascenders and descenders of characters.
5. Text spacing can be adjusted by changing the tracking, kerning, and leading,
6. Punctuation decisions for desktop publishing include use of capitals, use of spacing after end punctuation, and use of hyphens and dashes.

### Chapter 10: Print Graphics

1. Graphics may float over the page or be placed inline.
2. Text may be wrapped by maintaining a rectangular border between the text and the graphic or it may be wrapped so that the text and the graphic merge.
3. One use for drawing tools is to create a pull quote.
4. Watermarks are pale images placed on a page as if they were the lowest layer.
5. Some desktop publishing programs enable you to create artwork from actual text, converting words to images.

### Chapter 11: Print Design

1. When graphics are added to a page, the standard Z pattern can be altered. The page designer uses a focus plan in deciding the direction in which a reader gathers the information on a page.
2. White space (or sometimes negative space) acts as a design element of its own.
3. To create satisfying page layouts, use the rule of thirds, alignment, repetition, and symmetry.
4. Text may be balanced with other text or with a graphic.
5. Design elements should not seem to float off a page, so it's a good design technique to attach them to the page in some way.

### Chapter 12: Print Standards

1. Limit the number of fonts in a document to no more than three.
2. Include essential information, grouping together related information.
3. Long lines of body text should not run across a page.
4. Paragraphs should be indented an em space (the width of a capital *M*), rather than by keying five spaces.
5. Hanging punctuation should be placed outside the edges of a paragraph.
6. Curly quotes should be used for quotation marks in place of the straight marks.
7. Avoid widows, orphans, and tombstone headings.
8. Consider your audience when making type and layout decisions.
9. With Adobe Acrobat, you can create PDF documents that can be read on any platform (Macintosh or PC) and with any computer.

# Terms

**alignment** the placement of text on a line either to the left, to the right, centered, or justified

**ascender** the part of a lowercase letter that extends above the x-height, as in the letter *t*

**bleed** a layout design that places an image or block of color so that it ends at the exact edge of the paper

**clip art** a picture or drawing created with the intention that the artwork will be used by others; clip art is packaged with desktop publishing software or can be purchased separately

**curly quotes** rounded marks used for quotation marks and apostrophes

**descender** the part of a lower-case letter that extends below the baseline, as in the letter *g*

**desktop publishing** the use of word processing software or specialized desktop publishing software on a personal computer to create a document in which graphics and text enhance the message

**dingbats** graphic symbols or ornaments, rather than letters or numbers

**display fonts** fonts designed to attract attention to the design of the font, as well as to the words

**distiller** the software installed as part of Acrobat that converts documents into PDF files so that they can be read by Acrobat Reader

**drop cap** a large, often ornate, first letter of a paragraph.

**em dash** a line the width of the capital letter *M* in whatever font and point size are being used; indicates a break in thought.

**em space** a space the width of a capital letter *M* in the font and point size being used

**en dash** a line the width of the capital letter *N* in whatever font and point size are being used; it is used in ranges of numbers, letters, or dates

**en space** half the size of an em space; a space the width of a capital letter *N* in the font and point size being used

**focus plan** determines the path the eye will follow on a page

**font** originally included typeface, style, and size, but now the term is interchangeable with *typeface*

**greeking** the use of placeholder words that have no meaning to show where text is to be placed in a layout; also, the use of gray bars in some desktop publishing software to represent text that is too small to be legible on the screen

**grunge type** a modern typeface that appears "distressed," with letters oddly shaped and not completely formed

**gutter** a vertical column of white space

**hanging punctuation** punctuation such as quotation marks that needs to "hang" outside a paragraph rather than line up with the text below

**kerning** spaces certain characters closely enough that the smaller character fits under the larger

**layout** the arrangement on a page of all the key parts without regard to the specific content

**leading** the space between lines of text or between paragraphs

**ligature** two characters tied to each other in such a way that they appear to be one unit, such as *a* and *e* combined to form *æ*

**monospace font** a font that looks as if it were created with a typewriter because each character is given the same space

**orphan** a line of text that appears at the top of a column or page with the rest of the paragraph appearing at the bottom of the previous column or page

**PDF** the acronym for Portable Document Format; the file extension .pdf identifies a document encoded in this format; Adobe's Acrobat Reader enables you to read PDF files without having the original software installed on your computer

**point** a type measurement that equals 1/72 of an inch

**pull quote** a short text or article extract set off by rules or in a box

**reverse type** white type on a dark background, designed to make the type stand out

**rule** a horizontal or vertical line

**sans serif** a typeface without serifs

**serif** a typeface with extensions at the ends of the main strokes that define each letter; these extensions are called serifs

**text wrapping** moves text away from a graphic so that it flows around the image

**tombstone** a design in which two heads are "bumped" into each other across columns

**tracking** the amount of space between characters

**typeface** the design of the letters, numbers, and symbols that make up a font

**typography** the study of all elements of type including the shape, size, and spacing of the characters

**watermark** a pale image placed on the background of a page; often used for logos or other identification

**white space** the area on a page in which text or graphics are absent

**widow** a sentence at the bottom of the column or page that is separated from the rest of its paragraph

**WordArt** a desktop publishing option that creates a graphic out of text by using curves, colors, and other effects

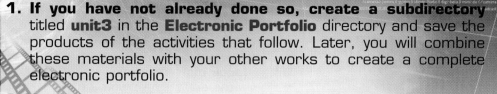

# ELECTRONIC PORTFOLIO

1. **If you have not already done so, create a subdirectory** titled **unit3** in the **Electronic Portfolio** directory and save the products of the activities that follow. Later, you will combine these materials with your other works to create a complete electronic portfolio.

2. Create a one-page newsletter on a subject of interest to you. Make design decisions based on a specific audience. Save the document as **newsletter1**.

3. On page two of the document, explain your choices of type, graphics, and design.

4. Using the same information included in **newsletter1**, create a second newsletter design for another audience and explain your choices of type, graphics, and design. Save this document as **newsletter2**.

5. Save both newsletters as PDF files.

6. Use the following chart to evaluate the quality of your portfolio material.

|  | Beginning | Developing | Accomplished | Exemplary | Score |
|---|---|---|---|---|---|
| Newsletter 1 | Newsletter demonstrates fewer than three concepts | Newsletter demonstrates fewer than six concepts | Newsletter demonstrates more than ten concepts | Newsletter demonstrates more than ten concepts and focuses effectively on the selected audience | |
| Newsletter 2 | Newsletter demonstrates fewer than three concepts | Newsletter demonstrates fewer than six concepts | Newsletter demonstrates more than ten concepts | Newsletter demonstrates more than ten concepts and focuses effectively on the selected audience | |

# Presentation Strategies

SOURCE: ©PHOTODISC

# Career Profile

Dr. Richard Wynn is not just a registered pharmacist. Dr. Wynn is one wired research scientist with a Ph.D. in pharmacology and an appointment at the University of Maryland Dental School in Baltimore, Maryland, in the Pharmacology department. Why, you ask, do we say that he is "one wired research scientist"? Let's put it this way: Dr. Wynn wows his audiences, whether they be dental students, pharmacy students, dental hygiene students, or the many other attendees (practicing dentists and hygienists) at the seminars he conducts around the country. How does he do this? Dr. Wynn uses his expertise in pharmacy and technology to bring to his audience up-to-date information in a variety of ways: in his research, in his teaching, in continuing education programs, and in his presentations.

SOURCE: ©PHOTODISC

**139**

(continued)

For his research activities, the variety of available tools is tremendous. Drug manufacturers, medical schools, and foundations often have statistical packages available for research. He also uses the Internet, entering search words to learn about new drug research or drug interactions quickly and efficiently. This same type of search can be conducted even the night before a lecture or a seminar so that Dr. Wynn can use any new information he finds to update his PowerPoint slide presentations. Talk about optimum use of Internet capabilities!

Along these same lines, he uses the Internet to e-mail students who query him about assignments and research. He can get back to them in minutes sometimes, because he has his laptop with him, even on the road. Medical professionals and students today often are equipped with a personal digital assistant (PDA) that contains a module of drug information that can be updated daily. Using electronic technology, Dr. Wynn can update the module. To do this, for example, he may receive a drug update from the Food and Drug Administration (FDA). He then enters it in Microsoft Word on his laptop, it gets converted to HTML, and the information is then revised into a main module of drug information. Users can then download the revised information in the main module from a Web site and to their PDAs so that they have the updated drug information for patient care or a research project.

Dick Wynn knows the importance of presentation planning and the effect the design of his presentations will have on his audience. Presenting to various audiences has led him from the simple transparencies he once used to a variety of multimedia in his presentations. His expert PowerPoint slide shows illustrate the field of dental technology, charting and graphing, and drug information on several screens. His laptop is also connected to the Internet, so he can switch back and forth between his PowerPoint presentation and the Internet to take advantage of the latest information he needs to convey to the audience.

To be effective, a PowerPoint slide show must take advantage of type size, fonts, colors, arrows, banners, and other stylistic techniques to keep an audience excited and interested. However, too much information on a slide, or a type font or color that is too difficult to read, will detract from any presentation. Dr. Wynn knows that animations and other fancy stylistic combinations take up large amounts of memory. He is therefore careful to use only what is necessary to avoid any slowdowns in performance of his computer.

Dental professionals value updating their skills and learning new competencies to enhance their expertise with their patients. They must know and understand how drugs interact with other medications that patients may be taking. Dr. Wynn uses his background in pharmacy to give dental professionals as well as his students the latest in dental/pharmacology-related technology. Dentists today must know how to use equipment such as digital cameras for oral photography, voice recognition software to dictate patient notes, and the Internet to obtain practical information on drugs and dental materials from manufacturers. Some manufacturers now supply information over the Internet as well as on CDs.

Being able to access dental and drug information in a variety of ways is critical to the performance of most dentists and pharmacists today. Keeping accurate patient records on a computer is essential so that patient histories and treatment data can be accessed rapidly. Medical profes-

(continued)

sionals now carry PDAs so that their patient records can be accessed at chairside or bedside. Drug databases, as noted earlier, can also be accessed on PDAs. Many of these palm-size computers can also be accessed by voice command.

You can imagine how exciting these innovations are to the field of dentistry and pharmacology. Being a dental professional today doesn't mean just filling or extracting teeth; being a pharmacist today doesn't mean just counting pills into a bottle. Patients today expect their medical professionals to be professionals—not only in their specialties but also in the technologies that will help them exercise their specialties for the betterment of their patients.

Throughout this course, you will learn how to design your presentations and use multimedia effectively. A good first step in the process is proper planning. As you complete this unit, you will learn more about effective design through the use of various media devices. You can also develop your skills to a high level—Dr. Wynn is a perfect example of taking presentation skills to the max! ■

Note: Dr. Richard Wynn is a real person in the pharmacology department at the University of Maryland Dental School in Baltimore, Maryland.

# Chapter 13
## Presentation Planning

SOURCE: ©DIGITAL VISION

## Objectives

- *You will learn how to research your audience.*
- *You will learn how to use outline functions to plan your presentation.*
- *You will learn how to structure your basic points.*
- *You will learn how to use the notes feature.*
- *You will learn how to arrange your slides to be most effective.*

## INTRODUCTION

According to statistics, the most frightening experience for a person is speaking in front of an audience. Most successful people in business, however, must do so at one time or another. The fear is founded on concerns about looking foolish—perhaps by forgetting important points or by not being able to make a point clear to the audience. Fortunately, with the technology available today, you can use presentation software to reduce your fear. With presentation software, your points are visible to everyone, your ideas have already been structured, and as a side benefit the audience's eyes are not always on you.

Almost anyone can create or **build** a presentation. The challenge is to create a good presentation—as John and Harriet Whitedeer, school building architects/contractors, discovered when they had to present a proposal to the local school board. They needed to convince this group that they were the right company to create the plans for a new elementary school to be built in the district.

## RESEARCH

Before you begin creating your presentation, you need to do some research about your audience so that you can be sure to include the information that is important to the group to whom you are speaking. It is easy to become so engaged in the production of your slide show that you forget that the message is more important than the medium. Doing the essential research before you begin, helps avoid this pitfall.

The widely used AUDIENCE formula will make it easy to know where to start by answering a series of questions about the audience and the facilities in which you will present.

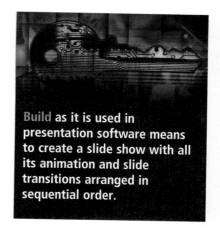

**Build** as it is used in presentation software means to create a slide show with all its animation and slide transitions arranged in sequential order.

**A**nalyze—Who is the audience? How can you "connect" with the members of this audience?

**U**nderstanding—What is the audience's level of knowledge of the topic of your presentation?

**D**emographics—What ages, gender, and educational backgrounds are represented in the audience?

**I**nterests—Are the members of the audience there because they chose to attend or because they were required to attend?

**E**nvironment—Will you have a cordless microphone? Is the platform or podium placed so that the audience can see the projection screen (ideally at least six feet off the floor)? Is your space limited? Will everyone be able to see and hear you? How big is the room, and how many chairs will it have?

**N**eeds—What does the audience need or want to get from the presentation?

**C**ustomization—What can you do to make the presentation appropriate for this particular audience?

**E**xpectations—What is the audience expecting?

SOURCE: ©PHOTODISC

Use the AUDIENCE questions to help you plan ahead. To answer the questions, you may have to contact the person who arranged the presentation or ask those who are planning to attend. As you get the answers to your questions, fill in a chart similar to the one shown in Figure 13.1.

The Whitedeers have spoken to school district personnel, and they know that their audience is the local school board and that this group does not consist of any architects, so the group's knowledge of design issues may be limited. They also know that the age

| Analyze | Who is the audience? How can you "connect" with the members of this audience? | |
|---|---|---|
| Understanding | What is the audience's level of knowledge of the topic of your presentation? | |
| Demographics | What ages, genders, and educational backgrounds are represented in the audience? | |
| Interests | Are the members of the audience there because they chose to attend or because they were required to attend? | |
| Environment | Will you have a cordless microphone? Is the platform or podium placed so that the audience can see the projection screen (ideally at least six feet off the floor)? Is your space limited? Will everyone be able to see and hear you? How big is the room, and how many chairs will it have? | |
| Needs | What does the audience need or want to get from the presentation? | |
| Customization | What can you do to make the presentation appropriate for this particular audience? | |
| Expectations | What is the audience expecting? | |

**Figure 13.1** Use of a chart such as this one makes it easy to keep in mind the essential questions to consider before preparing a presentation.

and education of the seven-member board are varied but that these men and women are very interested in seeing what plans are possible. District officials have assured them that the room will be large, with a projection system built in for optimum visibility, so it will be easy to use presentation software. The audience wants to see specific details, not just a broad overview. The hardest decision the Whitedeers have to make is how to connect to the audience. However, they know they have a well-thought-out plan and look forward to the challenge of making their presentation to the school board.

## THE **ETHICS** OF PRESENTATION HONESTY

As a speaker, you have an obligation to be honest with your audience. This need for honesty means you must check your facts carefully to ensure that they are accurate. It's easy to inflate figures and add details you are unsure of in order to make your presentation appear more valuable. Always double-check your facts and incorporate only information that you can verify. Your credibility will grow and your effectiveness as a speaker will grow at the same time.

## PREPARATION

Once you know the AUDIENCE answers, you can begin to prepare your presentation. In an earlier time, presentation speeches were created and then the audiovisual components were added. Today, speakers often use presentation software such as Microsoft PowerPoint as a planning tool. Even though this is a useful technological shortcut, don't fall into the trap of trying to plan your ideas and the **multimedia** elements at the same time. Instead, decide what you want to say and then decide how to enhance that message with the multimedia potential of the presentation software.

It's easy to want to rush the preparation process, but prior thought is essential for the success of your presentation. The time spent deciding what information to include is far more valuable than the time spent deciding on the perfect graphic. Your audience cares far more about what you are saying than how fascinating your PowerPoint slides may appear.

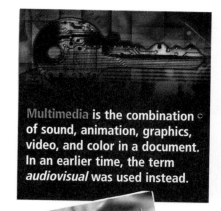

Multimedia is the combination of sound, animation, graphics, video, and color in a document. In an earlier time, the term *audiovisual* was used instead.

## OUTLINE

The general rule is that a visual presentation should be limited to three main ideas supported with several subpoints or explanations. The outlining view of PowerPoint and other types of presentation software makes it easy to work with your ideas before you begin to create the actual display. The outline should always be your starting point when you begin to prepare your presentation. Use of the outline encourages you to consider your content before thinking about design issues.

The software enables you to easily move ideas about until you are satisfied with the arrangement and have selected exactly the right information. If your presentation program doesn't provide an outline feature, then you should create an outline before moving to the next stage of preparation.

It's important to know that when using Microsoft PowerPoint (and some other software), you must select a slide type that includes both title and text in order for the outline to function as anticipated. Each time you press the Enter key, a new slide will appear with a new point. Pressing the Tab key will convert the title to a point. Pressing Shift + Tab reverses the process. As the outline points are entered, PowerPoint translates the information into a series of graduated steps that appear on the slides. Notice in Figure 13.2 that the bullets and dashes combined with the indenting of lines provide an outline-like view on the slides themselves.

## Good Business

### Teamwork

The team concept is becoming the workplace norm. People who have difficulty working with others are at a major disadvantage in the modern workplace. Your communication skills, your willingness to go the extra mile, your positive attitude, your time management skills—all of these elements and more will determine your value as a team member. It is not good enough simply to know how a few software programs work.

Team members must understand their roles and be aware of how they affect the rest of the team. They must also stay in frequent touch with one another to coordinate the work that needs to be done. For example, typesetting on a book cannot begin until the design has been finalized and the text written. The designer and the author cannot spend an excessive amount of time on their jobs and expect the typesetter to work hurriedly in the little time remaining in the schedule at the end. All must work together to ensure that enough time is allotted for each task.

**Digging deeper:** In a team with three or four classmates, create a small multimedia project of your choice. Team members will need to work together to select a topic, decide what kinds of elements to include, delegate tasks, and so forth. After you're finished, evaluate your success as a team.

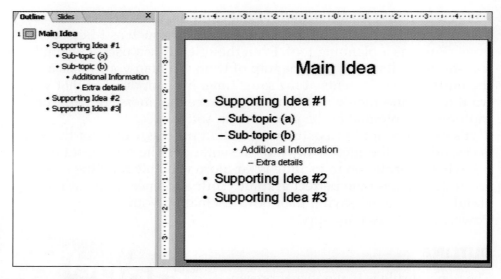

**Figure 13.2** The outline function of PowerPoint makes it simple to plan your presentation.

Begin your presentation planning by asking yourself what are the three most significant ideas that you want to get across to your audience. Then list them using the outline feature. Often at this stage of planning, you may find yourself with a long list of ideas that seem important. It is essential to pare this list down, or you will have a presentation that is nothing but a long list with no focus. To solve this problem, see if some of the points can be moved to become subpoints or gathered under a common topic. Use the outline feature to juggle ideas until you are satisfied with the outcome. Once you have decided on the major points, add supporting information. It is tempting to bypass this step, but if you spend the time at this stage to think through your ideas carefully, your presentation will be far more effective.

Some presentation designers create the entire outline on a single slide and then divide the points once the ideas are in place. Other designers prefer to create three slides (one for each main point) and then add their subpoints to those

**ERGO-TIPS ERGO-TIPS**

**LIMBER UP!**

Key each of these lines twice to exercise your fingers and to practice correct keying techniques. The sentences were constructed to give you practice in all letters of the alphabet.

1. Jack Faber was amazingly quiet during the extensive program.
2. Dixie quickly gave him two big prizes for completing a jump.
3. Jordan placed first by solving the complex quiz in one week.

slides. Regardless of the technique you use, once the outline is complete, you must then begin to decide how much information to include on each slide. A general rule is to limit the number of lines on a slide to no more than six, creating additional slides as needed. Depending on how long your presentation is and how much information you have, all the supporting ideas may appear on a single slide or each idea may need to appear on a slide of its own.

The Whitedeers meet to discuss the points they want to make. After much discussion, they decide to emphasize their history of reliability, their credentials, and their plans to use staff and community input in the design process. They had wanted to include their award-winning designs and their years of community involvement, but they decided to use those as sub-points under the credentials main topic.

While they were working on the slide for the design process, as shown in Figure 13.3, they realized they were quickly running out of space for all the sub-points. Rather than stop to create new slides, however, they continued to list at random all their ideas. Once they listed all the points they wanted to deliver, they considered the order in which to deliver them.

After the Whitedeers made all the decisions, they started to move the points to new slides. Once again, they realized they had too many points and stopped to gather these ideas into categories of their own. Fortunately, it was easy to move the points around on the page until the new organization was completed, as shown in Figure 13.4.

| Outline | Slides |
| --- | --- |

5 ▢ **Design Process**
- Staff Questionnaire
  - Wiring
    - Number of electrical outlets
      - Placement of outlets
    - Lighting options
      - Rheostats
      - Extra lighting in special places
    - Projection bay in ceiling
    - Mounted television
  - Physical Arrangement
    - Number of desks
    - Space for centers
    - Closets and storage
    - Windows
    - Floor covering
    - Blackboard or whiteboard
      - Height of blackboard
    - Counter top
      - Height of counter
      - Placement of counter

**Figure 13.3** It's often easier to list all your points before thinking about the slide arrangements.

## STRUCTURE

The basic guidelines of good presentation design limit you to no more than six lines of text per slide and no more than six words per line of text. This means you should keep your ideas brief rather than use long explanations. Complete sentences are generally not necessary or desirable.

In addition to limiting the number of words and lines on a slide, it's also a good idea to make your points grammatically parallel. **Parallelism** means that if you use a verb and a noun in supporting idea number 1, you should use the same grammatical structure in supporting idea number 2. It also means that if you capitalize all the terms in idea 1, you should do the same in idea 2. You do not have to make every statement parallel to every other one—merely to ones that are on the same level. Attention to this kind of detail will give your presentation a professional look and shine.

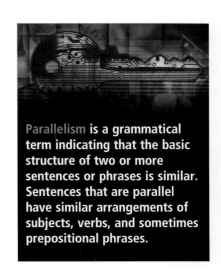

Parallelism **is a grammatical term indicating that the basic structure of two or more sentences or phrases is similar. Sentences that are parallel have similar arrangements of subjects, verbs, and sometimes prepositional phrases.**

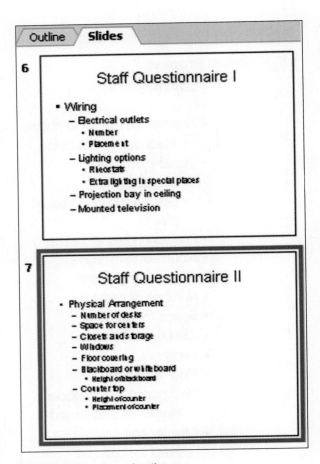

**Figure 13.4** Once details are decided, it's time to decide on the number and content of slides.

The Whitedeers checked their list of ideas for parallelism after they were satisfied they had included all the necessary details. They realized they had too many lines on some slides but decided that as long as the initial slides were brief, it would be okay to leave the supporting slides more complex.

## NOTES

Once the major ideas and subsequent points are in place, you may find yourself with information you want to include but don't want to list on the slides. It's not necessary to include every word of your presentation in your actual slides. If that were the case, then you could just hand your audience the printout and not need to give the presentation at all, although at times that may seem like an appealing choice. Limit your slide information to the major points and then add information orally. The notes option in Power-Point is a good place to jot down these ideas as they occur (see Figure 13.5). Later, you may want to add even more information as you complete the design of your presentation.

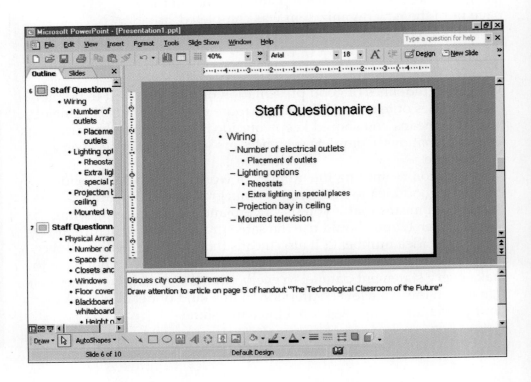

**Figure 13.5** The notes window in PowerPoint is a good place to store additional information.

# ARRANGEMENT

Once the content of the presentation is in place, it is time to decide on the movement of the slides. Generally, presentations move sequentially from one slide to another, but that is not the only option. With the use of **hyperlinks** (just like the ones found on a Web page), movement can be in any direction you want. This part of the planning process requires you to decide in exactly what order you want the audience to see each of your points.

PowerPoint provides a series of action buttons similar to those shown in Figure 13.6 to simplify movement from one slide to another. Placing these buttons on your page enables you to select the links you want them to activate, such as moving to a particular page or back to the first slide.

The Whitedeers decide to create a series of links from their master page to each of the subpoints. After each subpoint and its supporting information are completed, the presentation will then move back to the original slide. Returning to the original list after each topic is presented will continually reinforce their three major points. This process makes their presentation design more like a web. Figure 13.7 shows the anticipated movement from the opening points to the first major subpoints to more specific details and then back to the original slide.

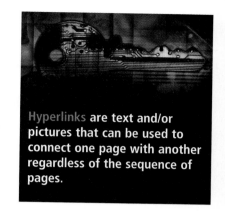

**Hyperlinks** are text and/or pictures that can be used to connect one page with another regardless of the sequence of pages.

SOURCE: ©MICROSOFT POWERPOINT

**Figure 13.6** PowerPoint provides action buttons to use as navigation tools.

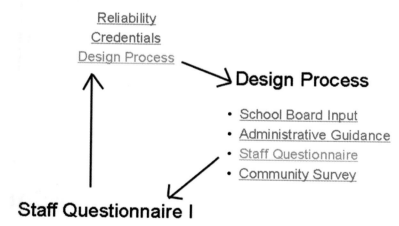

**Figure 13.7** Using links makes it possible to move back and forth between slides that are not sequential.

## SUMMARY

In this chapter, you have learned to plan presentations before beginning the graphically intense part of the process. You have learned that planning begins with research into the audience and its expectations. You also have learned how to compile significant points by using the outlining ability of PowerPoint. You have learned about adding notes and selecting the arrangement of the slides. Now it is time to add the multimedia features that are characteristic of PowerPoint keeping in mind the points listed in Figure 13.8.

**Figure 13.8** These four points provide guidelines you can use when creating the content for your presentation.

---

# Guidelines to Keep in Mind

- Three main points
- Six lines of text per slide
- Six words per line
- Parallel structures

---

Answer the following questions on your own computer.

1. What questions should you ask about the demographics of an audience?
2. What constitutes the environment of a presentation?
3. What does an audience care about more than interesting graphics in a presentation?
4. How many main points should be in a presentation?
5. What determines how many slides you will use?
6. What view is most useful when beginning to plan a presentation?
7. What purpose do the bullets and dashes serve in a PowerPoint slide?
8. How many lines of text should appear on a slide?
9. How many words should appear in a line of text on a slide?
10. How can you make ideas grammatically parallel?
11. What should be included in the notes on a slide?
12. Why shouldn't you include every detail on a slide?
13. What are two options available to you when deciding on the movement of slides?
14. What purpose do links serve on a slide?
15. Why did the Whitedeers decide to override the rules about the number of ideas on a single slide?

Discuss the following questions either as a class or as a written assignment.

1. What difference will it make in your presentation if the audience is attending by choice?
2. Why is planning content and multimedia effects at the same time not a good idea?
3. Why should a presentation be limited to three main ideas?
4. Why should you not include all your material on a PowerPoint slide?
5. Why does use of parallel grammar give a shine to a PowerPoint presentation?

1. Find the text of a famous speech such as John F. Kennedy's inaugural address (http://www.bartleby.com/124/pres56.html) or Martin Luther King Jr.'s "I Have a Dream" speech (http://web66.coled.umn.edu/new/MLK/MLK.html).

2. What answers would the speaker give to each of the **AUDIENCE** questions? Record them in a word processing document using a chart similar to the one shown in Figure 13.1.

3. Outline the speech, looking for the major points and subpoints. Record the points in a word processing document or in your presentation software.

4. Either using presentation software or on paper, determine which points should be included on a slide and which information should go into the notes.

5. Indicate the order of the slides and links (if appropriate) either on paper or in the presentation software.

## FURTHER EXPLORATION

Contact the chamber of commerce or an organization such as the Rotary club to find out when a presentation is going to be made that you could attend. Attend the presentation; observe the answers to the **AUDIENCE** questions and the format of the actual presentation. Speak with the presenter when the presentation is over and ask about the planning that went into it. If presentation software was used, ask what process was used in creating the slides and the name of the software. Give your classmates an overview of your findings.

# Chapter 14
# Presentation Design

ESTIMATED TIME

**2**

HOURS

SOURCE: ©PHOTODISC

## INTRODUCTION

Like characters moving onto a stage to speak the words the author has created, presentation design allows you to set the stage for these words. Your design can be elaborate or sparse, complicated or simple. Whatever choices you make, they should be selected based upon the need to convey your message in the best way possible. This may mean that you use few colors or many, images that appear and disappear, or fonts that attract attention. The design of a slide show or presentation provides you with many options.

Harriet Turnbow is faced with these decisions as she prepares a slide show for her father's Rotary club presentation demonstrating the work that was completed on a recent service project. The group had spent several weeks constructing a playground for a park that had fallen into disuse. A playground

## Objectives

- *You will learn how to use layout options such as templates, master slides, and color schemes.*
- *You will learn how to choose professional backgrounds, text, and bullets.*
- *You will learn how to add visual effects such as multimedia and white space.*

had once been located in the park, but over the years it had become unusable. Mr. Turnbow and several other Rotary members had decided to rebuild it and now they wanted to show the rest of the organization the results of their efforts. Harriet volunteered to help her father create a PowerPoint presentation.

## TEMPLATES

Once your message has been determined by your research and preparation steps, it is time to set the stage for your ideas. The quickest way to add visual effects to your presentation is to use one of the predesigned **templates** that come with your presentation software, similar to those shown in Figure 14.1. These templates contain backgrounds, font sizes and colors, and bullets already chosen for you. If time is a critical factor in your design process, use of templates is an excellent choice.

Microsoft has anticipated that many users of PowerPoint will be business professionals, and consequently, it has included a series of prepared slides designed to be used in typical situations such as those shown in Figure 14.2. This list appears when you use the AutoContent Wizard, which takes you through a series of steps before beginning the

**Templates** are document masters predesigned by professionals who have already chosen the background, font size and color, and bullets to be used.

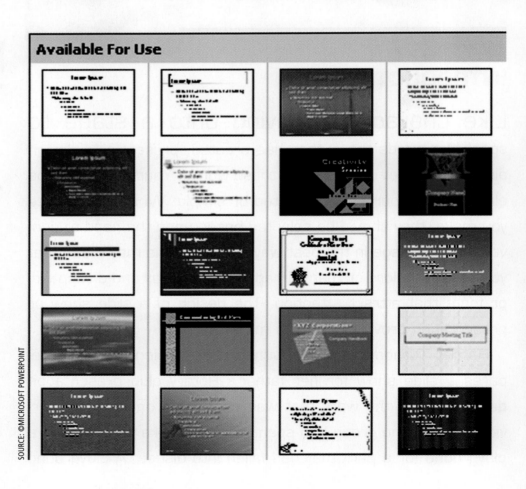

SOURCE: ©MICROSOFT POWERPOINT

**Figure 14.1** Templates such as these can make PowerPoint presentations easy to design.

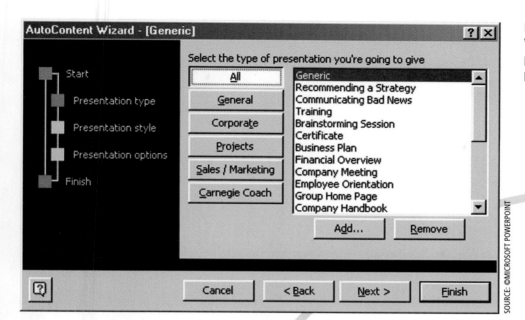

**Figure 14.2** The AutoContent Wizard makes it easy to create a presentation using a series of prepared slides.

process of adding information. If you have already planned what you want to include in your slides, it is easy to add this content to a prepared template. In addition, the details already included on the slides may trigger an awareness that you need to add additional information.

Microsoft templates have been created by professionals to be attractive and effective. One disadvantage of using them is that if your audience has frequently attended PowerPoint presentations, they may recognize a template from a previous experience. Your message may be "blurred" by this recognition factor. One solution is to use a template as a base for your design and then modify it to personalize it for your presentation. Another possibility is to use third-party designs such as Digital Juice, offered by Crystal Graphics. These are also created by professionals, but they are less likely to have been seen previously, and they include interesting backgrounds, animations, and photos to enhance your presentation.

Harriet's father had listed for her the construction plan, costs, and the names of the members who participated in the project. She created the content portion of her slide show using these three main points. Now she wanted to add visual elements, but her time was somewhat limited. She chose a basic template (shown in Figure 14.3) already identified as a template for a project postmortem (or results).

## THE **ETHICS** OF PRESENTATION VALUE

As a speaker, you have an obligation to provide value for the time your audience invests in your presentation. This obligation means you need to design slides the audience can see easily and understand quickly. It means you must spend your time preparing well so that each minute the audience spends with you offers them some useful or important idea. Too many slides that have only interesting pictures, or too few slides that have condensed text, waste your audience's time. If that happens, you have failed to meet your obligation to them.

**Figure 14.3** This opening slide is simple but effective

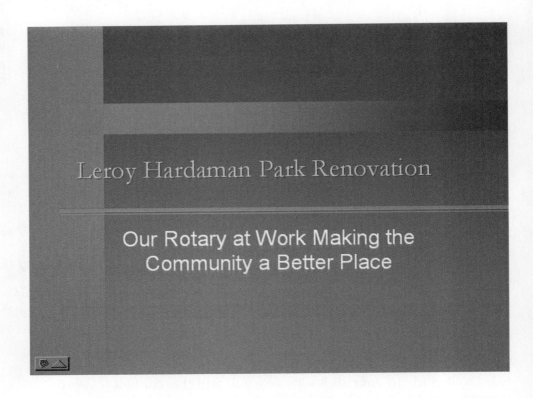

Leroy Hardaman Park Renovation

Our Rotary at Work Making the Community a Better Place

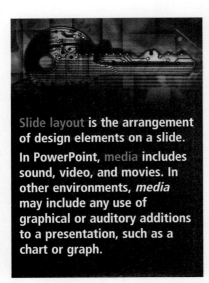

Slide layout is the arrangement of design elements on a slide.

In PowerPoint, media includes sound, video, and movies. In other environments, *media* may include any use of graphical or auditory additions to a presentation, such as a chart or graph.

## SLIDE LAYOUTS

Whether you use a prepared template or not, you will still need to decide what slides to use. When you created your outline, you had to use a slide that included a bulleted list, so you have already had some experience with choosing a slide layout. **Slide layouts** fall into three basic categories:

1. Title slide
2. Text slide
   - Single-bulleted list
   - Double-bulleted list
3. Multimedia slide
   - Table
   - Chart
   - Clip art
   - Picture
   - Diagram or organizational chart
   - Media (sound or movie)

As shown in Figure 14.4, each of these three slide types can appear in a variety of combinations, such as title, text, and clip art. **Media** slides that incorporate movies or sound are discussed later in more detail. Varying the slide layout helps in creating a presentation that is not monotonous. Harriet used the chart slide with a title to list the

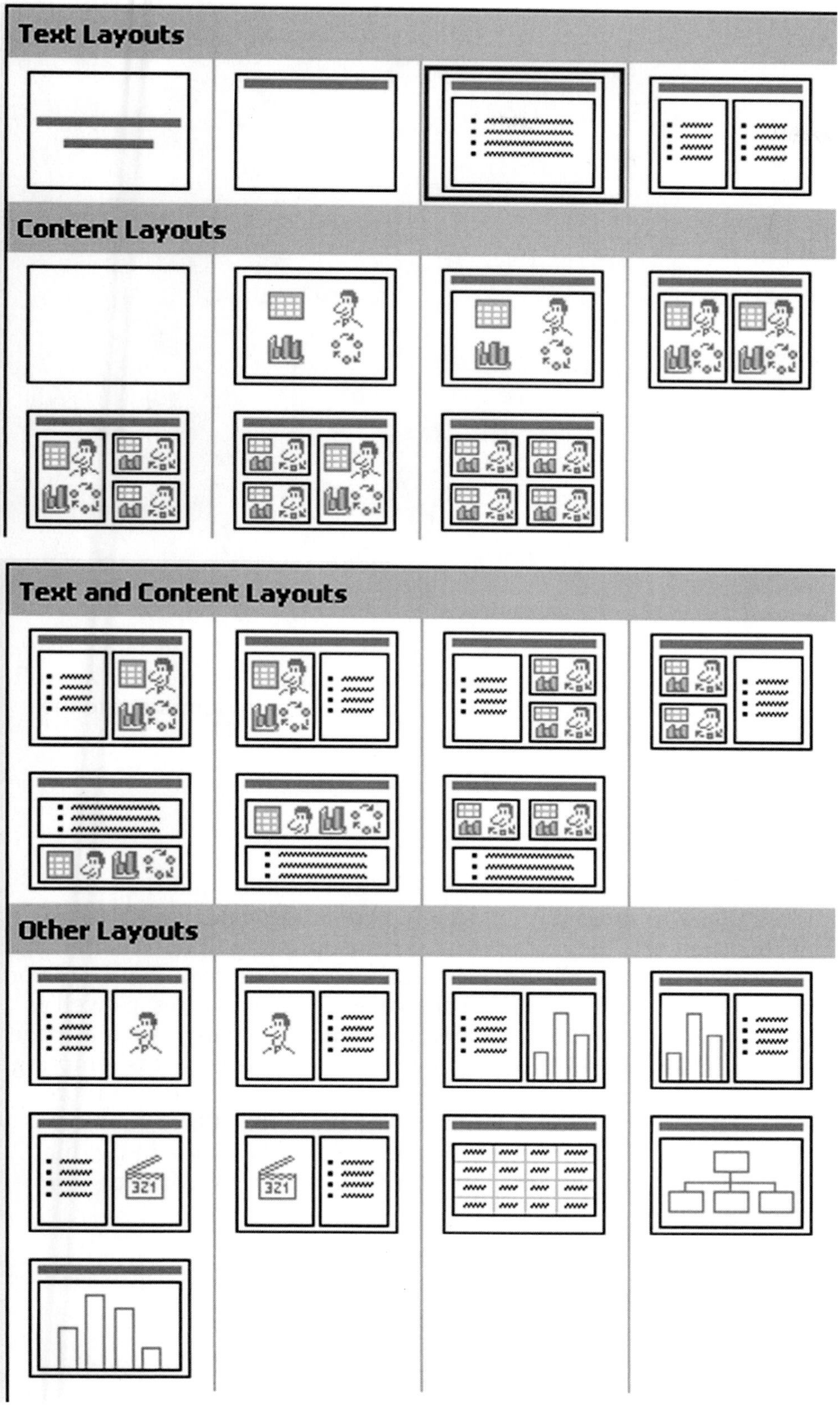

**Figure 14.4** Slide layouts offer a wide number of choices to help prevent audience boredom.

**Figure 14.5** Slides can include a variety of media options, such as this chart.

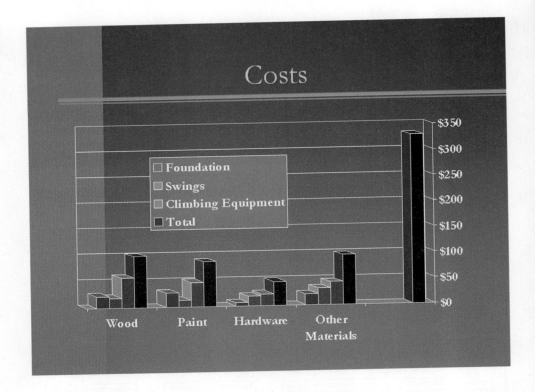

expenses associated with the project, as shown in Figure 14.5, as well as a variety of other slides such as bulleted lists to demonstrate the points of the project.

## MASTER SLIDES

In print design, you work to keep a consistent look, and the same should apply to presentation design. One of the easiest ways to establish consistency is to use the **master slide** option to make design choices that apply to all slides. With a master slide, you can decide on font size and style, background choice, and bullet choices, as well as other details. In addition, header and footer information such as page numbers is also included on the master slide. Although it is tempting to vary these design elements on every slide, you will have a more professional-looking presentation if you avoid this. Once a master slide is in place, all that's left is to add the details for the individual slides in your slide presentation. Harriet's master slide is shown in Figure 14.6.

A master slide is a single slide that can be designed once and then applied to many slides. PowerPoint enables the creation of multiple masters for use in different situations.

## COLOR SCHEMES

Color in presentations does more than just make the slides pretty. Color can increase learning retention and recall by nearly 80 percent. Use of color can increase comprehension by more than 70 percent. Color increases willingness to read by up to 80 percent and improves

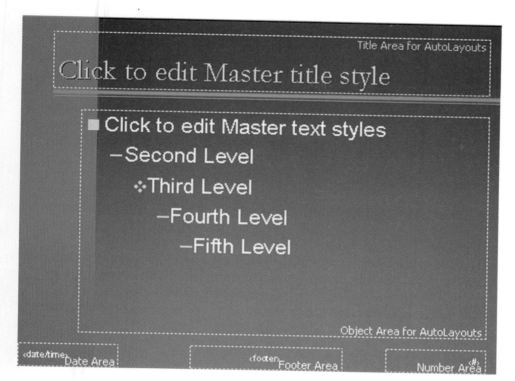

**Figure 14.6** A master slide such as this one from PowerPoint allows you to make "global" changes to all your slides at one time.

selling efficiency by nearly 85 percent. With this much power, color cannot be ignored. The choice of color must be made carefully, however, so that it reaches its maximum potential whether it is used as a background, as a font color, or in a graphic.

PowerPoint offers a series of **color schemes** designed to be effective in most situations (see Figure 14.7). Colors are assigned to the background, the title, and the bulleted text. Use of color schemes helps keep a presentation design consistent. If you do not want to use the options Microsoft provides, you can modify them or even create your own while keeping in mind the guidelines suggested here.

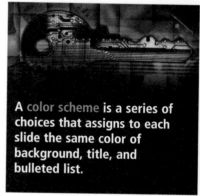

A color scheme is a series of choices that assigns to each slide the same color of background, title, and bulleted list.

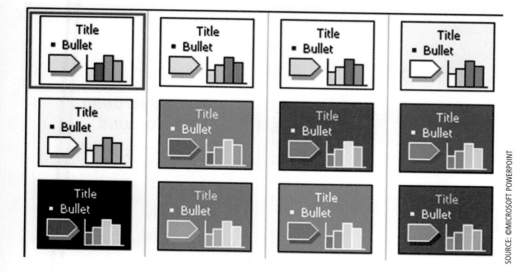

SOURCE: ©MICROSOFT POWERPOINT

**Figure 14.7** Color schemes are designed to simplify the color selection process.

Dark blue creates a stable, mature message. It has a calming effect on most audiences. Red or orange can cause excitement or create an emotional effect that makes it a good color to use to emphasize one word. Green can make audiences feel comfortable.

The most readable colors are yellow with black lettering. This is why school buses and some traffic signs are yellow. Keep in mind, though, that on a sign the color is paint, but on a screen the color is projected using light. What may work on a sign may not work as effectively on a display screen.

Audiences are better focused if the background is dark and the text and drawings are lighter colors. The eye is drawn to the lighter areas, and the use of contrast in colors creates an impact on the audience. Watch for color clashing, however, such as red text on a green background.

Harriet's template choice included a series of variations of blue and green with text colors of yellow and white. Since the message that was to be delivered did not require or need the excitement of emotional colors such as red, these are good choices for her design.

## BACKGROUNDS

Unlike desktop publishing, in which the background generally is white, presentation software allows you a free range of background choices. The **background** can be a single color, graduated colors, colored textures, or even a photograph, as shown in Figure 14.8. Although it is interesting to see all the possible background varia-

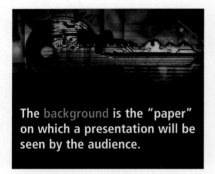

The background is the "paper" on which a presentation will be seen by the audience.

**Figure 14.8** Backgrounds are the "paper" on which a slide is presented. An infinite number of choices are available to you.

tions, use restraint in your choice. The background should not be so overwhelming that the words or the message drown in it. Instead, use a subtle background that supports your message. When making your choice, keep in mind how color influences your audience.

## TEXT

In designing a presentation, choosing the right font size is 90 percent of the job. Billboard painters have a rule for size of letters: A 1-inch letter is readable from 10 feet; a 2-inch letter is readable from 20 feet; a 3-inch letter is readable from 30 feet. A presentation screen is not a billboard, but if 72-point fonts are 1 inch high, then that gives you an idea how big the font should be to be read by the audience. Actually, you are generally limited to fonts no larger than 96 points.

Remember that PowerPoint builds in font size based on the amount of text on a page. If you have many lines, the font size will be smaller than if you have only a few lines. You can always change the font size yourself, but you need to be aware of the need to keep it as large as possible.

Just as you saw in the chapter on desktop publishing, font choices consist of serif, sans serif, and display. It's important to choose your font for readability rather than for style. If your audience must strain to figure out the words, they will not be paying attention to your message. Never sacrifice readability for style. Times New Roman may not seem to have enough "splash," but it is a good basic font to use.

Use text enhancements such as italics and bold on a limited basis. Underlining is particularly difficult to read onscreen and should be avoided. Other choices, such as embossing and shadowing, are also not easily visible. WordArt, which appears to be text, is actually a graphic and should be treated just as you would an image.

The template for the park renovation title used a 40-point Garamond (serif) type and a 32-point Arial (san serif) type for the points (see Figure 14.9). These will be easy for the Rotary audience to view from wherever they are in the room.

### Problem-Solving skills

Employees who can solve problems on the job are more valuable than those who are easily stumped by difficulties or new situations. So learn to approach problems in an organized and efficient way. Avoid quick fixes; they rarely solve problems in the long run. Take the time to consider the problem thoroughly. Be creative when you consider solutions; don't rule out ideas just because they're new or have never been tried.

You must first identify what's causing a problem before you can solve it. (For example, bad color in a scanned photo is a *symptom* of the problem; the *cause* might be faulty software or a missed step in the scanning process.) Then explore many possible solutions before selecting the best one. Input from your supervisor and co-workers can be very valuable at this stage. Finally, implement your solution and determine whether it will work; if not, select another from the alternatives you considered earlier. Be persistent.

**Digging deeper:** Use the Internet to research further the steps to take in solving a problem. Create a slide show to communicate your findings.

**Figure 14.9** Font size is an important consideration in a slide show.

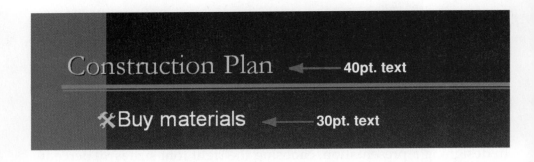

## BULLETS

Bullets are used as a standard feature in presentations to draw attention to specific points. Bullets can be standard round "dots," or they can be more decorative special shapes such as multicolored squares or even arrows. The choice is yours, but remember that you don't want the unusual nature of your bullets to detract from the message they are supposed to enhance. Harriet decided to modify her master slide so that the first-level bullet would be a crossed hammer and wrench, in keeping with the construction aspects of the project. Figure 14.9 demonstrates both the new bullet selection and the font sizes and colors used in the presentation.

## VISUAL EFFECTS

Other than text, your most important decision is what visual content to place on each slide. The content could be a table, a chart, clip art, a picture, a diagram, or media in the form of a movie or sound. When adding images such as clip art or video, it is easy to get so involved in the fun that the message gets lost. When considering what visual effects to include in your presentation, continually ask yourself the following two questions:

1. Does this element clarify the message?
2. Does this element make the presentation more effective?

Be particularly careful about your clip art choices. Just as with overused templates, overused clip art can create a "ho hum" response in your audience. It is often better to use a simple graphic that you created or a photograph that you have taken instead of work created by someone else. Your own work can have more impact than clip art that everyone has already seen.

Don't forget the drawing tools that are also available. Rules and autoshapes can provide effective graphics without obscuring your message.

Once you have decided that your choice of visual effect is appropriate and useful, you can easily insert the element onto a page and then resize or move it. Just as you limit the number of lines on a slide, you should limit the number of images on a slide to no more than three.

**Figure 14.10** Use of images such as this thank-you card can deliver a powerful message.

Harriet used a series of photographs to illustrate the construction process, interspersing each one between the content slides. These were important images because they helped the audience see the project at each stage as the park changed from a weed-infested sandy pit to a lively playground filled with children. The final slide (Figure 14.10) was a scanned image of the card signed by people in the neighborhood thanking the organization for their work.

## WHITE SPACE

As you have seen, the same rules apply for both page layout and presentation design. This means you shouldn't be afraid to leave white space on your slide. This openness will enhance your message and give your audience a breather. Avoid cluttering up your slide. Less is definitely more in presentation design. Notice in Figure 14.2 that only three lines of text send the message without cluttering the page.

## SUMMARY

In this chapter, you have seen how templates, slide layouts, master pages, and color schemes can be used to create professional presentations. You have also learned what makes good choices for backgrounds, text, and bullets. You have even looked at ways to add visual effects and white space to enhance your message.

**Chapter 14:** Presentation Design | **163**

**Answer the following questions on your own computer.**

1. Why are templates good design choices?
2. What is the disadvantage of using a template?
3. What are the three basic kinds of slide layouts?
4. What might a multimedia slide contain?
5. What is included in the term *media*?
6. What purpose does a master slide serve?
7. What can be included on a master slide?
8. What four positive results does color provide in a presentation?
9. What options does a color scheme provide?
10. What colors help keep an audience focused?
11. What are your background choices?
12. What happens to the size of the text on a PowerPoint slide if you add more text?
13. What is the most important criterion when choosing a font for a presentation?
14. What decision do you have to make regarding use of multimedia on a slide?
15. What design element on a slide can help prevent clutter on a slide?

## DISCUSSION

**Discuss the following questions either as a class or as a written assignment.**

1. Have you ever seen the same PowerPoint template used for two different presentations? What was your response? If you haven't, how do you think you would have responded?
2. How would you use a master slide and a color scheme?
3. What colors appeal to you? What is your response to red, blue, and green?
4. How big does text need to be for you to see it from the back of your classroom? What happens if the audience cannot see text well in a presentation?
5. What is your response to clip art that is used in a presentation more for show than for content?

1. On paper or your computer, sketch a master slide for use during the speech you selected in the previous chapter. Indicate the background selection; the font size, type, and color; and the bullet choice. Consider what colors would be most appropriate for your speech.

2. List the specific visual effects you would include in the speech. Consider what images, sounds, or other elements would be effective.

Research color responses to find out what colors are known to create certain responses. See if you can find out how researchers determined these responses (perhaps by emailing the authors). Design a way to test these theories yourself and then perform this test on a group of subjects. Write an article that outlines your test and explains your results. Find an Internet site to which you can post your article.

ESTIMATED TIME
**3**
H O U R S

# Chapter 15
## Presentation Effects

SOURCE: ©EYEWIRE

## Objectives

- *You will explore the use of slide transitions in presentations.*
- *You will learn how animation schemes can be used effectively.*
- *You will see ways to use a motion path in your presentation.*
- *You will consider how sound can enhance your presentation.*

## INTRODUCTION

Multimedia has transformed the world. No longer are messages delivered in black text on white paper; now they swirl onto the page in multicolor extravaganzas accompanied by music. This makes for an exciting and fun method of communicating with others. It also makes serious demands on your image management skills. In this chapter you will explore these possibilities as they relate to presentations.

## SPECIAL EFFECTS

Once you have decided on your message and have selected appropriate background, text, and images to use in your presentation, you have another set of decisions to make. Microsoft PowerPoint and similar software provide you with ample choices of ways to open your pages, to close them, and to activate those pages while they are visible. You can also use a variety of techniques to **animate** the text or images that appear on your slides.

Harve Hernandez owns a shop that provides pool and outdoor recreational supplies to homeowners. He wants to renovate his building but must seek approval from the planning and zoning commission at its next regular monthly meeting. He decides that he will use a slide presentation to enhance his message. The special effects are important to him because he believes this use of multimedia will make his request more appealing. He has already completed all the earlier preparation, but now he needs to decide which effects to use.

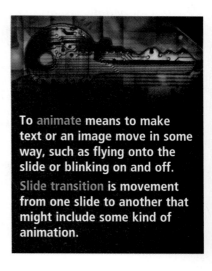

## SLIDE TRANSITIONS

**Slide transition** is the term used to describe movement from one slide to another and any effects that are used during that transition. The transition between slides can be simply moving from one to another or it can be an interesting special effect such as a clockwise spin. Movement between slides can occur on a mouse click or after a set period of time. It can be accompanied by special sounds, and the event can happen quickly or slowly. As shown in Figure 15.1, transition options are available to fit every situation.

**To animate** means to make text or an image move in some way, such as flying onto the slide or blinking on and off.

**Slide transition** is movement from one slide to another that might include some kind of animation.

SOURCE: ©MICROSOFT POWERPOINT

**Figure 15.1** Slide transitions can move slowly or quickly and with or without sound.

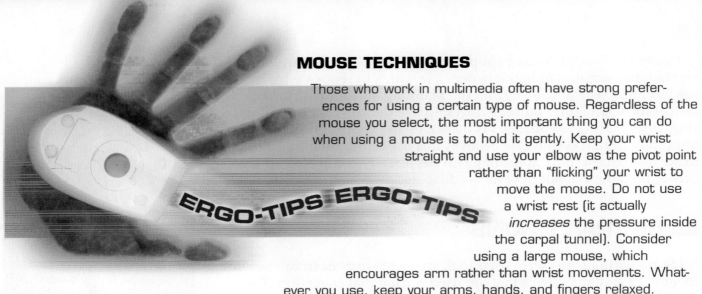

Those who work in multimedia often have strong preferences for using a certain type of mouse. Regardless of the
mouse you select, the most important thing you can do
when using a mouse is to hold it gently. Keep your wrist
straight and use your elbow as the pivot point
rather than "flicking" your wrist to
move the mouse. Do not use
a wrist rest (it actually
*increases* the pressure inside
the carpal tunnel). Consider
using a large mouse, which
encourages arm rather than wrist movements. Whatever you use, keep your arms, hands, and fingers relaxed.

Regardless of your choice, the same rules apply to the use of these
effects as to the use of colors and images in the previous chapter. You
must ask yourself whether this effect clarifies the message or makes
the presentation more effective. It is unlikely that a slide transition
will clarify a message, but a special effect might make the presentation more interesting. Because your goal is to have your message
heard, anything you can do to ensure that outcome will succeed in
making the presentation more effective. Appropriate use of slide transition effects can keep your audience engaged in the information on
the screen. Inappropriate effects may distract your audience.

Harve's slide show has twelve slides, and he decides to use a simple slow fade to black between each slide and to activate the change
with a mouse click.

## ANIMATION SCHEMES

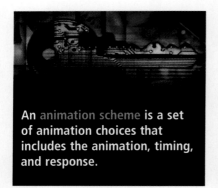

An animation scheme is a set
of animation choices that
includes the animation, timing,
and response.

**Animation schemes** apply to text or images that appear on a slide.
Endless options are available, limited only by your imagination.
PowerPoint 2002 even arranges the schemes by categories such as
basic, subtle, moderate, and exciting, as shown in Figure 15.2, to simplify the decision-making process. You can use the schemes as they
are designed, or you can modify them in any way you want using
custom animation similar to the ones shown in Figure 15.3. Schemes
can be selected as openings, as exits, or for emphasis. Once a custom
animation is selected, you can set options such as direction of activity,
speed, and means of activating (shown in Figure 15.4). An example of
ways to use custom animation is shown in Figure 15.5. The hammer
has been given an alternating rotating animation to make it appear to
be driving a nail.

Text animation can be set to appear all at once, by word, or by letter, using the text effects options shown in Figure 15.6. Bulleted points
can be set to appear line by line. These are very useful techniques

SOURCE: ©MICROSOFT POWERPOINT

**Figure 15.2** Animation choices can be set to apply to a single slide or to all the slides in the presentation.

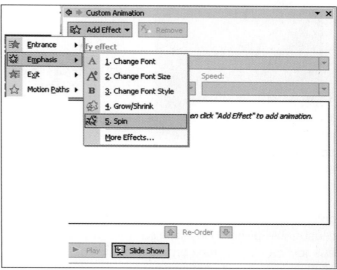

SOURCE: ©MICROSOFT POWERPOINT

**Figure 15.3** Custom animation is used for entrances, exits, and emphasis.

SOURCE: ©MICROSOFT POWERPOINT

**Figure 15.4** When you are using a custom animation, you have a variety of ways to animate the text or image.

SOURCE: ©MICROSOFT POWERPOINT

**Figure 15.5** Animation can be used to make a point, as well as to attract attention.

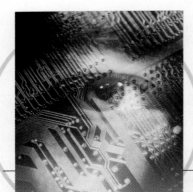

because they mean you can control exactly how much of the text your audience will see. Notice in Figure 15.7 that the animated text "Flying Title" is being dropped onto the page one letter at a time. Text colors can be animated so that when the text first appears it is one color but then changes color when the next word or line appears by setting the event that occurs after the animation appears. Notice in Figure 15.6 that the text will change to orange once the animation is completed. This technique can be quite effective because it keeps your audience focused on the particular point you are making, allowing previous points to lose impact.

Again, use of all these effects must be chosen with care and be based on their potential effectiveness. The division into categories such as subtle gives you an idea about appropriate situations in which to use each of the schemes. Subtle or "low-key" effects and basic effects can be used in formal situations. Exciting and moderate ones should be reserved for when more interesting effects will be appreciated.

## THE **ETHICS** OF MUSIC IN PRESENTATIONS

It's very tempting to copy music either from a CD or from the Internet to use in a presentation. The fair use rules that apply to schools allow you to use up to 30 seconds of such sound in a school presentation. This same law of fair use does not cross over into commercial use. If you need to use music for a business presentation, you must seek permission to include it. Another option is royalty-free music CDs that are available for purchase at reasonable prices. Royalty-free means you cannot sell the music but you can use if for commercial purposes. It's a good idea to have one or more of these CDs available if you do not want to have to acquire permission each time you want to use music in a presentation.

Keep in mind that while downloadable music on the Internet is often advertised as being free for all use, often this music has been pirated (stolen) and the site offering it to you does not own the music. Don't put your business or employer at risk by using music that has questionable ownership.

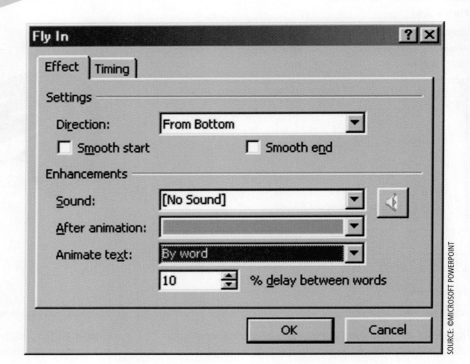

**Figure 15.6** Text effects is another way to customize animation of the points you are making in your presentation.

If less is better in the use of images and text, then it's surely true in the use of animation schemes. The use of a few schemes may help keep your audience's attention, but the use of too many will overwhelm them.

Harve decides to have his points appear line by line and to change color when he moves on to the next. He has included an artist's drawing of the renovated building and a chart showing the increase in taxable revenue that he anticipates. The drawing expands onto the page at a mouse click because he wants to draw attention specifically to it.

## MOTION PATHS

One of the more enticing animation options is **motion paths.** Creation of paths enables you to create a flying object or text line that moves across your slide in exactly the pattern you want. It can be quite effective as a means of grabbing attention, and the novelty of creating such paths can be appealing. Figure 15.8 shows the upwardly diagonal path that will be followed by the text box "Motion Path."

Motion path animation can be used rather creatively to accent a point or to simulate an event. For example, Harve decides that he wants an attention getter at the opening of his speech. Because he anticipates that his renovation will increase the number of customers, he creates a series of feet that automatically travel across his opening

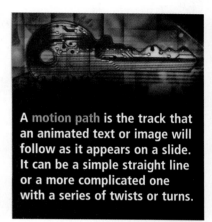

**Figure 15.7** Text boxes that appear slowly, such as this one, can help keep your audience focused on your message.

A **motion path** is the track that an animated text or image will follow as it appears on a slide. It can be a simple straight line or a more complicated one with a series of twists or turns.

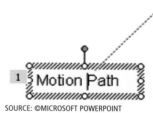

SOURCE: ©MICROSOFT POWERPOINT

**Figure 15.8** Motion paths let you decide exactly how text or images move onto a slide.

SOURCE: ©PHOTODISC

page according to the time he has set. One set of only two feet moves slowly to indicate his current business. The next set, consisting of several feet, moves quickly in order to make his point about the increase in people coming to his business.

## SOUND

In addition to motion, another option for both slide transitions and animation is sound. A series of sounds is built in, but you can also add your own that you or someone else has created. Sound can be a significant enhancement if used carefully. A few bars of music attached to an opening slide can set the mood or tone of your presentation. Splashes of sound effects as an animation occurs can draw additional attention to the visual effect, and voice can be used to add information. Short clips of someone else's ideas or thoughts can be a good way to add credibility to your own ideas.

You can add sound to a presentation slide in two ways. One option is to insert the sound much as you would an image; a speaker icon appears on the slide that can be assigned animation options such as timing and visibility. The second option is to attach sound to an image or text box by using the effects options so that the sound plays as the image or text appears on the slide. Your choice depends on your intended use of the sound, but often attaching sound to an object is the most effective use because the sound usually is not the primary focus of the slide.

Regardless of how you intend to use sound, be careful with the use of sound clips provided as part of the software package. Sound that has been used before in a presentation is even less appealing to your audience than reused clip art or templates. Annoying sounds should also be limited. A sound that seems interesting in the first few seconds can quickly become an irritating noise.

Harve is aware of the limitations of sound and uses it only in his opening slide. He has a recording of footsteps to add to his animated feet. He considered using clips of conversations from some of his customers encouraging him in his renovation, but he decided instead to use the quotes in text form.

## SUMMARY

In this chapter, you have looked at the special effects available in presentation software. You have seen that effects such as slide transitions, animations, and motion paths can be quite effective in keeping your audience's attention if used carefully. You have also seen ways that sound can be used to create a mood for your presentation.

### Time Management Skills

You may not realize it, but you already practice time management skills. It takes a lot of talent to squeeze homework assignments from three different classes, soccer practice, and your nightly chat room session into one single evening! Your success depends entirely on your ability to plan your time wisely. This is especially true in the workplace.

Time management on the job can be a bit tricky at first. If you've never tried to scan a batch of 50 photos at once, for example, you may not realize how long it can take. Your supervisor will give you some reasonable guidelines, but you'll soon learn yourself how to size up the work you have to do and what you need to get it done. Set priorities. Which tasks need to be finished first? Don't do the enjoyable work first and put off the less desirable tasks for later. Learn how to schedule your time.

**Digging deeper:** Create a grid for each day of the week, in 30-minute intervals, and record your activities during that time. At the end of one week, closely examine the grid to find ways to use your time more effectively.

**Answer the following questions on your own computer.**

1. What happens when you animate text?
2. What kinds of events occur when you create a slide transition?
3. What purpose could an animated slide transition serve?
4. To what do animation schemes apply?
5. What options do animation schemes provide?
6. What are your choices for text animation?
7. When would you use a subtle effect?
8. What does setting a motion path let you do?
9. What purpose can music serve on a slide?
10. Besides inserting a sound, what other ways can you use sound?

## DISCUSSION

**Discuss the following questions either as a class or as a written assignment.**

1. When a presenter uses a dramatic series of slide transitions, what response do you have?
2. Which slide transitions are most effective in a school setting? In a business setting? In a general-population presentation?
3. Which animation schemes do you prefer? Which do you like the least? Why?
4. Give three ways that a motion path could be used effectively in a presentation, other than as a means of creating an entrance.
5. What happens if a presenter selects sounds for a slide show that don't appeal to you or are irritating? How does that affect the message?

1. Once again, use the speech you selected in Chapter 13. List what slide transitions you would use and what animation effects would be appropriate.

2. Decide whether there is any need to use a motion path. Explain why and how you would use it.

3. Select at least one sound and one piece of music to use in the slide show. Indicate the title and placement.

**FURTHER
EXPLORATION**

Some interesting studies have been conducted on audience response to music based on their age. Find information on the different responses by searching the Internet or by surveying adults and students of different ages to find out their preferences. Create a short test by designing three slide shows with the same message but different types of music such as classical, rock, and country. Measure the response of three different age levels to see whether the music changes the response to the message. Create a presentation that demonstrates your findings.

ESTIMATED TIME

**3**

HOURS

# Chapter 16
# Presentation Media

SOURCE: ©PHOTODISC

## Objectives

- *You will learn how GIFs can be used to create animation.*
- *You will see how to create flash files with Flash and LiveMotion.*
- *You will learn how to place flash files into a PowerPoint presentation.*
- *You will investigate what flash tools can be used for animation.*

## INTRODUCTION

Characters and figures that move about the screen and even talk can be a lively addition to a presentation. No longer must your slides be limited to the actions provided by your presentation software. True multimedia is possible when you include animated images in your slide show.

## MEDIA ANIMATION

Functions that allow you to add animation such as spirals and fades are built into presentation software, but you can add animation to your presentation in other ways. The two most common ways are animated GIFs and Shockwave Files (SWF). Presentation software such as PowerPoint enables you to insert these animations into a slide show. You can use animations created by others (just as you would use clip art), or you can create your own. Either way, you will have animations that reflect exactly the message you want. If you want to add even more interest to your pages, you can also use animated characters that speak to your audience.

Ralph Garcia has found such animations to be very helpful when he creates presentations for use by his client, who sells wooden pallets. Before Ralph started working with the president of the pallet factory, Jamie Harrison found that his sales efforts were often met without much enthusiasm by potential clients who valued his product but frankly found the details boring. Ralph showed him how he could add interest while still providing the message that his pallets are a quality product.

# ANIMATED GIFS

**Animated GIFs** are the easiest way to create your own animations. You insert them just as you would any other graphic. If you have Jasc Paint Shop Pro, Animation Shop allows you to create your own animated GIFs. If you have Adobe LiveMotion or Macromedia Flash, you can save animations in a GIF format.

An animated GIF is merely a series of frames combined into a single GIF file (review Chapter 2 for more information on GIFs), much as a PowerPoint slide show gathers a series of slides into a single presentation. Figure 16.1 shows a series of images combined into an animated GIF. When the GIF becomes active, it cycles through each frame, making it appear that a single image is moving. In the example shown, when the GIF appears on the screen, the baby will seem to be actively yawning as she moves from sleep to wake and back.

The advantage of animated GIFs is that they are easy to use. Two disadvantages of using GIFs are that (a) they do not display extensive colors (they can show only 256) and (b) the file sizes can become quite large. To keep the file sizes of animations as small as possible, the software provides an optimizing option to simplify this process. **Optimization** is similar to the compression process discussed in Chapter 2 for JPG files that reduces the number of colors and the number of frames wherever possible.

With these limitations in mind, you can use GIFs quite effectively as a means of gathering your audience's attention or making a point.

Ralph originally created a series of animated GIFs that showed a pile of wooden slats being transformed into a pallet. The complexity

## Play to Your Strengths

Today more than ever, it's important to learn new skills. Anyone who resists technology and innovation will be left behind in the workplace. But it's also important to recognize that you're probably not great at everything. You might be a gifted graphic designer, for example, but not quite as good at creating presentations or slide shows. Another classmate might excel at that task. Maybe you have a special knack at getting the color just right on a scanned photo, but your friend's Web pages always seem to be just a little easier to use than yours. We all have our own special areas of strength.

The phrase "playing to your strengths" doesn't mean that you shouldn't try to improve your "weak" spots or that you should resist new learning. You can often discover new strengths you didn't even know you had. The phrase just means being confident in your particular abilities. Although your employer might expect you to be familiar with many different multimedia applications, you would be smart to focus on a special area at which you particularly excel. If you spend your day doing work that you're good at, your self-esteem level will stay high, you'll be more productive, and you'll likely be much happier on the job.

**Digging deeper:** Make a list of the three multimedia-related tasks at which you believe you're especially good. Compare your list with those of your classmates. How do your aptitudes differ?

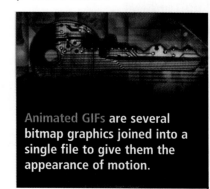

**Animated GIFs** are several bitmap graphics joined into a single file to give them the appearance of motion.

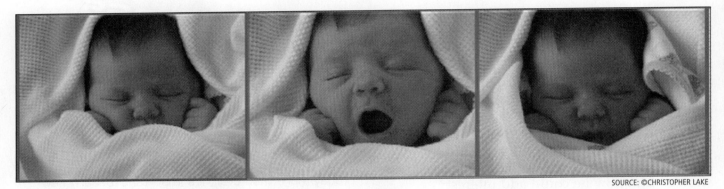

**Figure 16.1** Animated GIFs make it easy to add movielike features to a presentation by using a series of images combined into a single file.

of the image meant that the file was large enough that it couldn't be used easily on a Web site, but it worked well in a slide show, for which file size wasn't as much of an issue.

## SHOCKWAVE

Another form of animation is a Shockwave **flash** file (SWF) created with Macromedia Flash or Adobe LiveMotion. It's easy to get confused with the term *flash* because in one instance the term is used to describe software marketed by Macromedia and in another it is used to describe animated software in general. To avoid confusion, in this chapter the term *Flash* (capitalized) is used for the specific software and *flash* (lowercase) is used to indicate general-purpose software. The format for Flash is FLA; for LiveMotion, it is LIV. Each of these file types can be converted from the native format to SWF using animation software.

Shockwave or flash files (the terms are often used interchangeably) are created with vector graphics rather than with bitmap ones used in animated GIFs. Because of the vectors, the file sizes are much smaller so they load quickly and take up less computer memory. A disadvantage is that flash files require a plug-in in order to be seen if you're using a Web browser, although current browsers all include flash plug-ins automatically. With presentation software, viewing is not an issue. The steps to insert flash files into Microsoft PowerPoint are more complex than those required for animated GIFs. To add Flash files, you must follow a series of steps using the Control Toolbox.

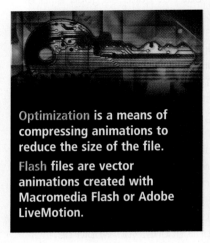

**Optimization** is a means of compressing animations to reduce the size of the file.

**Flash** files are vector animations created with Macromedia Flash or Adobe LiveMotion.

**Figure 16.2** The Control Toolbox is required to add Shockwave files to a presentation.

1. Record the location of the SWF file. The flash file should be in the same folder as your presentation. (You will have to type in the location later, rather than browse for it.)
2. Make the Control Toolbox visible by using the View Toolbars menu.
3. Click on the More Controls button, shown in Figure 16.2. The More Controls icon is the one in the lower right corner that is a hammer and wrench crossed.
4. Select the Shockwave Flash Object control from the list.
5. Draw a rectangle approximately the size you want for the image.

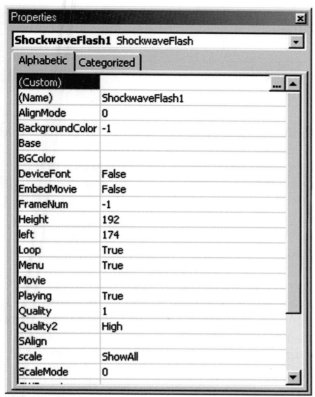

**Figure 16.3** The Custom line is used to enter the location of the Shockwave file.

**Figure 16.4** The property options allow you to choose exactly how your flash file will appear on the screen.

6. Right-click on the rectangle and select Properties.
7. Click on the Custom line and then on the ellipsis dots to the right as shown by the arrow in Figure 16.3.
8. Type in the location of your flash file and change the other properties such as quality and scale as shown in Figure 16.4.
9. Close the Control window. Your flash image will not appear until you run your presentation.

# FLASH TOOLS

The essential tool used to create flash movies is a **timeline,** which records when each event will occur and what actions will happen (see Figure 16.5). A **keyframe** is used to set the point at which a new action begins. Layers are used just as in other graphics programs to separate visual elements. Each layer can be assigned its own series of animations, so several events can be happening at the same time.

Objects in flash files can be changed in a variety of ways, called **transforming,** such as changing size or shape, taking new positions along a motion path, rotating or flipping, and changing color. Although flash files are vector in nature, bitmap graphics can be added to Shockwave files, and they too can be transformed. A motion

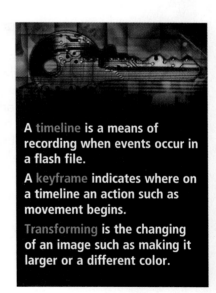

A timeline is a means of recording when events occur in a flash file.

A keyframe indicates where on a timeline an action such as movement begins.

Transforming is the changing of an image such as making it larger or a different color.

**Figure 16.5** A timeline is used to set up the movement of each event in a flash movie.

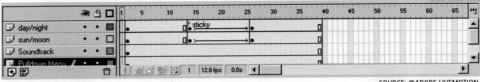

SOURCE: ©ADOBE LIVEMOTION

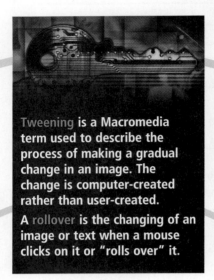

Tweening **is a Macromedia term used to describe the process of making a gradual change in an image. The change is computer-created rather than user-created.**

A rollover **is the changing of an image or text when a mouse clicks on it or "rolls over" it.**

path in flash is similar to the motion path you use in PowerPoint that allows you to choose the line of motion an object follows.

**Tweening** is a useful function that allows the software to make a series of gradual changes or transformations for you. For example, if you want an object to grow from small to large on the screen, setting it to tween from one point on the timeline to a later point means the object will automatically enlarge without your having to create a series of changing figures.

A common use for flash files is to create **rollovers.** Rollovers are "triggered" when a button is clicked or the mouse "rolls over" an image or text. Rollovers can be created in both LiveMotion and Flash. Rollovers are a common means of indicating to a viewer the location of the mouse pointer, as well as of attracting attention to an item.

Ralph decided to experiment with creating a flash movie for Mr. Harrison to use. The flash file would be smaller and could be incorporated as a sales tool in the company's Web site. He took the same images that he had used in the animated GIF and added details. What was once a simple movement from slats to pallet became a series of events that Mr. Harrison could trigger as he began his presentation. The first image that appeared was the single slat. Mr. Harrison clicked on the slat to show the wood in closeup to demonstrate the quality of the original component. This image was quickly replaced with the slat, giving him time to discuss the statistics that were important in his message. Next he clicked on a rollover button that triggered the rest of the sequence showing the construction process for the pallets.

## THE **ETHICS** OF PRESENTATION PIZZAZZ

As a speaker, you know that you must be honest with your audience. This honesty is not limited to the actual facts you cite but also applies to the way you present them. If you create a presentation that is all pizzazz and no content, then you are being dishonest with the people who have come to hear you speak. Remember that content must be the focus of any presentation. The "bells and whistles," such as animation, are there to enhance your message, not to replace it.

## ANIMATED CHARACTERS

One of the most interesting uses of animation within PowerPoint is created with the software Microsoft Agent Technology. This technology is used to animate characters such as the paper clip that appears on a Microsoft Office screen to ask if you need help. Special software can be purchased that makes it easy to add to your presentation **animated characters** and scripts of the narration you want the characters to speak, similar to the ones shown in Figure 16.6.

Animated characters are designed to interact with and talk to an audience by using voice technology. As with any other animation, it's important to consider the effectiveness of such characters. If they are being used to help bring your message to your audience, then they should be considered. If they are being used merely for novelty, then they should be avoided.

Ralph is considering creating a character to guide the audience throughout the presentation. He has discussed this with his client, who is interested in seeing a possible use of animated characters to add interest and details to his current slide show.

## SUMMARY

In this chapter, you have learned how animation can be added to a presentation. Your choices are to use animated GIFs or flash movies. Each has a different set of requirements and issues to consider. You have seen that GIFs are easy to create but may be large files. You have seen that flash files are smaller but require several steps to add to the presentation. You have also seen that animated characters can be used to add interest and information to a slide.

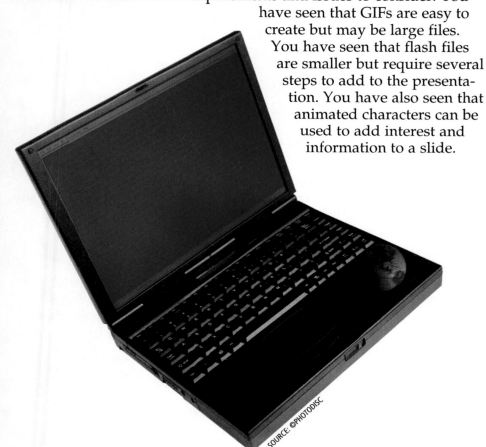

SOURCE: ©PHOTODISC

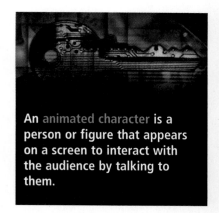

An animated character is a person or figure that appears on a screen to interact with the audience by talking to them.

We are animated characters created by Vox Proxy.

SOURCE: ©VOXPROXY

**Figure 16.6** Animated characters can add novelty and interest to a presentation while conveying information.

**Answer the following questions on your own computer.**

1. What programs can be used to create animated GIFs?
2. How do animated GIFs mimic movement?
3. What are some disadvantages to animated GIFs?
4. What purpose does optimizing serve?
5. What is the difference between Macromedia Flash and Shockwave flash?
6. Why are Shockwave files smaller than GIF files?
7. What is a disadvantage of using flash files on the Web?
8. What is a disadvantage of using flash in a presentation?
9. What does a timeline indicate?
10. Where are keyframes found?
11. In what ways can an image be transformed?
12. When is tweening useful?
13. What events can "trigger" a rollover?
14. What is an animated character?
15. What software is used to create animated characters?

## DISCUSSION

**Discuss the following questions either as a class or as a written assignment.**

1. When would it be important to use animation?
2. How long should an animation last before its effectiveness is reduced?
3. How are flash animations more or less effective than animations that can be created from within presentation software?
4. How much time should be "invested" in the creation of a presentation's message and how much in the creation of special effects such as flash animations?
5. Specialized software that creates animated characters must be purchased separately. How can you justify the cost of this kind of software?

1. Using the speech you found in Chapter 13, make a list of possible animated GIFs and flash animations that would be appropriate for the seriousness of the presentation.

2. Sketch at least three GIF frames you would use.

3. Draw a timeline that shows the images and changes you would use in your flash movie. Be sure to indicate the keyframes. Consider including a tweening event.

4. Find a figure or character that would make a good animated character for the speech. Write a short narration for the character to speak.

5. Sketch a design of your own flash opening to use in your electronic portfolio.

Search the Internet and find out how long it takes a professional designer to create a flash movie. Talk with a local designer, if one is available, to find out how long it takes to create a two-minute flash event. Find out how much a minute of flash would cost a company to purchase. Create a chart comparing all your findings and write up a proposal to justify or not justify the use of flash in a company's presentation.

# Unit 4: Summary

## Key Concepts

## Chapter 13: Presentation Planning

1. Use the AUDIENCE formula to help you begin preparing for a presentation.
2. Don't try to plan your ideas and the multimedia elements of a presentation at the same time.
3. Use the outline functions to list the three major points and additional subpoints.
4. Use no more than six words on each line.
5. Keep your points grammatically parallel.
6. Use the notes function of PowerPoint to include material you wish to present orally.
7. Use links to arrange slides if you do not wish to proceed sequentially.

## Chapter 14: Presentation Design

1. Use the predesigned PowerPoint templates to create slide shows quickly.
2. Slide layouts consist of three types: title, text, and multimedia.
3. Master slides are used to create a consistent design for all slides in a presentation.
4. Color is a powerful way to increase the effectiveness of a presentation, and color schemes make using them easy.
5. Backgrounds can be added to presentations to add interest, but they should not over-whelm the slide.
6. It's essential that text sizes be large and readable to ensure that the message is easily read by all viewers.
7. Bullets, white space, and other visual effects such as clip art should be used to help clarify the message and make the presentation more effective.

## Chapter 15: Presentation Effects

1. Slide transitions can be simple or complex and use sound and motion to build interest.
2. Animation schemes can be basic, subtle, moderate, or exciting, depending on the type and speed of action.
3. Text animation allows words to appear all at once or in sequence.
4. Motion paths allow the user to decide how an image will move in a presentation.
5. Sound can be added as a separate component to a slide or be attached to an image or text.

## Chapter 16: Presentation Media

1. Animated GIFs create motion by layering one image onto another saved into a single file.
2. Shockwave flash files are vector graphics that create the image of motion.
3. Placing flash files into a PowerPoint presentation requires use of the Control toolbar.
4. Timelines and keyframes are used to create flash files.
5. Tweening allows the flash software to make incremental changes in an image.
6. A rollover occurs when a mouse button is clicked or the mouse pointer is "rolled over" an image or text to create a sense of movement.
7. Animated characters talk to the presentation audience by using special software.

# Terms

**animate** to make text or an image move in some way, such as flying onto the slide or blinking on and off

**animated character** a person or figure that appears on a screen to interact with the audience by talking to them

**animated GIFs** several bitmap graphics joined into a single file to give them the appearance of motion

**animation scheme** a set of animation choices that includes the animation, timing, and response

**background** the "paper" on which a presentation will be seen by the audience

**build** a term used in presentation software meaning to create a slide show with all its animation and slide transitions arranged in sequential order

**color scheme** a series of choices that assigns to each slide the same color of background, title, and bulleted list

**flash** files that are vector animations created with Macromedia Flash or Adobe LiveMotion

**hyperlinks** text and/or pictures that can be used to connect one page to another regardless of the sequence of pages

**keyframe** where on a timeline an action such as movement begins

**master slide** a single slide that can be designed once and then applied to many slides

**media** in PowerPoint, a term that includes sound, video, and movies

**motion path** the track that an animated text or image will follow as it appears on a slide

**multimedia** the combination of sound, animation, graphics, video, and color in a document

**optimization** a means of compressing animations to reduce the size of the file

**parallelism** a grammatical term indicating that the basic structure of two or more sentences or phrases is similar

**rollover** the changing of an image or text when a mouse clicks on it or "rolls over" it

**slide layout** the arrangement of design elements on a slide

**slide transition** movement from one slide to another that might include some kind of animation

**template** document masters predesigned by professionals who have already chosen the background, font size and color, and bullets to be used

**timeline** a means of recording when events occur in a flash file

**transforming** changing an image, such as making it larger or a different color

**tweening** a Macromedia term used to describe the process of making a gradual change in an image

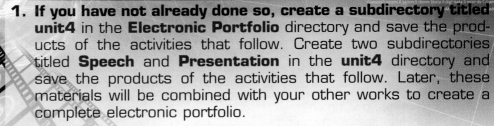

# ELECTRONIC PORTFOLIO

1. **If you have not already done so, create a subdirectory titled unit4** in the **Electronic Portfolio** directory and save the products of the activities that follow. Create two subdirectories titled **Speech** and **Presentation** in the **unit4** directory and save the products of the activities that follow. Later, these materials will be combined with your other works to create a complete electronic portfolio.

2. Use the sketches and ideas that you created for the speech you selected to create a PowerPoint presentation.

3. Create at least one animated GIF and one flash file for use within the presentation.

4. Save the presentation as **speech.ppt** to the speech subdirectory. Be sure to save into this folder all flash and sound files that you use.

5. Create a slide presentation for someone in your school or community to use. You might ask your principal, your superintendent, a school board member, or your teachers if there is a presentation they must make for which a slide show would be appropriate. The slide show should include at least eight slides and include some animation as appropriate. Use sound as appropriate. If you use a template or clip art, modify it using good design principles. Save this material into the **Presentation** subdirectory.

6. Use the following chart to evaluate the quality of your portfolio material.

|  | Beginning | Developing | Accomplished | Exemplary | Score |
|---|---|---|---|---|---|
| Speech | Speech contains fewer than five slides | Speech contains more than five slides | Speech contains more than five slides and includes at least one animation | Speech contains more than eight slides, includes at least one animation, and demonstrates awareness of good design choices |  |
| Presentation | Presentation contains fewer than five slides | Presentation contains more than five slides | Presentation contains more than five slides and includes at least one animation | Presentation contains more than eight slides, includes at least one animation, and demonstrates awareness of good design choices |  |

# Web Publishing

## Unit
# 5

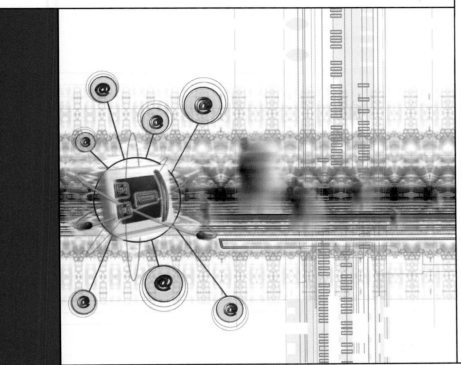

SOURCE: ©PHOTODISC

# Career Profile

Alan Baumgarten, information architect at Candesa in Provo, Utah, leads some kind of enchanted life. Can you imagine working on the Web site of a Hollywood motion picture? Alan doesn't have to imagine it—he actually does it! Wait until you read about the other exciting things he does as he provides expert navigation to the Web sites he scripts.

Alan received his bachelor's degree in liberal arts from Brigham Young University, majoring in writing and broadcasting. Early in his career, he worked in film and television production, including working as a cameraman for KBYU, the local PBS station. He also worked in Florida for a time, producing corporate videos for a small production company. And for a time he taught language arts at a middle school in Long Beach, California.

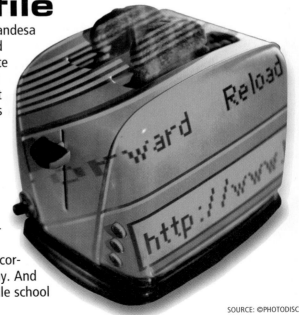

SOURCE: ©PHOTODISC

(continued)

Eventually, Alan's love of writing led him away from film, video, and teaching. He turned to writing full-time and authoring a few technology textbooks, as well as undertaking a few fun projects. A friend introduced him to Candesa, a Web development agency, where he has worked for the past several years.

Alan's work at Candesa is broad and varied. He works with clients to create engaging Web sites and helps them use digital technologies to improve their businesses. As an information architect, Alan makes sure Web sites are easy to navigate and don't leave users confused. He writes new content for Web sites and creates multimedia presentations for companies that want to communicate through new media.

Some of the software programs he uses are Photoshop, Dreamweaver, Visio for site maps, Microsoft Office for scripts and Web content, QuickTime, RealPlayer, and Windows Media Player.

Alan uses the Web constantly for his own research. He enhances his skills by using voice recognition software for Web content development. Dragon NaturallySpeaking voice recognition software is especially useful as he does multimedia scripting because he can generate multimedia scripting that sounds natural when it is recorded. Dragon makes it easier to create something that gives you a better match to normal conversational speech. In addition, he uses the playback in normal speech to make it easier to catch a missing word in the scripting.

Alan sees multimedia as a tool that all students can use in their personal lives, as well as in their workplaces. His belief in multimedia development and its usefulness is apparent. He emphasized, "Students must learn how to find information and apply it in the right way to give them a competitive advantage. Students need to be able to participate in multimedia-rich environments—audio, digital video, photography—not just as a consumer but as a contributor." Students need to learn to use digital cameras and speech recognition software so that they can acquire and generate information. They should understand that, in the modern workplace, everyone needs to be able to share information in a variety of ways.

Alan's work at Candesa includes information architecture, content development, usability studies, and instructional design. As you continue in this course, take advantage of innovations in the media world and learn how to use technologies to make your career exciting and ongoing—just as Alan does in his work. Maybe a Hollywood movie is just waiting for you to create its Web site! ■

Note: Alan Baumgarten, information architect at Candesa in Provo, Utah, is a real person, and his work with Web site scripting for Hollywood motion picture clients and others is real work.

# Chapter 17
# Web Editing

ESTIMATED TIME

2

HOURS

SOURCE: ©PHOTODISC

## INTRODUCTION

Multimedia and the Internet are peanut butter and jelly. Separately they are good. Together they are perfect for each other, enhancing the qualities of each. The ability to create or edit Web pages makes it possible for you to use multimedia on the Internet in exciting and interesting ways. However, before you begin the design process, it is important to know how Web pages are created and then transferred to the Internet.

Marcia Eubanks volunteers her time to a local museum and one of her contributions is to maintain the Web site for this group. The museum was established as a way to share with others a collection of items from drugstores, begun by Willard Jameson. His collection includes items that are over a hundred years old and are not usually seen today. The museum's

## Objectives

- *You will learn how HTML is written.*
- *You will learn the usefulness of Web editors.*
- *You will understand how Web pages provide universal access.*
- *You will see how to transfer files to the Internet.*

director knows that not everyone can visit the actual museum, so he would like to create a "virtual museum" on the Web. Marcia agreed to help and has begun the process of building a site that displays the museum's more interesting pieces.

# HTML

HTML is a universal code that allows anyone using browser software such as Microsoft Internet Explorer or Netscape Navigator to view documents created with the code. HTML files can be read by everyone regardless of the platform (Macintosh or PC) and regardless of the browser. Contrary to what many users believe, you do not have to be connected to the Internet to read HTML documents. Web documents can be read on any computer, much like a word processing document. This universal nature of the Web documents makes it a valuable business tool, as you will see.

**HTML** (Hypertext Markup Language) is a simple code designed to translate text and graphics into a viewable page. Text (usually written in all capital letters) enclosed in angle brackets is called a **tag** and provides the browser with the information it needs to display a page. This is the secret to its universal means of delivery.

Every Web page begins with an opening HTML tag (shown in red in Figure 17.1). The page then contains an opening HEAD (shown in green) followed by an opening TITLE (shown in pink) and then a closing TITLE and closing HEAD. Next appears the opening BODY (shown in blue), in which the majority of code is found. At the end is a closing BODY and then finally a closing HTML code. A forward slash (/) indicates a closing tag. The page that was created with this code is shown in Figure 17.2.

Other frequently used tags are IMG SRC (image source), P (paragraph), and A HREF (a link reference), as well as heading, alignment, and font tags.

HTML **stands for Hypertext Markup Language, the code used to create Web pages.**

A tag **is a specific piece of HTML code used to tell a Web browser how information should be displayed.**

## THE **ETHICS** OF CODE SHARING

It is easy to view the HTML code created by someone else. It's just as easy to copy that code and paste it into your own Web pages, and this is frequently done. When you discover an interesting technique, your inclination will be to use that same technique on your own pages. In this way, the Internet becomes a resource for everyone to use for inspiration and encourages the expansion of Web design. Although it is considered acceptable to use code in this way, the ethical decision becomes yours. How much code can you "borrow" before it is no longer your page? Is it important to give credit for innovative techniques? Does this borrowing hinder or encourage development of new ideas?

You can easily see the HTML code that is used for any Web page by clicking on View on the menu bar in Internet Explorer and then choosing Source (or Page Source in Netscape). The code will appear in Notepad format.

Marcia visited several museum Web sites to see what they included on their Web pages. She found several that were similar to what she needed and viewed their code to see what software they used. She also observed what she liked and disliked about the arrangement of the sites.

```
<HTML>
<HEAD>
<TITLE>Cooper Elementary</TITLE>
</HEAD>

<BODY BACKGROUND="elback.jpg">
<DIV ALIGN="center">
<IMG SRC="pirates.gif" WIDTH="327" HEIGHT="125" ALT="pirate logo"><BR>
<IMG SRC="movingline.gif" WIDTH="270" HEIGHT="8"><BR>
<H2>Lubbock-Cooper Elementary</H2>
<FONT COLOR="red">
<IMG SRC="1star.gif" WIDTH="14" HEIGHT="14">Rita McDaniel, Principal<BR>
<IMG SRC="1star.gif" WIDTH="14" HEIGHT="14">Jim Rose, Assistant Principal
</FONT>
<P>Welcome to the Cooper Elementary page. Click on the pirate below to enter our world.</P>
<P><A HREF="elemlist.html"><IMG SRC="pirwink.gif" WIDTH="128" HEIGHT="103"
ALT="winking pirate"></A></P>
</DIV>
</BODY>
</HTML>
```

**Figure 17.1** HTML code appears complex at first glance, but it is simple once you learn the meaning of the tags used in the development process.

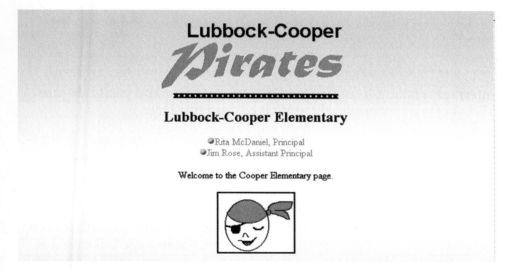

**Figure 17.2** This Web page contains all the basic elements found on most pages: background color, text choices, graphics, and links.

# WEB EDITORS

Although HTML is a not a difficult code to learn, most businesses find it easier to use specific Web design software such as Microsoft FrontPage, Macromedia Dreamweaver, Adobe GoLive, or even a word processing program such as Microsoft Word. Unlike desktop publishing software such as Microsoft Publisher, once you have created a Web page, the software is no longer needed to read pages created with it. This means that you can create a Web document and send it to someone else without worry that she or he may not have the necessary software to view it.

The software used to design a Web page is often called a **Web editor.** One advantage of using this software instead of writing code is that it provides a WYSIWYG (What You See Is What You Get)

A Web editor **is software that creates HTML code automatically as part of the Web design process.**

**Figure 17.3** Microsoft FrontPage is a good example of a WYSIWYG Web editor.

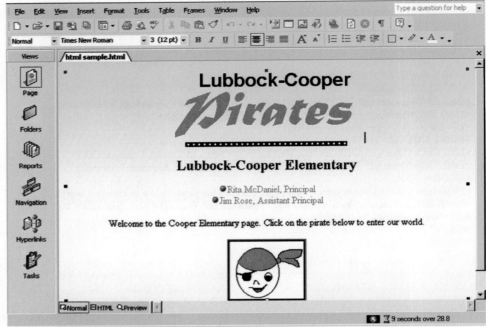

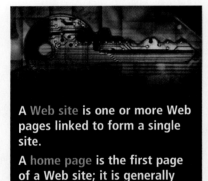

A Web site is one or more Web pages linked to form a single site.

A home page is the first page of a Web site; it is generally saved as *index*.

interface, making it easy to design pages quickly and easily. Figure 17.3 shows an example of the Web editor FrontPage.

Web editors are unlike other software in which you both create and view the files in the same software. With Web editing software, you create the file with one kind of software and then view the final product in another. Web editors provide temporary viewers so that you can see how your product is developing, but what you see is not designed for permanent viewing.

As Web pages are created, they are linked together to form a **Web site,** with the first page generally called the **home page** but saved as *index*. Because Web pages are linked, it's vitally important to ensure that each one works. Web editors often have a function to verify that all links are functioning. Whereas the first page is generally saved as *index*, each additional page should be saved in a way that makes it easy to know what is included on the page.

All Web editors are similar in that they enable you to create pages, link them together, and add content and graphics. They gather all the essential information into one or more folders to make it easy to transfer Web pages to the Internet. Make it a habit to save in the correct folder any files you intend to use on your Web site. Doing so will simplify the "gathering" process.

Marcia is familiar enough with HTML that she could create a site without a Web editor, but she also is aware that others who follow her may not be able to do the same. In addition, she has a limited amount of time to give to the project. Using a Web editor will speed up the process, so she asks the museum director to purchase the editor that she wants to use.

# UNIVERSAL ACCESS

The universal nature of Web pages means that any Web page created in one Web editor can be read and edited in another. Generally, Web editors provide tools to create the following effects:

- Backgrounds with color or graphics
- Text in colors and sizes
- Graphics including horizontal rules, bullets, rollovers, and image maps
- Wraparound text
- Links to other pages, including e-mail links
- Frames to gather separate pages into a single page

You will read more about these tools in the later Web chapters.

It is possible for everyone to view Web pages, but you need to be aware of certain limitations when creating pages. Some computers have larger display screens than others, some do not have the same fonts as yours, and some cannot display as many colors as yours. These and other limitations make it challenging to design a Web page that will appear exactly as you anticipate. Keep this idea in mind at all times when you are designing a Web page. Although you may have millions of colors displayed on a 17-inch monitor and a fast Internet connection, your audience may not. Your design choices must reduce the chance that your pages will not be seen as you want them to be seen.

One of the most important limitations is the speed with which your audience will be able to view your pages. Web editors will help you know how long it will take users with different access speeds to view your pages. If a user is able to load your pages through a high-speed connection such as DSL or cable modem, you will have fewer restrictions on your choices. If you know that many of your users will be limited to a modem, then you must think carefully about your choice of multimedia. If users are looking for information and they have to wait for a graphic to load, they may leave before they ever view your page.

In addition to concerns related to the hardware a viewer uses are the issues related to browser software. Some Web editors will help you make your choices by indicating whether

## Going the Extra Mile

Few employees—especially those just beginning their careers—walk into a company and immediately get all the glamorous jobs and plum assignments. Employers want to see what you can do when they hire you, and may start you out slowly. You may sometimes be asked to perform tasks you don't like or aren't particularly interested in. Yet these tasks contribute to the job as a whole, and your willingness to take on your share of them will impress your employer. It will also show your co-workers that you are a good team player who focuses on getting the job done.

Be willing to go the extra mile. Don't just meet the minimum requirements of your job—try to do a better job than expected. If you're working on a team-based project, try to make things easier for the person you hand the project off to. Be willing to help if you're asked to do something that isn't technically "your job." The next time, you may be the one who needs that extra assistance.

**Digging deeper:** Use the online edition of the *Occupational Outlook Handbook* (http://www.bls.gov/oco/) and find a description of a multimedia-related job that interests you. Then think of some extra tasks you could perform as part of that job in addition to those listed.

## ERGONOMIC KEYBOARDS

Ergonomic keyboards are designed to improve hand posture and make keying more comfortable. They usually have a split design with left and right banks and the ability to tilt or rotate the keyboard for comfort. You may find that using such a keyboard reduces the strain on your hands and wrists while you work.

ERGO-TIPS ERGO-TIPS

SOURCE: ©PHOTODISC

a particular function provided by the Web editor is not available to all browsers. When you begin the design process, it is important to be aware of these considerations. Never assume that just because you see a page in a particular way, everyone else will too. It's an excellent idea to check your completed Web pages using both Internet Explorer and Netscape to verify that your pages work as intended. Some Web designers keep several versions of each program installed on a computer for testing purposes. This helps them see if their Web pages are as effective in an early version as in a later one.

Several naming guidelines will help ensure that your pages can be viewed by everyone in your audience. The first is related to your extension options. Web pages are saved with .html or .htm extensions. Many Web editors automatically save as .htm; however, it is better to overwrite this default and save pages with .html to ensure that the pages can be read by all browsers. Some Web-hosting providers require you to use .htm on the index page but not on later pages. Check with your host to determine its requirements.

In addition to extension issues, naming is also important. We recommend that you use the following conventions when saving Web documents:

- Limit names to eight characters.
- Use lowercase letters.
- Include no spaces.
- Avoid slashes and hyphens.
- Use underscores to join names.

As browsers become more standardized, these problems will diminish, but until that happens, you need to make choices that ensure universal availability. Following these naming conventions will give your pages greater universal acceptance.

Marcia carefully follows the naming guidelines since she knows that her audience may not have the latest Web browsers on their computers. For the same reason, she also takes time to check her completed pages using older versions of both Netscape and Internet Explorer. She occasionally must make minor changes to her pages, but she is comfortable knowing that the museum's site can be viewed by the widest audience possible.

## FTP

Once a Web page or Web site is completed, you must transfer to the Internet the files you created. The transfer can be completed in several ways. One of the most common means of doing this is the use of **FTP** (File Transfer Protocol) software. FTP software allows a computer to connect to a **Web server** and then to transfer files directly to the server that will then broadcast to the world the contents of your pages.

Because you do not want others to be able to make changes to your Web pages without your permission (called **hacking a site**), Web servers require a login name and a password, as shown in Figure 17.4. Other information such as the host (Web server) name and type may also be needed. To prevent hacking, it's important to keep your login and password secure and to use a password that is not easily guessed.

Figure 17.5 demonstrates WS_FTP, a commonly used FTP program. The column on the left is a list of directories and files on the user's computer. The column on the right is a list of directories and files on the Web server, which may be anywhere in the world. The Web

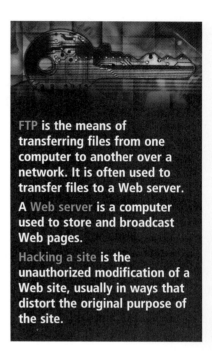

**FTP** is the means of transferring files from one computer to another over a network. It is often used to transfer files to a Web server.

A **Web server** is a computer used to store and broadcast Web pages.

**Hacking a site** is the unauthorized modification of a Web site, usually in ways that distort the original purpose of the site.

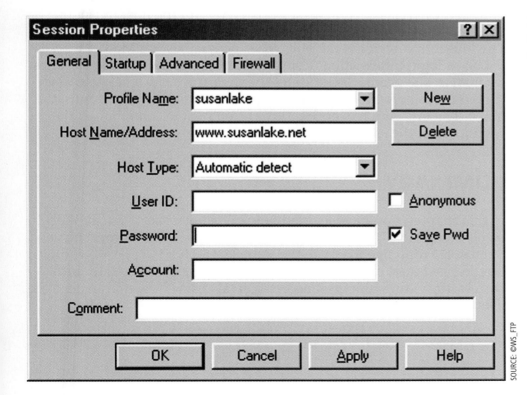

SOURCE: ©WS_FTP

**Figure 17.4** FTP login information should not be shared with anyone other than authorized personnel.

**Figure 17.5** FTP software such as WS_FTP allows you to transfer files to a Web server.

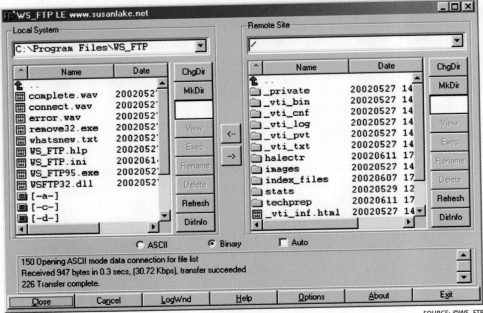

SOURCE: ©WS_FTP

server is connected through the Internet to the user's computer using this software. With this FTP software, files can be moved with ease from the user's computer to the Web server using the arrows found between the two columns.

Marcia's Web server is provided by a larger museum in Washington, D.C., that hosts other smaller museums such as hers. They provide this service to local nonprofit museums that can't afford to maintain their own server. When she registered with the host museum, they sent her an e-mail with all the login information that she needed. The museum director is the only other person besides Marcia who has the site's login information. Using FTP software, she can transfer files as often as she needs. She updates the museum's site weekly to keep it current, using both her home computer and the one at the museum office. The museum has noticed how often people comment on the usefulness of the site.

## SUMMARY

In this chapter, you have learned how HTML is used to create Web pages using tags. You then explored how to use Web editors such as Microsoft FrontPage to create the same pages in a WYSIWYG format. You learned how important it is to consider everyone in your audience by providing universal access. You also saw how to transfer Web files onto the Internet.

Answer the following questions on your computer.

1. What is the advantage of HTML code over other forms of software?
2. How does HTML function?
3. What function does a tag serve?
4. What tag opens and closes all Web pages?
5. How can you see the HTML code used to create a Web page?
6. What software can you use to create Web pages if you do not want to write your own code?
7. What is the advantage of using a WYSIWYG editor?
8. What makes Web editing software different from other publication software?
9. How is a home page generally saved?
10. What is FTP software used for?
11. What are some limitations you must consider when designing pages?
12. What should you never assume when designing a Web page?
13. What are the two extension options used for Web pages, and which should you use?
14. How many characters should you use in naming a Web page?
15. What punctuation should you avoid when naming a Web page?

Discuss the following questions either as a class or as a written assignment.

1. Should businesses use Web editors to create Web pages, or should they write their own HTML code?
2. How important is it to use different browsers to check Web pages? Explain your response.
3. How long will you wait to see a graphic load on a Web page?

## USE YOUR KNOWLEDGE

1. Compare the price and features of at least three major Web editors. Create a chart that includes this information.

2. Find a less well-known Web editor and add its features and price to your chart.

3. Look for reviews of each of the Web editors you have listed. Attach copies of the reviews to your chart.

4. Indicate in a summary statement which Web editor you would rather use and why. Use quotes from the reviews to support your statement.

5. Find information on at least two **FTP** software programs. Survey school personnel to find out which program they use. Look for reviews of **FTP** software. Compile this information and add it to your previous work.

## FURTHER EXPLORATION

1. Find out why it is standard practice to name the first page of a Web site as *index.*

2. Find out why you should use lowercase, no spaces, no slashes, and no more than eight characters when naming a Web page.

3. Find out why you should save as .html rather than as .htm.

4. Write a brief explanation of your findings and share them.

# Chapter 18
# Web Design

ESTIMATED TIME

2

HOURS

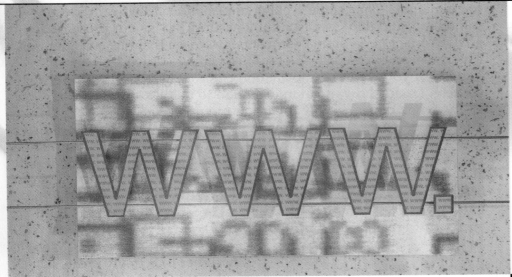

SOURCE: ©DIGITAL VISION

## INTRODUCTION

A decision about your Web editor has been made. You know how to get your Web pages onto the Internet. Now it's time to decide what to put on these pages. The place to begin is with ideas, not images.

Ralph Contreras owns a locksmith shop that cuts keys for both homes and businesses, but he has recently added a service providing specialty keys that many homeowners are showing an interest in purchasing. These keys are larger than standard keys, with large decorative motifs on them. He is the only dealer in the region with the franchise for these keys, and he knows that homeowners from out of his area may be interested in having keys made. Up until now, he didn't think a Web site would add much to his business, but this new addition has changed the way he anticipates doing business.

## Objectives

- *You will learn the importance of content in Web design.*
- *You will learn ways to create navigation links.*
- *You will learn how to be consistent in Web design.*
- *You will learn how Web pages differ from print pages.*

# CONTENT

When designing a Web page, it is easy to get so involved in the graphic design questions that you forget the most essential element of any Web page—the content. Without content, any Web page is just decoration. Without content, your audience will disappear. Without content, you have no reason to design a page. Always keep this in mind. Few if any business viewers come to a page just to see the colors or animations. They come seeking information. They want to know something, and they want to find it easily. That is your primary design goal. Every choice you make must be based on that one consideration. Continually ask yourself, "Does this meet my audience's needs?"

Gather your content information before you begin the design process. Decide how much information to deliver on each page. Generally, when deciding how to arrange content, keep the text concise on the opening pages and provide navigation links to more extensive text passages. While visitors to your page are looking for information, they usually don't want to read long passages trying to decide if this is the information for which they are looking. Good Web design generally recommends that opening pages require little or no scrolling. Later pages can be more text-intensive, because by then your audience knows that this is information they want.

## THE **ETHICS** OF WEB LINKS

Adding links to other sites outside your own is easy to do. The law is still unclear on the right of one person to include a link to another person's site without that person's approval. Generally, it's considered standard practice to request permission of the Webmaster of the site before adding the link.

The use of frames has presented an interesting ethical question for Web designers. It is possible to incorporate someone else's page within our own by using a framed link. Many Web sites object to this practice for several reasons. The most obvious concern is that of implied ownership. A greater concern, though, is the misrepresentation that is possible. For example, a general-purpose Web site that wants to sell a product such as a camera might include a framed link to the manufacturer of that camera. The camera manufacturer may not want to endorse this sales site, but it is no control over the link.

Search engines make it possible to see who has linked to your pages by typing the word *link* and then a colon followed by your Web address (link:www.mysite.com). If you discovered that your business page was linked to a site that you did not endorse, what would you do? If a Webmaster contacted you because you had included his or her Web site and asked you to remove the link, what would you do? How would you handle the use of a framed link? These business concerns will continue to be addressed in the future.

Ralph will use a local Web designer to actually create his pages, but he has learned that if he prepares his text in advance the cost will be significantly reduced. He begins by listing all the services he now provides with a description of costs. He realizes that the specialty key information is rather complex, since there are a wide variety of locks from which to choose. It takes him some time to gather together all the essential material.

## SPELLING

Spelling is an issue that often gets overlooked when creating the content for a page. In the early days of Web design, it was not uncommon to encounter spelling and grammatical errors on even professionally designed pages. That is no longer acceptable. Most Web editors have spelling checker options. Use them frequently. Consider spelling and grammar to be as important as the information you are delivering. Careless errors send a message of carelessness to your audience that can easily eliminate a business opportunity.

Don't rely on the built-in spelling and grammar tools of your software. Check all your work yourself, and always have someone else proofread your content before you deliver it to the Web.

# NAVIGATION

The need for navigation guides is essential in designing a Web page. It is the means of providing information for your customer. Sketching in advance on paper the links you intend to create from your content is an excellent habit to acquire. This will help ensure that links occur as you intend. If pages seem too dense with text, break the information into one or more pages. Once you know what your links will be, then it is time to create a navigation guide.

One common means of navigating is a series of links that act somewhat like an index calling up information selected. A simple set of **navigation links** is shown in Figure 18.1. Notice that clicking on *Blue*

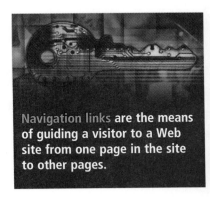

Navigation links are the means of guiding a visitor to a Web site from one page in the site to other pages.

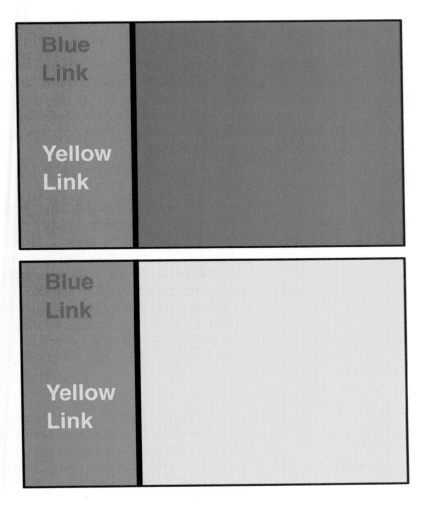

**Figure 18.1** Clicking on a link that is designed to be a navigation aid makes it easy to move around a business's Web site.

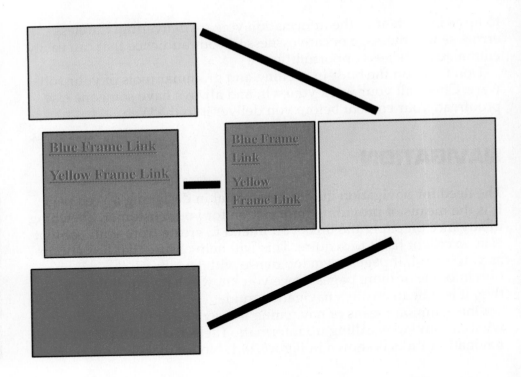

**Figure 18.2** Frames require the design of several Web pages in order to create the framed page.

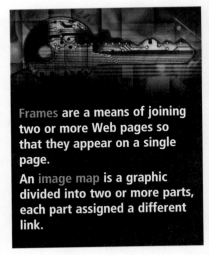

Frames **are a means of joining two or more Web pages so that they appear on a single page.**

An image map **is a graphic divided into two or more parts, each part assigned a different link.**

*Link* takes the reader to the blue page information. Clicking on *Yellow Link* takes the reader to the yellow page. The pages remain the same in design; only the linked information changes. Navigation links are generally found up the side, along the bottom, or across the top of the page; the design arrangement of links is repeated on every page to simplify movement from one page to another.

## FRAMES

Navigation linking was once accomplished by using **frames.** Frames are actually two or more Web pages joined to create another page. Each frame within the page displays a page that is created separately. Figure 18.2 demonstrates this process. Notice that three Web pages are required to create the final frame page. Because of the complexity of this arrangement and because some browsers don't handle frames, they are not as frequently used today as they once were. However, this design scheme is now reproduced by using designs similar to the one shown in Figure 18.1. In this Web page, clicking on *Yellow Link* replaces the complete page rather than just the interior frame.

## IMAGE MAPS

**Image maps** are useful design tools for navigation. Image maps are graphics that have been segmented, and each segment is assigned a different link. For example, if a drawing full of toys were used as an image map, clicking on each toy would take you to a page describing it. Image maps don't have to be images. They can be a simple graphic with a variety of words listed, as shown in Figure 18.3. Clicking on *Lenses* would take you to a page with images and prices for camera lenses. Image maps are very common ways of creating navigation links.

Ralph has seen pages that have navigation tools and he likes the way they look. He experiments with a picture of a series of keys to use as a navigation image and creates a drawing to give the designer some idea of what he wants.

## CONSISTENCY

When designing Web pages, you can format text as paragraphs with lines between them or into cells of a table. Paragraphs can be aligned right, left, or centered. Text can be wrapped around images, just as it can be in a word processing document. One great temptation is to use every design element possible to create pages so that each one has its own personality. Well-designed pages have simplicity as their basic structure, however, with the same design or elements recurring throughout each page so that the audience can anticipate what to expect as they change pages. The same design issues apply to printed books such as this text. Notice that elements are similar from one chapter to another, with fonts, sizes, features, and images placed in the same positions each time you encounter them. Those design tools should also be used when designing a Web site. Consistency of design is one way to make it easy for your audience to find what it is seeking.

**Photo Paper**

**Film**

**Camera Supplies**

**Lenses**

**Figure 18.3** Image maps once were difficult to create, but today's Web editing software makes them easy to make.

SOURCE: ©PHOTODISC

## CASCADING STYLE SHEETS

One way to create consistency is to use **cascading style sheets** (CSS). If you have ever used styles in a word processing program, you understand the concept of CSS. Text is assigned the same appearance every time it occurs and is based on the style to which it is assigned. That way, the style remains consistent throughout the entire page and Web site. Changing the style once automatically changes it everywhere.

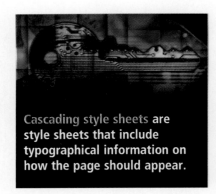

Cascading style sheets are style sheets that include typographical information on how the page should appear.

# DESIGN DIFFERENCES

Web pages may appear to be like print, but they have major differences. One difference is that each page is viewed as a single continuous block even though the page may print out on one or more sheets of paper. This means that issues such as page breaks, headers, and page numbering are not a consideration. Page links, instead, become the next page.

Just as there are no page breaks, there are no margins. The width of a Web page can be narrower than a standard 8.5-inch × 11-inch page or much wider. Often the width of a page is determined not by the designer, but by the width of the user's computer screen.

### TABLES

In addition, the use of columns (a common element in desktop publishing) is not possible when using today's HTML code; text usually spans the width of the screen. Designers of Web pages have discovered, however, that tables can be used to create the appearance of columns, as well as to provide spacing options for images. In Figure 18.4, the three "columns" of links are actually three cells of a single table, as shown in Figure 18.5. If you are viewing the code for a page using tables, the tag for tables is <TABLE>; for cells, <TD>; and for new rows, <TR>.

Use of tables is not as limiting as it may appear. Table borders can be visible, but they can also be invisible (their use does not have to be obvious to the casual observer). Changing **cell padding** (shown in orange in Figure 18.6) within each cell allows you to set the amount of space that borders the information in the cell. Setting the **cell spacing** (shown in green) determines the amount of space between cells. Cells in one row can also be set to span more than one column, so each cell does not have to be the same width, similar to those shown in Figure 18.7.

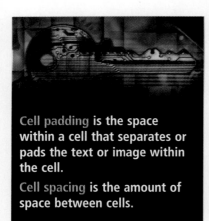

Cell padding is the space within a cell that separates or pads the text or image within the cell.

Cell spacing is the amount of space between cells.

### FONTS

Fonts provide an additional challenge. You may design a page with a particular font you chose for a specific impact. If your audience does not have that font, their computers will automatically substitute a generic font that may negate your intended effect. The user may also set font preferences that will override your selection. Font size can be set just as you would in desktop publishing, but a numbering system

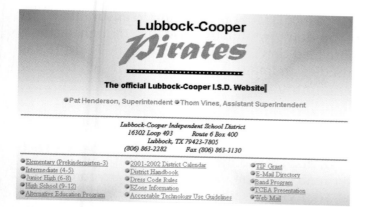

**Figure 18.4** Invisible tables can be used to create the appearance of columns.

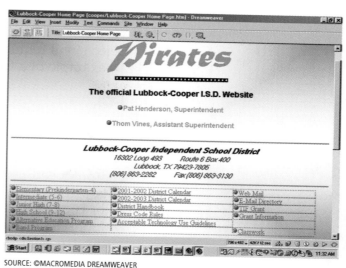

SOURCE: ©MACROMEDIA DREAMWEAVER

**Figure 18.5** Table cells such as these provide you with many design options.

**Figure 18.6** Cell padding and cell spacing give Web designers more control of tables.

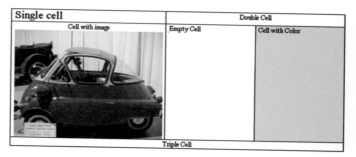

**Figure 18.7** Cells do not have to be the same width. Some can cover two or more columns.

from one to seven is more commonly used. The use of numbers allows the computer to enlarge the font proportionally on the basis of the computer user's display.

Font color choices require careful consideration. You want to select both font and background colors that offer high contrast, making them easy to read. Yellow on white is an example of a poor choice because it makes the text appear blurry. White text on a black background may be too stark. Choose colors based upon how well they work together.

You can incorporate specific fonts into your Web page in a variety of ways, but they require the loading of special scripts using fonts provided by specific Web sites. Generally, it's better to assume that special fonts are not available for use on your Web pages. (You can create an image using a particular font if you want to ensure that viewers see that font. You don't want to overuse this, though, as the objects will require more load time.) The word *Pirates* in Figure 18.4 is an example of a font used as an image.

## COLOR

Colors of images and backgrounds, as you learned in an earlier chapter, fall into three categories: millions of color choices, 256 colors, and 16 colors. The video card, display monitor, type of computer, and computer settings determine what the viewer will see. If you design a page with the idea that your viewers will be able to appreciate your color choices based on millions of colors available but your audience cannot see them, once again your intended effect will be lost. The use of the 216 Web-safe colors limits your choices, but helps guarantee that all colors will be seen by all users.

Colors are usually identified with HTML code using a set of three hexadecimal equivalents—one for red, one for green, and one for blue. A color that is R-62, G-122, and B-171 has a hexadecimal number of 3E7AAB. This *hex number* is generally provided by most graphics programs such as Photoshop. Web editors set the hex number for you when you select a color.

You may have previously used a color wheel that allows you to compare millions of colors (discussed in more detail in Chapter 21), but some color wheels include only the 216 Web-safe colors. A color wheel for the Web is useful in that it provides you with a color sample as well as the hexadecimal number used to indicate the HTML color. It also lets you see what colors work well together or complement each other.

SOURCE: ©PHOTODISC

When selecting colors for your Web pages, keep in mind a few simple basic color rules:

Blue is relaxing and a popular choice.
Red is visible and powerful.
Purple gives a sense of importance to a page.
Yellow and green are well received.
Brown can be used to simulate wood or leather, providing a sense of dignity.

When Ralph brings in his sketch of the site, he has included several columns and specific placement of images. He isn't aware that he can't use columns in his page design, but the designer assures him that tables can provide the same look. Ralph isn't particularly concerned about the fonts that will be used, but he does want his pages to appear to be solid and somewhat elegant. The designer suggests a background color of brown with darker flecks to appear like leather.

## IMAGES

To meet the needs of your audience, you do not have the same choices that you have in print, such as font selections. However, you do have the ability to create interesting backgrounds and to add animated images, much as you do in presentation software. The difference is that presentations are generally limited to small audiences, whereas Web pages can reach a world audience. This larger audience is a powerful force for any business.

Images can include JPG, PNG, or GIF graphics (standard, transparent, or animated), horizontal rules, bullets, flash files, and video.

A standard technique when using large images is to create **thumbnails,** smaller versions that can be clicked on to reveal the full-size image (Figure 18.8). Many Web editors provide thumbnail capabilities, making it easy to create them. Don't forget that although it is possible to reduce the size of an image or to crop it within a Web editor, doing so is not a good idea. Instead, to make the file size as small as possible, reduce the size in your image software before adding it to a page.

An interesting combination of text and graphics is a **scrolling marquee.** Marquees run text across the page much like a weather warning

### Customer Service Skills

Customers are the lifeblood of a business. *Customer service* means giving customers what they want and need. Top-notch customer service exceeds a customer's expectations. Employees who practice good customer service skills help build repeat business by building customer loyalty. If you directly work with clients, you *are* the company in the eyes of customers. Listen to them, anticipate their needs, and find ways to help them. Make it easy for the customer to do business with you.

Even if you don't come into direct contact with clients, you can still practice good customer service simply by doing quality work and delivering it on time. A Web designer who creates poorly planned pages, for example, can negatively affect a customer's feelings about a company without ever having met the customer. All employees and departments must cooperate to provide good service to clients. (Do you see a relationship between teamwork and customer service?)

**Digging deeper:** Imagine that you operate a midsized design and print shop. Use the Internet to research good customer service practices. Create a newsletter communicating these practices to your employees.

Thumbnails **are small versions of larger images. They speed up the download process by allowing viewers to choose whether they want to see the larger image.**

**Figure 18.8** If you plan to include large images on your Web site, it is a courtesy to your audience to provide thumbnails first to allow them the choice of what size to view.

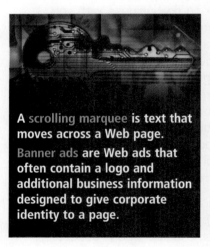

A **scrolling marquee** is text that moves across a Web page.

**Banner ads** are Web ads that often contain a logo and additional business information designed to give corporate identity to a page.

that appears at the bottom of your television screen. Even though this is text, treat it more like a graphic because of the animation involved.

Images can also be used to create rollovers. With one type of rollover, the image changes when the mouse rolls over it. This technique is generally used to indicate that an action is occurring, such as a button being selected. With the other type of rollover, often seen in **banner ads,** a series of images appears in sequence without any user intervention. Rollovers like this are often used to reveal more than one image without cluttering up the page.

Ralph has provided his designer with several photographs of the specialty keys. The designer recommends that the basic page contain small copies of the images that will load quickly. Someone interested in a particular key can then click on the thumbnail to see a full-screen version. Before Ralph leaves, he asks to have a printed copy of every page before it is loaded onto the Internet because he wants to proofread it carefully. The designer assures him that at least two members of his staff check all copy, but he will also send a copy to Ralph as the final check.

## SUMMARY

In this chapter, you saw the importance of making content decisions before making design decisions. You learned that navigation using repeating links, frames, or image maps was a second consideration. The need for consistency was stressed, and you learned the differences between the way print and Web pages are designed. You also learned ways that images can be used on a Web page.

Answer the following questions on your own computer.

1. What is your primary design goal when creating a Web page?
2. How much text should appear on the opening pages of a Web site?
3. Where can you place text-intensive information?
4. What is as important as the information you are trying to deliver?
5. Where are navigation links usually located?
6. What design tool is no longer used as frequently to create navigation links?
7. What purpose do image maps serve?
8. How are image maps created?
9. What is a characteristic of a well-designed Web page?
10. What is a tool for creating consistency of design?
11. What often determines the width of a Web page?
12. How do Web page designers create columns of text?
13. What options are available when designing a table?
14. What limitations do fonts provide?
15. What does a scrolling marquee do?

DISCUSSION

Discuss the following questions either as a class or as a written assignment.

1. Do you think spelling or grammatical errors change your impression of a Web site? Explain your response.
2. What kind of linking arrangements do you prefer on a Web site?
3. What problems does a user encounter when using an image map?
4. What resolution does your computer display when you are viewing a Web page?
5. Do you find thumbnails to be a useful courtesy on a Web page? Explain.

1. Search for three Web pages that contain tables. Print a copy of the pages. At least two of the pages should be using invisible tables.

2. Using the View Source menu option, print the code used for each of these pages. Highlight the tags used to create the tables.

3. Find three Web pages that have navigation links. Print a copy of the pages.

4. Indicate whether the pages are using repeating links, frames, or image maps.

## FURTHER EXPLORATION

Use the search tool that allows you to check links to a page address (link:www.mysite.com).

1. Check the links that connect your personal or school Web site.

2. List the links and describe the type of site, such as educational or business-related.

3. Find out whether each of these sites has sought permission to create the link.

4. Write a proposal to indicate ways to increase the number of links to the site.

# Chapter 19
# Web Media

ESTIMATED TIME

2

HOURS

SOURCE: ©PHOTODISC

## INTRODUCTION

The nature of Web pages is that they are dynamic (moving) rather than static (still). Static pages can become dynamic in several ways. The most obvious way is the use of interactive links that allow the user to view a new page. Another way is to use animations such as flash files or animated GIFs, which you have seen previously in presentation software; these animations were first developed to create dynamic Web pages. Sound, video, and dynamic HTML are other ways to create active pages.

Samantha Medina has learned the value of dynamic Web sites in her job as an administrative assistant for the mayor of a moderate-sized city. One of her tasks is to see that the mayor's **intranet** (a Web site available only to those within the mayor's office) is kept current. Samantha doesn't have to do the actual

SOURCE: ©MICROSOFT SOUND RECORDER

**Figure 19.1** Sound Recorder is an applet built into the Windows operating system that enables you to record sound.

site development, but she does have to keep the information up to date and make design decisions.

## SOUND

Sound files are not visible like other forms of multimedia, but they are an integral part of the dynamic nature of Web pages. Just as with image files, there are several sound formats, including WAV, AU, AIFF, MID, RA, and MP3. Sound files are often quite large and must be loaded from the Web page on which they are stored in order to be heard. Slow connections make the download process time-consuming. **Streaming audio** is a process developed by RealAudio that allows sound to begin to play before it has completely loaded onto a Web page; thus, the sound begins to play more quickly.

The biggest issue, other than download time, for designers of Web pages who want to use sound is the personal nature of music. The music that appeals to a 20-year-old may not appeal to someone even a few years older or younger. Another issue is the invasiveness of sound in a business environment. Pages that suddenly begin to play sounds may be a distraction to other workers. As a result, give careful consideration to the use of sound, particularly music, before including it in a page.

Sound can be recorded and edited with Microsoft Sound Recorder (shown in Figure 19.1) or with full-featured programs such as Sonic Foundry Sound Forge. Sound files can also be downloaded from the Internet or purchased in a CD format and used immediately.

Samantha (Sammie to her friends) has included on the Web site a digital recording of the mayor's acceptance speech. She didn't want to include the entire speech, so she had it edited to include only the five major goals the mayor outlined in his plan for the city. When viewers click on one of his goals, they can hear the mayor make his point. It is a brief clip that quickly establishes the mayor's position on each item.

### WEB SITES

You will be working at a computer for many hours every day if you pursue a career in multimedia. That's why good posture at your workstation and proper mouse/keyboard techniques are so important. Improper techniques put you at risk for developing carpal tunnel syndrome and repetitive stress injury. Learn more about proper mouse and keyboard use at:

http://kidshealth.org/kid (search for *ergonomics*)
http://www.healthycomputing.com
http://www.me.berkeley.edu/ergo (follow the *Computer Use Tips* link)
http://www.office-ergo.com

## PLUG-INS

Some sound formats, such as RA (RealAudio), require that a **plug-in** be loaded to be played. However, plug-ins are not limited to sound files. A plug-in is an add-on to an existing software program that gives the software additional functions. A plug-in for RA allows the browser to play music created with that program. Usually, when a feature is activated that requires a plug-in, a message appears giving you the option to download the plug-in to your computer immediately. For many users, this option creates problems. One issue is the concern that they are being asked to load unfamiliar software they may not want on their computers—or may not even be allowed to load, depending upon company policy. Another problem is the time required to download the plug-in. Consider both of these issues when designing pages that require plug-ins of any kind.

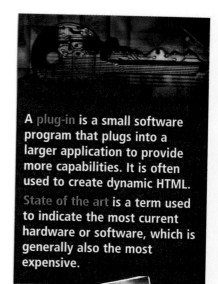

A **plug-in** is a small software program that plugs into a larger application to provide more capabilities. It is often used to create dynamic HTML.

**State of the art** is a term used to indicate the most current hardware or software, which is generally also the most expensive.

## VIDEO

Video and movies create the same problems as sound when loading onto a Web page. The file sizes are large, and download time can be a barrier. The file types for movies fall into three basic categories: Apple QuickTime (MOV), Windows Media Player (MPG and AVI), and RealPlayer (RAM). Windows Media Player (shown in Figure 19.2) can be used for both video and sound. It is generally already loaded onto computers with Windows operating systems. Apple QuickTime is generally already loaded onto Macintosh computers. A Windows version of QuickTime is available, but it must be loaded before videos can be viewed. Video is quite memory-intensive and requires computers that are usually considered **state of the art.**

Movies can be created and edited with programs such as Macromedia Director (which also creates Shockwave files) and Adobe Premiere. You can also capture action with a digital camera or convert nondigital movies with special hardware and software. Just as it's important to be able to stream audio, **streaming video** is becoming more important to allow larger video files to be viewed more easily on Web pages.

Sammie has included a link to a video clip of recent press conferences the mayor has held. These clips are streamed, making them appear

### Leadership Skills

Good leaders don't order people around and bark out commands like a drill sergeant, and they don't micromanage every little detail of a job. Instead, good leaders motivate people to do their best work at all times. They delegate work and authority, trusting that employees are professionals who want to do a good job. A good leader builds teamwork and encourages employees to be independent rather than to constantly look for direction.

If you find yourself in a leadership position at work—either as a supervisor or as the head of a work team—be sure to reinforce good ideas and build up your employees. Make them *want* to work for you, rather than *forcing* them to work for you. Treat employees the way you would want to be treated. You'll be surprised at the results.

**Digging deeper:** Suppose you are leading a four-person group responsible for producing a 128-page workbook for an important client. The workbook contains many pieces of art and photos. How will you delegate the tasks so that the workbook can be completed in two weeks? Discuss in class.

**Figure 19.2** Windows Media Player is designed to provide Windows users with a means to play sound, music, and video.

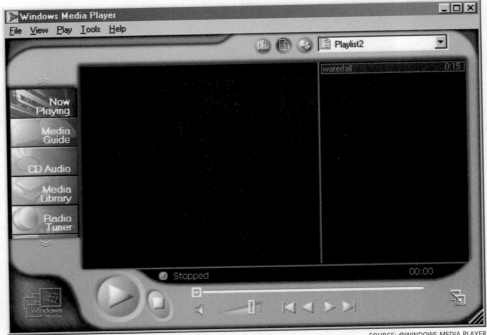

SOURCE: ©WINDOWS MEDIA PLAYER

**Streaming video** is a technique that enables the viewing of a movie before it has completely loaded and without placing as many demands on computer resources.

A **cookie** is computer code that stores information about a visitor to a Web site.

**Dynamic HTML** is any of several software functions that enable Web pages to be interactive.

**Client-side access** refers to dynamic HTML code that stores information on the user's (client's) computer.

**Server-side access** refers to dynamic HTML code that stores information on the server computer.

quickly. Because she knows that all the computers in the mayor's office have the same configuration, she is not concerned about software issues. Being able to see the press conferences at their leisure means that all the office personnel know what was said if any questions come up.

## DYNAMIC HTML

One of the biggest changes in Web design is a movement to dynamic pages that are modified each time they are viewed or that allow users to interact with the page such as by filling out forms. The words "Good morning, Sam" might appear on a dynamic page when Sammie first opens it. The page "knows" the time, and from a previous visit she made it will know her name. Her name and other information about her may have been stored on her computer or on a Web server in a **cookie** created by the HTML code.

**Dynamic HTML** takes many forms. It can be created with tools such as ActiveX, JavaScript, CSS (Cascading Style Sheets), Java applets, CGI (Common Gateway Interface) scripts, and SSI (Server-Side Include). Some of these tools, such as ActiveX, create interaction from within the user's computer by using **client-side access.** Others create these changes by accessing the Web server (**server-side access**) where the Web page is stored. CGI scripts are an example of dynamic HTML that require server-side access. As a nonprofessional designer of Web pages, you will not likely use many of these tools yourself; however, as a member of the business community you will need to be aware of their possibilities and to understand how they can be used to enhance your business.

Sammie has used several dynamic HTML features to make the intranet site valuable to everyone. One way is to have an interactive calendar available to everyone in the office. This means that anyone with password access can add information to the calendar and can see what events are coming up. This calendar has greatly simplified the process of keeping staff informed of city events such as parades, conferences, and conventions. Sammie continues to look for ways to incorporate the dynamic options into the Web site.

It is important to understand that each form of dynamic HTML has limitations. Client-side HTML must "take over" the user's computer in order to function. Many **firewalls** and browser restrictions prevent this from occurring; they protect the integrity of the data on a computer. The issue of computer viruses has become such a concern that users are wary of allowing outside computers access to business and personal computers. This wariness may limit the usefulness of this form of dynamic page design.

Server-side HTML requires a **Web hosting server** to allow server-side code to have access to its computers. Just as individual users are concerned about allowing others access to their computers, so are the administrators of Web servers. Poorly written code can create internal problems when the software code is activated and can make the server computer vulnerable to abuse by outsiders. Consider concerns such as these before choosing server-side dynamic HTML.

As the use of Web pages and the Internet continue to grow as an important part of the business world, however, issues such as these will be resolved and greater use of dynamic Web pages will become more important.

A **firewall** is blocking software that prevents certain actions from occurring within a server. A firewall often blocks access to files without a password.

A **Web hosting server** is the computer on which a Web site is stored and that is accessed whenever someone enters the site's address in a browser.

# SUMMARY

In this chapter you saw ways to add dynamic events to a Web page, including sound, video, and streaming media. You investigated dynamic HTML, which uses both client- and server-side access. In each of these areas, you learned the drawbacks and advantages of using dynamic media in a Web page.

## THE **ETHICS** OF SOUND AND VIDEO

The use of sound and video on a Web page creates the same ethical dilemma that comes with the use of still images. It is easy to copy these media from existing Web pages. It's also easy to copy music from CDs. Just as it's important to keep in mind copyright and ownership issues that apply to still graphics, it's equally important to remember that these same rights apply to sound and video. You can purchase music from royalty-free sites for use on a Web site, and these are good resources. There are few royalty-free options for video. Video clips will generally come from media created by you or your representative either as a Shockwave/flash file or recorded live.

Answer the following questions on your own computer.

1. What is the difference between dynamic and static?
2. In what ways can Web pages be made dynamic?
3. What file formats are used for sound?
4. What are the limitations on using sound?
5. Name and describe one technique that is used to make sounds play more quickly.
6. Describe one problem that occurs when using music on a Web page.
7. What purpose does a plug-in serve?
8. What are the three basic file types for movies?
9. How can movies be created for the Web?
10. What does a cookie do?
11. What is dynamic HTML?
12. List types of dynamic HTML.
13. What is the difference between client- and server-side access?
14. Why do users sometimes prevent client-side dynamic HTML from being used?
15. What problems can dynamic HTML cause for a Web server?

## DISCUSSION

Discuss the following questions either as a class or as a written assignment.

1. How long will you wait to download music or sound files?
2. If the music that plays on a Web site is a type that does not appeal to you, what is your response?
3. What is your response when a plug-in message appears asking for permission to load additional software?
4. What kinds of dynamic responses on a page do you want to see? Which ones do you find annoying?
5. What kind of dynamic responses make you return to a Web site you have previously visited?

1. Locate sites that provide royalty-free music for sale. List the Web address and the prices being charged.

2. Most music sites have samples of the music they provide. Listen to the music and rate its usefulness for a business Web page.

3. Look for sites that provide free animated GIFs and flash animations. Copy an example of each that might be of use on a business Web page.

4. Find out the restrictions on the use of the GIFs and flash. Include them with your examples.

5. Find a site with free video clips that would be appropriate in a business environment. Record the Web address, describe the clips, list any restrictions on use, and rate their usefulness in a business environment.

Find out if your school or organization has a firewall and what its restrictions are.

1. Does it allow server-side access?

2. Contact the Webmaster of a professional site and ask about his or her use of dynamic HTML. What restrictions is the Webmaster under in the use of dynamic design elements?

# Chapter 20
## Web Standards

SOURCE: ©PHOTODISC

## Objectives

- *You will learn how the W3C influences Web design.*
- *You will learn the importance of Section 508.*
- *You will consider what are the expectations for Web pages.*
- *You will learn how to ensure that your Web pages are found.*

## INTRODUCTION

The Internet appears to be free and open for anyone who wants to use it. However, as the use of the Web matures and continues to grow, it becomes important to make sure that growth is orderly and pages are accessible to as many people as possible. One of the ways to make this happen is through the use of standards and acceptable practices. Awareness of these standards and practices is important to businesses that want to acquire customers and meet their needs. As a result, students of image management who understand these standards will find their skills to be much in demand.

Miranda Yee is very aware of the Web standards issue as the director of the Homes for Families agency, which helps families find affordable housing. She had been surprised how often families have contacted her for help via the agency's Web site, until she learned that the local library had a list of resources posted on the computers available for patrons. When she contacted the librarian, she found that more and more people were beginning to use the Web as a primary means of getting information, instead of picking up brochures as they had once done.

# WORLD WIDE WEB CONSORTIUM

One of the ways that Web standards are established and maintained is through the **World Wide Web Consortium** (W3C). Unlike other forms of software that are developed and maintained by specific companies, HTML is not created by specific companies. Instead, the World Wide Web Consortium, an independent nonprofit organization, oversees and monitors the creation of Web design code. The W3C acts as the standards agency to keep changes orderly.

As individuals or businesses develop new and improved forms of HTML, they can submit their ideas to the W3C for approval. Once the changes have been accepted, developers of browser software begin to integrate these modifications into their programs. This means that users with older versions of browser software may not be able to use fully all the features available to them. Cascading style sheets, discussed in a previous chapter, are an excellent example of W3C-accepted modifications that may not be available to those using an older browser. This is one reason that businesses need to know the pros and cons of using the most current HTML options and understand what standards are guiding their choice.

Web designers and even those in business who must direct the work of those creating Web pages need to know what changes the W3C has approved. For this reason, it's important to keep up to date on the changes approved by the W3C in order to know what new tools are available. It is easy to fall behind quickly in the fast-changing world of Web design. Information about the World Wide Web Consortium can be found at http://www.w3.org.

Miranda knows that many of her clients have older computers and that the library computers are also not always up to date. With this in mind, she has frequently turned down

W3C **is an organization that approves changes to HTML code.**

## Good Business

### Multiculturalism in the Workplace

The United States has become a truly multicultural society; this is increasingly reflected in the workplace. Not everyone you work with will be exactly like you. You will almost certainly work with people from a wide variety of ethnic, cultural, and religious backgrounds. This variety can enhance a workplace and bring different perspectives to a job, but some employees may be intimidated by it.

Take opportunities to learn about your co-workers' traditions. For example, if you hear a co-worker talking about celebrating Cinco de Mayo, Juneteenth, or St. Patrick's Day, ask a few friendly questions. Most people enjoy talking about their heritage. This is not only a good way to make friends and learn something, but it can also build teamwork on the job. The more you know and like your co-workers, the easier it will be to work together with them when the time comes.

**Digging deeper:** Use the Internet to research a holiday from a culture different from your own. Write a one-page summary of your findings; include a link to a pertinent Web page and at least one other related element (image, sound file, and so on).

opportunities to add features to the agency's Web site in favor of older browsers. She has learned to read about the new browser features and to carefully measure their worth against the needs of her audience.

## THE **ETHICS** OF SECTION 508

Section 508 has caused considerable concern in the Web development community. It requires Web designers to consider carefully how they use their tools—particularly the more dynamic ones. It is easy for Web designers to think they must restrict their creativity if they cannot use tables or flash files to enhance their pages without excluding some readers. It is also easy for them to think it is too much trouble to build more than one set of pages so that readers with disabilities can have equal access to information.

As Web developers become more adept at using their software and as new software takes into account all users, these issues should become less important. Until then, no business should ignore the needs of its customers. Just as you would not place a barrier at the door of your business requiring only the agile to leap over it to get in, you should not place other kinds of barriers between your Web site and anyone who wants to get in.

Section 508 **is a law that requires federal agencies to make their Web sites accessible to all users, regardless of abilities.**

## SECTION 508

While the W3C is concerned about maintaining stable HTML code that can be used by as many browsers as possible, other groups are concerned about making sure that as many people as possible, regardless of their abilities, can use the Internet. There is a growing concern that standards be developed for those who design or authorize Web sites to ensure that all users, regardless of their vision or hearing abilities, be able to access the information found on Web sites.

For those designing for governmental agencies, the issue has become crucial as a result of **Section 508** of the Rehabilitation Act. This act requires access to electronic and information technology offered by federal agencies. Although currently these restrictions do not apply to sites created by businesses, this is a standard to consider so that all members of your audience are included when you are constructing Web pages.

How do you know if your Web site meets Section 508 requirements? One way to find out is to use the following list of questions. Another way is to use Web sites developed specifically to test for noncompliance, including color blindness. Entering your site address will return a report with the infractions listed. The Bobby site (http://www.cast.org/bobby/) is one of the most frequently used for this purpose. A third way is to download a reader and test for yourself how logical your page sounds. One of the most frequently used readers is JAWS, which can be found at http://www.freedomscientific.com.

### USEFUL WEB SITES

http://www.cast.org/bobby/ (Section 508 check)
http://www.temple.edu/inst_disabilities/piat/wave/yindex.html (Section 508 check)
http://www.freedomscientific.com/fs_downloads/jaws.asp (JAWS reader)
http://www.vischeck.com (color-blind check)

## SECTION 508 QUESTIONS

1. For all images, is alternative text provided?
2. For all applets, are alternative text and content provided?
3. For all image map links, is alternative text provided?
4. If server-side image maps were used, are text links provided for each hotspot in the image map?
5. For all graphical buttons, is alternative text provided?
6. Is there an absence of ASCII art, and, instead, are images and alternative text used?
7. If OBJECT was used to incorporate an image, applet, or script into a page, is the information also conveyed in an alternative means in cases where the OBJECT cannot be perceived, such as with "title" or within the body of the OBJECT element?
8. Are long descriptions provided of all graphics that convey important information?
9. For stand-alone audio files, are textual transcripts of all words spoken or sung as well as all significant sounds provided?
10. For audio associated with video, are captions—textual transcripts of dialogue and sounds—synchronized with the video?
11. Where sounds are played automatically, are visual notification and transcripts provided?
12. For short animations such as animated GIFs, are alternative text and a long description provided, if needed?
13. For movies, are auditory descriptions provided and synchronized with the original audio?

SOURCE: ©PHOTODISC

14. If color is used to convey information, is the information also clear from the markup and/or text?
15. Are foreground and background color combinations used that provide sufficient contrast when viewed by someone with color blindness or when viewed on a black-and-white screen?
16. For auto-refreshing or timed response pages, is a second copy of the page provided where refresh only happens after a link has been selected (until user agents provide this ability themselves)?
17. Is the Web page free from any blinking or updating of the screen that causes flicker?
18. Is a fallback page provided for pages that contain frames?
19. For scripts that present critical information or functions, is an alternative, equivalent presentation or mechanism provided?
20. For pages that use style sheets, are the contents of each page ordered and structured so that they read appropriately without the style sheet?
21. If frames are used, are titles provided so that users can keep track of frames by name?
22. Do you provide a "text only" alternative page to the original page?
23. If you provide a "text only" alternative page, does it contain substantially the same information as the original page?
24. If you provide a "text only" alternative page, is it updated as often as the original page?

As you can see from the list of Section 508 questions, one of the most significant standards is one that identifies images for those with vision problems. This is achieved by including the image ALT (or alternate) tags available in HTML, as shown in Figure 20.1. ALT tags are included when you insert an image onto a page. Web editors provide this as part of the design option. Software programs designed to "read" Web pages use the ALT tags to identify an image.

**Figure 20.1** ALT tags serve several purposes, including providing access to the page for those with disabilities.

```
<HTML>
<HEAD>
<TITLE>Cooper Elementary</TITLE>
</HEAD>

<BODY BACKGROUND="elback.jpg">
<DIV ALIGN="center">
<IMG SRC="pirates.gif" WIDTH="327" HEIGHT="125" ALT="pirate logo"><BR>
<IMG SRC="movingline.gif" WIDTH="270" HEIGHT="8"><BR>
<H2>Lubbock-Cooper Elementary</H2>
<FONT COLOR="red">
<IMG SRC="1star.gif" WIDTH="14" HEIGHT="14">Rita McDaniel, Principal<BR>
<IMG SRC="1star.gif" WIDTH="14" HEIGHT="14">Jim Rose, Assistant Principal
</FONT>
<P>Welcome to the Cooper Elementary page. Click on the pirate below to
enter our world.</P>
<P><A HREF="elemlist.html"><IMG SRC=pirwink.gif" WIDTH="128" HEIGHT="103"
ALT="winking pirate"></A></P>
</DIV>
</BODY>
</HTML>
```

SOURCE: ©PHOTODISC

Other ways to provide information is to create alternate pages that have few if any special features such as animations, frames, or image maps. More and more sites automatically provide a text-only path for those who need that option.

Miranda is particularly concerned about the standards outlined in Section 508. She knows that many clients may have poor sight, particularly those who are elderly. She has used the Bobby site several times to see if her Web pages comply. She wants to make sure that no one is excluded from receiving the information they need to help them find housing. While this at times means that the Web designer has to make changes to the site, Miranda knows that in the long run what might be lost in creativity is won in more users.

## PAGE EXPECTATIONS

Another area in which Web designers provide a courtesy to their readers is by maintaining certain page conventions or expectations. Some of these conventions include providing the last date that a page has been updated as well as a copyright date. Pages should also have links back to the home page in the event that a reader has come to a page from a search engine and cannot "back up" to the index page. It is also expected that the home page will have an e-mail link to the Web editor to simplify the process of contacting the editor.

Businesses and organizations that have contact with the public should always include information about their physical address (including state and country) as well as a telephone number. Detailed maps indicating a way to reach the business are particularly helpful. It's easy for Web designers to forget that customers may use Web sites as a means of verifying the existence of a business or to actually drive to its physical location. While everyone in the area may know

that the Washington Irving State Park is in Massachusetts, those who visit the Web site will have no way to learn that unless it's made very clear. Even highway designations can be a problem since Interstate highways cross state lines; just giving the information that the park is off I-44 is not enough information.

Miranda knows that her clients often must visit her agency in person. She includes a map showing the location of her office as well as step-by-step instructions that could be printed out for someone who must provide this information for a driver. She has verified that all pages have links back to her home page and the index page includes a link to all essential e-mail addresses, including her own. On the page that indicates current housing information, she makes sure that the date is continually updated so those people using the page will know if the information is up to date.

## GETTING FOUND

A feature of Web pages that is not an obvious standard is designed to help Web sites get "found." It serves no purpose to have the finest Web site that offers the most carefully prepared message if no one comes to the page. Being found can be accomplished in several standard ways. The most obvious, of course, is to advertise in print or other media, and this should always be considered. This solution means it's essential that your message always include the address of your business's Web site on documents such as business cards, forms, print ads, brochures, and invoices. This also means that media ads, whether on television or radio, should contain the address.

The next most obvious way of being found is through **search engines** such as Yahoo and Excite. One way to "help" a search engine find you is to submit your Web site to search engines by yourself or through a paid service. The following list of engines is a good place to begin:

http://www.altavista.com
http://www.excite.com
http://www.hotbot.com
http://www.infoseek.com
http://www.lycos.com
http://www.google.com
http://www.webcrawler.com

There are other standard ways, however, that Web designers can improve the chances of their sites being found by building information into the HTML code. Search engines are designed to roam the sites on the Internet, looking for information to add to the engine's database. Computer programs called **spiders** do the roaming and then send back to the search engine database the results of their encounters. Their searches focus on the **meta names,** titles, and headings that are included in Web pages. The code for meta names is placed in the heading, as shown in Figure 20.2, but does not appear on the page seen by viewers. **Keywords** found within the meta name tags are specifically indexed so that if someone is looking for that word, your site's address will appear.

It is obvious that if a Web site is going to be found, the keywords selected are very important. They should be the ones you would anticipate in a search. Creative Web designers learn to think beyond the obvious and to include words that might help someone stumble upon the site even by accident. Another issue, though, is the use of keywords that are not directly related to the actual content of the site but that might attract attention. This is a fairly common technique that should be avoided by businesses that want their audience to take their site seriously. It should be considered a business standard that only legitimate keywords be included in the header.

**Search engines** are programs that search for keywords in documents or in a database; databases that store information about Web sites.

A **spider** is software that roams the Internet, searching for information about Web sites that it then sends to a search engine database.

A **meta name** is an HTML tag that stores information about a Web site.

**Keywords** are terms used to identify and locate a particular Web site.

```
<HTML>
<HEAD>
<META NAME="description" content="Lubbock-Cooper Elementary, an award
winning school">
<META NAME="keywords" content="school, Lubbock, Cooper, Elementary, award,
winning, Texas, TAAS">
<TITLE>Cooper Elementary</TITLE>
</HEAD>

<BODY BACKGROUND="elback.jpg">
<DIV ALIGN="center">
<IMG SRC="pirates.gif" WIDTH="327" HEIGHT="125" ALT="pirate logo"><BR>
<IMG SRC="movingline.gif" WIDTH="270" HEIGHT="8"><BR>
```

**Figure 20.2** Meta names provide information that is used by search engines and browsers.

The Homes for Families agency had a contest when the agency's Web site was first being designed. The person with the most possible keywords was awarded a special plaque, and it was considered to be money well spent. The winner was able to think up 112 keywords that someone might use to locate the site. Some were quite surprising, such as "dog," but as someone pointed out, pets and families do go together. Meanwhile, the number of "hits" indicating how often someone finds the Web site continues to grow each year. Miranda feels that good keywords have made a difference.

## SITE EVALUATIONS

Designing quality Web pages requires you to keep many features in mind. The following chart has a series of questions designed to help you ensure that you have met acceptable standards and created an effective site. It is also a good guide to use when evaluating the content and design of other sites.

| Criteria (Assign a score from 1 to 4, with 4 indicating exceptional work) | Score | Comment |
|---|---|---|
| Is it easy to navigate from page to page? | | |
| Is it easy to find information? | | |
| Are links easy to locate? | | |
| Are links useful? | | |
| Do all links work? | | |
| Do all pages have a link back to the home page? | | |
| Does the site engage the reader? | | |
| Is the page visually appealing? | | |
| Is the text easy to read with a contrasting background? | | |
| Are opening pages short enough that extensive scrolling is not necessary? | | |
| Is the content on each page identified? | | |
| Is the content on each page useful? | | |
| Is the text free of grammar, spelling, or punctuation errors? | | |
| Is the text free of errors in factual information? | | |
| Does information appear quickly, even using a modem? | | |
| Do graphics load quickly? | | |
| Is there alternate text for graphics and image maps? | | |
| Does the home page have a contact person and e-mail address? | | |
| Is there information indicating when the site was last updated? | | |
| Is there information about the site such as a physical address? | | |
| TOTAL SCORE | | |

SOURCE: ©PHOTODISC

## SUMMARY

In this chapter on standards, you saw how the World Wide Web Consortium acts as a monitor for HTML development, making decisions on features that will eventually be incorporated into browsers. You saw the importance of creating Web sites that can be accessed by anyone seeking your services or site by considering the requirements outlined in Section 508. You also saw what expectations are provided as a courtesy to viewers of Web pages. In addition, you learned ways to ensure that your business's Web site will be found by users looking for information you can provide.

Answer the following questions on your own computer.

1. What is the purpose of the W3C?
2. What occurs after the W3C approves new HTML code?
3. What is Section 508?
4. What tag is useful in helping make your Web site more accessible to the visually impaired?
5. How do the visually impaired know what is on a Web page?
6. How can you know if your site meets Section 508 requirements?
7. What is Bobby?
8. What date information should be included on a home page?
9. How can a viewer contact a Web editor?
10. What business information should be included on a Web page?
11. Why should Web pages have links back to the home page?
12. What is the most obvious way to ensure that people learn about your Web site?
13. How can you help search engines find your Web site?
14. What is another way that search engines find your site?
15. What code helps search engines find and catalog your site?

## DISCUSSION

Discuss the following questions either as a class or as a written assignment.

1. Why is an organization like the W3C necessary?
2. Should Web browsers incorporate HTML changes before the W3C approves them?
3. What words are most often "found" by using a search engine? Should these words be included as keywords by businesses to help ensure that their sites are noticed?
4. Who should create a list of keywords for a business site? How many should be listed?
5. Should Web developers limit their creative designs to ensure that everyone can use their pages?
6. What courtesies should Web designers use when designing pages in order to make sites and the information on them easy for readers to use?

1. Locate three business sites by using a search engine and words that will likely direct you to them.
2. Using the View Source option, see if these words are included in their meta names.
3. Check these sites to see if they have used **ALT** tags for the visually impaired.
4. Using the **24-point checklist**, evaluate the accessibility of each site.
5. Enter the addresses of these sites at the Bobby site. Print out the report on the accessibility of the sites.
6. Evaluate the sites to see what information they have included as a courtesy to the reader.
7. Use the chart in this chapter to measure the overall quality of the site.
8. Create a report indicating how well these sites meet the requirements of business standards.

Explore the information available on the World Wide Web Consortium (http://www.w3.org). Read the list of specifications that currently apply to HTML code.

1. What are the major areas of discussion?
2. What else is available at the W3C Web site?
3. Present your information to the class.

# Unit 5: Summary

## Key Concepts

## Chapter 17: Web Editing

1. HTML is a universal code that allows anyone using browser software to view documents created with the code.
2. One advantage of using a Web editor instead of writing code is that WYSIWYG makes it easy to design Web pages.
3. One of the most common means of transferring Web files to a Web server is to use FTP (File Transfer Protocol) software.
4. Although it is possible for everyone to view Web pages, you need to be aware of certain limitations such as displays, browsers, and connection speed when you're creating pages.

## Chapter 18: Web Design

1. Your primary design goal is to meet your audience's need for information.
2. Navigation guides are essential in designing a Web page.
3. Well-designed pages have simplicity as their basic structure.
4. Designers of Web pages use tables to create the appearance of columns.
5. Web images can include JPG, PNG, or GIF graphics (standard, transparent, or animated), horizontal rules, bullets, flash files, or video.

## Chapter 19: Web Media

1. Sound formats include WAV, AU, AIFF, MID, RA, and MP3.
2. The file types for movies fall into three basic categories: Apple QuickTime (MOV), Windows Media Player (MPG and AVI), and RealPlayer (RAM).
3. One of the biggest changes occurring in Web design is a movement to dynamic pages.
4. Dynamic HTML falls into two categories: client-side access and server-side access.
5. Each form of dynamic HTML currently has limitations.

## Chapter 20: Web Standards

1. It is important to keep up to date on the changes approved by the W3C in order to know what new tools are available.
2. Older versions of browser software may not be able to use fully all the features available to them.
3. A growing concern for those who design Web sites is the need for all users, regardless of their vision or hearing abilities, to be able to access the information found on those sites.
4. There are several ways to check whether your Web site meets 508 requirements.
5. Web pages should be designed with certain expectations provided as a courtesy to the reader, such as dates and links to the Web editor.
6. Search engines are designed to roam the Internet, looking for Web sites.

# Terms

**banner ads** Web ads that often contain a logo and additional business information designed to give corporate identity to a page

**cascading style sheets** style sheets that include typographical information on how the page should appear

**cell padding** the space within a cell that separates or pads the text or image within the cell

**cell spacing** the amount of space between cells

**client-side access** dynamic HTML code that stores information on the user's (client's) computer

**cookie** computer code that stores information about a visitor to a Web site

**dynamic HTML** any of several software functions that enable Web pages to be interactive

**firewall** blocking software that prevents certain actions from occurring within a server; it often blocks access to files without a password

**frames** a means of joining two or more Web pages so that they appear on a single page

**FTP** the means of transferring files from one computer to another over a network; it is often used to transfer files to a Web server

**hacking a site** the unauthorized modification of a Web site, usually in ways that distort the original purpose of the site

**home page** the first page of a Web site; generally saved as *index*

**HTML** Hypertext Markup Language; the code used to create Web pages

**image map** a graphic divided into two or more parts, each part assigned a different link

**intranet** a network designed for providing information within a company or an organization; it functions much as the Internet does for the world

**keywords** terms used to identify and locate a particular web site

**meta name** an HTML tag that stores information about a website

**navigation links** the means of guiding a visitor to a web site from one page in the site to other pages

**plug-in** a small software program that plugs into a larger application to provide more capabilities; often used to create dynamic HTML

**scrolling marquee** text that moves across a Web page

**search engines** programs that search for keywords in documents or in a database; databases that store information about Web sites

**Section 508** a law that requires federal agencies to make their Web sites accessible to all users, regardless of abilities

**server-side access** dynamic HTML code that stores information on the server computer

**spider** software that roams the Internet, searching for information about Web sites

that it then sends to a search engine database

**state of the art** a term used to indicate the most current hardware or software, which is generally also the most expensive

**streaming audio** a technique that enables sound to be heard before the complete file has been loaded onto the user's computer

**streaming video** a technique that enables the viewing of a movie before it has completely loaded and without placing as many demands on computer resources

**tag** a specific piece of HTML code used to tell a Web browser how information should be displayed

**thumbnails** small versions of larger images; they speed up the download process by allowing viewers to choose whether they want to see the larger image

**W3C** an organization that approves changes to HTML code

**Web editor** software that creates HTML code automatically as part of the Web design process

**Web hosting server** the computer on which a Web site is stored and that is accessed whenever someone enters the site's address in a browser

**Web server** a computer used to store and broadcast Web pages

**Web site** one or more Web pages linked to form a single site

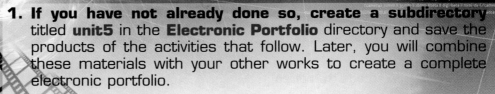

# ELECTRONIC PORTFOLIO

1. **If you have not already done so, create a subdirectory** titled **unit5** in the **Electronic Portfolio** directory and save the products of the activities that follow. Later, you will combine these materials with your other works to create a complete electronic portfolio.

2. Create a business-related Web site with at least three pages, including tables as part of the design of at least one page.

3. Create a consistent design for all pages, adhering to the courtesies expected by your reader.

4. Include navigation links, which can be an image map.

5. Include at least one dynamic element other than links.

6. Make sure keywords are entered into the heading.

7. Use the Section 508 guidelines to ensure that the Web site is accessible to all.

8. Save the site to the **unit5** directory. Be sure to save the first page as **index.**

9. Use the following chart to evaluate the quality of your portfolio material.

| | Beginning | Developing | Accomplished | Exemplary | Score |
|---|---|---|---|---|---|
| Web page design | Site contains fewer than three pages | Site contains at least three satisfactory pages | Site contains at least three pages with a consistent design | Site contains at least three pages with a consistent and creative design and courtesy elements | |
| Web page elements | Site includes navigation links | Site includes navigation links and another dynamic element | Site includes navigation links, another dynamic element, and keywords | Site includes navigation links (image map), another dynamic element, and creative keywords, and meets Section 508 requirements | |

# Oral and Other Professional Communications Skills

SOURCE: ©PHOTODISC

## Career Profile

Patrick Cannon, the son of Patsie and Carroll Cannon, knows what it means to discuss his qualifications to be judged to compete in an event. Therefore, competition is no stranger to Patrick. He has competed in various 4-H events and mastered in most of them. Doing so often means he has to submit a portfolio (his qualifications, photos, and other materials) that he prepares on the computer. He must make his portfolio a sales presentation—one that sells his accomplishments. His portfolio must demonstrate his ability to present himself well in an event he plans to enter. Patrick realizes that good oral communication skills are also important in a presentation.

Using a computer and sending materials to a printer are standard tasks for his parents as well, who own Cannon Marketing, a successful Ty Ty, Georgia, auctioneering company for purebred cattle. For each auction sale they coordinate and present to buyers, they not only must schedule the dates and places for the sale but also provide catalogs, advertising, and other print materials to showcase the cattle that will be at the sale. Cataloging each animal is a large

SOURCE: ©PHOTODISC

233

SOURCE: ©PHOTODISC

(continued)

responsibility for Cannon Marketing, a process that takes time and skill in checking each animal's birth date, identification, pedigree, performance data, and reproductive status. Each sales piece is actually a sales presentation designed to show each animal at its best and to create the desire for a buyer to bid on that animal at the auction.

Patsie's main contribution is preparing the catalogs and advertising for print. She has to select not only the photos that portray the cattle in their best light but also those that will print with the greatest reproduction quality. Therefore, she works constantly hand-in-hand with the local printer to select type fonts, styles, photos, colors, and other print specifications.

Patsie knows that her degrees in business have helped provide the skills she uses daily: keyboarding, copy writing, editing, proofreading, and attention to detail.

Carroll, an auctioneer licensed in several states, knows how important an accurate and clear catalog is so that buyers will see the cattle and want to attend the sale. The same as for Patsie, Carroll's degree in animal science prepared him for the details of marketing that are crucial to a successful sale. His presentation skills must be honed to perfection as an auctioneer. Not only must his skills be top-notch as a registered auctioneer, but his oral presentation skills must also meet the challenges that a sale of purebred cattle entails. He knows how important oral communication skills are in sales presentations and demonstrations.

Cannon Marketing must create reports immediately after the sale for its business records. These reports reflect the sales data and other important information that will be needed for future sales, as well as for banking and taxation purposes.

Being successful in a career means developing your skills and continuing to perfect them. You, too, can use your skills learned in your business, technical, and multimedia courses to excel in a career you like, just as the Cannons have. ■

Note: Patrick Cannon and his parents are real people, and Cannon Marketing, based in Ty Ty, Georgia, is a real business.

SOURCE: ©PHOTODISC

# Chapter 21
# Communication Preparation

ESTIMATED TIME
3
HOURS

SOURCE: ©EYEWIRE

## INTRODUCTION

Images are not created or managed in a vacuum. In business, images are used to communicate—often as a sales or informational tool. Before this is possible, however, significant planning must occur. Those who find planning the easiest are the ones who build in time for things to go wrong by accomplishing as much as possible before the final product is needed.

One way to plan ahead is to anticipate what images will be needed. Needed items might include business cards, logos, letterhead, coupons, handouts, or even maps. Having preliminary models of each of these image "events" means you are not rushed to create or manage material when you are pressed for time.

Marcella Johnson learned this while working at Copy Services, Inc. She saw that the customers who had planned ahead

## Objectives

- *You will learn to how to create the components of a presentation.*
- *You will learn details to include in preparing for a presentation.*
- *You will learn about voice recognition technology.*

left with materials that were more professional and satisfying. Customers who rushed in at the last minute with materials to be reproduced often discovered too late that their work didn't completely meet their expectations. While it was not the responsibility of Copy Services to provide proofreading or camera-ready materials, Marcella tried to smooth the way for many harried executives.

# PRESENTATION COMPONENTS

## LOGOS

A **logo** is an image designed to convey a corporate or business identity. The Thomson logo shown in Figure 21.1 is a good example of a simple, straightforward logo that is easily recognizable. Logos such as this one can be created with text, vector graphics, bitmap graphics, or more often a combination of these tools. Logos are used in a variety of ways, and so the designer must be able to create logos that can be used effectively in both black and white and in color, in display and in print, and in all sizes. It is often necessary to design logos that can be used horizontally as well as vertically and in different file formats.

The nature of logos is that they are simple and symbolic; they send a message through the image. A logo should be timeless so that the image created today will be just as effective in the future. Good logo design requires balance, parallelism, repetition, and contrast. Color is often an essential part of the message and requires you to have a working knowledge of color theory.

Marcella learned to warn her customers that simple is better. Too often she saw logos that were complex and multicolored. She knew from experience that these complicated logos often didn't stand the test of time. The logos that used effective color theory had a lasting power that sometimes even surprised her.

## COLOR THEORY

**Color theory** consists of an understanding of the relationship of color by using a color wheel, shown in Figure 21.2. Colors opposite each other on the wheel, called **complementary colors,** can be combined effectively to be seen as attractive or pleasing

A **logo** is a graphical symbol that uses both text and graphics to convey the identity of a business.

**Figure 21.1** Good logos such as the Thomson one allow for easy recognition of a product.

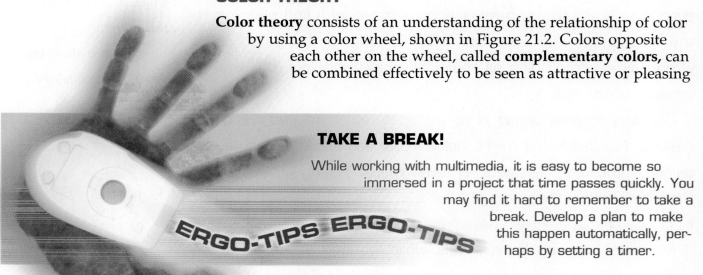

### TAKE A BREAK!

While working with multimedia, it is easy to become so immersed in a project that time passes quickly. You may find it hard to remember to take a break. Develop a plan to make this happen automatically, perhaps by setting a timer.

ERGO-TIPS ERGO-TIPS

to the viewer. In addition, **analogous colors,** those next to each other on the wheel, can be combined successfully. When you select color, keep in mind that a carefully selected color or set of colors will not appear the same in different situations. Color seen outside in sunlight may appear quite different from color seen under fluorescent light or incandescent light. You have already seen that color may be different from one display monitor to another.

Color itself communicates a message that depends on the age, gender, and culture of the person viewing it. Different colors can be expected to send different messages or to create different effects. For example, the following colors often generate these reactions:

Blue—creates tranquility or peacefulness but also sadness
Green—gives a soothing feeling
Orange—increases mental sharpness
Pink—provides a subdued response
Red—stimulates
Yellow—creates harmony or anxiety, depending on the brightness

## BUSINESS CARDS

Development of a business card often requires the use of a logo, as well as knowledge of layout, discussed in an earlier chapter. A business card should be simple, be easy to read, and have significant white space. The choice of paper and ink colors can send an important message, depending on the business for which it is used. More formal business cards limit their paper choice to white and print to

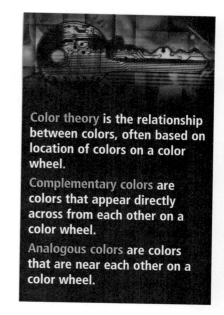

**Color theory** is the relationship between colors, often based on location of colors on a color wheel.

**Complementary colors** are colors that appear directly across from each other on a color wheel.

**Analogous colors** are colors that are near each other on a color wheel.

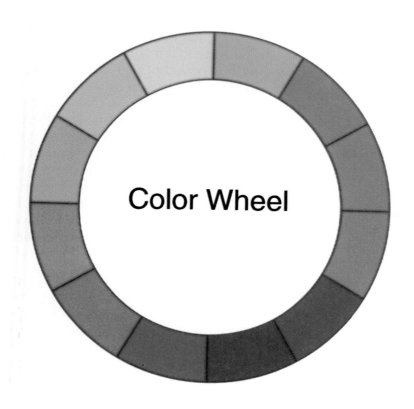

Color Wheel

**Figure 21.2** A color wheel such as this one enables you to see the relationship of various colors.

black. Less formal business cards may use **colored stock,** photographs, or nonstandard typography and ink colors to make an impression. You must think carefully about your audience before making a design decision.

Marcella saw in her work that some businesses used perforated, preprinted stock for business cards. These 8-1/2 × 11-inch sheets are designed to be passed through a copy machine. The color design has been preprinted, providing ten business cards to a sheet. All that remains is for information to be reproduced ten times. The advantage of using preprinted stock is that design and color have been created by professionals and short runs can be done quickly. The disadvantages are that the distinctiveness of a design is lost, long runs of cards are expensive, and sometimes the photocopied text flakes off.

## LETTERHEADS

Development of a business letterhead requires the same knowledge of design used in development of a business card. Once again, a logo may be part of the design. Formal letterheads place essential information across the top, often centered. Less-formal letterheads may place the information along a side margin or at the bottom of the page. Paper choices are often similar to those used in business cards and may act as a way to provide a consistent look. A company logo, business cards, and letterhead are frequently designed as a package to establish an identity for the company early in the startup process. Having your logo, business card, and letterhead in place removes some of the time pressure later when print or Web communication is required.

Just as some businesses use predesigned business cards, they can also use the same designs for their letterheads. Marcella knew that some small businesses used a package that included the same design for letterhead that they used for business cards. In addition, these same designs are also available for use as brochures or other types of print documents, so that design continuity continues. Marcella knew that when the business grew, the cost might become unnecessarily expensive. But for companies that needed only a small number of letterhead sheets or brochures, this was a good way to have a professionally designed package.

## THE **ETHICS** OF TRADEMARKS AND LOGOS

Trademarks and logos are distinctive symbols that represent a company and its products. Use of such trademarks or logos by others is restricted by law. Once you have created a logo for your own company, you will want it protected in the same way, for the symbol becomes a part of your business's identity. Companies work hard to keep their logos and trademarks from being infringed upon by others. For this reason, in print documents you will often see the TM symbol next to a brand name, or you will see a generic term used instead, such as the word *tissue* used instead of *Kleenex™*. Keep this in mind whenever you are creating a print document, a presentation, or a Web page. These restrictions apply in every situation.

## COUPONS

One presentation component most often ignored is a coupon. Coupons can be enclosed in thank-you letters to ensure repeat customers, or they can be used to encourage new customers. They

**Figure 21.3** Promotional products attract attention and increase the likelihood that your logo will remain visible to your customer.

can also be handed out much like business cards. Coupons are designed with the same skills used in creating business cards—incorporating white space, logos, and color choices into the appropriate look.

## PROMOTIONAL PRODUCTS

Notepads, pencils, rulers, key chains, and even balloons or stress balls (shown in Figure 21.3) that are used to advertise a company must be designed in preparation for events. These promotional items, sometimes called **schwag,** can be an important way to keep a company's name in front of its customers. The choice of color, size, and placement of information is an important image management decision. Even providing logo-bearing pencils and pads at a presentation is a good way to continually reinforce a message.

**Schwag is promotional products such as fuzzy animals, calculators, and other items designed to carry a company logo.**

## PRESENTATION PREPARATION

### MAPS

Often, part of the preparation for a presentation requires the design of materials for use before or at the time of the presentation. These materials may include a map that gives the location of either the physical address or the location of a specific room. Never assume that "everyone knows where it is." Having maps available in advance simplifies the preparation process, whether you are sending a letter notifying someone of a meeting, publicizing an event, or even placing an ad in the phone book.

You have already seen in an earlier chapter how to create maps and insert them into documents. It is important to remember that, once again, simple is better. When designing a map, eliminate as many details as possible; leave only essential information. For example, if only one major highway is generally used to access the road on which your business is located, include only the portion of the map that is needed once the highway exit has been reached. Include a text statement indicating the major highway used to reach the exit.

If there are several ways to reach your location, use the highlighting tool provided in most mapping programs to indicate the best choice. It's usually considered a standard convention to indicate north on maps. Be sure also to include any other helpful information such as distances between major points.

## INFORMATION PACKETS

Most presentations require print information. This information may include a single-page handout, a **seminar notebook,** or a catalog. Development of each of these print documents requires the knowledge of design and layout that you studied earlier. Keep the following guidelines in mind as you design the information:

- For handouts that you anticipate your audience will make notes on, allow space at the sides.
- For notebooks, use tabs to help the audience quickly find information as you address each point.
- For catalogs, include on the back cover mailing information that meets postal requirements.
- For any information that must be bound, allow enough of an inner margin for binding.

# PRINTING PREPARATION

While many business documents are produced using a photocopier, many more are sent to professional printing services. An area of preparation that is often overlooked by those planning presentation materials (or any print document) is a **pre-press check.** In order for a printer to be able to print a document successfully, the printer must have not only the page files, but also the graphics files and the fonts that were used to create those pages. During a pre-press check all of these files are collected for transmittal to the printer. This process is often referred to as *preflighting.* For documents that are to be printed in color, the pre-press check also includes checking color separations to ensure that colors will be reproduced properly in the printing process.

Specialized software, such as Extensis Preflight, is available to simplify this process. If your business intends to use a printing service, it is important to be aware of printing issues and to be prepared to work with the professionals producing your printed documents.

Marcella saw these problems all too often. Printing jobs became much more expensive for businesses until their employees learned to do preflight checking. Once they learned to verify use of fonts and to check on how images would print, the printing process became much

A seminar notebook is a bound document, often in a binder, that contains all the printed information needed for a conference or meeting.

A pre-press check verifies that all files and fonts needed to print a document by a printing service are present.

less of a problem. Documents were printed on the deadline that was needed and costs were kept within expectations.

# VOICE RECOGNITION

One technology tool available to you as you create materials for presentations is **voice recognition** software. With this software, you can easily add text to long or short documents without the use of a keyboard. Currently, three major types of voice recognition software are available: IBM ViaVoice, ScanSoft Dragon Naturally Speaking, and voice recognition software that comes built in as part of Windows XP and Office XP.

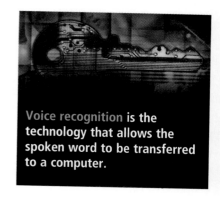

**Voice recognition is the technology that allows the spoken word to be transferred to a computer.**

All voice recognition software functions with similar features. They all anticipate that you will use a headphone-microphone combination (shown in Figure 21.4), although a microphone alone can be used. In addition, for each one you must teach the software to recognize your particular voice pattern by speaking a series of passages. The more passages you use, the better the recognition. It's important to learn to speak in a way that the software can recognize, which requires the use of phrases rather than single words strung together. A little practice makes it easy to speak in a way that the computer can record accurately.

Once the voice recognition software has been installed, a toolbar similar to the one shown in Figure 21.5 will appear. With the toolbar, you can turn the microphone on or off and activate other functions.

Voice recognition software also enables you to use voice commands to perform basic functions such as open and save, as well as to input words. Image management choices such as font type, size, and style can also be made with the software commands.

One aspect of voice recognition that many users don't anticipate is the need to insert punctuation and to move to a new paragraph using commands. This means that if you were using voice recognition software to record this paragraph you would have to tell it to place a period at the end of this sentence and to start a new paragraph for the one that follows.

Capitals at the beginning of sentences are created automatically, as are capitals of common nouns such as a person's name. However, words that the computer cannot anticipate as being

## Good Business

### Managing Stress on the Job

It can sometimes be difficult to manage the demands of a job, family, friends, and your personal life. Everyone has a bad day every now and then, but sometimes the pressure can get to be a little difficult to handle. If you get too stressed over your job, unfortunately your work will suffer—which in turn will simply increase your anxiety.

It is possible to take your work seriously but not become overly stressed about it. When you feel overburdened, try a few simple tactics to relieve the pressure: Keep your sense of humor, take a coffee break with a co-worker, go for a walk, or listen to music. Try to stay focused and use your time wisely. Above all, make sure to eat right and exercise daily; good nutrition and physical fitness are great stress-busters.

**Digging Deeper:** What do you do to relieve stress? Create a one-page newsletter to share your ideas with the class.

**Figure 21.4** A combination headphone-microphone similar to the one shown here makes it easier to use voice recognition software because your hands remain free at all times.

**Figure 21.5** Voice recognition toolbar such as this one from Dragon NaturallySpeaking provides quick access to all essential functions.

capitals will not be capitalized automatically. Instead, you must instruct the software to capitalize such words.

Use of voice recognition can speed up the creation of the text files you need for all your presentation documents, as well as for other text-based material. It is software that is becoming more valuable as the accuracy and ease of use continues to improve. The future business world could see a time when keyboarding accuracy and speed is no longer as important as the ability to use voice recognition software with ease and accuracy.

## SUMMARY

In this chapter, you learned how to create presentation components such as logos, business cards, letterhead, coupons, and promotional products. You saw how planning ahead by creating maps and information packets can make for more effective communication. You saw how voice recognition technology can be used to simplify the process of converting ideas to text.

**Answer the following questions on your own computer.**

1. What visual design demands are involved when creating a logo?
2. What is the difference between complementary colors and analogous colors?
3. What issues do you face when designing a business card?
4. What connection do logos, business cards, and letterheads have?
5. For what purposes can a coupon be used?
6. Why are promotional items important?
7. What is the design rule for maps?
8. Why should dividers be used in a presentation notebook?
9. Why should you allow extra space at the sides when designing a handout?
10. Why do you have to read passages when you set up voice recognition technology?

DISCUSSION

**Discuss the following questions either as a class or as a written assignment.**

1. How much information should be included in a logo for it to be effective?
2. How do you respond to the colors listed: blue, green, orange, pink, red, yellow?
3. What is your response to a coupon you receive in the mail?
4. What schwag would appeal to you enough to keep it visible on your desk?
5. How much information do you need on a map to reach your destination?

1. Select three logos from products you are familiar with. How many colors are used in each? If more than one color is used, are the colors analogous or complementary? What font is used in the text? What graphics are used? Are these logos basically vertical or horizontal? How "timeless" do they seem to be? Write a short description of each and then compare them to evaluate their effectiveness.

2. Use the Internet to locate three companies that sell promotional products. What types of schwag are available? How much does a typical product cost? Which ones appeal to you? What design options are available? Write a memo recommending the purchase of a promotional product; explain the cost per product, the advantage of the product, and the time it will take for delivery. Include any additional details that appear to be a significant part of the decision process.

3. Compare the features of at least two types of voice recognition software. Create a chart that indicates the differences. In one column, indicate differences that seem significant.

## FURTHER EXPLORATION

Explore the history of voice recognition software. Who first developed it? What problems did they encounter? What is the future of this technology? What additional features would you like to see included? Share your findings with your instructor or class.

# Chapter 22
# Synchronous Communication

**ESTIMATED TIME**
**3**
**H O U R S**

SOURCE: ©EYEWIRE

## INTRODUCTION

**Synchronous** communication occurs in real time. It is the sales presentation you give to a live audience. It is the report you deliver to a committee or group. It is the meeting you hold to discuss a new product. With synchronous communication, you can observe your audience's reaction, answer questions immediately, and get feedback about the information you are providing. In the next chapter, you will read about asynchronous communication, which is the opposite of synchronous communication.

Charlotte Jamison has begun to learn the importance of synchronous communication in her new position selling cosmetics. She has just become a part-time sales consultant working out of her home at night while she continues in her day job as a receptionist at a bank. She decided to see whether she likes

- *You will learn how to manage synchronous communication in a sales presentation.*
- *You will learn the importance of images and reports.*
- *You will learn how to deliver a presentation.*
- *You will learn how to use Pack and Go.*

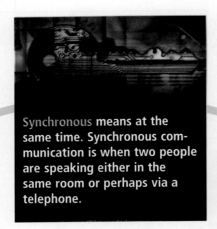

Synchronous means at the same time. Synchronous communication is when two people are speaking either in the same room or perhaps via a telephone.

sales work before committing to sales full time, and this has been a good solution. Until now, her bank position has not required her to do presentations to a group of any size, but as a sales consultant she must now present to both small and large groups. It is an interesting challenge for her, but she is enjoying the chance to build her own business.

# TYPES OF SYNCHRONOUS COMMUNICATION

You have many opportunities to communicate in real time. Any time you are engaged in a conversation with another person, you are participating in an informal synchronous communication. In the business world, interviews, sales presentations, demonstrations, and reports are four important types of synchronous communication and each requires image management skills.

## INTERVIEWS

An interview is one of the most frequent forms of synchronous communication. In order to be hired for any position, you must meet with a perspective employer; this meeting requires you to use your most effective presentation skills. You must keep a number of points in mind if you want a successful interview for employment.

1. Be on time.
2. Dress appropriately.
3. Use the initial handshake and later eye contact to make a good impression.

## THE **ETHICS** OF POLITICAL CORRECTNESS

One issue to keep in mind in any form of communication is political correctness. Political correctness includes use of nongender-specific terms, appropriate ethnic designations, and nondemeaning age designations. Other areas to be aware of include religious affiliations, political alliances, and socioeconomic levels. Political correctness is often discussed as if it were a contrived response to unnecessary demands. This is not the case at all. Care in use of politically correct terms demonstrates that you respect your audience and their point of view. Your ability to communicate to any group will be more successful if you are aware of and use politically correct terms.

Laughter is an essential component of all presentations, making your listeners more comfortable and more interested in what you have to say. However, the use of jokes and humor is a particularly difficult area in which to be politically correct. As a presenter you must measure carefully your audience's response. Avoid humor that ridicules any single group of people.

4. Have your résumé with you even if you have already sent one in advance. Refer to it when indicating information that you want noted and be prepared to answer questions about the information you have included.
5. Be prepared to answer questions that indicate your strengths, your weaknesses, and your ability to contribute to the success of the company.
6. Talk about your accomplishments without inflating them.
7. Be positive, enthusiastic, and confident.
8. Research the position for which you are applying. Indicate your understanding of the company and its product or services.

9. Ask questions that will complete your knowledge of the position for which you are applying. Never respond with a no when you are asked if you have questions.
10. Send a follow-up thank-you note after the initial interview.

## SALES PRESENTATION OR DEMONSTRATION

A sales presentation is one of the most common types of communication that require image management. You must manage your own personal image, the image of your product, and even the image of the location in which the presentation is held. The materials you have developed beforehand, such as logos and business cards, all play a part, but the presentation itself goes beyond that.

Charlotte has a set of business cards with all her information. The cosmetics company she represents gave her a template that only required her to add her personal information; she didn't have to design her own. As a receptionist, she is used to managing her personal image by dressing professionally. However, she has had to find a way to carry her cosmetics samples into homes in such a way that they deliver an effective image.

The most important rule of any sales presentation is to demonstrate the benefit and relevance of the product. You must develop an image that makes that point clear. You must do it with an image of confidence and control. You must project a sense of order, clarity, and credibility.

Charlotte has studied extensively all the information provided by the cosmetics company. She has developed a strong belief that these products are excellent and provide good value for her customers. Because of this belief, it is easy for her to talk to customers about the benefits of her products, and her credibility is demonstrated when she can show them test results comparing her products to the products of other companies.

Your challenge when creating a sales presentation is to determine how to convey these messages. A slide show presentation is one way. A Web site can be another, or you may limit your information to print documents. Remember that no matter what your choice is, you want to communicate, not impress. Customers will not make purchases because you have the flashiest PowerPoint presentation. Customers make purchases because you have a product they need.

## Good Business

### International Business Etiquette

Are you aware how important business cards are in Japan? Would you know what refreshments to offer—and what not to offer—a business associate from Saudi Arabia? Is it appropriate to send a gift to a customer in Germany? Is it expected? Should you express your annoyance if a customer from Mexico arrives late for a business meeting? How hard should you press a client from South Korea for a yes-or-no answer?

More and more companies—particularly cutting-edge, high-tech companies—are doing business with people from other countries. But "doing business" means different things in different countries. Knowing how to treat foreign customers and business associates is not only polite, but it's also good business. It builds trust and shows that you care enough to make them comfortable. Successful business relationships can be fashioned simply by knowing a little bit about the other person's culture.

**Digging Deeper:** Use the Internet to research common business practices in a country of your choice. Create a simple Web page to present your findings.

Jargon is specialized words used within a particular industry, often incorporating acronyms as shortcuts. W3C (World Wide Web Consortium) is an example of an acronym used in the Web design community.

Charlotte has purchased a slide show presentation, as well as print documents, developed by the cosmetics company. She uses a laptop computer to demonstrate before-and-after makeovers, as well as short video clips of the national sales meeting fashion show introducing new products. She doesn't need a projector often because of the one-on-one nature of her business. Occasionally, however, she meets with several women in a party atmosphere, and for that meeting she rents a projector.

Not everyone has the same needs; you must find out what these individual needs are. One way is by asking questions. You must be able to ask and answer questions intelligently as they arise, perhaps in a spur-of-the-moment response. To make this happen, you must manage your list of benefits without the use of **jargon** or terms that can confuse.

In addition, in a global economy, communication is no longer between people from the same region who may have similar needs. You must consider the diverse needs of a global audience.

Charlotte is very aware of the change to a global economy because of her experience at the bank, where she daily answers calls from other countries. Even in her new business, she has several customers who have moved into her community from these countries. As a result, she has learned that the questions she gets are often different from one culture to another. She is proud that she has learned how to deal with the unexpected and has learned how to address the needs of each customer.

When creating your presentations, you must keep all these elements in mind. Ask yourself what images clarify, what colors promote the response you want, and what typestyle and size make it easiest for your audience to understand the message. Bringing together all you have learned in image management is a way to do all this and more.

SOURCE: ©PHOTODISC

## REPORT

Another form of communication is a report. Reports can be presented in person (synchronously) or as a submitted document. Synchronous reports differ from sales presentations in that generally they are given to an audience within an organization rather than outside an organization. A synchronous report requires presentation skills similar to the ones you use in a sales presentation, and you have the same image management tools at hand such as a slide show and handouts.

What is different is your audience's need, which is to gather information. You have information they want to know. Your challenge is to provide that information as succinctly as possible. A report requires the ability to summarize key points, list relevant details, and help your audience draw a conclusion. Just as with a sales presentation, however, you must deliver your presentation with a sense of order, clarity, and credibility.

Charlotte meets once a month with other sales consultants to report their successes. This is a way to help others benefit from what each has learned. Her report is brief, but in it she outlines a situation she has encountered, explains what she did to address the problem, and then explains the outcome. A short question session follows her report. She has experimented with different ways to present her information, including a short slide show, but now she usually provides a printed handout. Several other consultants have commented that they have found several of her reports to be quite valuable.

SOURCE: ©PHOTODISC

## DELIVERY

You may create a fine presentation in isolation, but the delivery is the deciding factor in its success. One essential means of improving delivery is to send your audience the message that you are organized. One way you can convey this sense of order in your delivery is to rehearse your presentation, paying particular attention to timing, movement, and even the lighting.

Timing can be as simple as knowing when to start and stop, or it may be more complex, including details such as when to ask for questions. Movement includes details such as where in the room you will deliver the presentation and how you will move there. It also might include concerns such as when and how to hand out materials. Lighting is always an important consideration when using projectors. It is often necessary to dim or turn off lights. Make sure you know how doing so will affect the room. Make sure you also know where the controls are. As simple as this seems, fumbling for a switch can ruin even a well-prepared presentation.

In addition, keep in mind the following points:

- If you are using a projector, make sure you know how to set it up.
- If you are using a laptop, you may have to toggle between the laptop screen and the projection screen in order to see both displays.
- Check that your presentation can be seen from all points in the room.
- If you are using sound, make sure it is loud enough. Remember that an empty room will echo sound that will be absorbed when people are in the room.
- Make sure all the files needed in your presentation are on your laptop or CD. A presentation that works fine on the computer on which you created it may not work as well on another if files such as sound are not included.

Charlotte has learned the hard way how important delivery is. Even though she knows she has a product that sells itself, when she first began meeting with customers she spent several disorganized minutes setting up her cosmetics and connecting her laptop. She always thought it was wasted time and didn't provide the impression she wanted. She has now learned to display her products quickly and easily no matter what the setting is. Sometimes it is a kitchen where no electrical outlet is nearby. Sometimes she is perched on an overstuffed chair in a living room, using only her lap.

SOURCE: ©PHOTODISC

## PACK AND GO

One technology tool available to you in presentation software such as PowerPoint is the **Pack and Go** feature. With this wizard, shown in Figure 22.1, you can create a PowerPoint presentation and package it to be placed on media such as a floppy disk, a CD, a laptop hard drive, or even a USB device. Once you are ready to use the presentation, you can click on the packed presentation to play it easily because all essential files such as type, sound, and graphics are included. In addition, a player can be

**Figure 22.1** The Pack and Go wizard makes it easy to compress your PowerPoint slide show.

included so that it is not necessary to have specific software on the computer from which it is being displayed.

Charlotte has received several of the corporate-produced slide shows in a Pack and Go format. She downloaded these files using her modem, which would be very time-consuming without the compression features. Recently, she created a PowerPoint presentation of her own, using photographs she took with a digital camera; she then packaged it and gave it to another consultant to use.

## SUMMARY

In this chapter, you learned ways to use image management skills in presentations and reports to create synchronous communication. You looked at ways to ensure that your delivery is successful. In addition, you looked at Pack and Go, a technology tool that simplifies the process of transferring a presentation to another computer.

**Pack and Go is a feature of Microsoft PowerPoint that compresses a presentation for ease of transfer to another computer. It may also include a reader that lets you view the presentation even if you do not have PowerPoint on your computer.**

**Answer the following questions on your own computer.**

1. When does synchronous communication occur?
2. How does image management relate to synchronous communication?
3. What is the most important rule of a sales presentation?
4. What image must you develop for a sales presentation?
5. Why do customers make purchases?
6. Give two examples of ways to create a presentation that communicates benefits.
7. What is the focus of a report?
8. What does an audience need in a report?
9. When checking for sound in a room before a presentation, what concern should you have?
10. What is the advantage of using the Pack and Go feature in PowerPoint?

## DISCUSSION

**Discuss the following questions either as a class or as a written assignment.**

1. What is your response to someone who admits in a presentation that she or he is not prepared?
2. When would jargon be appropriate in a presentation?
3. How would you respond to a presentation handout that is a poor photocopy with misspelled words and dense text?
4. How long should a report last?
5. What was the best presentation you have ever seen? What made it memorable, and what set it apart from others you may have seen?

1. Choose a product you would like to sell. It can be a product that is on the market or one that you create. List three benefits that make this product valuable to a customer. List five questions a customer might ask about this product, and supply answers to these questions.

2. Create a short slide show (at least five slides) or Web page you could use in a sales presentation, as well as a print handout. Include the three benefits and at least two answers to the questions you addressed.

3. Give a three- to five-minute sales presentation using your materials. Be sure to demonstrate order, clarity, and credibility during your presentation.

4. When all the sales presentations are complete, gather into groups of five members. Each person in the group should report on his or her presentation, explaining the following: problems encountered, solutions, and results. One member from the group should record this information. A second member should enter the notes into a compiled report incorporating the information. A third member should create a brief handout as an overview of the results. A fourth member should present the findings in a report to the entire class. The fifth member should field questions from the class.

5. As a member of the report audience, direct at least one question to the individual group report.

Research the concept of political correctness. When did the term first appear and in what situation? What is considered politically correct? Find examples of situations in which someone has not spoken in a politically correct manner. Give details of the consequences. Write a policy statement for a business that outlines what is politically correct for this business.

# Chapter 23
# Asynchronous Communication

SOURCE: ©PHOTODISC

## Objectives

- *You will learn how to manage the image of a résumé.*
- *You will learn what to include in a business plan.*
- *You will learn the importance of a kiosk.*
- *You will learn how an interactive CD-ROM can be used in asynchronous communication.*
- *You will learn how to burn a CD.*

## INTRODUCTION

Although you may think of most presentations as being "eyeball-to-eyeball," many more will be **asynchronous,** meaning that your presentation will have to make your points for you because you will not be there. Asynchronous communication can occur when a visitor to your Web site reads about your latest product. It might happen during a kiosk display of a Power-Point presentation. It can also happen when a banker reads your bound business plan or a potential employer reads your résumé.

David Wallace, a pharmacist, has learned how to use asynchronous communication effectively. His job is not your typical behind-the-counter position seen as the role of pharmacists in previous generations. Today he and many other pharmacists actively interact with those who bring prescriptions to be filled. Frequently, he must help them understand the importance of completing the dosage schedule and returning for follow-ups. He must also help them understand side effects and interactions with other medications.

# TYPES OF ASYNCHRONOUS COMMUNICATION

## RÉSUMÉ

A résumé is a sales tool. Instead of selling a company's product, you are selling yourself. And you must often do the selling in an asynchronous mode. Your only means of making the sale is through the pages you create. Everything you have already learned about typography, color, and paper choices will apply, but there is one more essential tool. The nature of a résumé is that it must be brief. You do not have the luxury of page after page demonstrating your skills and abilities. You must find a way to convey your message in as few words as possible. Use of bullets and short points is the standard means of succeeding at this, as shown in Figure 23.1.

A résumé should include the following:

- Job objective
- Educational experience
- Job experience, including brief descriptions of your contributions
- Recognition and awards
- Organizations and activities that demonstrate your skills and interests
- References (either listed or indicated as available)

With the introduction of Web and CD résumés, it is now possible to create one with links that can supplement your primary résumé with additional information. Although this is useful and to your advantage, the initial page must still be condensed. Do not rush the preparation of your résumé. Allow plenty of time to gather information, and after you are finished encourage others to critique it for you. Check for errors in both details and spelling. Errors send the wrong message about your attention to detail.

David used his image management skills before he even took the position he currently

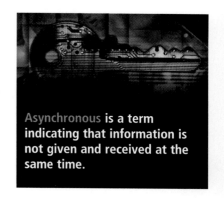

Asynchronous **is a term indicating that information is not given and received at the same time.**

## Good Business

### Résumé Skills

Think of your résumé as a marketing tool—and the product being marketed is you! Your résumé will likely be your first contact with a prospective employer, so strive to make a good first impression. Avoid grammatical mistakes, rambling descriptions, irrelevant personal information, and questions about salary. And above all, be honest.

Well-produced résumés emphasize the future, not the past. They focus on what you have done and what you want to do for the employer. Your résumé should stress the job you are seeking, your applicable skills, your accomplishments, your previous employment, and your education and training. Electronic résumés—résumés that can be delivered to prospective employers via the Internet—are becoming increasingly popular. An e-résumé would enable a graphic designer, for example, to include a link directing a prospective employer to her Web site, where samples of her design work can be examined.

**Digging Deeper:** Using the skills you have learned in this class, create a résumé that will help you get an entry-level job in the multimedia-related field of your choice. If necessary, use the Internet or library to learn more about résumés before you begin. Have your instructor critique your résumé.

**Figure 23.1** Résumés need to be easy to read and succinct in the presentation.

Education
- Vocational Endorsement                                                          July 1996
- Information Processing Technology EXCET                                         May 1996
- M. A. in English                              Texas Tech University              1977
- B. A. in English                              Texas Technological College        1969

Professional  Experience
- Lubbock-Cooper I. S. D.
  - District Technology Education Specialist (central office)    2000 - present
  - Computer Education Teacher (high school)                     1996 - 2000
    - Business Computer Information Systems
    - Desktop Publishing
    - Multimedia
    - Web Mastering
    - Computer Maintenance and Repair
  - English Teacher (high school)                                1992 - 1996
  - Public Relations Coordinator (central office)                1987 - 1992
  - English, History, and Journalism Teacher (high school)      1979 - 1987

Publications
- South-Western Educational Publishing Co.        Cincinnati, Ohio
  - *Multimedia: Ten Hour Series* (author)                                      2002
  - *E-Terms: A Dictionary for the 21st Century* (fee writer)                   2001
  - *Scheduling with Outlook: Ten Hour Series* (author)                        2001
  - *Electronic Mail: Ten Hour Series* (author)                                2000
  - *Desktop Publishing: Ten Hour Series* (author)                             1999
  - *Microsoft Publisher 3.0/97: QuickTorial* (consulting editor)              1997
  - *PageMaker 6.0 for Windows 95 and Macintosh: Quicktorial* (fee writer)     1996
  - *PageMaker 5.0 for Windows 95 and Macintosh: Quicktorial* (fee writer)     1995
  - *Express Publisher: Tutorial and Applications* (fee writer)                1994
- Eagle Press                                     Beaufort, South Carolina
  - *Unit Based Planning: A Handbook for English Teachers* (author)            1993

holds by creating a CD résumé as well as a printed version. On the CD, he included his résumé, but David also added a clip demonstrating his counseling technique and samples of instructional material he has developed. The résumé has links to several articles he has written for pharmaceutical journals and awards he has received. He has also created a link to an online résumé that he can add to whenever necessary.

David's ability to use multimedia tools impressed his potential employer, who was looking for someone who could go beyond the traditional role of a pharmacist. His CD résumé made it clear to them that he had these skills.

## BUSINESS PLAN

A business plan allows you to think through all the issues relevant to the creation of a new business. The plan can develop interest in the business and help secure financing for it. The image your plan projects is essential to its success. A sloppily bound, visually unappealing document will seriously limit acceptance of your new venture. Remember that you will not be there to make an impression—your document must speak for you. A well-developed plan may include the following:

- A cover or title page
- A table of contents
- An overview of the plan
- Information about your business experience (perhaps in a résumé format)
- An analysis of the market, including strengths and weaknesses
- Strategies for success
- Financial information, including profit potential and projected income

A **kiosk** is a freestanding computer used by visitors.

In your plan, keep in mind all the issues you would address if you were there. Build in answers to the questions the reader might ask. Be politically correct and globally aware. Use informational images to make your points clear. Think about the impact of color and paper choice. Consider your audience. Does your reader expect your presentation to be formal or more creative? All the questions you have learned to ask about image management apply in this situation.

Once Dave was hired he did not need to create a business plan, but he was expected to create a report that told his employers what his plans were. He had to consider strategies, costs, and benefits in order to get approval for the ideas he had. He carefully analyzed the market and the customer base. He looked at what other in-house pharmacies had to offer and how offering more could increase traffic and sales. His employers saw that his plan was well researched and gave him approval to proceed with the changes he wanted.

## KIOSK DEMONSTRATION

A **kiosk** version of a sales demonstration is becoming more common. A kiosk is a freestanding computer display that is considered robotic in nature because it communicates and interacts with a user.

Kiosks are of two types: passive and interactive. A passive kiosk uses software such as PowerPoint that has been designed to run continuously without user intervention. Each slide is timed to move at the pace you have selected. Kiosks of this type are used in such places as museums and stores. The issue with this type of demonstration is that you must anticipate how fast your

## THE **ETHICS** OF RÉSUMÉS

Résumés create ethical dilemmas for many people. The nature of a résumé requires you to demonstrate your skills in the most positive way possible. The question becomes how you can do that without distorting the truth. For example, if one week out of the year while your employer was on vacation you were responsible for receiving shipments and recording the inventory, can you indicate on a résumé that you had that responsibility without indicating the limited duration?

A more important issue is complete fabrication of information such as schools attended or degrees earned. Statistics indicate that this deception is a chronic problem in the résumés received by many potential employees.

In the first example, you actually had the experience and presumably acquired skills as a result, even if for a short time. In the second situation, no judgment is needed. This is clearly wrong.

Not only is lying on a résumé ethically wrong, in the long run it can destroy a career when the falsehood is discovered. Search for ways to maximize your image, but avoid including any information that is untrue.

**Figure 23.2** Kiosks are becoming common methods of supplying information, even money, using an interactive computer. The design of their screens requires image management knowledge to encourage ease of use.

audience will read the material, how much material they are willing to read, and how long you can hold their attention. This is an image management situation in which flashy can be an important addition. Sound and video can also be used effectively as a means of conveying information without requiring the audience to read. If sound is too intrusive, however, personnel who work near the demonstration and must listen to it continuously may disable this feature.

An interactive kiosk allows the user to make selections, often with a touch screen. Your audience can find information and even print it out. Kiosks of this type are used in such places as libraries, gift registries, and information booths. Perhaps the most common kiosks are automated bank teller machines, similar to the one shown in Figure 23.2. The image design issues here are related to ease of use. Mice and keyboards are replaced with touch screen buttons. These buttons must emit sounds to indicate to the user that he or she has interacted with the display screen. The process must be easy to use and intuitive. Hardware issues become a major concern to ensure that the kiosk always works.

David had installed a kiosk that allows his customers to print out information of interest to them. He provided a series of diets for a variety of needs, warning signs for various illnesses, and a schedule of immunization requirements. He also included a blank printout for patients to use to list their medications and dosages. He knows that his elderly patients are often on many drugs and cannot provide this essential information quickly when they enter the hospital or visit a physician. This kiosk has become very popular and he plans to continue adding information as it becomes available.

## INTERACTIVE CD-ROM

Another form of asynchronous communication can be through an interactive CD-ROM. This medium can be distributed and installed on a user's computer to provide information, to answer questions, or to provide a demonstration. It becomes a personal kiosk that can be a great sales tool. An interactive CD can allow users to view all the features of a product at their leisure. It is even possible to create a package that enables users to view the same product with different enhancements. For example, suppose you are selling sweaters in several colors; rather than show six different sweaters on the same page, you can enable users to select the sweater color of their choice.

SOURCE: ©PHOTODISC

Interactive CDs can be created with a wide variety of software packages. You can create a Web page that can be viewed without an Internet connection. You can include a PowerPoint presentation, or you can use specialized authoring software. Regardless of the software you choose, image management will play a significant part in the design.

One part of David's plan was to create a separate kiosk center that could be used by customers as they waited for their prescriptions to be filled. David didn't anticipate doing the actual kiosk design, but he did know what he wanted. He knew that these "waiting" minutes could be a valuable tool to get information to his customers. He created a series of designs that included material provided by drug companies as well as those provided by the Food and Drug Administration. Many of the presentations only required a Web link to a demonstration that had already been created. Others he had to have designed for him.

In addition, he has learned that this kiosk can be used as a counseling tool when he needs to work with a patient. The screen and prepackaged content means that he does not have to set up a separate area. One thing he and his patients also like is that returning to the kiosk for a refresher is easy. David anticipates a growing interest in this use of multimedia technology in his field.

## CD CREATION

One of the most common ways to distribute asynchronous communication is on CDs (compact disks). Unlike the process used to transfer

data to a floppy disk, copying information to a CD requires "burning" the data to the disk. The burning process requires special software that is usually supplied by the manufacturer of the CD burner, such as Easy CD Creator (originally marketed by Adaptec but now owned by Roxio). Writable CDs fall into two categories: CD-R and CD-RW. CD-R disks do not allow information to be removed once it has been written; CD-RW disks can be erased and written again. CD-R disks are much less expensive than CD-RW, and so they are the type most often used.

When copying data to a disk, several variations are possible. You can encode data, music, or a mixture of the two. CD writing software makes a distinction between the two and will ask you what type of information you are copying. In addition, for a CD to be read by all CD readers, you must take a step to close the CD. Every CD writer has a different way of allowing this, and as a final step in the burning process you will often be asked you if you want this option. Some CD-writing software now allows you to set up a CD so that data can be transferred by dragging documents to the CD, much as you would with a floppy disk. This makes it easier to use a CD for storage purposes, but once again, before the CD can be read by another reader, a closing step must be performed.

The speed at which you burn information to a CD is important. Older CD readers cannot read disks recorded at a high speed. Some older writers cannot burn a CD at the high speed modern disks allow. It becomes a juggling act to determine what speed and what kind of CD will be most appropriate for your equipment. If you are unsure what speed to use, 4× will generally serve most purposes. One way you can ensure that your disk will burn successfully is to allow your burner to test the CD before beginning. Although this step adds to the time it takes to create a CD, it helps prevent *coasters*, or unusable CDs.

The next generation of disks is the DVDs (digital versatile disc or digital video disc), which are similar to older CDs but are faster and can hold more data. The ability to copy and write to DVDs is not as common today, but you can anticipate that in time the versatility of this medium will replace standard CDs.

## SUMMARY

In this chapter, you learned about various means of communicating in an asynchronous manner. These means included résumés and business plans, usually distributed in print, and kiosks and interactive CD-ROM disks, which are hardware solutions. You also learned how CDs can be created as a means of copying the information used in asynchronous communication.

Answer the following questions on your own computer.

1. What is the limitation of asynchronous communication?
2. Why is a résumé a sales tool?
3. What is the one essential component of a résumé?
4. What happens when you have spelling errors in a résumé?
5. What are two uses of a business plan?
6. What is one way you can answer questions that come up while someone else is reading your business plan?
7. What are the two types of kiosks?
8. What are some of the problems you face when trying to design a passive kiosk?
9. What is the design issue when considering how people use an interactive kiosk?
10. What is a time advantage of an interactive CD-ROM?

Discuss the following questions either as a class or as a written assignment.

1. What skills do you need to create an effective résumé?
2. Why is a written business plan used instead of a direct plan?
3. What kinds of kiosks have you used? What did you like and dislike about them?
4. If an interactive CD-ROM arrives in the mail as a sales presentation, do you install it onto your computer? Why or why not? How can the business ensure that more people will install it?

1. **Create a résumé for a movie character of your choice. Be sure to select a character you know enough about to be able to include a complete résumé. For areas about which you know no details, make up information that can be supported from what you do know.**

2. **For this same character, select a business venture he or she might want to start. Create a business plan from the information you have or can logically support. Include the character's résumé in the plan.**

3. **Include in the business plan a description of a kiosk you could use as a means of enhancing the business.**

4. **Convert the business plan into a PDF document.**

5. **Copy this information to a CD.**

**Research kiosks. Find out how much a kiosk costs to establish and maintain. Find out what kinds of software options are available to use to develop software. Find out what physical options are available. Find information on the growth of the use of kiosks in national and international business. Use the information you have found to write a report that predicts the future of kiosks.**

# Chapter 24

## Video Communication

**ESTIMATED TIME**

**3 HOURS**

SOURCE: ©DIGITAL VISION

## INTRODUCTION

One of the most interesting changes in business communication has been the movement to the use of video. Video can be used to provide both synchronous and asynchronous communication. Synchronous communication can be used to hold video conferences or even video sales demonstrations. Asynchronous communication with video can be used on a Web page or on an interactive CD.

Sarah Volcancik never saw herself as a movie producer. She had done some work with multimedia while in school, but video seemed out of her realm of expectations. That was the case until she took a position as the director of patient records for five hospitals. Each of these hospitals is located in a remote area and has joined a consortium to cut costs in the maintenance of

## Objectives

- *You will learn ways to improve your presentation during a video conference.*
- *You will learn other ways to use video for communication.*
- *You will learn options to incorporate video for different presentation modes.*
- *You will learn about the tools used to create videos.*

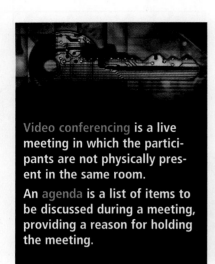

patient records. Sarah must meet with several contacts at each hospital at least once a week.

# VIDEO CONFERENCING

**Video conferencing** is a live meeting between two or more people who are not in the same location. A video camera or Web cam is used to span the distance between the members attending the meeting. These conferences may be meetings held at regular intervals for co-workers who work in different cities, or they may be single events held for participants who have not met previously. The same issues one must address in holding a meeting in which everyone is in the same room apply to video conferencing, but with additional image management concerns.

Initially, Sarah was spending hours traveling to each of the hospitals for which she was providing services. Often she found that the same problems were appearing in more than one location and she wished for a way to have all the members of the consortium meet on a regular basis. Video conferencing turned out to be the answer.

## PREPARATION

If you are responsible for setting up a video conference, one essential item to include in your preparation is an **agenda.** An agenda should include the following:

- Name of the group
- Date and starting/ending times
- Means of making the video connection (indicate any special setups necessary for the user's computer)

SOURCE: ©PHOTODISC

- Purpose of the meeting
- List of those invited to attend (include a short informational paragraph about each person if appropriate)
- Items to be addressed (include approximate time and name of person responsible for providing information)

In live meetings in which not all members may know each other, name tags or nameplates are usually used. In video conferencing, such identification may not be as easily accomplished. If you do use name tags, they must be large enough to be visible onscreen. A possible solution is to include a digital photograph on the agenda of each person invited.

Sarah's first video conference required considerable preparation. Everyone was rather nervous about the use of new technology, but the setup and implementation went well. She kept the agenda short for the first meeting, knowing that introductions and adjustments would take up more time initially.

## CLOTHING

If you do participate in a video conference, consider the color of the clothes you select. Although professional dress is always appropriate, within that category certain colors are more effective onscreen than others. There are actually more "don'ts" than "do's" in your color selection. Your best choice is shirts or blouses in solid pastels with darker pants or skirt. For best result, it is helpful to do a "trial run" to observe how your color choices will appear onscreen.

Avoid the following:

- Bright colors such as red, because they tend to "bleed" onscreen
- White, because it can cause you to be "lost" in the image
- Patterns such as checks and stripes
- Clothing that is all one color, particularly those that are very light or very dark, because the camera will respond to the predominant color, making you appear washed out or in shadow

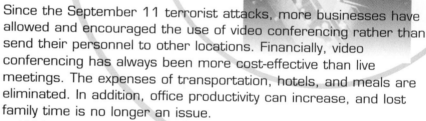

## THE **ETHICS** OF VIDEO CONFERENCES

Since the September 11 terrorist attacks, more businesses have allowed and encouraged the use of video conferencing rather than send their personnel to other locations. Financially, video conferencing has always been more cost-effective than live meetings. The expenses of transportation, hotels, and meals are eliminated. In addition, office productivity can increase, and lost family time is no longer an issue.

With all the advantages, it would seem that most meetings should be held in this way. The issue, though not one of right or wrong, is one of effectiveness. Although business personnel time is increased, personal contact with the other members of the meeting is lost. There are advantages to meeting people in person. It is easier to understand other people's cultures, beliefs, and points of view when you see them in their own environment. In addition, video conferences are rather rigidly controlled. There is little time for friendly exchanges before or after the meeting that can often pave the way for later conversations or smooth over possible conflicts.

One often unspoken concern about video conferences is the permanence. In live meetings, what is said is often not recorded other than by notes. In a video conference, this is not the case. A comment you might not want recorded can easily be distributed to those who you would rather not have access to this information. For this reason, it is important to have a policy about the archiving of video conferences so that all members will be comfortable in providing whatever information is essential for the meeting to be effective.

Sarah advised the participants in advance that certain clothing colors would make them less visible. Several of her contacts usually wore white lab coats and she was concerned about this. She suggested they might want to check this on their equipment to see if it was a problem.

## MOVEMENT

Cameras used in video conferencing have a limited range of motion, so restrict movement to a very small area. Also avoid the use of hands while speaking. Although use of hands may be effective in "live" exchanges, it is less so in a video conference.

The need to restrict movement can easily make a speaker appear to be a **talking head,** which can be quite boring. One way to avoid this is to limit the amount of time any one person speaks. Long presentations should be broken up by comments or additions from other speakers or by the use of graphics such as charts, bulleted lists, or other informational pieces. Technology tools such as whiteboards or Smart Boards can be used effectively for demonstration purposes.

It took several meetings before the participants began to learn how to respond to the movement issues. Initially some members of the consortium moved too rigidly and some too much. Within a short time, however, they all adjusted to the new technology.

## SOUND

In a video conference, sound becomes an important consideration. You must keep distractions to a minimum even more so than if you

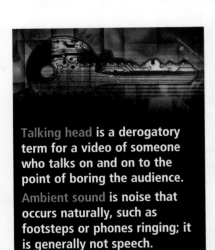

**Talking head** is a derogatory term for a video of someone who talks on and on to the point of boring the audience.

**Ambient sound** is noise that occurs naturally, such as footsteps or phones ringing; it is generally not speech.

were attending the meeting in person. Turn off cell and land phones. Avoid rooms that echo or that will be subjected to outside noises. Avoid distracting sounds such as pencil tapping, coughing, or a squeaking chair. These become magnified by the microphone, which picks up all **ambient sound** as well as speech.

Don't interrupt the person speaking. Although such interruptions may not be a problem in "live" exchanges, the **lag time** between transmittal of sound in a video conference makes interruption awkward. Wait for an appropriate moment to interject your comments.

## VISUALS

If you use visuals, image management decisions become very important. Choose the type size and style that will make the information easy to read on a computer screen. Choose colors that will increase visibility. If you are creating a chart, limit the essential details. If you are using a bulleted list, limit the number of points to three. Use wide margins to ensure that part of your visual is not cut off.

Remember that your audience may not have your visual available to refer to later. Rather than returning to your visual several times, complete all references to it before moving on to another point.

Sarah used visuals in her video conference, but she also sent copies in advance to the consortium. This way each person would have a copy on which to make notes and to refer to as they met. Often she emailed a copy that they could print out before the meeting. She still adhered to the policy of completing a discussion of a visual rather than moving back to it several times. She discovered that video conferencing does not provide the same visual cues one gets in a live demonstration. When using visuals, she was particularly aware of this problem.

## OTHER VIDEO USES

The same rules used in video conferencing apply to other forms of synchronous use of video, with one important consideration. The nature of video conferencing is that all members are expected to provide input and to be part of the interactive event. Other uses of video often are more one-sided, such as in a sales

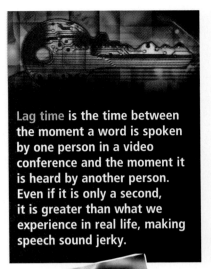

**Lag time** is the time between the moment a word is spoken by one person in a video conference and the moment it is heard by another person. Even if it is only a second, it is greater than what we experience in real life, making speech sound jerky.

# Good Business

## Communication Skills

In the workplace, you need the ability to communicate your ideas clearly. Customers and co-workers must be able to understand you. They will have difficulty doing so if you use vague or incorrect language or if you use unfamiliar words and phrases.

Use grown-up language on the job, with both customers and co-workers. You'll be more likely to be treated as an adult if you talk like one. In written communications, check and double-check your spelling and grammar. Errors signal that you do not care enough about your work to do a good job. A company's image—particularly a multimedia company, whose very existence revolves around communicating—can be severely damaged by employees who do not use language properly.

**Digging Deeper:** Examine advertisements, company signs and billboards, and other business-related communications for spelling and grammatical errors. Create a presentation highlighting your findings. (If possible, include scans of the advertisements, digital photos of the signs, and so on.) Did the errors affect your opinion of these businesses?

demonstration or other forms of instruction. In these situations, it is particularly important to be aware of the "talking head" problem. To be more effective, find ways to encourage those watching to interact—perhaps with questions directed to them.

Use of video on a CD-ROM or a Web page does not allow for live interactions. As a result, video information on these media should be designed carefully. Limit use of talking heads to only a few minutes at a time. Include graphics, sound, and other visuals as often as possible. Even the simplest use of interaction, such as having the user click on a Continue button, will increase the effectiveness of the presentation by engaging your audience.

Sarah found another use for video that simplified her job. She quickly learned that members of the consortium changed frequently, which required her to bring the new participants up to date. She used short clips from some of the video conferences as well as prepared demonstration clips to provide each new member with "live" information. She found that in a 20-minute streaming video she could cover far more information than in several print packets.

## DELIVERY

Videos can be created with a variety of camera options such as an analog video camera, a digital video camera, or even a simple Web cam. For use on a computer, analog video must be converted to digital with special hardware and software. Digital video can be transferred directly to the computer in the format in which it is created by using a connection such as **FireWire** (also known as IEEE 1394). Web cams plug directly into a computer and are inexpensive and simple to use. Even today, computers are being marketed with built-in Web cams to simplify the process of video exchange between two people.

As video conferencing and other forms of synchronous communication become more common, businesses will be able to provide more professional means of delivery, including specially designed rooms that can send out video of such high quality that this type of exchange will seem more like meetings held in one's presence. Streaming video already reduces the lag time between one person speaking and another hearing the conversation. The use of video promises to be one of the most important forms of communication in the future, and the ability to manage effectively all components by using multimedia skills will become just as important. Meanwhile, setup and delivery can be quite demanding, with a different set of technical requirements in every situation.

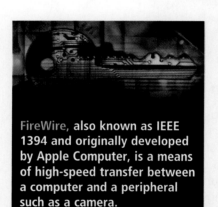

FireWire, also known as IEEE 1394 and originally developed by Apple Computer, is a means of high-speed transfer between a computer and a peripheral such as a camera.

## VIDEO PRODUCTION

Creation of a video requires knowledge of many of the tools you have already studied, such as graphics, sound, and animation. To create a

SOURCE: ©PHOTODISC

video requires you to pull together these and other skills. A video integrates all these activities into a single event that often requires high-end computer hardware and software. Adobe Premiere, Macromedia Director, Ulead VideoStudio, Final Cut Pro, iMovie, and MGI VideoWave are software video editing packages often used by businesses. In addition, Microsoft Windows XP has a limited editing program—MovieMaker—provided as a utility program.

When you open image editing software, you will see a series of options to choose based on what format you intend to work (see Figure 24.1). The numerous options are based on audio quality, size of screen, and format. Some formats you will encounter are PAL, NTSC, SECAM, and QuickTime. PAL (Phase Alternating Line) and SECAM (sysème electronique couleur avec memoire) are formats used in Europe. NTSC (National Television Standards Committee) is an American standard. QuickTime is a standard developed by Apple Computer.

Videos are actually a series of still images linked together along a continuous path. Because each image or frame is projected only briefly, the images appear to be moving. As a result, one significant issue is the tracking of frames within a video, for each frame represents a point much like pixels in a still image. Because generally there are 30 frames in each second of video, rather than noting individual frames, you track each second of video. When the video is recorded, a **timecode** is set as each second passes. It is often important to keep track of your start and stop timecode to know what segments you

A timecode is a means of tracking groups of frames within a video.

**Figure 24.1** Video editing software requires you to make initial choices about the format in which you intend to work.

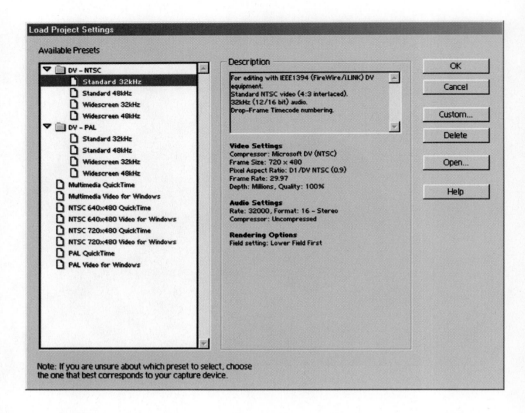

Load Project Settings

Available Presets

- DV – NTSC
  - Standard 32kHz
  - Standard 48kHz
  - Widescreen 32kHz
  - Widescreen 48kHz
- DV – PAL
  - Standard 32kHz
  - Standard 48kHz
  - Widescreen 32kHz
  - Widescreen 48kHz
- Multimedia QuickTime
- Multimedia Video for Windows
- NTSC 640x480 QuickTime
- NTSC 640x480 Video for Windows
- NTSC 720x480 QuickTime
- NTSC 720x480 Video for Windows
- PAL QuickTime
- PAL Video for Windows

Description

For editing with IEEE1394 (FireWire/iLINK) DV equipment.
Standard NTSC video (4:3 interlaced).
32kHz (12/16 bit) audio.
Drop–Frame Timecode numbering.

**Video Settings**
Compressor: Microsoft DV (NTSC)
Frame Size: 720 x 480
Pixel Aspect Ratio: D1/DV NTSC (0.9)
Frame Rate: 29.97
Depth: Millions, Quality: 100%

**Audio Settings**
Rate: 32000, Format: 16 – Stereo
Compressor: Uncompressed

**Rendering Options**
Field setting: Lower Field First

OK    Cancel    Custom...    Delete    Open...    Help

Note: If you are unsure about which preset to select, choose the one that best corresponds to your capture device.

SOURCE: ©PHOTODISC

particularly want. Just as you used keyframes in working with animation software, you will also use keyframes in video to indicate changes in clips or audio. Figure 24.2 is an example of the timeline used in a video editing program to track events.

Videos can be edited in interesting ways, including transition effects and fades similar to those you learned to used in slide show presentations. You can cut and paste segments to enhance the effectiveness of your video, as well as to remove material that is not significant. Once a video has been completed, you will export it from its native format into one that can be read by the anticipated software. The export process uses compression algorithms similar to the ones used to create JPG images, making the file sizes smaller to increase transmission speed. Your choice of export format may be based not only on soft-

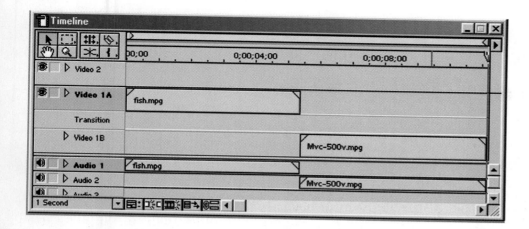

**Figure 24.2** Video timelines track both the visual and audio portions of the movie.

ware options but also on means of delivery. In some instances, it may be necessary to export in a variety of formats to meet every need. Video is a growing field of image management that requires you to stay aware of the frequent changes in the industry.

## SUMMARY

In this chapter, you learned how to present yourself most effectively in video conferencing. This includes preparation, choice of clothing, restriction of movement, and use of sound and visuals. In addition, you learned other uses of video, as well as ways to deliver and create video.

Answer the following questions on your own computer.

1. What is the difference between an ordinary conference and a video conference?
2. What is one essential item to include when preparing a video conference?
3. What is often used in ordinary meetings that is difficult to duplicate in a video conference?
4. What is your best choice of clothing during a video conference?
5. What happens when you use bright colors such as red in a video conference?
6. Why should you restrict movement during a video conference?
7. What problem can restricted movement possibly create in a video conference?
8. What is ambient sound?
9. What is the one image management issue that you face when creating visuals for a video conference?
10. What is expected of everyone who attends a video conference?
11. What is FireWire?
12. What programs can be used to edit video?
13. How are images made to appear to be moving in a video?
14. How many frames are generally included in a second of video?
15. What is a timecode?

DISCUSSION

Discuss the following questions either as a class or as a written assignment.

1. Why is an agenda important when you have a video conference or any other kind of meeting?
2. What happens if someone wears as color such a white during a video conference? Why does it happen?
3. Why are talking heads boring?
4. What problems does lag time cause during a video conference?
5. Why is interaction so important during asynchronous communication?

1. Create an agenda for a meeting between the character you selected in the previous chapter, yourself, another student in class, and the character that student selected. The meeting will be a discussion of ways the group can form a working team.

2. Create a visual for use in the meeting that demonstrates the strengths of each team member; use either a chart or a graph.

3. If you have a Web cam or a video camera, record yourself welcoming everyone to the meeting and introducing each member. Be sure to dress appropriately. If you can transmit the image, create a live conference with the other member in class.

4. Watch the tape, listening for ambient sound. Write a review of the effectiveness of your welcome. Include comments about your appearance, noise problems, quality of transmission, and visibility of the visual you created.

5. Create a short edited video of the meeting. Use techniques such as transitions and fades to enhance the effectiveness of the presentation.

FURTHER
EXPLORATION

Find out what is involved in creating streaming video, including software and hardware options. List the advantages of streaming video over other types. Write a letter to the members of your class, explaining to them the advantages and disadvantages.

# Unit 6: Summary

## Key Concepts

## Chapter 21: Communication Preparation

1. The nature of logos is that they are simple and symbolic; they send a message through the image.
2. Color theory consists of understanding the relationship of color by using a color wheel.
3. A business card should be simple, be easy to read, and have significant white space.
4. Logos, business cards, and letterhead are frequently designed as a package to establish an identity for a company.
5. When designing a map, eliminate as many details as possible; leave only essential information.
6. A pre-press check ensures that fonts, images, and other elements are present and available for use by the printing company producing the document.
7. Use of voice recognition can speed up the creation of the text files you need for all your presentation documents, as well as for other text-based material.

## Chapter 22: Synchronous Communication

1. The most important rule of any sales presentation is to demonstrate the benefit and relevance of the product.
2. A report requires the ability to summarize key points, list relevant details, and help your audience draw a conclusion.
3. One essential means of improving delivery is to send your audience the message that you are organized.
4. Pack and Go is a feature of Microsoft PowerPoint that compresses a presentation for ease of transfer to another computer.

## Chapter 23: Asynchronous Communication

1. The nature of a résumé is that it must be brief.
2. A business plan can develop interest in the business and help secure financing for it.
3. A kiosk is a freestanding computer display that is considered robotic because it communicates and interacts with a user.
4. Interactive CD-ROMs can be distributed and installed on a user's computer to provide information, to answer questions, or to provide a demonstration.

## Chapter 24: Video Communication

1. Video can be used to provide both synchronous and asynchronous communication.
2. The same issues one must address in a meeting in which everyone is in the same room apply to video conferencing, but with additional image management concerns.
3. Your best choice when being filmed for a video conference is shirts or blouses in solid pastels.
4. The need to restrict movement during a video conference can easily make a speaker appear to be a talking head.
5. During a video conference, you must keep distracting sounds to a minimum.
6. Videos can be created with a variety of camera options such as an analog video camera, a digital video camera, or even a simple Web cam.
7. Videos are actually a series of still images or frames projected only briefly so that they appear to be moving.

# Terms

**agenda** a list of items to be discussed during a meeting, providing a reason for holding the meeting

**ambient sound** noise that occurs naturally, such as footsteps or phones ringing; it is generally not speech

**analogous colors** colors that are near each other on a color wheel

**asynchronous** term indicating that information is not given and received at the same time

**colored stock** paper that may range from a pale off-white to a vivid color

**color theory** the relationship between colors, often based on location of colors on a color wheel

**complementary colors** colors that appear directly across from each other on a color wheel

**FireWire** also known as IEEE 1394 and originally developed by Apple Computer; a means of high-speed transfer between a computer and a peripheral such as a camera

**jargon** specialized words used within a particular industry, often incorporating acronyms as shortcuts; W3C (World Wide Web Consortium) is an example of an acronym used in the Web design community

**kiosk** a freestanding computer used by visitors

**lag time** the time between the moment a word is spoken by one person in a video conference and the moment it is heard by another person

**logo** a graphical symbol that uses both text and graphics to convey the identity of a business

**Pack and Go** a feature of Microsoft PowerPoint that compresses a presentation for ease of transfer to another computer; it may also include a reader that lets you view the presentation even if you do not have PowerPoint on your computer

**pre-press check** verifies that all files and fonts needed to print a document by a printing service are present.

**schwag** promotional products such as fuzzy animals, calculators, and other items designed to carry a company logo

**seminar notebook** a bound document, often in a binder, that contains all the printed information needed for a conference or meeting

**synchronous** at the same time; synchronous communication is when two people are speaking either in the same room or perhaps via a telephone

**talking head** a derogatory term for a video of someone who talks on and on to the point of boring the audience

**timecode** a means of tracking groups of frames within a video

**video conferencing** a live meeting in which the participants are not physically present in the same room

**voice recognition** the technology that allows the spoken word to be transferred to a computer

# ELECTRONIC PORTFOLIO

1. **If you have not already done so, create a subdirectory** titled **unit6** in the **Electronic Portfolio** directory and save the products of the activities that follow. Later, you will combine these materials with your other works to create a complete electronic portfolio.

2. Create a logo for a business of your choice.

3. Use the logo to create a business card, letterhead stationery, a coupon, and a promotional product.

4. Create a map demonstrating the location of the business.

5. Create a slide show for a sales presentation for the business and package it to Pack and Go.

6. Create a business plan that includes résumé information to support it.

7. Save the business plan as a PDF file.

8. Create a short video in which you report on the progress of your business. Include an agenda.

9. Save the documents and files to the **unit6** directory.

10. Use the chart on the following page to evaluate the quality of your portfolio material.

| | Beginning | Developing | Accomplished | Exemplary | Score |
|---|---|---|---|---|---|
| Logo design | Demonstrates knowledge of basic design elements | Uses color effectively in design | Incorporates color and design elements | Demonstrates exceptional creativity in choice of design | |
| Business card design | Demonstrates knowledge of basic card design | Uses color effectively in design | Incorporates color and design elements | Demonstrates exceptional creativity in choice of design | |
| Letterhead design | Demonstrates knowledge of basic letterhead design | Uses color effectively in design | Incorporates color and design elements | Demonstrates exceptional creativity in choice of design | |
| Coupon design | Demonstrates knowledge of basic coupon design | Uses color effectively in design | Incorporates color and design elements | Demonstrates exceptional creativity in choice of design | |
| Promotional product design | Demonstrates knowledge of basic product design | Uses color effectively in design | Incorporates color and design elements | Demonstrates exceptional creativity in choice of design | |
| Map | Includes basic mapping elements | Includes effective details | Includes details and appropriate additional information | Demonstrates exceptional design | |
| Slide show | Consists of a basic presentation | Consists of a presentation with sufficient slides | Consists of a presentation that demonstrates use of all design elements | Consists of a presentation that demonstrates exceptional design | |
| Business plan | Contains minimal elements | Contains essential elements | Contains all elements | Contains all elements presented with exceptional design | |
| Video clip | Contains minimal information | Contains essential information | Contains extensive information | Contains extensive information attractively presented | |

# UNIT 7

# The Changing Business Environment

SOURCE: ©PHOTODISC

# Career Profile

Do you think outside the box? Mari Ann Binder Futty—the owner of The Creative Cookie in Columbus, Ohio—does. Her creative juices must flow constantly, as you can imagine. Together, Mari Ann and her company's designer, Lisa Fulcher, design and sell specialty cookies to companies, professional organizations, and others. How did all this come to be?

Mari Ann has a degree in journalism from Ohio University, with media coursework, such as advertising, news and magazine writing, and public relations. She specialized in public relations and hoped that her love for creative writing would lead her to new means and ends. And that it did!

Mari Ann went to work looking for a way to market her idea, a different type of cookie. She designed the company logo herself (a cookie with a bite missing and with crumbs that form the second C in "The Creative Cookie") and then

SOURCE: ©PHOTODISC

278

(continued)

set out to get a printer and an artist to help her get her ideas into final format. Out of that collaboration came her business card, a product list, and a thriving business. Just to give you an idea what she does: Various organizations (such as manufacturers, country clubs, hospitals, home and garden exhibitors, vacation and boat exhibitors) and professionals (such as optometrists, cancer benefit organizers, nurses) want specialized cookies for their meetings, outings, or special benefits. That is where The Creative Cookie comes in.

These organizations want a particular theme, and they want a particular style of cookie to illustrate that theme. Mari Ann and Lisa go to work, often batting ideas around for hours (or even days) until they settle on just the right look. Then the cookie is molded (they often design the mold) and the icing or frosting is put on so that the little cookie looks just like a salad dressing bottle, a tennis or golf shoe, an airplane, or whatever else the client wants so that the workplace standards are met.

The training that Mari Ann had in her courses, as well as the natural talent she and Lisa have (Lisa's grandfather was a professional artist), come in handy. The two women are working on expanding the business and have several decisions to make in the future. They are thinking about using their computer technology in new ways to advertise the business. For example, they are designing a sticker with the company logo, name, address, and phone number and that will affix quickly to the cookie bag. This sticker will be an advertisement in itself besides being a functional element of the bag.

The decision-making and problem-solving skills that Mari Ann learned in school, as well as being honed through experience with Lisa, work well with this pair of entrepreneurs. Mari Ann said rather pointedly, "I need to use my computer more and get my database of names of clients in order for follow-up sales. Also, I have several great ideas for a Web site, and that is certainly in the future as well." She has a terrific idea for marketing on the Internet a ready-made gingerbread kit for children.

As you perfect your skills in solving problems and in working with creative ideas gathered throughout this course, you may take many different paths in the multimedia field. These paths can help you use your talents in multimedia as you work with designers, vendors, and clients. Just think outside the box! You, too, can create special effects through media enhancements.

As you have progressed through this course, you have learned why workplace standards are important and how you can work effectively with suppliers, vendors, and customers in the workplace, just as Mari Ann does every day. The future will see additional changes in the business environment brought about by the impact of technology; being able to adapt and work with those changes will be part of your successful business strategy. ∎

Note: Mari Ann Binder Futty is a real person, and her company, The Creative Cookie, based in Columbus, Ohio, is a real business.

ESTIMATED TIME
**6**
HOURS

# Chapter 25
## Team Building

SOURCE: ©PHOTODISC

## Objectives

- *You will learn to build a team.*
- *You will learn to participate as a team.*
- *You will learn to use a team to create a multimedia product.*

## INTRODUCTION

Quality multimedia products are not often created by a single person. You have seen in the preceding chapters that a diverse set of skills is needed that often requires the work of a team. Teamwork is not simply a matter of gathering a group of people and asking them to complete a task. Functioning as a team requires specialized skills on the part of both the team leader and the team members. Just as it is important to learn how to manage images, perfect presentation skills, and design effective Web pages, it is also a vital multimedia skill to know how to add your expertise to that of others in order to produce a product.

In this chapter you will learn team skills while you explore the impact of technology on business—two areas that will become more important to you when you enter the world of work.

# STAGES OF TEAM DEVELOPMENT

Teams generally go through the four stages shown in Figure 25.1: forming, storming, norming, and performing. Each stage is fairly predictable and the issues that arise must be addressed in order for your team to be successful. Learning to recognize and work through each stage will give you a stronger team.

SOURCE: ©DIGITAL VISION

- *Forming* represents the creation stage when a team is formed. Members are assigned to a team and introductions are made.
- *Storming* represents the stage in which personalities begin to mesh, sometimes with initial conflict. This stage often occurs almost as soon as forming is completed. It's easy for those unused to working together to feel ill at ease with each other.
- *Norming* represents the stage during which conflicts are resolved and plans are begun. The movement from storming to norming is the point at which the future success or failure of the team is often determined.
- *Performing* is the moment when the team becomes a functioning productive group. This stage should represent the majority of the team's working time. The previous three stages are merely preambles to the important work that must be accomplished.

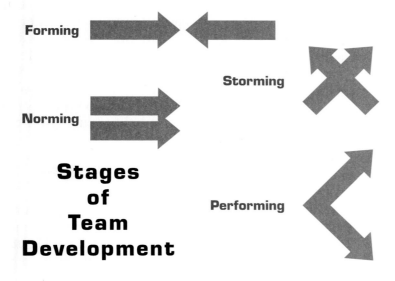

**Stages of Team Development**

Forming

Storming

Norming

Performing

**Figure 25.1** Teams go through four expected stages of development.

# TEAM CHARTER

A team charter specifically identifies the team's goals, values, and approach to handling the task at hand.

Beginnings are important times for teams. As a general rule, groups should be created quickly and begin to work as soon as possible after they have formed. If extended periods of time are allowed to elapse between creation and work, the energy of the team can become lost.

Once a team starts to work, it must understand its purpose. A team with a fuzzy focus cannot be expected to accomplish much of importance. Part of a team's responsibility is to learn why it was formed. When it knows its reason for existence, then it must establish a **team charter** to specifically identify its goals, its values, and its approach. While this may seem pointless, in the long run a team will achieve much more if it uses the time at the beginning to clearly identify the path it plans to follow. The following areas should be addressed in the team charter:

- Why was the team created?
- What is the team to accomplish?
- How will the team track its progress?
- What will the team members gain from working on this team?
- What happens when team members need help?

## THE **ETHICS** OF CONFLICT

Conflict is usually seen as undesirable and to be avoided. It is true that physical conflict is not desirable, but this is not the case with a conflict of ideas. The importance of teamwork is to bring into the open all possible ideas in order to provide as many solutions as possible. As a member of a team, you have to learn not to see a difference of opinion as a personal attack. If everyone in a team tries to "play nice" by not countering one idea with another, then the team will lose its force. This does not mean that ideas should be presented in an argumentative manner. Verbal fighting is not the answer. Instead, you must learn to present your ideas and to accept the ideas of others without creating a negative environment for others.

Another way that teams often come into conflict is when a member of the team shares information gained in team meetings with those outside the team. This failure to keep information confidential seriously erodes honest communication within a team. At no time should comments from team members be revealed to others unless the team agrees. Maintaining team confidentiality is essential to avoiding conflict and increasing team effectiveness.

All these issues provide an ethical challenge for everyone in the team.

## TEAM BUILDING

Teams comprise many individuals, each with different ideas, experiences, and concerns. Teams must gather each person into the group by meshing all the personalities in order for them to function as a single entity. One of the best ways for this to happen is to include team-building activities into the function of the team. These activities are generally recreational, giving members time to get to know each other and develop a trust. Food, games, and recognition activities are frequently used to build team spirit and to help reduce conflict.

## TEAM LEADER

Every member of a team is important and should contribute in a significant way. The team leader is merely one member of the group—not someone special. The team leader's significant function is to facilitate communication. A good team leader encourages communication, enhances team productivity, and provides essential structure and organization. Selection of a team leader should be based upon these skills and not on how well the person is liked.

In some organizations the team leader is selected by an immediate superior, or the task is assigned as part of the job responsibility. If this is the case, the team leader needs to be aware of the essential skills of a good leader and work on acquiring those skills in which he or she may be weak.

# TEAM COMMUNICATION

Communication within a team is essential to the success of the organization. Too often fear of ridicule prevents team members from adding essential information. Others fear entering into conflict with members of the team. Some members so strongly want to see their point accepted that they refuse to allow others to add ideas. These and other problems of communication can destroy the effectiveness of a team. Members must be encouraged to listen to each other, be open in their opinions, and be willing to accept diversity of opinions. The team leader is an important component in this process.

# TEAM MEETINGS

One of the activities that a team engages in is to meet and report on the progress and concerns of its members. These meetings should have beginning and ending times and clearly stated purposes. As a good team member, do not keep the others waiting. In addition, do not prolong the meeting past the time it should end.

An agenda is the guiding hand at team meetings. With a well-thought-out agenda, members know the subjects to be discussed and the material to have present. Agendas should be delivered before the meeting so that everyone is prepared.

## Good Business

### Office Politics

When you start a new job, you may discover—to your dismay—that not all employees work together well or even like each other. Sometimes one group of employees gossips and complains incessantly about another group. Sometimes employees complain about their jobs or the boss or the company. All of this is unfortunate, but you need to know that it does happen.

So what do you do? The best thing to do, at least at first, is to stay out of it as much as possible. Don't get drawn into gossip and complaints. But *do* keep your eyes and ears open. You also don't want to be completely out of the loop; sometimes important, valid information is spread by the employee grapevine and you don't want to miss out on that. If you observe your co-workers closely, though, you'll soon learn who the hard workers are and who the complainers are. If you want to do well on the job and advance your career, you'll pattern yourself after the first group.

**Digging Deeper:** Use the Internet to research ways to deal with office politics. Then create a brief animation to show what you've learned.

These meetings are not chat sessions or recreation. Members should keep discussion centered on the purpose for which the meeting was called and not deviate to other issues unless appropriate. While meetings are designed to allow members to give their opinions, you should not go into long, rambling speeches. Limit your discussion to the essential points. Often individual discussions that may take up the time of the team can be better held outside the meeting.

Good team members adhere to rules that make meetings productive. They include the following:

- Be on time.
- Start on time and end promptly.
- Use agendas that include the purpose, time for discussion, and desired outcome of the meeting.
- Come prepared with the information needed by others.
- Stay on task.

## TEAM DECISIONS

As part of any meeting, decisions must be made by the team. It is during this decision-making process that conflict can arise. Learning to make decisions as a team is a skill that can reduce long-term conflict and increase the team's effectiveness. As part of the decision-making process, everyone in the team should understand the issues related to the decision, including the following questions:

- What are the specific details of the decision to be made?
- What is the deadline for the decision?
- What impact will the decision have on the team?
- Who will be involved in the outcome of the decision?
- How will the decision be made?

There are a number of ways to make a decision. The two most frequently used means of reaching agreement are to gain a consensus or to allow the majority to rule. **Consensus building** requires that everyone or nearly everyone agree with the final decision. Majority rule requires most of the members to agree but not all. Some decisions are made by a small subgroup of team members or by a single member once the team as a whole contributes their ideas. Each means of making a decision can be appropriate at various times. Your team must should consider each option and its consequences whenever making a decision.

When you are a member of the team making a decision, it is important that you listen carefully to all points. When giving your opinion, don't seek conflict, but don't avoid it to keep peace. Everyone should participate, even those whose opinions go against the feelings of the majority. The leader and others in the team should check often for understanding by restating the points being made to ensure that everyone understands all the issues. Continually search for alternative solutions that meet the goals of all members. The purpose of a team decision is to use the all the ideas that can be generated, rather than those of a single person.

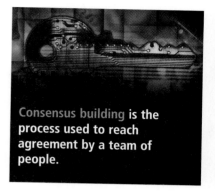

**Consensus building** is the process used to reach agreement by a team of people.

## COLLABORATIVE TOOLS

Collaborative computing is growing in importance as software is developed to encourage its use as part of a team activity. Technology has provided teams with ways to collaborate even if the team does not meet in person. You have seen in a previous chapter how video conferencing is used to provide people with a means of meeting using a video camera. Teleconferencing using phone lines is another way. Calendars and databases that can be accessed by everyone in a team are another useful collaborative tool.

Any software that facilitates gathering ideas and tracking information can be an important collaborative tool. Brainstorming software such as Inspiration is sometimes used to gather ideas and then to sort them.

SOURCE: ©PHOTODISC

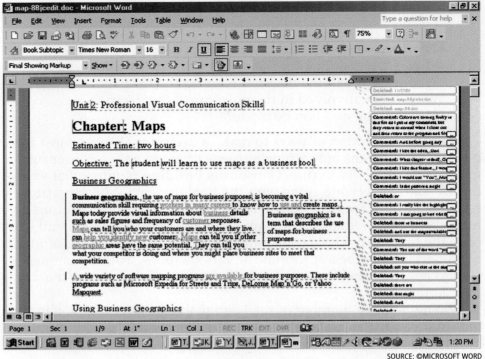

SOURCE: ©MICROSOFT WORD

GroupSystems is designed for strategic planning, product development, problem solving, and other business processes. SolvingRight software pulls together facts and consensus ideas to develop a problem statement and analysis. MeetingPro keeps meetings on track, supports group decisions, tracks action items, and distributes meeting notes. Microsoft PowerPoint is also used to brainstorm, and its notes features can be used to add ideas as they occur to a group.

Software such as Microsoft Word allows you to create a document, send it on to others for their comments, and then use the Reviewing toolbar to accept or reject the suggestions. Figure 25.2 demonstrates how this was done during the creation of your textbook. Notice the revisions as well as comments on the right side of the document. With collaborative tools such as these, teams can be far more productive than in the past. It is just one way that technology has had an impact on business.

## SUMMARY

In this chapter you explored ways to function as part of a team. You saw that there are stages to team development and ways to build consensus. You looked at the rules good team members follow to make meetings and communication work more efficiently. You also saw that technology can play a part by making collaboration easier even if team members cannot meet in person.

Answer the following questions on your own computer.

1. What are the four stages of team development?
2. During what stage does conflict most often occur?
3. What purpose does a team charter serve?
4. What type of activities are used to build a team's spirit?
5. What is the purpose of a team leader?
6. What is one of the reasons that team members do not contribute ideas?
7. What is the purpose of a meeting agenda?
8. What speaking limitations should members of a team place upon themselves during meetings?
9. What ways can be used to reach a decision in a team meeting?
10. Give an example of a way that technology can be used as part of the collaborative process.

Discuss the following questions either as a class or as a written assignment.

1. What problems occur as a team begins to function?
2. What are ways that all members of a team can be encouraged to participate?
3. What happens if a member of a team doesn't fulfill his or her tasks? How can this be avoided?
4. Why is a team more effective than single members completing single tasks?
5. What kinds of tasks are most appropriate for a team?

1. Create a team of four to eight members. Assign people to act as project manager, research director, writer, artist/animator, sound specialist, Webmaster, desktop publisher, and presentation expert. Depending upon the number of people in your team, some members may need to be assigned more than one area of responsibility.

2. Write a charter indicating the group's goals, values, and work approach. Build a consensus so that everyone understands what is to be expected.

3. Research the impact of technology on business today and in the future. Use Web sources, personal interviews, and personal experiences. Take into consideration international business influences.

4. Select a single product or event that your team believes will be significant in the business world of tomorrow based upon your research.

5. Produce a multimedia production that demonstrates the following:
   a. Why your group believes this is a significant product or event
   b. What research supports your ideas
   c. What the long-range impact will be of this product or event

6. Create a print document that summarizes your information and includes appropriately cited sources. Design the document using your desktop publishing skills.

7. Create a single Web page that includes the information in your presentation.

8. Make sure that both the multimedia production and Web page include sound and graphics that enhance the message you are sending.

9. Give a team presentation of your multimedia production.

10. Create a chart to evaluate the overall effectiveness of your team's work. Include at least five areas that you believe are important in the functioning of a team. Have all members of the team complete the evaluation and then compile the results.

**FURTHER EXPLORATION**

Create a new team and gather all the Web pages created by the members of the class. Design a Web page to act as an entry page to make the team's pages available to everyone.

# Chapter 26
# Multimedia in the Corporate World

ESTIMATED TIME
**3**
H O U R S

SOURCE: ©PHOTODISC

## INTRODUCTION

The changing business environment is apparent in everything you encounter today. Businesses that at one time were considered invincible are now in bankruptcy. You have seen other businesses explode with growth and then deflate. In the years to come, you will likely see more such events.

Technology will be the deciding factor in many of these occurrences. The quality and effectiveness of multimedia and image management (significant technology components) will contribute to the success or failure of businesses.

Your hard work to develop essential multimedia skills with this book will be invaluable to your future. In this chapter, you will bring your image management skills together. Then you can take your knowledge with you into your career of choice.

## Objectives

- *You will research a corporation while focusing on multimedia and image management issues.*
- *You will synthesize information from your research using a series of questions.*
- *You will develop a project to demonstrate your multimedia skills and your ability to draw conclusions.*
- *You will demonstrate your knowledge of the changing business environment.*

# PROJECT OVERVIEW

You have looked at image management procedures, print publishing, slide show presentations, and Web publishing. You have also looked at ways to communicate using multimedia tools. Now you want to investigate how these tools are used in the real world by observing how others have used the same skills you have been studying.

You will begin by selecting a product or service that is recognized internationally, such as a McDonald's Big Mac or perhaps a Harley-Davidson motorcycle.

Then you will research in depth to answer a series of questions about the company that markets your chosen product. Once you have gathered the necessary information, you will create a new product to demonstrate your ability to draw conclusions from your research and present the product in a professional manner. Enjoy the exploration and learn from it. Carry the knowledge you learn from this experience into the awaiting business world.

# COMPANY INFORMATION

Use Yahoo financial information at http://finance.yahoo.com (or a comparable Web site) to locate financial information about your product's company. You may have to use the Symbol Lookup feature to find the stock symbol for the company. Read about the company and look for any information that indicates a change the company may be experiencing.

Copy the five-year linear chart (similar to the one shown in Figure 26.1) of the company's stock price to show its performance during the time period. Save it as **chart.gif** or **chart.png**.

Locate the company profile information. Copy the business summary information into a word processing document. Then copy and paste the financial summary below the business summary. Include the complete Web site address from which you copied the information and paste the address at the end of the document for documentation. Save the summaries as **profile.doc**.

Has the company's stock improved or declined over the five-year time period? Has the change been dramatic with many peaks or valleys, or has it been a gradual change? In the information provided on the Web site, is

## THE **ETHICS** OF CYBERSQUATTING

Cybersquatting or domain name grabbing is the practice of registering a Web address that may be wanted by another person. This activity is not limited to corporate or product name grabbing. Some people register names they believe might be valuable in the future, such as www.camera.com, in hopes of selling the domain for an inflated price. This is an example of the entrepreneurial spirit responding to emerging technology.

Some argue that these name grabbers are taking advantage of the situation. Others argue that they are merely smart or early adopters. The courts have ruled that trademark infringement can apply in these situations and restrict the opportunities for cybersquatting. However, people will continue to see how change can be used to their advantage. As technology continues to change the way business operates, new opportunities will present themselves to you or others who are alert to possibilities.

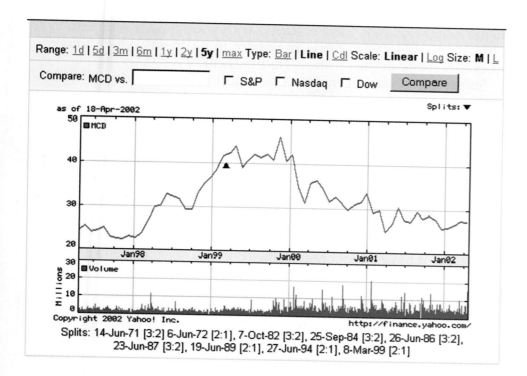

Range: 1d | 5d | 3m | 6m | 1y | 2y | **5y** | max Type: Bar | **Line** | Cdl Scale: **Linear** | Log Size: **M** | L

Compare: MCD vs. [           ]  ☐ S&P  ☐ Nasdaq  ☐ Dow   [Compare]

as of 18-Apr-2002                                    Splits: ▼

**Figure 26.1** Financial charts make it easy to see changes in stock prices. Source: Reproduced with permission of Yahoo! Inc. ©2000 by Yahoo! Inc. YAHOO! and the YAHOO! logo are trademarks of Yahoo! Inc.

Splits: 14-Jun-71 [3:2] 6-Jun-72 [2:1], 7-Oct-82 [3:2], 25-Sep-84 [3:2], 26-Jun-86 [3:2], 23-Jun-87 [3:2], 19-Jun-89 [2:1], 27-Jun-94 [2:1], 8-Mar-99 [2:1]

there any indication of what impact technology has on this business? What changes has the company been experiencing, and what changes does it anticipate experiencing? In your own words, explain your observations and any conclusions you draw from your reading. Focus on these questions, but include any other pertinent business information. Save your observations as **company.doc**.

## GENERAL SEARCH

Search other Web sites for information about the company you chose. Are there Web sites designed to create a negative image of the company or its products? What is used as a basis of complaint? Explain what negative publicity is available on the Web about your company and save the explanation as **negative.doc**.

# DOMAIN NAME

Locate the Web site of this company. How did you find it? What other addresses might the company have used other than the one you found? Do they use more than one address?

The name of a Web site is called a **domain name**. Domain names are registered to protect the Web site from use by others. Companies did not always register domain names, and private individuals claimed the right to them instead. As you can imagine, this caused problems for companies who realized too late that their Web address had already been registered. Search for information about domain

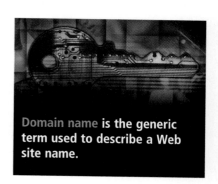

**Domain name is the generic term used to describe a Web site name.**

name issues that may have occurred with your chosen company. How do domain issues cause an impact on business? What change does this create in the business environment?

Summarize your information and save it as **domain.doc**.

## PAGE DESIGN

Look carefully at the opening page of your company's Web site and consider all the design elements you have studied. Ask yourself the following questions, then summarize your observations. Save the document as **design.doc**.

- How quickly does the page load?
- Does it have a login requirement?
- What colors are used on the opening page?
- What psychological impact or emotional impact do these colors have?
- What size and type of font appear on the page?
- What is the primary focus of the page?
- What types of multimedia are used?
- Is there sound on the page?
- Are there navigation tools?
- Does the page use frames?
- Does the page meet disability requirements?
- How effective is the page in keeping your attention?
- Is the page friendly and easy to use?
- Reveal the code used to create the page. Can you tell what software was used to create the page?
- What keywords are included for search engines?

SOURCE: ©DIGITAL VISION

## LOGO

Is there a corporate logo? How is the logo integrated into the page? What colors are used? What impact do the colors have? Is the logo memorable? Why do you think the logo was designed this way? What file format is the logo saved as? Has technology made any change in the logo? What technology, such as Flash, might impact the logo at a later time? Describe your responses to the logo and save it as **logo.doc**.

Use your image management software to duplicate the logo, including the colors. Save your duplicated logo as **logo.gif** or **logo.jpg**. What image tools are most useful to create the logo?

## WEB DESIGNER

Is there information on the page to indicate who designed or manages the page? Is there a contact e-mail address? Is there information to indicate the most recent update? Does the page appear to be current? If possible, e-mail the site designer to ask for information about his or her credentials, experience, and contributions to the design. Make a copy of the e-mail you sent. If you receive an e-mail response, make a copy of the response and save both as **mail.doc**.

# WEB CONTENT

Consider the audience who would use this corporate Web page. Who is this page designed to attract? Why would they come to this site? Would it meet their needs? What is the purpose of this site? Has the company fully used the power of Internet technology?

## INFORMATION

What information is available on this site? How many links are there? What information appears on these linked pages? Does the opening page provide a site search engine?

## CULTURAL ISSUES

Does the site appear to be usable for those in other countries? Which countries? If this site is country-specific, can you locate corporate sites designed for another country?

## Continuing Your Education

You're probably aware of how quickly technology can change. Today's hot new trend or product can become obsolete almost overnight. In fact, some of the information in this textbook may become outdated in just a few years. To keep your career moving ahead, then, you need to keep abreast of the innovations in your field.

There are some simple ways to stay on top of technology changes. One of the most enjoyable is to get together with colleagues from time to time and chat about your work; you'll be surprised at the new things you can learn. Consider subscribing to magazines that relate to your fields of interest. Internet discussion groups are also excellent sources of new information. You should also plan to take relevant classes on an ongoing basis, just to make sure you don't get left behind on anything. Consider yourself a lifetime learner!

**Digging deeper:** Use the Internet to compile a list of information sources (such as discussion groups, magazines, classes at a local community college) on the multimedia topic of your choice. Present your findings in a chart. Be specific.

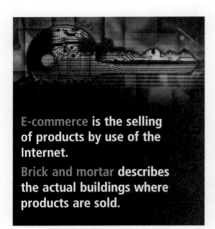

E-commerce **is the selling of products by use of the Internet.**

Brick and mortar **describes the actual buildings where products are sold.**

### E-COMMERCE

Many corporate Web sites are created as a means of selling the company's product. Use of the Internet for sales purposes is called **e-commerce.** Is this site designed to market a product? How easy is it to use? Does the site content explain shipping and taxes before you have to order? How fast does shopping information load? Do prices appear to be more or less than you would purchase in a **brick and mortar** store?

Use the answers to your Web site content questions to write a summary discussing the usefulness and effectiveness of the pages. Use your knowledge of the Internet and image management skills to include suggestions about how to improve the page. Include observations of how technology has impacted this business and how the business environment is changing. Save your summary as **content.doc**.

# PRODUCT

Now gather your information and observations to create a product to demonstrate your knowledge of business image management and its impact. Your product will consist of three parts: a series of Web pages, a slide show, and a print document in PDF format. Use the following chart to ensure that you include all essential components. Points will be applied based on inclusion of the necessary components and the quality of the information provided. Present your product to your class, other students, faculty members, parents, and members of the business community in order to gather their feedback.

SOURCE: ©PHOTODISC

### WEB PAGES

Your Web pages should be saved in a folder titled **chngbus**. Begin by creating an opening page that includes color, animation, your title, your name, and navigation links. Select colors that will convey the message you intend. Your animation can be created using the corporate logo you re-created as **logo.gif** or **logo.jpg**. The title should reflect your opinion of the site's image management and its impact on the business you chose.

The second page should include an explanation of your overall conclusions. The page should also include links to each of the following pages:

- Company Information (include **chart.gif**, **profile.doc**, **company.doc**, and **negative.doc**)
- Domain Name (include **domain.doc**)
- Page Design (include **design.doc**, **logo.doc**, and **logo.gif** or **logo.jpg**)
- Mail Response (optional; include **mail.doc**)
- Content (include **content.doc**)

If you have the capabilities, include sound and video somewhere within the site. If these pages will be placed on a live Web site, keep in mind that download time should be a consideration. If these pages will not be live, you have more flexibility in the length of the video and the amount of sound. Photographs of the actual product should also be included on the site. Video, sound, and photographs should demonstrate your knowledge of the editing tools available to you.

## SLIDE SHOW

Use the information you developed for the Web pages to create a slide show with a similar design. Set up the presentation to be used as an independent running show without intervention (as in a kiosk). Save the presentation as **changingbusiness.ppt**.

## PRINT DOCUMENT

Use the information you developed for the Web pages to create a desktop-published document. Save the document as **changing business.doc**. Convert the document to a PDF file and save it as **changingbusiness.pdf**.

| CHANGING BUSINESS PROJECT | Points Possible | Points Earned |
|---|---|---|
| **Web Pages Criteria** | | |
| Pages saved to a folder called **chngbus** | 5 | |
| Opening page contains title demonstrating changing business | 5 | |
| Opening page contains effective color | 5 | |
| Opening page contains appropriate animation | 5 | |
| Opening page contains navigation links | 5 | |
| Opening page contains student name | 5 | |
| Summary page contains overall conclusions | 5 | |
| Summary page contains links to pages | 5 | |
| Summary page contains navigation links | 5 | |
| Company information page contains chart graphic | 5 | |
| Company information page contains profile information | 5 | |
| Company information page contains company information | 5 | |
| Company information page contains negative information | 5 | |
| Domain name page contains domain information | 5 | |
| Page design page contains design information | 5 | |
| Page design page contains logo information | 5 | |
| Page design page contains logo graphic | 5 | |
| Content page contains content information | 5 | |
| All pages have functional navigation links | 5 | |
| Page design demonstrates knowledge of image management | 5 | |
| Total for Web Pages | 100 | |
| | | |
| **Slide Show Criteria** | | |
| Opening page contains title demonstrating changing business | 5 | |
| Opening page contains effective color | 5 | |
| Opening page contains appropriate animation | 5 | |
| Opening page contains student name | 5 | |
| Summary page contains overall conclusions | 5 | |
| Company information page contains chart graphic | 5 | |
| Company information page contains profile information | 5 | |
| Company information page contains company information | 5 | |
| Company information page contains negative information | 5 | |
| Domain name page contains domain information | 5 | |
| Page design page contains design information | 5 | |
| Page design page contains logo information | 5 | |
| Page design page contains logo graphic | 5 | |

| CHANGING BUSINESS PROJECT *Contd.* | Points Possible | Points Earned |
|---|---|---|
| Content page contains content information | 5 | |
| Presentation demonstrates knowledge of image management | 20 | |
| Presentation requires no intervention | 10 | |
| Total for Slide Show | 100 | |
| **Print Document Criteria** | | |
| Opening page contains title demonstrating changing business | 5 | |
| Summary page contains overall conclusions | 5 | |
| Company information page contains chart graphic | 5 | |
| Company information page contains profile information | 5 | |
| Company information page contains company information | 5 | |
| Company information page contains negative information | 5 | |
| Domain name page contains domain information | 5 | |
| Page design page contains design information | 5 | |
| Page design page contains logo information | 5 | |
| Page design page contains logo graphic | 5 | |
| Content page contains content information | 5 | |
| Document demonstrates knowledge of desktop publishing | 30 | |
| Document converted to PDF file | 15 | |
| Total for Print Document | 100 | |
| **TOTAL PROJECT GRADE** | | |

# SUMMARY

In this chapter, you used business image management skills to explore ways technology has created an impact on a specific corporation and ways the business environment is changing for your chosen company. You looked into the financial side of the company and investigated its Web site. You drew conclusions using your knowledge and experience. You then demonstrated this knowledge by creating a series of Web pages, a slide show, and a print document.

## REVIEW

Answer the following questions on your own computer.

1. What financial information on a company can be found on the Internet?
2. What graphics can provide financial information?
3. What are the issues with domain name registrations?
4. What is e-commerce?
5. What does *brick and mortar* mean?

## DISCUSSION

Discuss the following questions either as a class or as a written assignment.

1. Can companies grow without a Web site?
2. Will customers use a corporate Web site to make purchases?
3. How could a company encourage customers to visit corporate Web sites?
4. Should Web sites be allowed to present a negative side to a product?
5. How much can you trust both the positive and negative information about a product that is found on the Internet?

1. Compare the information you gathered with information gathered by the other members of your class. Rank the corporate sites based upon the following criteria:
   - Effectiveness using the power of the Internet
   - Attractiveness of site design
   - Usefulness of site content

2. Use the rankings to determine the best Web site. Add your results to the class results to determine a "Best in Class," and perhaps "Best Overall" using the results from several classes.

3. Create a "Best in Class" Web site award. Notify the Web site administrator of the award.

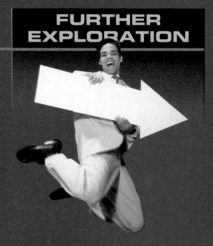

Select a product that does not currently have a Web presence (or use an imaginary product). Choose a domain name that would be appropriate for the product. Check to see if that name is already in use. Create a Web site for that product using your knowledge from the sites you have observed. Consider ways to make the site accessible for the disabled as well as for those from other countries. Include information that will draw people to the site and ways to purchase your chosen product.

# Unit 7: Summary

## Key Concepts

## Chapter 25: Team Building

1. Teams generally go through four stages: forming, storming, norming, and performing.
2. When a team knows its reason for existence, then it must establish a charter to identify specifically its goals, its values, and its approach.
3. Team-building activities are generally recreational, giving members time to get to know each other and develop a trust.
4. The team leader's significant function is to facilitate communication.
5. Ways must be found to encourage members to listen to each other, to be open in their opinions, and to be willing to accept diversity of opinions
6. An agenda is the guiding hand at team meetings.
7. There are a number of ways to make a decision: majority rule, general consensus, small group, or single member.
8. Collaborative computing is growing in importance as software is developed to encourage its use as part of a team activity.

## Chapter 26: Multimedia in the Corporate World

1. The changing business environment is apparent in everything you encounter today.
2. The quality and effectiveness of multimedia and image management (significant technology components) will contribute to the success or failure of businesses.
3. Yahoo financial information at http://finance.yahoo.com (or a comparable Web site) can provide you with financial information about a product's company.
4. Domain names are registered to protect the Web site from use by others.
5. Many corporate Web sites are created as a means of selling the company's product.

## Terms

**brick and mortar** describes the actual buildings where products are sold

**consensus building** the process used to reach agreement by a team of people

**domain name** the generic term used to describe a Web site name

**e-commerce** selling products via the Internet

**team charter** specifically identifies the team's goals, values, and approach to handling the task at hand.

SOURCE: ©PHOTODISC

# ELECTRONIC PORTFOLIO

1. **Create a master portfolio Web page that includes each of** the six areas that you have studied: Image Management Procedures, Professional Visual Communication Skills, Print Publishing Systems, Presentation Systems, Web Publishing Systems, and Oral and Other Professional Communication Skills. Also include Team Building covered in Chapter 25 and Multimedia in the Corporate World from Chapter 26.

2. Make the master page an interesting gateway to your portfolio using all your design skills and knowledge.

3. Include links to each of the portfolio areas. Make sure that all your links work.

4. Gather all files into a single folder and burn the folder material to a CD to use as a reference demonstrating your multimedia skills.

| | Beginning | Developing | Accomplished | Exemplary | Score |
|---|---|---|---|---|---|
| Gateway Page | Demonstrates knowledge of basic design elements | Uses color effectively in design | Incorporates color and design elements | Demonstrates exceptional creativity in choice of design | |
| Image Management Procedures | | | Functional link | Demonstrates exceptional creativity | |
| Professional Visual Communication Skills | | | Functional link | Demonstrates exceptional creativity | |
| Print Publishing Systems | | | Functional link | Demonstrates exceptional creativity | |
| Presentation Systems | | | Functional link | Demonstrates exceptional creativity | |
| Web Publishing Systems | | | Functional link | Demonstrates exceptional creativity | |
| Oral and Other Professional Communication Skills | | | Functional link | Demonstrates exceptional creativity | |
| Team Building | | | Functional link | Demonstrates exceptional creativity | |
| Multimedia in the Corporate World | | | Functional link | Demonstrates exceptional creativity | |

# Appendix A
## Career Appendix

Welcome to the world of careers and career information. This appendix has been compiled to give you up-to-the minute ways and means to advance your studies of multimedia and image management and to prepare you for the world of work. The information is organized into six different categories:

**Category 1** • High school courses that will be of benefit to your multimedia career

**Category 2** • Career opportunities and related careers in multimedia technology

**Category 3** • College programs with course descriptions that you may be interested in

**Category 4** • Workshops, seminars, and advanced studies you may participate in

**Category 5** • Internships, job shadowing, and on-the-job training

**Category 6** • Job search skills and résumé building

This is a working appendix. What, you ask, is that? In addition to the information provided, you may add to this appendix as you progress through the course and as you progress in continued educational programs and your career. If you discover a neat Web site, workshop, seminar, or advanced educational program or certification, add it to your Career Appendix, even if you cannot take part in it at the time. Save it for later. Use this Career Appendix as a career reference section. You will be glad you did!

# CATEGORY 1 • HIGH SCHOOL COURSES

Now, let's discover some high school courses that may be valuable for a degree or emphasis in various technology and telecommunications programs. These courses will also form a good foundation for your initial employment in many multimedia fields.

- Business courses—Accounting, finance, introduction to business, management, and various office-related courses (filing and records management, office procedures) will be relevant to your continued education and/or job entry.
- Computer applications—courses such as beginning computer applications, databases, and Web design will be useful in a multimedia career.
- Design—Students who feel the creative juices flowing will find courses in design not only fun but also challenging. These courses will form a good basis for further academic courses or a career.
- English—Basic grammar, spelling, punctuation, letter/report writing, and oral communication skills are mandatory for job success.
- Graphics—Being able to produce not only useful but attractive graphic presentations is a qualification that you will find valued by many companies.
- Keyboarding—Being able to type with proficiency will help you as you work on many different types of equipment.
- Photography—Companies often need photos of special events, promotions, and other happenings; this skill can make you a valued addition to a staff.
- Speech—Communication skills are needed in every job or educational program you will seek, whether you communicate orally or with sign language; being able to communicate is important.

# CATEGORY 2 • CAREER OPPORTUNITIES AND RELATED CAREERS

Many occupations and job categories will draw on your expertise from your multimedia courses as well as from your other areas of study. Here are some occupations for you to consider:

## OCCUPATIONAL CATEGORIES

- Computer graphics producer
- Desktop publishing specialist
- Desktop video editor
- Electronic imaging technician
- Graphic arts technician
- Instructional developer

- Interactive multimedia producer
- Multimedia producer
- Technology specialist
- Training program developer
- Virtual effects producer
- Webmaster

## RELATED OCCUPATIONS

- Computer-mediated training
- Graphics designer
- Internet
- Marketing
- Production specialists
  - TV and radio staff and specialists
  - Special effects and graphics specialists
  - Directory and information staff
  - CD-ROM technologists and designers
  - Multicultural interactions representatives and specialists

Sounds exciting, doesn't it? Other related occupations can be found in various types of organizations. Additional career paths will be identified as you review the rest of the Career Appendix.

# CATEGORY 3 • COLLEGE PROGRAMS WITH COURSE DESCRIPTIONS

Many colleges and universities as well as career and vocational schools and distance education organizations offer various courses, degree programs, certificate programs, and certifications in multimedia and technology areas. Many of these organizations offer both campus-based programs and online programs. In addition, many schools offer not only bachelor's degree programs but also master's programs. A few offer doctoral programs as well. A separate section herein lists another venue for job skill certifications in addition to those offered by educational institutions.

If you are interested in advancing your education and becoming more skilled in multimedia and various technologies, you are sure to find some program, course, or certification that will appeal to you. Be sure to add to the following list as you learn of additional educational opportunities that you may want to remember for later.

## DEGREE AND CERTIFICATE PROGRAMS AND CERTIFICATIONS IN MULTIMEDIA/TECHNOLOGY

### Western Illinois University
1 University Circle, 115 Sherman Hall, Macomb, IL 61455
http://www.wiu.edu/

The Instructional Technology & Telecommunications Department, College of Education and Human Services, offers degree programs whose graduates are in demand for careers in government and military operations; law enforcement and nonprofit agencies; and graphic design, multimedia, and video production firms. Hospitals and health education providers and various telecommunications entities also provide employment opportunities. Graduates of this program can then pursue advanced degrees in instructional design, human resource development, instructional technology and telecommunications, and related fields. Internships, projects, and practice provide students with opportunities to apply their skills in real-world settings.

Western Illinois University, Engineering Technology Department, offers a bachelor of science degree in Graphic Communication. The department focuses on techniques using the computer and a variety of software to produce printed and video materials. Graduates of this program are prepared for careers in graphics and printing industries. Internships are available in this option as well.

## Tennessee Board of Regents Online Degree Programs

1415 Murfreesboro Street, Suite 324, Nashville, TN 37217
http://www.tn.regentsdegrees.org

The Tennessee Board of Regents colleges, universities, and technical centers join to offer the Regents Online Degree Program (RODP) for associate, bachelor, and master degree programs. One such program is the associate of applied science degree in Information Technology (60 credit hours). Courses include the following:

- Networking and PC Communications
- Web Page Design and Development
- Computer Graphics
- Java Programming
- Data Structures

## DeVry University

Online, undergraduate, and graduate courses in many areas around the country
http://www.devry.edu/index.html

DeVry offers many programs, such as undergraduate degrees in:

- Computer Technology
- Information Technology
- Network Systems Administration
- Technical Management
- Telecommunications Management

See the Web site for a list of campuses and a map showing all the campuses and centers in the United States, as well as DeVry online courses.

## Santa Barbara City College
721 Cliff Drive, Santa Barbara, CA 93109
805-965-0581
http://multimedia.sbcc.net/courses.html

Santa Barbara City College offers multimedia arts degrees and intensive certificates:

- Digital Design Certificate
- Web Development Certificate
- Video: Broadcast Design or Production Certificate
- Sound Design Certificate
- Animation Certificate

For students desiring a major in multimedia that will transfer to a four-year program, an associate of arts degree in Multimedia is offered. Courses offered include the following:

- Introduction to Multimedia
- Survey of Multimedia Applications
- Digital Art Tools and Techniques
- Web Design Tools and Techniques
- Introduction to Photoshop
- Introduction to Illustrator
- Introduction to Dreamweaver
- Introduction to Nonlinear Editing
- Introduction to Director
- Introduction to Flash
- Creative Thinking
- Computer Interface Design/Advanced Photoshop
- Introduction to Web Design, Advanced Web Design
- Computer Animation I and II, Animation III
- Development of Online Learning Materials
- Game Design
- Writing for Multimedia
- Multimedia for Advertising
- Cinematography
- Digital Video Editing
- Motion Graphics & Compositing
- Film and Video Production I
- Introduction to Audio and Video for Multimedia
- Principles of Audio Production
- Webcasting: Broadcasting on the Web
- Topics in Multimedia
- Multimedia Arts Practicum
- Portfolio Development
- Advanced Nonlinear Editing
- Advanced Photoshop
- Advanced Motion Graphics
- Film and Video Production II
- Work experience/internships in multimedia (see the Internships section for additional information). General education and other courses comprise the program as well as the preceding courses.

Santa Barbara City College also offers a graphic design and photography program. See http://www.sbcc.net/gdp/prgmcrses.html.

## Southwest Florida College

10210 Highland Manor Drive, Suite 200, Tampa, FL 33610
1685 Medical Lane, Fort Myers, FL 33907
http://www.swfc.edu/graphic.htm

Southwest Florida College offers an associate of science degree in Graphic Design (96 quarter hours). Some of the graphic design courses are as follows:

- Drawing I and II
- Introduction to Graphic Design
- Photography
- Typography
- Computer Illustration
- Image Editing
- Digital Composition
- Web Page Design
- Portfolio Presentation
- Desktop Publishing

Southwest Florida College mentions on its Web site that upon successful completion of the program, graduates can pursue entry-level positions as a graphic designer, artist, or cartoonist. General education courses as well as electives are required in the program.

## Miami-Dade Community College

11380 NW 27th Avenue, Miami, FL 33167-3418
(North Miami location)
305-237-0000 (Call for all campus locations)
http://www3.mdcc.edu/programs/
http://www3.mdcc.edu/contacts/#information

The Miami-Dade Community College offers an associate of science degree in Graphic Arts Technology (64 credit hours) that contains the following courses:

- Introduction to Graphic Communication
- Graphic Design I
- Introduction to Graphic Imaging
- Offset Strip (Imposition)
- Graphic Arts Estimating
- Electronic Publishing
- Computer Assisted Graphic Design
- Color Tech I
- Electronic Photoshop
- Advanced Electronic Photoshop 2
- Offset Presswork 1 and 2
- Digital Graphic Painting
- Graphic Arts Estimating 2
- Professional Desktop Publishing Media

The program also includes a co-op work experience. The program gives students hands-on experience with graphic design, estimating, color theory, electronic scanning, page makeup, imposition, electronic color retouching, and presswork.

Miami-Dade Community College offers an additional degree in Graphic Design Technology (64 credits). General education courses and electives also are components of each program. This degree is to prepare students for employment in the printing, publishing, electronic communication, design, and advertising industries.

### Keiser College
Locations in Fort Lauderdale, Daytona Beach, Sarasota, Lakeland, Melbourne, Kendall, and Tallahassee, Florida
800-749-4456
http://www.keisercollege.cc.fl.us/prog.htm

Keiser offers associate of science degrees in Computer Graphics and Design as well as in Computer Animation and Design. Keiser mentions on its Web site that graphic designers are in demand in commercial, government, and educational organizations. Various employment opportunities are available for graphic designers, including with advertising and marketing companies, print and electronic publishing, video and film production, and in-house graphics departments. Opportunities also abound for free-lance graphic artists.

The associate of science degree in Computer Graphics and Design (72 credit hours) includes the following courses:

- Introduction to Computer Information Systems
- Introduction to Design
- 2D Illustration and Image Editing I and II
- Layout and Composition for Print Publication I and II
- 3D Modeling and Animation for Graphics Design I and II
- Multimedia Production I and II
- Delivery Systems for Electronic Publication I and II.

Students complete a portfolio that becomes a major component in their employment package. Students also take general education and elective courses in the programs.

### Tarrant County College
5301 Campus Drive, Fort Worth, TX 76119
http://somedia.tccd.net/programs

Tarrant County College offers degree programs in Graphic Communication. The associate of applied science degree (70 semester hours) contains courses such as the following:

- Introduction to Graphic Arts and Printing
- Introduction to Computer Graphics—Print
- Design I
- Drawing I
- Digital Imaging I and II
- Object Oriented Computer Graphics

- Electronic Publishing I and II
- Photography I
- Web Page Design I
- Basic Animation
- Design Communication I
- Computers in Video Production I

A capstone/portfolio is also required in the course selection. Electives and general education courses are also part of this program.

## Texas State Technical College, Abilene Campus

650 East Highway 80, Abilene, TX 79601
915-672-7091
http://www.westtexas.tstc.edu/abilene/index.html

Texas State Technical College offers a Digital Imaging and Design Technology program, which includes coursework as follows:

- Theory
- Typography
- Layout principles
- Digital manipulation of both vector and raster art
- Presentation applications
- Video editing
- Animation
- CD-ROM authoring

Students may select a Level 1 Digital Imaging and Design Specialist Certificate as well as an associate of applied science degree in Digital Imaging & Design Technology. A portfolio of projects is required for the end-of-course job preparation. Students will also participate in a capstone, which includes working collaboratively with an outside company or organization. The average time to complete the program is five semesters. These courses will prepare students for work in the field of graphic arts, Web page design, videography, and other multimedia-oriented careers. Texas State Technical College states that the *Bureau of Labor Statistics Occupational Handbook* indicates there will be 79,000 new positions within the field by 2008.

## Westwood College of Technology, LBJ-635 and 75N, Dallas, Texas

(Other programs on Anaheim Campus, Chicago–DuPage Campus, Chicago–River Oaks Campus, Denver–North Campus, Denver–South Campus, Fort Worth Campus, Inland Empire Campus, Los Angeles Campus)
http://aviationandtechtraining.com

Technical and general education courses help students prepare for jobs such as graphic designer, production artist, Web page designer, and multimedia designer. Degree programs for associate of arts in Graphic Design and Multimedia are available.

## ITT Technical Institutes
Over 70 schools nationwide in 28 states
http://www.tech-programs.com

ITT offers associate degree programs in Information Technology. For example, the Houston North Campus (Texas) offers an associate of applied science degree in Information Technology—Multimedia (8 quarters). These associate degree programs prepare students to perform tasks that deal with multimedia communication. The programs consist of general education and computing courses for a foundation, followed by advanced studies in multimedia applications. Courses include the following:

- Software scripting
- Multimedia languages
- Database development
- Other technical subjects

## University of Phoenix Online
P.O. Box 52031, Phoenix, AZ 85072-9352
http://online-learning-info.com

Earn a bachelor's degree in Information Technology, a master of business administration degree in Technology Management, or a master of science degree in Computer Information Systems. All courses and programs are completely online. See their site for complete information and course descriptions.

## Columbus State Community College
550 East Spring Street, Columbus, OH 43215
http://www.cscc.edu

According to researchers at Columbus State Community College in Columbus, Ohio, the market for multimedia products and services is growing rapidly. Project management, scripting/authoring of programs, media acquisition and manipulation, and user interface or navigation design are just some of the areas in which skilled multimedia technicians work. Positions for which you may qualify are media specialist, digital prepress technician, instructional designer, programs specialist, computer graphic artist, 3-D computer animator, digital journalist, and interactive systems designer. Programs such as the associate degree in Multimedia Production Technology offer students the option of selecting the Authoring Systems track or the Computer Graphics track.

The Interactive Multimedia Technology associate degree program (108 credit hours) offered by Columbus State provides the following courses:

- Beginning Composition
- PC Applications I
- The World of Multimedia
- CIV I/II/III or Am. History I, II, III
- Two-Dimensional Design

- Essay & Research
- Introduction to Computer Graphics
- Business and the Internet
- The Digital Revolution
- Color Composition
- Speech
- Design & Typography
- Electronic Imaging
- Communication for Mass Media
- Project Management
- Advanced Scripting
- Dynamic Graphics
- Creating Vector Graphics
- Designing in 3D Dimension
- Web Animation
- Controlling Web Page Layout
- Technical Elective
- Social Science
- Building Hierarchical Websites
- Interactive CD Development
- Multimedia Practicum
- Multimedia Seminar

Columbus State also offers a Macromedia Web Design Series I Certificate (10 credit hours), including the following courses:

- Flash Fundamentals
- Flash/Advanced
- Fireworks
- Dreamweaver 3 Fundamentals
- Dreamweaver 3/Advanced

## Delaware Joint Vocational School

4565 Columbus Pike, Delaware, OH 43015-8969

http://www.delawarejvs.org

Delaware JVS, like many other joint vocational schools, offers many programs that you may find interesting. Here are a few of its offerings:

- Adobe Illustrator
- Basic 35mm and Digital Photography
- Network+ Boot Camp
- A+ Boot Camp
- Internet+ Boot Camp
- Web Page Design
- MS Excel, Access, PowerPoint
- Photo Imaging
- Computerized Keyboarding
- MS Publisher

Certification programs include the following:

- Cisco Certified Network Professional (CCNP)

- Cisco Certified Network Administrator (CCNA)
- Microsoft Officer User Specialist (MOUS)

## Sessions.edu, Inc.
476 Broome Street, Fourth Floor, New York, NY 10013
http://www.sessions.edu/certificates/multimedia.html

Sessions.edu offers training in the latest multimedia technologies and applications. Students choose four required courses and five electives, at a cost of $1,759. Multimedia courses and certificates offered by the Online School of Design cover the following topics:

- Graphics
- Web design
- Digital design
- Multimedia

See the Web site for a complete listing of courses and registration information.

## National Center for Telecommunications Technologies (NCTT)
Springfield Technical Community College, One Armory Square, Springfield, MA 01105
800-421-9556
http://www.stcc.edu/academics/programlist.html

STCC offers a Multimedia Technology option to its Teleproduction & Multimedia Technology program that leads to an associate of science degree in Teleproduction and Multimedia Technology (65 credit hours). The program consists of the following courses:

- Microcomputer Applications for Windows
- Introduction to Multimedia
- Video Technology
- Video Production
- Introduction to Mass Communication
- Typography & Layout
- Internet Multimedia
- Design: Introduction to Art
- English Comp 2
- General Elective
- Optics & Image Recording
- Digital Full-Motion Editing
- Digital Sound & Video Design
- Interactive Multimedia Design
- General Social Science Elective
- Visual Quality & Aesthetics
- Multimedia Interactive Authoring
- Digital Animation
- Digital Arts
- Experimental Computer Imaging 2

The Teleproduction Technology option leads to an associate of science degree in Teleproduction and Multimedia Technology (66 credit hours). The difference in this program compared with the preceding program is its emphasis on television, mass media, video design, and speaking on television.

Springfield Technical Community College also offers certificate programs in Desktop Publishing (27 credit hours) and in Graphic Arts Technology (27 credit hours).

## ADDITIONAL CERTIFICATION

### Brainbench Certification

http://brainbench.com/xml/monster/main.xml

Some Brainbench certification tests are free; you can view information on all tests, certification preps, pricing plans, and so on. Categories of tests include the following:

- Computer software: AutoCAD 2000, Excel, Photoshop, PowerPoint
- Information technology
- Office skills
- Management

### Microsoft Training & Certification

http://www.microsoft.com/traincert

This site contains various links to information on examinations and training needs; click on "Microsoft Certifications" for a detailed review and description of the many certifications offered by Microsoft. Links provide not only information on the type of examination but the opportunity to read about the benefits of certification and a link to frequently asked questions.

### CIW Certification

http://www.ciwcertified.com

Technology demands individuals who have solid technical skills and abilities and proof of their expertise in various electronic media, such as the Internet. Certification in these areas has become necessary so that organizations can be competitive in the marketplace and so that individuals can secure their expertise in the electronic world. Therefore, the Certified Internet Webmaster (CIW) program was born and continues to thrive. What does CIW mean?

"CIW is an information technology job curriculum and certification for the knowledge economy," states the ciwcertified.com Web site. "It is designed to help career changers enter the IT industry and experienced vendor-certified professionals build on existing IT skills."

Who needs CIW certification? You do if you want to get the education, experience, and skills you need to reach your technical goals. Certification will direct you toward better jobs and better on-the-job performance.

Whether you are a professional who uses the Internet or a Webmaster, graphic designer, system administrator, software developer, Java developer, Certified Novell Administrator or Engineer, or IT

Security Officer—to name a few job titles—certification is for you. Go to the CIW FAQ to find a certification track that is right for you. Note that certification relates to job titles, since CIW is built around job roles.

To start up the certification path, take the basic certification—the CIW Foundations exam. After successful completion of the Foundations exam, you will be awarded a CIW Associate certification. You can then choose from four Master CIW certifications. Other certificates include the CIW Security Analyst Specialization, which denotes that you have achieved a level of competency in specific areas of Internet specialization.

The CIW Internet Skills programs develop and substantiate skills that are essential to implement business solutions—helpful to you as you advance in the business world. The certification program is endorsed by the International Webmaster Association (IWA) and the Association of Internet Professionals (AIP).

Educators have a great opportunity to achieve certification also. The CIW Faculty Institute is designed to facilitate CIW training for educators. A network of 15 regional training centers is available for training for IT educators. These Authorized Academic Partners help secondary and postsecondary educators to become certified. Go to http://www.ciwcertified.com/program/aaprogram.asp for more information.

What steps should you take to be certified? Simple.

- Determine which certification is the one for you.
- Study at home or take classes to prepare yourself for the exams.
- Then register and take and pass the exams.

That's all there is to it! Get started on the road to CIW certification now!

# CATEGORY 4 • CONFERENCES, WORKSHOPS, AND SEMINARS

Conferences, workshops, and seminars are offered by many institutions and organizations, both online and at various site locations around the country. Here are a few examples of the types of nontraditional training sessions that have been offered in the past. Many of these or other similar sessions are sure to be offered in the future. Be sure to add these to the list as you progress in your studies and/or career.

### Conference for Adobe Photoshop Users
A one-day, multisession conference for graphics, design, and Web professionals at all experience levels. $199. Presented by CompuMaster, 6900 Squibb Road, P.O. Box 2973, Mission, KS 66201-1373. http://www.compumaster.net

## Web Site Development and Design Conference
Creating a successful Web site: search engines, JavaScript, FrontPage 2000, Adobe GoLive, Macromedia Dreamweaver, Macromedia Flash, Macromedia Fireworks, XML, and other information. $199. Offered by CompuMaster, 6900 Squibb Road, P.O. Box 2973, Mission, KS 66201-1373.
http://www.compumaster.net

## Microsoft Excel
A one-day comprehensive workshop. Offered in several areas around the country at different times. $139; advanced workshop, $139; both days, $228. Offered by CompEd Solutions, P.O. Box 419107, Kansas City, MO 64141-6107.
http://www.natsem.com

## The Digital Design Camp
A one- or two-day workshop and conference covering QuarkXPress, Illustrator, Photoshop, Dreamweaver, Flash and Fireworks. Prices vary depending on days selected—$198, conference; first day plus two second-day workshops, $348; first day plus one second-day workshop, $298.50; second-day workshops only, $199. Offered by CompEd Solutions, P.O. Box 419107, Kansas City, MO 61141-6107.
http://www.natsem.com

## Dreamweaver & Flash
A two-day workshop covering basic and advanced techniques. $199 for each day or both for $348. Offered at many locations around the country by CompEd Solutions, P.O. Box 419107, Kansas City, MO 64141-6107.
http://www.natsem.com

## MacAcademy and WindowsAcademy
Offers various computer and software training: QuarkXPress, InDesign, Illustrator, FileMaker, Mac OS, Windows, Acrobat, Access, Excel, PowerPoint, Word, Appleworks, VectorWorks, RenderWorks, Entourage, Photoshop, PageMaker, Final Cut Pro, Premiere, After Effects, FrontPage, Web Development, Dreamweaver, Director, Flash, GoLive, FileMaker Pro Boot Camp. Visit the Web sites for information and pricing.
http://www.macacademy.com
http://www.windowsacademy.com

## Powerful Business Writing Skills
A one-day workshop that emphasizes writing, proofreading, and basic skills to build writing credibility. $199. Offered around the country at various locations by National Seminars Group, P.O. Box 419107, Kansas City, MO 64141-6107.
http://www.natsem.com

### How to Negotiate with Vendors and Suppliers
A one-day workshop. $149. Offered by SkillPath Seminars, 6900 Squibb Road, P.O. Box 2768, Mission, KS 66201-2768.
http://www.skillpath.com

### Santa Fe Workshops
Custom photography workshops; includes darkroom and chemicals. Alan Ross "crash" courses and two- to five-day custom workshops. Prices from $450 per day plus application fee and tax to $2135+ for a five-day workshop. See Web site for further information.
http://www.sfworkshop.com

### Basic Book Manufacturing Seminar
Seminar on electronic imposition, prepress, press, bindery, and materials in Ann Arbor. $150. Offered by Edwards Brothers Incorporated, 2500 South State Street, Ann Arbor, MI 48104.
http://www.edwardsbrothers.com

# CATEGORY 5 • INTERNSHIPS, JOB SHADOWING, AND ON-THE-JOB TRAINING

In order to further your academic studies with practical experience, get a feel for what a job entails, or actually learn on the job, you may find many opportunities in the business world in which you can enhance your academic studies. These opportunities may take you to an internship, a job shadowing situation, or to on-the-job training once you are hired. As you locate additional resources, add them to your Career Appendix.

## INTERNSHIPS

Internships are practical job experiences in which an organization agrees with an academic institution to accept one or more students for a set number of weeks/months. During this time the student works in a particular job setting or in some cases rotates throughout the organization in order to get varied work experience. Internships can be paid or unpaid.

Here are examples of internships that you may find interesting.

### Association for Multimedia Communications
P.O. Box 10645, Chicago, IL 60610
773-276-9320
http://www.amcomm.org

Students interested in internships, part-time work, or volunteering for jobs that use multimedia skills can contact the association via its Web site. Jobs are also posted in the Classifieds section.

## Santa Barbara City College
721 Cliff Drive, Santa Barbara, CA 93109
805-965-0581
http://multimedia.sbcc.net/internships.html

Santa Barbara City College invests in students who want to get practical experience by providing internship opportunities via course MAT 290, as part of the Multimedia Arts program. A Multimedia Arts and Graphics intern will put multimedia theory and skills to practice in real-world applications.

## San Jose State University
Department of TV, Radio, Film, Theatre
One Washington Square, San Jose, CA 95192
408-924-1000
http://info.sjsu.edu/web-dbgen/catalog/departments/
TA-courses.html

San Jose State University offers internships in radio, television, or theatre through the Department of TV, Radio, Film, and Theatre.

## Multimedia Internships
http://www.tvradiofilmtheatre.org/internship/mmedia.html

If you are interested in internships in television, radio, film, theatre, and the like, this site lists company names, addresses, contact persons, and phone numbers along with the type of internship the organization offers.

## Western Illinois University
1 University Drive, Macomb, IL 61455
309-298-1414
http://www.wiu.edu/itt/employers/employers.htm

Western Illinois University's Web site enables employers to post available jobs and internships in their companies as well as to choose from a wide variety of prospective employees. These potential employees are qualified in various skills from instructional design and Web development to multimedia and graphic design.

## National Museum of American History
On the National Mall, 14th Street and Constitution Avenue, NW, Washington, DC 20560
http://americanhistory.si.edu/interns/design.htm

The National Museum of American History provides internships throughout the year for various job categories: junior designer, design assistant, typesetter, model maker, digital imaging specialist, and graphic designer, to name a few. Go to the Web site for contact information and qualifications for internships posted.

**The Thomson Corporation**
Metro Center, One Station Place, Stamford, CT 06902
203-969-8700
http://www.thomson.com/Career/01_4_career.htm

The Thomson Corporation has intern-level opportunities for college sophomores and juniors, focusing on technology, liberal arts, or finance and accounting.

Thomson's focus, according to its Web site, is to expand the internship programs both in volume and areas of concentration along with providing on-the-job training and coaching.

The Thomson Web site states, "The Thomson Internship Program provides full-time students with real-world experience, classroom analysis, and the opportunity to work with some of the best and brightest professionals in their fields with one of our Thomson companies located throughout the world."

## JOB SHADOWING

Job shadowing can provide you an opportunity to work with or beside a professional in various types of organizations. You will follow your assigned professional throughout the day, perhaps being assigned a variety of tasks that encompass the job that the person holds.

### Monster.com
Sponsors Virtual Job Shadowing, which allows students anywhere in the country with Internet access to shadow working professionals online. They can see what these professionals do on a daily basis; more than 20 professionals are available, from doctors to zookeepers.
http://www.jobshadow.org/virtual_jobshadow/
virtual_jobshadow.html

### Groundhog Job Shadow Day
Monster.com also is a proud sponsor of Groundhog Job Shadow Day. For a How-to-Guide and online training presentation on how to coordinate job shadowing, visit the Web site.
http://www.jobshadow.org

### Huntington (West Virginia) Regional Chamber of Commerce
304-525-5131
Another virtual shadowing opportunity; you can select from a large variety of job titles.
http://huntingtonchamber.org/vjs/default.htm

### Directories of Job Shadowing Opportunities
Listed by occupational category, presenter, and geographic area.
http://www.reachoutmichigan.org

## Dryden Job Shadowing Program
Mail Stop 4839A, NASA Dryden Flight Research Center
P.O. Box 273, Edwards, CA 93523
661-276-2004

Offers educators a chance to visit with NASA engineers and technicians. Contact Ronnie.Boghosian@dfrc.nasa.gov.
http://www.dfrc.nasa.gov/trc/Teacher/shadow.html

## Michigan State University Career Development Center
65 Student Services Bldg., East Lansing, MI 48824
517-355-9510, Ext. 335
Provides its MSU Career Portfolio Guide and Career Exploration, a complete guide with worksheets; includes job search skills, job shadowing, and other information.
http://www.csp.msu.edu/cdc

## ON-THE-JOB TRAINING

One of the best ways for you to enhance your knowledge and skills is through on-the-job training. These programs are provided at various organizations and companies for employees to broaden their skills and increase their productivity. To read more about how a program should be set up, go to http://www.doi.gov/training, a site hosted by DOI University, National Business Center, U.S. Department of the Interior.

## Film & TV Connection
24-hour number: 800-755-7597
This entertainment industry school, a division of Career Connection, Inc., will train you in film and broadcasting and help you get a job in the field. They provide on-the-job training in major film/video studios and television stations. They state the following on their Web site:

- No experience required.
- Learn the latest digital technology.
- Train as an apprentice in a film studio or a TV station in your town.
- Part-time, nights, weekends.
- Train around your current job!
- Available everywhere in the U.S.A. and Canada.

http://www.film-connection.com

## Apprentice Mentor Association
Works with students who want to become an apprentice in radio, television stations, or recording studios/record companies, as well as video and film production companies worldwide. The nonprofit association contracts with companies that have current openings and a need to hire beginners and want to train and mentor them. The site

provides complete details on the mentor process, fees, payment plans, and how to register.

The association professes that the likelihood of obtaining a position increases with an apprentice who is already on the job and is a known entity by the hiring manager.
http://www.getamentor.com.

### Teach-nology
An excellent site to locate organizations and associations that provide training opportunities. The Apprentice Mentor Association is just one of the many organizations listed.
http://www.teach-nology.com/teachers/vocational_ed

### Texas Workforce Commission
Employers' Hotline 800-832-9394
Employees' Hotline 800-832-2829
The site provides links for business and employers, job seekers and employees, service providers, and the like: http://www.twc.state.tx.us. Veterans Education Institutes and apprenticeship programs are provided as a link at the following site:
http://www.twc.state.tx.us/svcs/vetsvcs/tsaa/vainst.html

### RAND Graduate School
1700 Main Street, P.O. Box 2138,
Santa Monica, CA 90407-2138
310-393-0411
RAND Graduate School gives students a chance to enter a community of practice and gather professional skills and tacit knowledge that courses alone can't convey, as aptly stated on the site. The school awards doctoral degrees in policy analysis and offers students the opportunity to engage in policy research; scholarships are available.
http://www.rgs.edu/ojt

# CATEGORY 6 • JOB SEARCH SKILLS AND RÉSUMÉ BUILDING

Most students and adults will need career information at some point. The following information should give you valuable tips that you can use in your job or career search by using some of the Online Searches or finding information in the textbooks suggested for your use. You may also contact your instructor or career counselor at school for suggestions on the job search procedure.

## ONLINE SEARCHES

### AOL Careers
http://jobs.hiresystems.com/aol_36/SearchOpenings.cfm

This site provides the opportunity to search by selecting various options:

- Job Category
- Brand
- Country/State
- Position Type

This site is of value to job seekers as it provides links to:

- Job Listings
- Résumé Center
- Get Jobs E-Mailed to You

## Vault: The Insider Career Network

http://www.vault.com

Provides links to finding a job, résumés, cover letters, interviewing, thank-you letters, and so on. Career Tools are also provided on this site:

- Salary Calculator
- Day in the Life—read real career stories
- Relocation Tools
- Member Network
- Job Search Survival—résumés, letters, etc.
- Ask Our Experts
- How's My Résumé?

## Monster

http://www.monster.com

Monster provides valuable data and search information opportunities as follows:

- Research companies you are interested in
- Company profiles by alphabet
- Job opportunities by U.S. state

Links are also available to My Monster:

- Become a monster member, register free and create your free account, post your résumé so that 1000s of hiring employers will have it available
- Apply to jobs online; receive job alerts, free newsletters, chats or message boards to network with peers

Monster also provides job skill certification information, including a link to Brainbench certification tests. Some tests are free; you can view information on all tests, certification preps, pricing plans, and so on. Categories of tests include the following:

- Computer software: AutoCAD 2000, Excel, Photoshop, PowerPoint
- Information Technology
- Office Skills
- Management

You can also access Brainbench Certification at http://brainbench
.com/xml/monster/main.xml.

### JobWeb

http://www.jobweb.com

Articles on résumés, internships, and job search-related information.
JobWeb finds what matters most to college students and new graduates and includes it on the site. The "Résumés & Interviews" section
has lots of information links and help on résumé writing and successful interviewing. Click the "What Employers Want in a Resume" link
to read a helpful article. The "Sample resumes" link contains the
following:

- Four sample résumés
- Seven sample résumés by format and major
- Sample cover letter 1: Conservative/Formal
- Sample cover letter 2: Creative/Informal—sample letter for a
  graphics designer position
- Sample thank-you letter 1: Conservative/Formal
- Sample thank-you letter 2: Creative/Informal

### Contractedwork.com

http://www.contractedwork.com

If you want to explore freelance opportunities such as contracted
work, this site provides the following links:

- Web Design & Web Designers
- Writing & Writers
- Administrative
- Legal
- Personal
- Software & Programmers
- Graphic Design & Designers
- Business
- Multimedia
- Miscellaneous

You can post your project and receive bids from professionals, search
talent, or provide service. These links are provided as well.

## TEXTBOOKS

The following textbooks, which may be located in bookstores or
libraries or from the publisher, may provide job search information
and résumé-building practice. Your instructor may also be able to
help you in locating these and other resources.

*How to Find and Apply for a Job*, 0-538-69845-4, © 2000–2001, South-
Western Educational Publishing/Thomson Learning, 800-477-3692

*Your Career: How to Make it Happen*, 0-538-72191-X, © 2000 South-
Western Educational Publishing/Thomson Learning, 800-477-3692

*Better Resumes in 3 Easy Steps*, 0-7668-1563-3, © 2000 South-Western Educational Publishing/Thomson Learning, 800-477-3692

*Basics of Employment Communication*, 0-538-72297-5, © 2001 South-Western Educational Publishing/Thomson Learning, 800-477-3692

Good luck in your career and further activities, whatever they are. Be sure to add any additional information to this appendix: Make it work for you!

NOTE: Sites are often changed, removed, or repositioned by their sponsors or hosts and may not be available as listed. You may use a search engine to locate similar or alternate sources of information should any of the sites not be available.

# Appendix B
# Copyright Basics

SOURCE: **Library of Congress, United States Copyright Office, 101 Independence Avenue, S.E., Washington, D.C. 20559-6000,** *www.copyright.gov.* **Rev. June 2002**

## WHAT IS COPYRIGHT?

Copyright is a form of protection provided by the laws of the United States (title 17, U.S. Code) to the authors of "original works of authorship," including literary, dramatic, musical, artistic, and certain other intellectual works. This protection is available to both published and unpublished works. Section 106 of the 1976 Copyright Act generally gives the owner of copyright the exclusive right to do and to authorize others to do the following:

- *To reproduce* the work in copies or phonorecords;
- To prepare *derivative works* based upon the work;
- *To distribute copies or phonorecords* of the work to the public by sale or other transfer of ownership, or by rental, lease, or lending;
- *To perform the work publicly,* in the case of literary, musical, dramatic, and choreographic works, pantomimes, and motion pictures and other audiovisual works;
- *To display the work publicly,* in the case of literary, musical, dramatic, and choreographic works, pantomimes, and pictorial, graphic, or sculptural works, including the individual images of a motion picture or other audiovisual work; and
- *In the case of sound recordings, to perform the work publicly by means of a digital audio transmission.*

In addition, certain authors of works of visual art have the rights of attribution and integrity as described in section 106A of the 1976 Copyright Act. For further information, request Circular 40, "Copyright Registration for Works of the Visual Arts."

It is illegal for anyone to violate any of the rights provided by the copyright law to the owner of copyright. These rights, however, are not unlimited in scope. Sections 107 through 121 of the 1976 Copyright Act establish limitations on these rights. In some cases, these limitations are specified exemptions from copyright liability. One major limitation is the doctrine of "fair use," which is given a statutory basis in section 107 of the 1976 Copyright Act. In other instances, the limitation takes the form of a "compulsory license" under which certain limited uses of copyrighted works are permitted upon payment of specified royalties and compliance with statutory conditions. For further information about the limitations of any of these rights, consult the copyright law or write to the Copyright Office.

# WHO CAN CLAIM COPYRIGHT?

Copyright protection subsists from the time the work is created in fixed form. The copyright in the work of authorship *immediately* becomes the property of the author who created the work. Only the author or those deriving their rights through the author can rightfully claim copyright.

In the case of works made for hire, the employer and not the employee is considered to be the author. Section 101 of the copyright law defines a "work made for hire" as:

1. a work prepared by an employee within the scope of his or her employment; or
2. a work specially ordered or commissioned for use as:
   - a contribution to a collective work
   - a part of a motion picture or other audiovisual work
   - a translation
   - a supplementary work
   - a compilation
   - an instructional text
   - a test
   - answer material for a test
   - a sound recording
   - an atlas

if the parties expressly agree in a written instrument signed by them that the work shall be considered a work made for hire....

The authors of a joint work are co-owners of the copyright in the work, unless there is an agreement to the contrary.

Copyright in each separate contribution to a periodical or other collective work is distinct from copyright in the collective work as a whole and vests initially with the author of the contribution.

## TWO GENERAL PRINCIPLES

- Mere ownership of a book, manuscript, painting, or any other copy or phonorecord does not give the possessor the copyright. The law provides that transfer of ownership of any material object that embodies a protected work does not of itself convey any rights in the copyright.
- Minors may claim copyright, but state laws may regulate the business dealings involving copyrights owned by minors. For information on relevant state laws, consult an attorney.

## COPYRIGHT AND NATIONAL ORIGIN OF THE WORK

Copyright protection is available for all unpublished works, regardless of the nationality or domicile of the author.

Published works are eligible for copyright protection in the United States if *any* one of the following conditions is met:

\* A treaty party is a country or intergovernmental organization other than the United States that is a party to an international agreement.

- On the date of first publication, one or more of the authors is a national or domiciliary of the United States, or is a national, domiciliary, or sovereign authority of a treaty party,\* or is a stateless person wherever that person may be domiciled; or
- The work is first published in the United States or in a foreign nation that, on the date of first publication, is a treaty party. For purposes of this condition, a work that is published in the United States or a treaty party within 30 days after publication in a foreign nation that is not a treaty party shall be considered to be first published in the United States or such treaty party, as the case may be; or
- The work is a sound recording that was first fixed in a treaty party; or
- The work is a pictorial, graphic, or sculptural work that is incorporated in a building or other structure, or an architectural work that is embodied in a building and the building or structure is located in the United States or a treaty party; or
- The work is first published by the United Nations or any of its specialized agencies, or by the Organization of American States; or
- The work is a foreign work that was in the public domain in the United States prior to 1996 and its copyright was restored under the Uruguay Round Agreements Act (URAA). Request Circular 38b, "Highlights of Copyright Amendments Contained in the Uruguay Round Agreements Act (URAA-GATT)," for further information.
- The work comes within the scope of a Presidential proclamation.

# WHAT WORKS ARE PROTECTED?

Copyright protects "original works of authorship" that are fixed in a tangible form of expression. The fixation need not be directly perceptible so long as it may be communicated with the aid of a machine or device. Copyrightable works include the following categories:

1. literary works
2. musical works, including any accompanying words
3. dramatic works, including any accompanying music
4. pantomimes and choreographic works
5. pictorial, graphic, and sculptural works
6. motion pictures and other audiovisual works
7. sound recordings
8. architectural works

These categories should be viewed broadly. For example, computer programs and most "compilations" may be registered as "literary works"; maps and architectural plans may be registered as "pictorial, graphic, and sculptural works."

# WHAT IS NOT PROTECTED BY COPYRIGHT?

Several categories of material are generally not eligible for federal copyright protection. These include among others:

- Works that have *not* been fixed in a tangible form of expression (for example, choreographic works that have not been notated or recorded, or improvisational speeches or performances that have not been written or recorded)
- Titles, names, short phrases, and slogans; familiar symbols or designs; mere variations of typographic ornamentation, lettering, or coloring; mere listings of ingredients or contents
- Ideas, procedures, methods, systems, processes, concepts, principles, discoveries, or devices, as distinguished from a description, explanation, or illustration
- Works consisting *entirely* of information that is common property and containing no original authorship (for example: standard calendars, height and weight charts, tape measures and rulers, and lists or tables taken from public documents or other common sources)

# HOW TO SECURE A COPYRIGHT

## COPYRIGHT SECURED AUTOMATICALLY UPON CREATION

The way in which copyright protection is secured is frequently misunderstood. No publication or registration or other action in the

Copyright Office is required to secure copyright. (See following NOTE.) There are, however, certain definite advantages to registration. See "Copyright Registration" on page 336.

Copyright is secured *automatically* when the work is created, and a work is "created" when it is fixed in a copy or phonorecord for the first time. "Copies" are material objects from which a work can be read or visually perceived either directly or with the aid of a machine or device, such as books, manuscripts, sheet music, film, videotape, or microfilm. "Phonorecords" are material objects embodying fixations of sounds (excluding, by statutory definition, motion picture sound-tracks), such as cassette tapes, CDs, or LPs. Thus, for example, a song (the "work") can be fixed in sheet music ("copies") or in phonograph disks ("phonorecords"), or both.

If a work is prepared over a period of time, the part of the work that is fixed on a particular date constitutes the created work as of that date.

## PUBLICATION

Publication is no longer the key to obtaining federal copyright as it was under the Copyright Act of 1909. However, publication remains important to copyright owners.

The 1976 Copyright Act defines publication as follows:

> "Publication" is the distribution of copies or phonorecords of a work to the public by sale or other transfer of ownership, or by rental, lease, or lending. The offering to distribute copies or phonorecords to a group of persons for purposes of further distribution, public performance, or public display constitutes publication. A public performance or display of a work does not of itself constitute publication.

A further discussion of the definition of "publication" can be found in the legislative history of the 1976 Copyright Act. The legislative reports define "to the public" as distribution to persons under no explicit or implicit restrictions with respect to disclosure of the contents. The reports state that the definition makes it clear that the sale of phonorecords constitutes publication of the underlying work, for example, the musical, dramatic, or literary work embodied in a phonorecord. The reports also state that it is clear that any form of dissemination in which the material object does not change hands, for example, performances or displays on television, is *not* a publication no matter how many people are exposed to the work. However, when copies or phonorecords are offered for sale or lease to a group of wholesalers, broadcasters, or motion picture theaters, publication does take place if the purpose is further distribution, public performance, or public display.

NOTE: Before 1978, federal copyright was generally secured by the act of publication with notice of copyright, assuming compliance with all other relevant statutory conditions. U.S. works in the public domain on January 1, 1978, (for example, works published without satisfying all conditions for securing federal copyright under the Copyright Act of 1909) remain in the public domain under the 1976 Copyright Act.

Certain foreign works originally published without notice had their copyrights restored under the Uruguay Round Agreements Act (URAA). Request Circular 38b and see the "Notice of Copyright" section on page 331 of this publication for further information.

Federal copyright could also be secured before 1978 by the act of registration in the case of certain unpublished works and works eligible for ad interim copyright. The 1976 Copyright Act automatically extends to full term (section 304 sets the term) copyright for all works, including those subject to ad interim copyright if ad interim registration has been made on or before June 30, 1978.

Publication is an important concept in the copyright law for several reasons:

- Works that are published in the United States are subject to mandatory deposit with the Library of Congress. See discussion on "Mandatory Deposit for Works Published in the United States" on page 340.
- Publication of a work can affect the limitations on the exclusive rights of the copyright owner that are set forth in sections 107 through 121 of the law.
- The year of publication may determine the duration of copyright protection for anonymous and pseudonymous works (when the author's identity is not revealed in the records of the Copyright Office) and for works made for hire.
- Deposit requirements for registration of published works differ from those for registration of unpublished works. See discussion on "Registration Procedures" on page 337.
- When a work is published, it may bear a notice of copyright to identify the year of publication and the name of the copyright owner and to inform the public that the work is protected by copyright. Copies of works published before March 1, 1989, *must* bear the notice or risk loss of copyright protection. See discussion on "Notice of Copyright" below.

## NOTICE OF COPYRIGHT

The use of a copyright notice is no longer required under U.S. law, although it is often beneficial. Because prior law did contain such a requirement, however, the use of notice is still relevant to the copyright status of older works.

Notice was required under the 1976 Copyright Act. This requirement was eliminated when the United States adhered to the Berne Convention, effective March 1, 1989. Although works published without notice before that date could have entered the public domain in the United States, the Uruguay Round Agreements Act (URAA) restores copyright in certain foreign works originally published without notice. For further information about copyright amendments in the URAA, request Circular 38b.

The Copyright Office does not take a position on whether copies of works first published with notice before March 1, 1989, which are distributed on or after March 1, 1989, must bear the copyright notice.

Use of the notice may be important because it informs the public that the work is protected by copyright, identifies the copyright owner, and shows the year of first publication. Furthermore, in the event that a work is infringed, if a proper notice of copyright appears on the published copy or copies to which a defendant in a copyright infringement suit had access, then no weight shall be given to such a defendant's interposition of a defense based on innocent infringement in mitigation of actual or statutory damages, except as provided in section 504(c)(2) of the copyright law. Innocent infringement occurs when the infringer did not realize that the work was protected.

The use of the copyright notice is the responsibility of the copyright owner and does not require advance permission from, or registration with, the Copyright Office.

## FORM OF NOTICE FOR VISUALLY PERCEPTIBLE COPIES

The notice for visually perceptible copies should contain all the following three elements:

1. *The symbol* © (the letter C in a circle), or the word "Copyright," or the abbreviation "Copr."; and
2. *The year of first publication* of the work. In the case of compilations or derivative works incorporating previously published material, the year date of first publication of the compilation or derivative work is sufficient. The year date may be omitted where a pictorial, graphic, or sculptural work, with accompanying textual matter, if any, is reproduced in or on greeting cards, postcards, stationery, jewelry, dolls, toys, or any useful article; and
3. *The name of the owner of copyright* in the work, or an abbreviation by which the name can be recognized, or a generally known alternative designation of the owner.

Example: © 2002 John Doe

The "C in a circle" notice is used only on "visually perceptible copies." Certain kinds of works—for example, musical, dramatic, and literary works—may be fixed not in "copies" but by means of sound in an audio recording. Since audio recordings such as audio tapes and phonograph disks are "phonorecords" and not "copies," the "C in a circle" notice is not used to indicate protection of the underlying musical, dramatic, or literary work that is recorded.

## FORM OF NOTICE FOR PHONORECORDS OF SOUND RECORDINGS*

The notice for phonorecords embodying a sound recording should contain all the following three elements:

1. *The symbol* ℗ (the letter P in a circle); and
2. *The year of first publication* of the sound recording; and
3. *The name of the owner of copyright* in the sound recording, or an abbreviation by which the name can be recognized, or a generally known alternative designation of the owner. If the producer of the sound recording is named on the phonorecord label or container and if no other name appears in conjunction with the notice, the producer's name shall be considered a part of the notice.

Example: ℗ 2002 A.B.C. Records Inc.

* Sound recordings are defined in the law as "works that result from the fixation of a series of musical, spoken, or other sounds, but not including the sounds accompanying a motion picture or other audio-visual work." Common examples include recordings of music, drama, or lectures. A sound recording is not the same as a phonorecord. A phonorecord is the physical object in which works of authorship are embodied. The word "phonorecord" includes cassette tapes, CDs, LPs, 45 r.p.m. disks, as well as other formats.

## POSITION OF NOTICE

The copyright notice should be affixed to copies or phonorecords in such a way as to "give reasonable notice of the claim of copyright." The three elements of the notice should ordinarily appear together on the copies or phonorecords or on the phonorecord label or container. The Copyright Office has issued regulations concerning the form and position of the copyright notice in the *Code of Federal Regulations* (37 CFR Section 201.20). For more information, request Circular 3, "Copyright Notice."

## PUBLICATIONS INCORPORATING U.S. GOVERNMENT WORKS

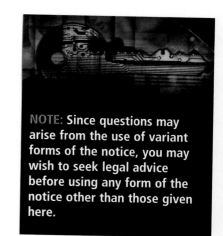

NOTE: Since questions may arise from the use of variant forms of the notice, you may wish to seek legal advice before using any form of the notice other than those given here.

Works by the U.S. Government are not eligible for U.S. copyright protection. For works published on and after March 1, 1989, the previous notice requirement for works consisting primarily of one or more U.S. Government works has been eliminated. However, use of a notice on such a work will defeat a claim of innocent infringement as previously described *provided* the notice also includes a statement that identifies either those portions of the work in which copyright is claimed or those portions that constitute U.S. Government material.

> Example: © 2002 Jane Brown. Copyright claimed in Chapters 7–10, exclusive of U.S. Government maps

Copies of works published before March 1, 1989, that consist primarily of one or more works of the U.S. Government *should* have a notice and the identifying statement.

## UNPUBLISHED WORKS

The author or copyright owner may wish to place a copyright notice on any unpublished copies or phonorecords that leave his or her control.

> Example: Unpublished work © 2002 Jane Doe

## OMISSION OF NOTICE AND ERRORS IN NOTICE

The 1976 Copyright Act attempted to ameliorate the strict consequences of failure to include notice under prior law. It contained provisions that set out specific corrective steps to cure omissions or certain errors in notice. Under these provisions, an applicant had 5 years after publication to cure omission of notice or certain errors. Although these provisions are technically still in the law, their impact has been limited by the amendment making notice optional for all works published on and after March 1, 1989. For further information, request Circular 3.

# HOW LONG COPYRIGHT PROTECTION ENDURES

## WORKS ORIGINALLY CREATED ON OR AFTER JANUARY 1, 1978

A work that is created (fixed in tangible form for the first time) on or after January 1, 1978, is automatically protected from the moment of its creation and is ordinarily given a term enduring for the author's life plus an additional 70 years after the author's death. In the case of "a joint work prepared by two or more authors who did not work for hire," the term lasts for 70 years after the last surviving author's death. For works made for hire, and for anonymous and pseudonymous works (unless the author's identity is revealed in Copyright Office records), the duration of copyright will be 95 years from publication or 120 years from creation, whichever is shorter.

## WORKS ORIGINALLY CREATED BEFORE JANUARY 1, 1978, BUT NOT PUBLISHED OR REGISTERED BY THAT DATE

These works have been automatically brought under the statute and are now given federal copyright protection. The duration of copyright in these works will generally be computed in the same way as for works created on or after January 1, 1978: the life-plus-70 or 95/120-year terms will apply to them as well. The law provides that in no case will the term of copyright for works in this category expire before December 31, 2002, and for works published on or before December 31, 2002, the term of copyright will not expire before December 31, 2047.

## WORKS ORIGINALLY CREATED AND PUBLISHED OR REGISTERED BEFORE JANUARY 1, 1978

Under the law in effect before 1978, copyright was secured either on the date a work was published with a copyright notice or on the date of registration if the work was registered in unpublished form. In either case, the copyright endured for a first term of 28 years from the date it was secured. During the last (28th) year of the first term, the copyright was eligible for renewal. The Copyright Act of 1976 extended the renewal term from 28 to 47 years for copyrights that were subsisting on January 1, 1978, or for pre-1978 copyrights restored under the Uruguay Round Agreements Act (URAA), making these works eligible for a total term of protection of 75 years. Public Law 105-298, enacted on October 27, 1998, further extended the renewal term of copyrights still subsisting on that date by an additional 20 years, providing for a renewal term of 67 years and a total term of protection of 95 years.

Public Law 102-307, enacted on June 26, 1992, amended the 1976 Copyright Act to provide for automatic renewal of the term of copyrights secured between January 1, 1964, and December 31, 1977.

Although the renewal term is automatically provided, the Copyright Office does not issue a renewal certificate for these works unless a renewal application and fee are received and registered in the Copyright Office.

Public Law 102-307 makes renewal registration optional. Thus, filing for renewal registration is no longer required in order to extend the original 28-year copyright term to the full 95 years. However, some benefits accrue from making a renewal registration during the 28th year of the original term.

For more detailed information on renewal of copyright and the copyright term, request Circular 15, "Renewal of Copyright"; Circular 15a, "Duration of Copyright"; and Circular 15t, "Extension of Copyright Terms."

# TRANSFER OF COPYRIGHT

Any or all of the copyright owner's exclusive rights or any subdivision of those rights may be transferred, but the transfer of *exclusive* rights is not valid unless that transfer is in writing and signed by the owner of the rights conveyed or such owner's duly authorized agent. Transfer of a right on a nonexclusive basis does not require a written agreement.

A copyright may also be conveyed by operation of law and may be bequeathed by will or pass as personal property by the applicable laws of intestate succession.

Copyright is a personal property right, and it is subject to the various state laws and regulations that govern the ownership, inheritance, or transfer of personal property as well as terms of contracts or conduct of business. For information about relevant state laws, consult an attorney.

Transfers of copyright are normally made by contract. The Copyright Office does not have any forms for such transfers. The law does provide for the recordation in the Copyright Office of transfers of copyright ownership. Although recordation is not required to make a valid transfer between the parties, it does provide certain legal advantages and may be required to validate the transfer as against third parties. For information on recordation of transfers and other documents related to copyright, request Circular 12, "Recordation of Transfers and Other Documents."

## TERMINATION OF TRANSFERS

Under the previous law, the copyright in a work reverted to the author, if living, or if the author was not living, to other specified beneficiaries, provided a renewal claim was registered in the 28th year of the original term.* The present law drops the renewal feature except for works already in the first term of statutory protection when the present law took effect. Instead, the present law permits termination of a grant of rights after 35 years under certain conditions by serving written notice on the transferee within specified time limits.

* The copyright in works eligible for renewal on or after June 26, 1992, will vest in the name of the renewal claimant on the effective date of any renewal registration made during the 28th year of the original term. Otherwise, the renewal copyright will vest in the party entitled to claim renewal as of December 31st of the 28th year.

For works already under statutory copyright protection before 1978, the present law provides a similar right of termination covering the newly added years that extended the former maximum term of the copyright from 56 to 95 years. For further information, request Circulars 15a and 15t.

## INTERNATIONAL COPYRIGHT PROTECTION

There is no such thing as an "international copyright" that will automatically protect an author's writings throughout the entire world. Protection against unauthorized use in a particular country depends, basically, on the national laws of that country. However, most countries do offer protection to foreign works under certain conditions, and these conditions have been greatly simplified by international copyright treaties and conventions. For further information and a list of countries that maintain copyright relations with the United States, request Circular 38a, "International Copyright Relations of the United States."

## COPYRIGHT REGISTRATION

In general, copyright registration is a legal formality intended to make a public record of the basic facts of a particular copyright. However, registration is not a condition of copyright protection. Even though registration is not a requirement for protection, the copyright law provides several inducements or advantages to encourage copyright owners to make registration. Among these advantages are the following:

- Registration establishes a public record of the copyright claim.
- Before an infringement suit may be filed in court, registration is necessary for works of U.S. origin.
- If made before or within 5 years of publication, registration will establish prima facie evidence in court of the validity of the copyright and of the facts stated in the certificate.
- If registration is made within 3 months after publication of the work or prior to an infringement of the work, statutory damages and attorney's fees will be available to the copyright owner in court actions. Otherwise, only an award of actual damages and profits is available to the copyright owner.
- Registration allows the owner of the copyright to record the registration with the U.S. Customs Service for protection against the importation of infringing copies. For additional information, request Publication No. 563, "How to Protect Your Intellectual Property Right," from: U.S. Customs Service, P.O. Box 7404, Washington, D.C. 20044. See the U.S. Customs Service Website at *www.customs.gov* for online publications.

Registration may be made at any time within the life of the copyright. Unlike the law before 1978, when a work has been registered in unpublished form, it is not necessary to make another registration when the work becomes published, although the copyright owner may register the published edition, if desired.

# REGISTRATION PROCEDURES

## ORIGINAL REGISTRATION

To register a work, send the following three elements *in the same envelope or package* to:

Library of Congress
Copyright Office
101 Independence Avenue, S.E.
Washington, D.C. 20559-6000

1. A properly completed application form.
2. A nonrefundable filing fee of $30 (effective through June 30, 2002) for each application.
3. A nonreturnable deposit of the work being registered. The deposit requirements vary in particular situations. The *general* requirements follow. Also note the information under "Special Deposit Requirements" on page 338.
   - If the work is unpublished, one complete copy or phonorecord.
   - If the work was first published in the United States on or after January 1, 1978, two complete copies or phonorecords of the best edition.
   - If the work was first published in the United States before January 1, 1978, two complete copies or phonorecords of the work as first published.
   - If the work was first published outside the United States, one complete copy or phonorecord of the work as first published.
   - sending multiple works, all applications, deposits, and fees should be sent in the same package. If possible, applications should be attached to the appropriate deposit. Whenever possible, number each package (e.g., 1 of 3, 2 of 4) to facilitate processing.

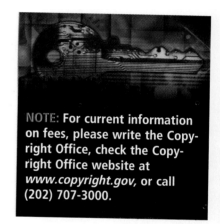

NOTE: For current information on fees, please write the Copyright Office, check the Copyright Office website at *www.copyright.gov*, or call (202) 707-3000.

## WHAT HAPPENS IF THE THREE ELEMENTS ARE NOT RECEIVED TOGETHER

Applications and fees received without appropriate copies, phonorecords, or identifying material will **not** be processed and ordinarily will be returned. Unpublished deposits without applications or fees ordinarily will be returned, also. In most cases, published deposits received without applications and fees can be immediately transferred to the collections of the Library of Congress. This practice is in accordance with section 408 of the law, which provides that the published deposit required for the collections of the Library of Congress may be used for registration only if the deposit is "accompanied by the prescribed application and fee...."

After the deposit is received and transferred to another service unit of the Library for its collections or other disposition, it is no longer available to the Copyright Office. If you wish to register the work, you must deposit additional copies or phonorecords with your application and fee.

## RENEWAL REGISTRATION

To register a renewal, send:

1. A properly completed application Form RE and, if necessary, Form RE Addendum, and
2. A nonrefundable filing fee of $60 without Addendum; $90 with Addendum for each application. Filing fees are effective through June 30, 2002. Each Addendum form must be accompanied by a deposit representing the work being renewed. See Circular 15, "Renewal of Copyright."

## SPECIAL DEPOSIT REQUIREMENTS

Special deposit requirements exist for many types of works. The following are prominent examples of exceptions to the general deposit requirements:

- If the work is a motion picture, the deposit requirement is one complete copy of the unpublished or published motion picture *and* a separate written description of its contents, such as a continuity, press book, or synopsis.
- If the work is a literary, dramatic, or musical work *published only in a phonorecord*, the deposit requirement is one complete phonorecord.
- If the work is an unpublished or published computer program, the deposit requirement is one visually perceptible copy in source code of the *first 25 and last 25 pages* of the program. For a program of fewer than 50 pages, the deposit is a copy of the entire program. For more information on computer program registration, including deposits for revised programs and provisions for trade secrets, request Circular 61, "Copyright Registration for Computer Programs."
- If the work is in a CD-ROM format, the deposit requirement is one complete copy of the material, that is, the CD-ROM, the operating software, and any manual(s) accompanying it. If registration is sought for the computer program on the CD-ROM, the deposit should also include a printout of the first 25 and last 25 pages of source code for the program.

In the case of works reproduced in three-dimensional copies, identifying material such as photographs or drawings is ordinarily required. Other examples of special deposit requirements (but by no

NOTE: Complete the application form using black ink pen or type. You may photocopy blank application forms. However, photocopied forms submitted to the Copyright Office must be clear, legible, on a good grade of 8 1/2-inch by 11-inch white paper suitable for automatic feeding through a photocopier. The forms should be printed, preferably in black ink, head-to-head so that when you turn the sheet over, the top of page 2 is directly behind the top of page 1. Forms not meeting these requirements may be returned resulting in delayed registration.

means an exhaustive list) include many works of the visual arts such as greeting cards, toys, fabrics, and oversized materials (request Circular 40a, "Deposit Requirements for Registration of Claims to Copyright in Visual Arts Material"); video games and other machine-readable audiovisual works (request Circular 61); automated databases (request Circular 65, "Copyright Registration for Automated Databases"); and contributions to collective works. For information about deposit requirements for group registration of serials, request Circular 62, "Copyright Registration for Serials."

If you are unsure of the deposit requirement for your work, write or call the Copyright Office and describe the work you wish to register.

## UNPUBLISHED COLLECTIONS

Under the following conditions, a work may be registered in unpublished form as a "collection," with one application form and one fee:

- The elements of the collection are assembled in an orderly form;
- The combined elements bear a single title identifying the collection as a whole;
- The copyright claimant in all the elements and in the collection as a whole is the same; and
- All the elements are by the same author, or, if they are by different authors, at least one of the authors has contributed copyrightable authorship to each element.

An unpublished collection is not indexed under the individual titles of the contents but under the title of the collection.

# EFFECTIVE DATE OF REGISTRATION

**A copyright registration is effective on the date the Copyright Office receives all the required elements in acceptable form,** regardless of how long it then takes to process the application and mail the certificate of registration. The time the Copyright Office requires to process an application varies, depending on the amount of material the Office is receiving.

If you apply for copyright registration, you will not receive an acknowledgment that your application has been received (the Office receives more than 600,000 applications annually), but you can expect:

- A letter or a telephone call from a Copyright Office staff member if further information is needed or
- A certificate of registration indicating that the work has been registered, or if the application cannot be accepted, a letter explaining why it has been rejected.

Requests to have certificates available for pickup in the Public Information Office or to have certificates sent by Federal Express or another mail service cannot be honored.

**NOTE: A Library of Congress Control Number is different from a copyright registration number. The Cataloging in Publication (CIP) Division of the Library of Congress is responsible for assigning LC Control Numbers and is operationally separate from the Copyright Office. A book may be registered in or deposited with the Copyright Office but not necessarily cataloged and added to the Library's collections. For information about obtaining an LC Control Number, see the following homepage:** *http:// pcn .loc.gov/pcn.* **For information on International Standard Book Numbering (ISBN), write to: ISBN, R.R. Bowker, 630 Central Ave., New Providence, NJ 07974. Call (877) 310-7333. For further information and to apply online, see** *www.isbn.org/ standards/home.* **For information on International Standard Serial Numbering (ISSN), write to: Library of Congress, National Serials Data Program, Serial Record Division, Washington, D.C. 20540- 4160. Call (202) 707-6452. Or obtain information from** *www.loc.gov/issn.*

If you want to know the date that the Copyright Office receives your material, send it by registered or certified mail and request a return receipt.

## CORRECTIONS AND AMPLIFICATIONS OF EXISTING REGISTRATIONS

To correct an error in a copyright registration or to amplify the information given in a registration, file a supplementary registration form—Form CA—with the Copyright Office. The filing fee is $100. (See Note on page 337.) The information in a supplementary registration augments but does not supersede that contained in the earlier registration. Note also that a supplementary registration is not a substitute for an original registration, for a renewal registration, or for recording a transfer of ownership. For further information about supplementary registration, request Circular 8, "Supplementary Copyright Registration."

## MANDATORY DEPOSIT FOR WORKS PUBLISHED IN THE UNITED STATES

Although a copyright registration is not required, the Copyright Act establishes a mandatory deposit requirement for works published in the United States. See the definition of "publication" on page 330. In general, the owner of copyright or the owner of the exclusive right of publication in the work has a legal obligation to deposit in the Copyright Office, within 3 months of publication in the United States, two copies (or in the case of sound recordings, two phonorecords) for the use of the Library of Congress. Failure to make the deposit can result in fines and other penalties but does not affect copyright protection.

Certain categories of works are *exempt entirely* from the mandatory deposit requirements, and the obligation is reduced for certain other categories. For further information about mandatory deposit, request Circular 7d, "Mandatory Deposit of Copies or Phonorecords for the Library of Congress."

## USE OF MANDATORY DEPOSIT TO SATISFY REGISTRATION REQUIREMENTS

For works published in the United States, the copyright law contains a provision under which a single deposit can be made to satisfy both the deposit requirements for the Library and the registration requirements. In order to have this dual effect, the copies or phonorecords must be accompanied by the prescribed application form and filing fee.

# WHO MAY FILE AN APPLICATION FORM?

The following persons are legally entitled to submit an application form:

- **The author.** This is either the person who actually created the work or, if the work was made for hire, the employer or other person for whom the work was prepared.
- **The copyright claimant.** The copyright claimant is defined in Copyright Office regulations as either the author of the work or a person or organization that has obtained ownership of all the rights under the copyright initially belonging to the author. This category includes a person or organization who has obtained by contract the right to claim legal title to the copyright in an application for copyright registration.
- **The owner of exclusive right(s).** Under the law, any of the exclusive rights that make up a copyright and any subdivision of them can be transferred and owned separately, even though the transfer may be limited in time or place of effect. The term "copyright owner" with respect to any one of the exclusive rights contained in a copyright refers to the owner of that particular right. Any owner of an exclusive right may apply for registration of a claim in the work.
- **The duly authorized agent** of such author, other copyright claimant, or owner of exclusive right(s). Any person authorized to act on behalf of the author, other copyright claimant, or owner of exclusive rights may apply for registration.

There is no requirement that applications be prepared or filed by an attorney.

# APPLICATION FORMS

## FOR ORIGINAL REGISTRATION

Form PA: for published and unpublished works of the performing arts (musical and dramatic works, pantomimes and choreographic works, motion pictures and other audiovisual works)

Form SE: for serials, works issued or intended to be issued in successive parts bearing numerical or chronological designations and intended to be continued indefinitely (periodicals, newspapers, magazines, newsletters, annuals, journals, etc.)

Form SR: for published and unpublished sound recordings

Form TX: for published and unpublished nondramatic literary works

Form VA: for published and unpublished works of the visual arts (pictorial, graphic, and sculptural works, including architectural works)

Form G/DN:   a specialized form to register a complete month's issues of a daily newspaper and newsletter when certain conditions are met

Short Form/SE and Form SE/GROUP: specialized SE forms for use when certain requirements are met

Short Forms TX, PA, and VA: short versions of applications for original registration. For further information about using the short forms, request publication SL-7.

Form GATT and Form GATT/GRP: specialized forms to register a claim in a work or group of related works in which U.S. copyright was restored under the 1994 Uruguay Round Agreements Act (URAA). For further information, request Circular 38b.

## FOR RENEWAL REGISTRATION

Form RE:   for claims to renew copyright in works copyrighted under the law in effect through December 31, 1977 (1909 Copyright Act) and registered during the initial 28-year copyright term

Form RE Addendum: accompanies Form RE for claims to renew copyright in works copyrighted under the 1909 Copyright Act but never registered during their initial 28-year copyright term

## FOR CORRECTIONS AND AMPLIFICATIONS

Form CA:   for supplementary registration to correct or amplify information given in the Copyright Office record of an earlier registration

## FOR A GROUP OF CONTRIBUTIONS TO PERIODICALS

Form GR/CP: an adjunct application to be used for registration of a group of contributions to periodicals in addition to an application Form TX, PA, or VA

## HOW TO OBTAIN APPLICATION FORMS

See "For Further Information" on page 344.

You must have Adobe Acrobat Reader® installed on your computer to view and print the forms accessed on the Internet. Adobe Acrobat Reader may be downloaded free from Adobe Systems Incorporated through links from the same Internet site from which the forms are available.

Print forms head to head (top of page 2 is directly behind the top of page 1) on a single piece of good quality, 8-1/2-inch by 11-inch white paper. To achieve the best quality copies of the application forms, use a laser printer.

# FILL-IN FORMS AVAILABLE

All Copyright Office forms are available on the Copyright Office Website in fill-in version. Go to *www.copyright.gov* and follow the instructions. The fill-in forms allow you to enter information while the form is displayed on the screen by an Adobe Acrobat Reader product. You may then print the completed form and mail it to the Copyright Office. Fill-in forms provide a clean, sharp printout for your records and for filing with the Copyright Office.

# FEES

All remittances should be in the form of drafts, that is, checks, money orders, or bank drafts, payable to: **Register of Copyrights**. Do not send cash. Drafts must be redeemable without service or exchange fee through a U. S. institution, must be payable in U.S. dollars, and must be imprinted with American Banking Association routing numbers. International Money Orders and Postal Money Orders that are negotiable only at a post office are not acceptable.

If a check received in payment of the filing fee is returned to the Copyright Office as uncollectible, the Copyright Office will cancel the registration and will notify the remitter.

The filing fee for processing an original, supplementary, or renewal claim is nonrefundable, whether or not copyright registration is ultimately made.

**Do not send cash**. The Copyright Office cannot assume any responsibility for the loss of currency sent in payment of copyright fees. For further , request Circular 4, "Copyright Fees."

## CERTAIN FEES AND SERVICES MAY BE CHARGED TO A CREDIT CARD

Some fees may be charged by telephone and in person in the office. Others may only be charged in person in the office. Credit card payments are generally authorized only for services that do not require filing of applications or other materials. An exception is made for fees related to items that are hand-carried into the Public Information Office.

**Certifications and Documents Section:** These fees maybe charged in person in the searching, locating and retrieving deposits; certifications; and expedited processing.

**Public Information Office:** These fees may only be charged in person in the office, not by phone: standard registration request forms; special handling requests for all standard registration requests; requests for services provided by the Certifications and Documents Section when the request is accompanied by a request for special handling; search requests for which a fee estimate has been provided; additional fee for each claim using the same deposit; full term retention fees; appeal fees; Secure Test processing fee; short fee payments when accompanied by a Remittance Due Notice; in-process retrieval fees; and online service providers fees.

**Reference and Bibliography Section:** Requests for searches on a regular or expedited basis can be charged to a credit card by phone.

**Records Maintenance Unit:** Computer time on COINS, printing from the Optical Disk, and photocopying can be charged in person in the office.

**Fiscal Control Section:** Deposit Accounts maintained by the Fiscal Control Section may be replenished by credit card. See Circular 5, "How to Open and Maintain a Deposit Account in the Copyright Office."

NIE recordations and claims filed on Forms GATT and GATT/GRP may be paid by credit card if the card number is included in a separate letter that accompanies the form.

NOTE: Copyright Office fees are subject to change. For current fees, check the Copyright Office website at *www.copyright.gov*, write the Copyright Office, or call (202) 707-3000.

## SEARCH OF COPYRIGHT OFFICE RECORDS

The records of the Copyright Office are open for inspection and searching by the public. Moreover, on request, the Copyright Office will search its records for you at the statutory hourly rate of $75 for each hour or fraction of an hour. (See note above.) For information on searching the Office records concerning the copyright status or ownership of a work, request Circular 22, "How to Investigate the Copyright Status of a Work," and Circular 23, "The Copyright Card Catalog and the Online Files of the Copyright Office."

Copyright Office records in machine-readable form cataloged from January 1, 1978, to the present, including registration and renewal information and recorded documents, are now available for searching on the Internet via the Copyright Office website at *www.copyright.gov*.

## FOR FURTHER INFORMATION

**Information via the Internet:** Circulars, announcements, regulations, other related materials, and all copyright application forms are available on the Copyright Office website at *www.copyright.gov*.

**Information by fax:** Circulars and other information (but not application forms) are available by using a touchtone phone to access Fax-on-Demand at (202) 707-2600.

**Information by telephone:** For general information about copyright, call the Copyright Public Information Office at (202) 707-3000. The TTY number is (202) 707-6737. Information specialists are on duty from 8:30 a.m. to 5:00 p.m., eastern time, Monday through Friday, except federal holidays. Recorded information is available 24 hours a day. Or, if you know which application forms and circulars you want, request them 24 hours a day from the Forms and Publications Hotline at (202) 707-9100. Leave a recorded message. 707-3000.

## INFORMATION BY REGULAR MAIL:

Library of Congress
Copyright Office
Publications Section, LM-455
101 Independence Avenue, S.E.
Washington, D.C. 20559-6000

For a list of other material published by the Copyright Office, request Circular 2, "Publications on Copyright."

The Copyright Public Information Office is open to the public 8:30 a.m. to 5:00 p.m. Monday through Friday, eastern time, except federal holidays. The office is located in the Library of Congress, James Madison Memorial Building, Room 401, at 101 Independence Avenue, S.E., Washington, D.C., near the Capitol South Metro stop. Information specialists are available to answer questions, provide circulars, and accept applications for registration. Access for disabled individuals is at the front door on Independence Avenue, S.E.

The Copyright Office is not permitted to give legal advice. If information or guidance is needed on matters such as disputes over the ownership of a copyright, suits against possible infringers, the procedure for getting a work published, or the method of obtaining royalty payments, it may be necessary to consult an attorney.

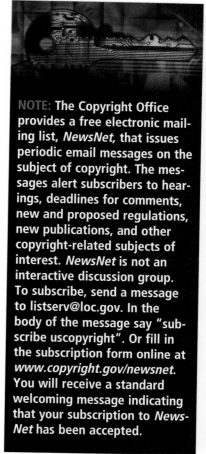

NOTE: The Copyright Office provides a free electronic mailing list, *NewsNet,* that issues periodic email messages on the subject of copyright. The messages alert subscribers to hearings, deadlines for comments, new and proposed regulations, new publications, and other copyright-related subjects of interest. *NewsNet* is not an interactive discussion group. To subscribe, send a message to listserv@loc.gov. In the body of the message say "subscribe uscopyright". Or fill in the subscription form online at *www.copyright.gov/newsnet.* You will receive a standard welcoming message indicating that your subscription to *NewsNet* has been accepted.

# Appendix C
## Activities
## Manual Sampler

## WHAT IS THE ACTIVITIES MANUAL SAMPLER?

The *Multimedia and Image Management* program consists of two teaching/learning resources: the Student Text and the Activities Manual. The Student Text emphasizes concepts while the Activities Manual focuses on developing skills within specific software applications. These two components may be used together or they may be used independently of one another.

The purpose of including Appendix C in this text is to provide the Instructor and the student with a sample from the Activities Manual.

## WHAT SOFTWARE APPLICATIONS ARE COVERED IN THE ACTIVITIES MANUAL?

The Activities Manual is organized into units and parts. Each part is designed to develop basic skills within a specific software application. The software applications covered in a given unit are all related. For example, in Unit 3 Print Publishing, the four parts covered are

Microsoft Publisher, Adobe PageMaker, QuarkXPress, and Adobe Acrobat. A complete table of contents follows.

# WHAT ARE THE SPECIAL FEATURES OF THE ACTIVITIES MANUAL?

As you will see in the sample on the following pages, students *learn by doing.* Each activity is designed to produce a specific end product such as a flyer, a brochure, or a newsletter. Each activity begins with a list of the specific skills that students will learn to use. Each of these skills is then developed step-by-step and makes use of documents and templates that are provided on the accompanying Student Data CD. Each activity ends with a mini-project in which students apply what they have learned. Once all activities have been completed, students are presented with a simulation which requires that they draw on *all* of their newly-acquired skills. Both the activities and the simulations include evaluation criteria so that both the Instructor and students can evaluate the work.

QuarkXPress, Part 3 of Unit 3, Print Publishing from *Multimedia and Image Management Activities* follows on pages 348–76.

# Part 3

# QuarkXPress

**QuarkXPress**
**Publisher: Quark Technology Partnership**
QuarkXPress is high-end desktop publishing software used extensively for publishing books and other documents in the publishing industry.

## ACTIVITY 1 • FLYER

In this activity, you will become familiar with:

- Document Setup for Flyers
- Publication Window
  - ○ Document
  - ○ Rulers
- Preferences
- Tools Palette
- Item Tool
- Content Tool
- Text Box Tool
- Styling Text
- Resizing Text Boxes
- Background Color
- Moving Text Boxes
- Zoom Tool
- Undo
- Frame
- Picture Box Tool
- Rotation Tool
- Color Palette
- Character Attributes
- Setting Formats
- Hyperlinking
- Changing Shapes

### Document Setup for Flyers

1. Go to the menu bar and choose File > New > Document.
2. In the New Document dialog box, you can adjust the page size and orientation, column guides, and margin guides. For this activity, accept the defaults by clicking OK.
3. Go to the menu bar and choose File > Document Setup. Note that in the Document Setup dialog box, you can change some of the same things as in the New Document dialog box. Click Cancel to make no changes.

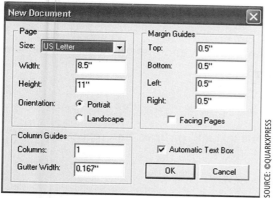

New Document

Document Setup

Ruler Origin Box
SOURCE: ©QUARKXPRESS

# Publication Window

## *Document*

1. The document opens in Actual Size view. Go to the menu bar and choose View > Fit in Window.
2. The blue box around the inside of the document is the guides that represent the margins. These can be toggled off by going to the menu bar and choosing View > Hide Guides. Toggle them back on by choosing View > Show Guides.

## *Rulers*

1. Go to the menu bar and choose View > Hide Rulers. You can toggle them back on by choosing View > Show Rulers.
2. Click in the Ruler Origin box. This is the area where the horizontal and vertical rulers intersect.
3. Hold down the left mouse button and drag the crosshairs so that the vertical and horizontal rulers are set on zero at the margin guides.

# Preferences

1. Go to the menu bar and choose Edit > Preferences > Preferences.
2. Note that there are Application and Document Preferences.
3. In the Preferences dialog box, click on Display under Application Preferences.
4. Change the guide colors for the margin, ruler, and grid. Adjust these colors to your personal preferences.
5. Choose View > Show Baseline Grids. Note that the color is your choice.
6. Choose View > Hide Baseline Grids.

# Tools Palette

1. The Tools palette should be on your document window. If it is not, go to the menu bar and choose View > Show Tools. You can also press F8 to toggle the Tools palette on and off.
2. The Tools palette shown to the right is vertical. If you want to change the orientation of the Tools palette to horizontal, press the Ctrl key and double-click the title bar of the palette.
3. Go to the menu bar and choose Help > Help Topics.
4. Click on the Index tab. Type "Tools palette" in the box. Double-click Tool overview.
5. Read the overview of all the tools in the palette.

Tools Palette
SOURCE: ©QUARKXPRESS

**Item Tool**
SOURCE: ©QUARKXPRESS

**Content Tool**
SOURCE: ©QUARKXPRESS

## Item Tool

1. Click on the Item tool.
2. The Item tool is used to select, move, resize, and reshape items such as boxes, lines, text paths, and groups.

## Content Tool

1. Click on the Content tool.
2. The Content tool imports and edits text and pictures, and repeats some of the same tasks as the Item tool.

## Text Box Tool

1. Click on the Text Box tool. Hold down the mouse button on the icon to see all the choices.

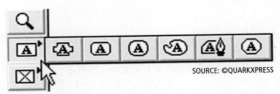

SOURCE: ©QUARKXPRESS

Text Box Tools

2. The Text Box tool creates rectangular text boxes as well as other shapes of text boxes.
3. Click on the Text Box tool and use the default rectangle shape.
4. Click on the upper left corner of the margin guides. Drag to draw a rectangular box across the entire horizontal margin and down to 2 inches on the vertical ruler.
5. Click on the Content tool.
6. Type "SAT Prep Classes." You may want to go to the menu bar and choose View > 75% so you can see the letters.
7. Use the Content tool to select the text.

## Styling Text

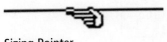

**Sizing Pointer**
SOURCE: ©QUARKXPRESS

1. Go to the menu bar and choose Style > Size > 60.
2. Go to the menu bar and choose Style > Font. Choose an appropriate font to get someone's attention.
3. Go to the menu bar and choose Style > Alignment > Centered.
4. Go to the menu bar and choose Style > Color > Red.

## Resizing Text Boxes

1. Click on the Content tool or the Item tool.
2. Hover the mouse pointer on one of the handles of the text box. The Sizing pointer appears.
3. Hold down the mouse button and drag the box up to resize it appropriately for the text inside.

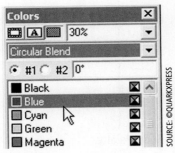

SOURCE: ©QUARKXPRESS

**Color Palette**

## Background Color

1. With the text box selected, click on Blue on the Color palette.
2. Click on the Shading drop-down box and choose 30%.
3. Click on the Color Blend drop-down box and choose Circular Blend.

4. Note that in the Color Blend Box, you can choose a second color. Choose a second color. Leave the Color Blend angle at 0 degrees.

## Moving Text Boxes

1. Click on the Item tool then click on the text box.
2. Drag the text box down to the middle of the document.
3. Resize the text box so that the text is on two different lines.
4. Resize the text box back to fit horizontally across the entire document.
5. Move the text box back to the top of the document, snapping it to the top margin.
6. The text box should now be back in its original position and size.

## Zoom Tool

1. Click on the Zoom tool.
2. The Zoom tool magnifies your document in 25% increments each time you click on the document.
3. You can also zoom in or out by going to the menu bar and choosing View. The first six options on the menu are for changing the view size of your document.
4. You can also change the view by clicking on the percentage in the status bar at the lower left corner of your screen.
5. Change the zoom in tool to zoom out by holding down the Alt key while clicking the zoom tool.

Zoom Tool
SOURCE: ©QUARKXPRESS

## Undo

1. Go to the menu bar and choose Edit > Undo.
2. This action will undo the last action taken.
3. Go to the menu bar and choose Edit > Redo.
4. Redo only remembers your last action.

## Frame

1. Use the Item or Content tool to click on the rectangular box.
2. Go to the menu bar and choose Item > Frame.
3. In the Modify dialog box, click on the drop-down box for Width and choose 4 pt.

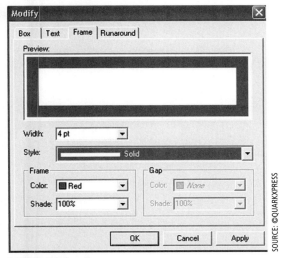

Modify Dialog Box

4. In the Frame section in the Modify dialog box, click the drop-down Color box and choose Red. Click on Apply and OK.
5. Go to the menu bar and choose File > Save As. Name the file *SATPrepFlyer.qxd*.

## Picture Box Tool

1. Click on the Picture Box tool. Hold down the mouse button on the icon to see all the choices. Select the beveled-corner Picture Box tool.

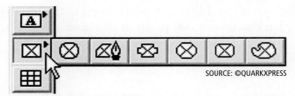

Picture Box Tools

2. Click on the document underneath the rectangle with the title in it. Drag the mouse pointer out to 4 inches on the horizontal ruler and 4 inches down on the vertical ruler.
3. Go to the menu bar and choose File > Get Picture.
4. Browse in your collection of clip art and select a picture of food.
5. Use the Content tool to move the picture up toward the top left side of the picture box to make room for a text box. See the Sample Picture Box.
6. Click on the Text Box tool and choose the rounded-corner Text Box tool.
7. Use the Content tool to type "Lunch Served at Noon."
8. Go to the menu bar and choose Style > Size. Change the size to an appropriate size for the area.
9. Go to the menu bar and choose Style > Type Style > Bold.
10. Go to the menu bar and choose Style > Alignment > Centered.

## Rotation Tool

1. Click on the Rotation tool.
2. The Rotation tool rotates items manually.
3. Hold the Rotation tool down in the middle of the text box. When it turns into the cursor seen in the figure to the left, drag the box to the angle you desire.

## Color Palette

1. Click on the Background Color icon in the Color palette.
2. Choose Red for the background color.
3. Click on the Text Color icon in the Color palette.
4. Change the text color to White.
5. Draw a rectangular text box on the right side of the picture box. Fill the area left on the right side with the box.
6. Type the following in the rectangular text box:
   Saturday
   February 23, 2XXX
   8 A.M. to 4 P.M.
   Cost: $20.00

## Character Attributes

1. Use the Content tool to select the text you typed in the rectangular text box.
2. Go to the menu bar and choose Style > Character. Note that "Character" has an ellipsis after the word, which means that a dialog box will be available to make

**Sample Picture Box**
SOURCE: ©QUARKXPRESS

**Rotation Tool**
SOURCE: ©QUARKXPRESS

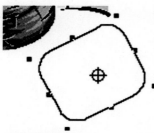

**Rotation Cursor**
SOURCE: ©QUARKXPRESS

**Background Color**

SOURCE: ©QUARKXPRESS

changes. You can make these changes individually on the Style menu, but by opening the Character Attributes dialog box, you can make several changes to fonts at one time.

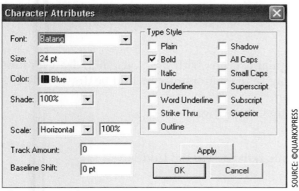

Character Attributes

3. Change the font to Batang, the size to 24 pt. and the color to Blue.
4. Change the type style to Bold. Click on Apply and OK.
5. Go to the menu bar and choose Style > Alignment > Centered.
6. Go to the menu bar and choose Item > Frame.
7. In the Modify dialog box, change the width to 2 pt and the frame color to Red.
8. Click on Apply and OK.

## Setting Formats

1. Click on the Text Box tool and choose Rectangle.
2. Draw a rectangular text box from the left to the right margin and from 4 inches to 7 inches vertically.
3. Type the following in the rectangular text box:
   NOTES:
   Get plenty of rest before the class.
   Eat a good breakfast.
   Bring pens, highlighters, and paper.
   Dress comfortably.
4. Select the text and change the size to 28 pt. and the color to Blue.
5. Go to the menu bar and choose Style > Tabs.
6. In the Paragraph Attributes dialog box, choose the Left tab, type ".5" for Position, and click on Set. Click on Apply and OK.
7. With the Content tool, select the NOTES line and the first enumeration.

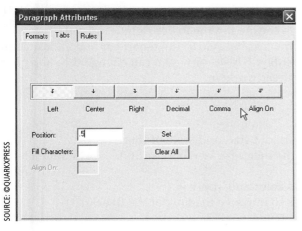

Paragraph Attributes

8. Go to the menu bar and choose Style > Formats. In the Space Before box, type ".25."
9. Click on Apply and OK.
10. In the Color palette, click on Background Color.
11. Choose Red at 10% shading.

## Hyperlinking

1. At the left below the rectangular text box with the Notes in it, draw a rounded-corner text box. It should snap to the bottom margin and be drawn to 4-1/2 inches on the horizontal ruler.
2. Type the following information in the box:
   Your High School Name
   City, State Zip
   Your School Phone Number, including Zip Code
   For More Information:
   www.kaplan.com
3. Use the Content tool to select the text.
4. Go to the menu bar and choose Style > Character. Choose Comic Sans MS, Size 24, 70% shaded Blue. Click on Apply and OK.
5. Go to the menu bar and choose Style > Alignment > Centered.
6. Select the word "Information," including the colon. Change the font color to Red.
7. Select the Web address for Kaplan Test Prep.
8. Go to the menu bar and choose Style > Hyperlink > New.
9. In the New Hyperlink dialog box, type in the following URL: http://www.kaplan.com.

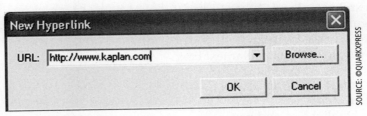

New Hyperlink

10. Go to the menu bar and choose Item > Frame. Change the frame to 2 pt. with Red as the color.
11. Move the text box as needed within the area.

## Changing Shapes

1. Click on the text box tool.
2. Draw a rectangular text box in the area in the lower right.
3. Use the Item tool to click on the text box. Go to the menu bar and choose Item > Shape > Concave-Corner Text Box. This is how you can change the shape of the picture or text box after it is already drawn.
4. Type the following in the box:
   Presented by
   Kaplan Inc.
5. Decide on an appropriate font, font size, and style of font.
6. With the text selected, go to the menu bar and choose Style > Alignment > Centered.
7. Determine a frame width and color and apply it.
8. Make any formatting changes to improve the look of the flyer.
9. Save the document.

## ACTIVITY 1 • MINI-PROJECT

### Create a Flyer for a Newspaper Advertisement

1. Use the skills you learned in creating a flyer to create a flyer that can be used in a newspaper advertisement.
2. Go to http://www.graphicsetc.net. Click on Flyer Samples. There are six examples of excellent flyers used in advertising situations. Choose one of the flyers. Print it out to use the information on the flyer. Re-create the flyer. It does not have to be exact, but it should be close. Use your own images from clip art or the Internet, or use scanned or digital images. If the Web site is no longer available, go to a search engine and search for "Sample Flyers." Get the flyer approved by your instructor before beginning.
3. Save the flyer as *Advertisement.qxd*.
4. The following criteria should be met:
   - ☐ Replication of sample flyer demonstrated attention to detail.
   - ☐ No errors on flyer.
   - ☐ Colors are close or follow design rules.
   - ☐ Font choices create a similar image to the original flyer and are sized appropriately.
   - ☐ Images of good quality with correct size and type.
   - ☐ Effort demonstrated on the flyer.
   - ☐ Flyer effects a positive image.

## ACTIVITY 2 • BROCHURE

In this activity, you will become familiar with:

- Document Setup for Brochures
- Inserting Pages
- Deleting Pages
- Resizing Pictures
- Get Text
- Drop Cap
- Line Tool
- Bring Forward
- Changing Pages
- Line Text-Path Tool

### Document Setup for Brochures

1. Go to the menu bar and choose File > New > Document.
2. In the New Document dialog box, change Orientation to Landscape and Column Guides to 3.
3. Click on Facing Pages.
4. Clear the Automatic Text Box check box. This box can be used to fill the entire page with color if desired, but you will not be using it. You can easily delete this box using the Item tool if you decide after the Document Setup that you do not need it.
5. Click OK.
6. Go to the menu bar and choose View > Fit in Window.

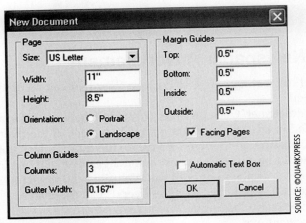

SOURCE: ©QUARKXPRESS

Brochure Specs

## Inserting Pages

1. Go to the menu bar and choose Page > Insert.
2. In the Insert Pages dialog box, type "2" in the box for the number of pages to insert.

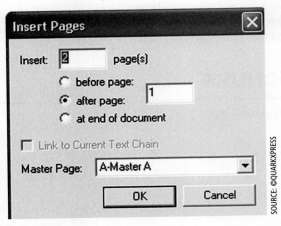

SOURCE: ©QUARKXPRESS

Insert Pages

3. Do not make any other changes to the other defaults. Click OK.

## Deleting Pages

1. Go to the menu bar and choose Page > Delete.
2. In the Delete Pages dialog box, type "3" in the box for the page number to delete.

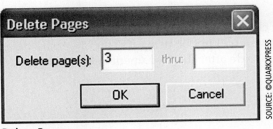

SOURCE: ©QUARKXPRESS

Delete Pages.

3. Click OK.

# Resizing Pictures

1. Click in the Ruler Origin area and drag the crosshairs so that the horizontal and vertical rulers are both on 0 at the top and left margin guides.
2. Click on the Picture Box tool.
3. At the top half of the third column, draw a picture box.
4. Begin at 7-1/2 inches on the horizontal ruler and drag over to approximately 9-1/2 inches. On the vertical ruler, begin at 1 inch and drag down to approximately 2-1/2 inches.
5. Go to the menu bar and choose File > Get Picture.
6. Browse to the CD and double-click on *WaterLily.jpg*.
7. Go to the menu bar and choose Style > Center Picture.
8. Go to the menu bar and choose Style > Fit Picture to Box.
9. Drag on the bottom right handle to decrease the size of the box. Notice that the image does not resize with the box. Click Undo.
10. Hover the mouse pointer over the bottom right handle. Hold down the Ctrl key. Drag to increase the size of the picture box. Notice that holding down the Ctrl key also increases the size of the picture with the box.
11. Resize the picture box appropriately for the area at the top of the front page of the brochure.
12. Use the Item tool to reposition. Reminder: The Item tool moves the box, whereas the Content tool moves the picture inside the box.
13. With the picture box selected, go to the menu bar and choose Item > Shape. Select the circular shape.
14. Save the brochure as *Quark.qxd*.
15. Create a text box with the text "Quark, Inc." inside it.
16. Fill the text box with yellow, Linear Blend.
17. Change the font size, color, and type.
18. Change the alignment to Centered for the text.
19. Rotate the text box and place it on the right edge of the water lily image.
20. Add a text frame to the text box that is the same color as the text.

# Get Text

1. Use the Rectangular text box tool to draw a text box beginning at 4 inches on the vertical ruler. Snap the text box to the bottom margin.
2. Use the Content tool to click inside the box.
3. Go to the menu bar and choose File > Get Text.
4. Browse to your CD to get *WaterLily.doc*.
5. Select the text that you imported.
6. Change the font type.

# Drop Cap

1. Go to the menu bar and choose Style > Formats.
2. In the Paragraph Attributes dialog box, click on drop caps.
3. Leave the Character Count at 1. Change the Line Count to 2.
4. Go to the Internet and search for articles on water lilies. Add two more sentences to the article on water lilies that tie in with the positive image this company has created.
5. You can add another image of a water lily from your available clip art or the Internet if appropriate.

# Line Tool

1. Draw a rectangular text box in the first column. Snap the rectangular box to all the margins.

2. Fill the entire text box with Yellow, shaded at 20%.
3. Type "History" at the top of the rectangular box. Format "History" in Size 36 font.
4. Change the font color to Pink.
5. Change the alignment to Centered.
6. Click on the Line tool.
7. Draw a line below the title from the left margin to the right margin.
8. With the line still selected, go to the menu bar and choose Style > Line Style. Change the line style to Thin-Thick.
9. Go to the menu bar and choose Style > Line Style. Change the width to 4 pt.
10. Go to the menu bar and choose Style > Color > Magenta.

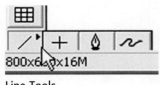

Line Tools

## Bring Forward

1. With the line selected, go to the menu bar and choose Item > Bring Forward.
2. Use the Content tool to click in the area below the line.
3. Go to the menu bar and choose File > Get Text. Browse to your CD and locate *History.txt*.
4. Change the font color to Blue and the font size to 12 and choose a font type.
5. Select all the text and change the after paragraph spacing to .125 and the first line indent to .25.
6. Save the file.

## Changing Pages

1. On the status bar at the bottom left of the Quark screen, click on the right arrow next to the page number box.
2. You should see three pages. The left page with the "A" on it represents the Master Page. Click on the page with the number 2 on it.

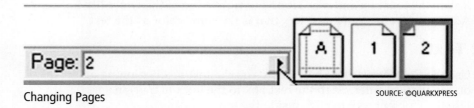

Changing Pages

## Line Text-Path Tool

1. Click on the Line Text-Path tool.
2. Draw a line at an angle across the middle column at the bottom half of the column.
3. Type "Be a Star!" on the line.
4. Format the text size, color, and font type.
5. Go to the menu bar and choose Style > Width. Change the width to 4 pt.
6. Go to the menu bar and choose Style > Color. Change the color of the line.
7. Draw a picture box near the angled line.
8. Get the picture *Star.gif* from your CD.
9. With the picture selected, go to the menu bar and choose Style > Fit Picture to Box.
10. Use the Line Text-Path tool to add a straight line below the picture. Hold down the Shift key while drawing the line to get a perfectly straight line.
11. Type the text "Join the Quark Team!" on the line.
12. Format the text as appropriate.

Line Text-Path Tools

Star

13. In the left column, draw a text box and type the title "Getting Hired." Format the font appropriately for color, size, and type. Center the title horizontally.
14. Draw a text box down to 5 inches on the vertical ruler. Snap the text box to the right margin of the column.
15. Go to the Quark Web site at http://www.quark.com. Write an article in the text box answering these questions:

    What are the hiring policies of Quark?

    What does it take to advance at Quark?
16. At the bottom of this column, add a digital picture of someone at your school working.
17. In the middle column, add a text box and title it "Dress Code Policy." Write an article explaining the Quark dress code policy.
18. In the third column, draw a text box in the entire column. Title the article "Building a Work Team."
19. Write an article explaining the following:

    Name at least three things that Quark believes are important to building a successful team.

    Describe some other company policies that help to build the team.
    *Hint:* These specifically revolve around food.
20. Change font types, color, and size as appropriate. Use alignment, fill color, and box color to enhance the brochure.
21. Save the document.

## ACTIVITY 2 • MINI-PROJECT

## Create a Brochure to Sell a Multimedia Book

1. You are an employee of South-Western Publishing Company, the publisher of your textbook. Create a brochure to assist in selling the textbook to teachers. Plan the brochure before beginning. Include as a minimum the following details:
   a. Name of textbook
   b. Authors
   c. Publication date
   d. Listing of units covered
   e. Special features in the textbook
   f. Overall mission statement of what the book is attempting to accomplish
2. Include scanned pictures from the textbook.
3. Save as *MultimediaText.qxd.*
4. The following criteria should be met:

   ☐ Minimum details required are included.

   ☐ Information displayed on the brochure in an organized manner.

   ☐ Colors appropriate and used effectively.

   ☐ Images appropriate size and type and of good quality.

   ☐ Fonts varied and appropriate type, size, and color.

   ☐ Minimum of one stacked text box and/or picture box with use of Bring Forward.

   ☐ Minimum of one use of Line tool.

   ☐ Minimum of one use of Line Text-Path tool.

   ☐ No errors on the brochure.

# ACTIVITY 3 • NEWSLETTER

In this activity, you will become familiar with:

- Document Setup for Newsletters
- Creating Style Sheets
- Scissors Tool
- Tabs
- New Colors
- Linking Text Boxes
- Freehand Line Tool
- Rules
- Cutting and Pasting Text
- Runaround
- Anchor
- Spelling
- H&Js
- Master Pages
- Tables
- Bullets

## Document Setup for Newsletters

1. Go to the menu bar and choose File > New.
2. In the New Document dialog box, change to portrait orientation, clear the Facing Pages check box, select the Automatic Text Box check box, and type 2 in the number of columns box.
3. Click OK.
4. Go to the menu bar and choose View > Fit in Window.
5. Drag the Ruler Origin crosshairs to 0.
6. Save the document as *XPert Publishing.qxd*.

## Creating Style Sheets

1. Go to the menu bar and choose Edit > Style Sheets.
2. In the Style Sheets for *XPert Publishing.qxd* dialog box, click on New, then Character.

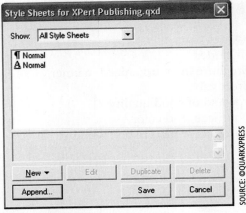

Style Sheets

SOURCE: ©QUARKXPRESS

Masthead

3. Make the changes in character style seen in the figure to the left. Name the style "Masthead." You do not need to type anything in Keyboard Equivalent.

4. Click on Save.
5. Use the Rounded-Corner Text Box tool to draw a Text Box across the top margin from left to right and down to 1-1/4 inches on the vertical ruler.
6. Type "XPert Publishing" in the text box.
7. Use the Content tool to select the text.
8. Go to the menu bar and choose Style > Character Style Sheet > Masthead.

## Scissors Tool

1. Click on the Scissors tool.
2. Use the Scissors tool to click on the top left corner of the rectangular text box. You will get the warning seen below.

Scissors Tool
SOURCE: ©QUARKXPRESS

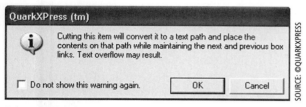

**QuarkXPress (tm)**

Cutting this item will convert it to a text path and place the contents on that path while maintaining the next and previous box links. Text overflow may result.

☐ Do not show this warning again.    OK    Cancel

SOURCE: ©QUARKXPRESS

Scissors Warning

3. Click OK.
4. Use the Item tool to click on the bottom part of the rectangular text box and press Delete to remove it. See below for an example of your finished masthead. It does not have to look exactly like the figure.

Volume 1, Issue 1                                April 10, 20XX

XPert Masthead

SOURCE: ©QUARKXPRESS

5. Format the line for 2 pt width, cyan color.

## Tabs

1. Use the Rounded Rectangular Text Box tool to draw a rounded-corner picture box about 1/2-inch long. The width should extend from the left to the right margin.
2. Use the Content tool to click within the rounded-corner picture box.
3. Go to the menu bar and choose Style > Tabs.
4. In the Paragraph Attributes dialog box, click on Right and type in the position 7.0.

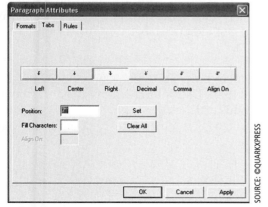

**Paragraph Attributes**

Formats  Tabs  Rules

Left    Center    Right    Decimal    Comma    Align On

Position:  7"        Set
Fill Characters:      Clear All
Align On:

OK    Cancel    Apply

SOURCE: ©QUARKXPRESS

Tabs

5. Click on Set.
6. In the rounded-corner picture box, type at the left margin "Volume 1, Issue 1."
7. Press the Tab key once. Type the current date.
8. Use the Content tool to select the text you typed and change the font to Batang or a similar font.

## New Colors

1. Go to the menu bar and choose Item > Frame.
2. Change the width to 2 pt.
3. Click in the Color drop-down list and choose Other.
4. In the New Color dialog box, type "Purple" for the name and choose a purple color from the color wheel.

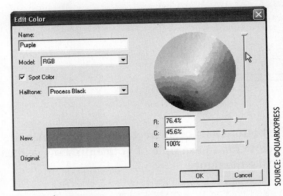

New Color

5. Click OK.
6. Draw a rounded-rectangle text box to place behind the company name.
7. Use the new color Purple for the background at 30% shading.
8. Add a 2 pt cyan border to the rounded-rectangle text box.
9. Go to the menu bar and choose Item > Send Backward.
10. Save the document.

## Linking Text Boxes

1. Use the Rectangular Text Box tool to draw a text box in the first column. Draw a second text Box in the second column.
2. Click on the Content tool.
3. Choose File > Get Text.
4. Browse to your CD and double-click on *Typefaces.doc.*
5. Note that at the bottom of the first column, the red box appears indicating more text that did not fit in that column. See the figure labeled More Text.
6. Click on the Linking tool.
7. Click anywhere in the first column to establish the beginning link.
8. Click anywhere in the second column to link to the first column.
9. Click in front of Typeface and type a title. Use your creativity to come up with a title for the first four paragraphs of this article.
10. Change the font to a sans serif font, Size 18. Center the text horizontally. Change the color to one of the two colors used in the masthead.

## Freehand Line Tool

1. Click on the Freehand Line tool.
2. Draw a squiggly line from the left to right margin underneath the title you created.

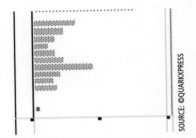

More Text

Linking Tool

SOURCE: ©QUARKXPRESS

Free Hand Line Tool

SOURCE: ©QUARKXPRESS

3. Choose Style > Color and choose one of the two colors that were used in the masthead.
4. Use the Content tool to click in front of the "T" in "Typeface."
5. Go to the menu bar and choose Style > Formats. Set a drop cap for the first paragraph.
6. Select the "T" in "Typefaces" and change the font to a fancy font.
7. Use the Content tool to click in front of "Size of your font . . . "
8. Use your creativity to come up with a title for the rest of the paragraphs in the article.
9. Change the font to a sans serif font, Size 18. Use a color to offset the colors already used on the page.

## Rules

1. With your cursor at the end of the title you created, go to the menu bar and choose Style > Rules.
2. Click on Rule Below.
3. Change the width to 2 pt. and choose a color.

## Cutting and Pasting Text

1. Select the third paragraph of the article.
2. Go to the menu bar and choose Edit > Cut.
3. Click on the Concave-Corner Text Box tool.
4. Draw a concave-corner text box from the right margin to the left margin, about 2 inches high.
5. With the Content tool inside the text box, go to the menu bar and choose Edit > Paste.
6. Resize the text box as needed.
7. Change the style of the frame to All Dots, 4 pt. width.
8. Decide on a fill color. Shade to 30%.

## Runaround

1. Go to the menu bar and choose Item > Runaround.
2. In the Modify dialog box, click the Runaround tab.

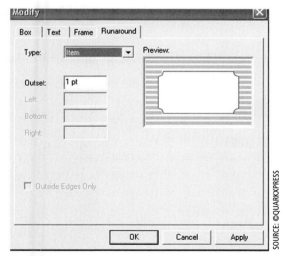

SOURCE: ©QUARKXPRESS

Runaround

3. In this case, the runaround has defaulted to wrapping the text around the box. Even though you have made no changes, click OK.

## Anchor

1. Use the Item tool to click on the freehand line you drew in column 1.
2. Go to the menu bar and choose Style > Anchor.
3. Click on New.

New Anchor

4. In the New Anchor dialog box, type in the name "Freehand" and click OK.
5. Change the first line indent on all paragraphs to .25.

## Spelling

1. Go to the menu bar and choose Utilities > Check Spelling > Document.

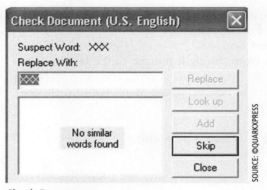

Check Document

2. In the Check Document dialog box, verify any words that were suspect. Make changes as needed.

## H&Js

1. Go to the menu bar and choose Edit > H&Js. (Hyphenation and Justification)
2. In the H&Js dialog box, double-click on Standard.

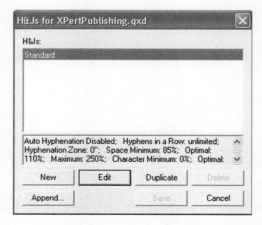

H&Js

SOURCE: ©QUARKXPRESS

3. In the Edit Hyphenation dialog box, clear the Auto Hyphenation check box. Note the other choices in the dialog box for future use.

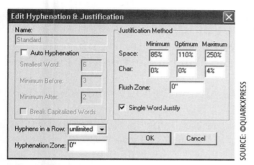

Edit Hyphenation

4. Click OK.
5. In the H&Js dialog box, click on Save to make the hyphenation change to your document.
6. Save the document.

## Master Pages

1. Use the Item tool to select the rounded-corner rectangle text box with the volume, issue, and date information in it.
2. Copy the rectangular text box.
3. Click on the Master Pages by going to the status bar and clicking on the drop-down arrow next to the page number.
4. Paste the rectangle on the Master Page, then drag the rectangle to snap it to the top margin.
5. You may need to delete the automatic text boxes before pasting.
6. Go to page 2 of the document. Note that the element you placed on the Master Page is now on page 2 of the document. It will also appear on any subsequent pages you add. Add a page to try it. Delete the extra page.

## Tables

1. Go to page 2 of the document.
2. Click on the Tables tool.
3. Draw a table that almost touches the left and the right margin and goes down 2 inches vertically.
4. In the Table Properties dialog box, type "6" for Rows and "6" for Columns.
5. Click OK.
6. Select the entire table by clicking and dragging the mouse.
7. Change alignment to Centered and size of the font to 18.
8. With Caps Lock on, type the following letters one per table cell:

    F O N T S P
    A G A E D O
    C O L O R I
    E X T P O N
    S A N S P T
    S E R I F X

## Bullets

1. Create a rectangular text box below the table you created.
2. Type in the text box: "Find the following words in the word search above:"

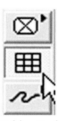

Tables Tool
SOURCE: ©QUARKXPRESS

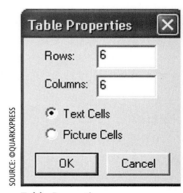

Table Properties

3. Go to the menu bar and choose Style > Tabs.
4. In the Paragraph Attributes dialog box, click in the Position box and type ".25," then click on Set. Be sure the Left button is clicked so that you are setting a Left Tab.
5. Type "1.75" in the Position box and click on Set.
6. Type "2.0" in the Position box and click on Set.
7. To create a bullet, hold down the Alt and Shift keys and press 8. Press Tab before typing "Fonts."
8. Press Tab again to 1.75. Hold down the Alt and Shift keys and press 8. Tab again to 2.0. Type "Color."
9. Hold down the Alt and Shift keys and press 8. Type "Serif." Tab to 1.75. Hold down the Alt and Shift keys and press 8. Tab to 2.0. Type "Faces."
10. Repeat this process to add "Sans" and "Point" with bullets in front of them.
11. Create a table with picture cells. The table should have one row and three columns.
12. Place a digital picture of yourself and two friends in each of the cells in the top row.
13. Below the table, draw another table that is the same size and specifications. This one should be for text.
14. Type the student names in the new table. Format the student names as needed.
15. Underneath the table, draw a line text path across from the left to the right margin.
16. Type on the text path: "Desktop Publishing Team."
17. Format the text, making effective choices for a headline.
18. Go to the Internet and search for "QuarkXPress tips" or "desktop publishing tips."
19. Complete the second column of the newsletter with articles or lists of tips. The following elements should be met:
    ☐ Headline in correct font and size with appropriate color.
    ☐ Minimum of two text boxes, appropriately placed and sized, one shaded in color.
    ☐ Minimum of two picture boxes; appropriate images, size, and placement.
    ☐ Bulleted list.
    ☐ Drop cap with fancy font.
    ☐ Minimum of one rule, either above or below.
    ☐ Minimum of one color change with appropriate color.
    ☐ Error-free.
    ☐ Design pleasing to the eye.
    ☐ No hyphenation.
    ☐ Freehand Line tool used with change in line width and color.

## ACTIVITY 3 • MINI-PROJECT

### Create a Newsletter on the Smithsonian Institution

1. Visit the Smithsonian Institution Web site at http://www.si.edu. Peruse the Web site, taking notes on announcements. You could also use an electronic encyclopedia to do research on the Smithsonian or visit a library. Organize your notes on 3 × 5 or 4 × 6 index cards that will be turned in to your instructor as part of the project. Decide on a longer article that can be written and two short articles. Be sure to explore the links to gather your information.
2. Use the Smithsonian logo on the newsletter. You may need to save the file from the Internet, then open it in your image management software and use your image management skills to make it appropriate for placement on your newsletter. Save as *SmithsonionLogo.gif*.

3. Study the image that the Web site has created for the Smithsonian Institution. Attempt to create a similar image for continuity.
4. Save as *SmithsonianNews.qxd*.
5. The following criteria should be met:
   - ☐ Index cards are organized and demonstrate evidence of note-taking that was used in the creation of the newsletter.
   - ☐ Colors appropriate for the topic.
   - ☐ Fonts appropriate in size, type, and color.
   - ☐ Images of quality and appropriate in size and type.
   - ☐ Logo altered effectively for this newsletter.
   - ☐ Creation of a style sheet.
   - ☐ Minimum of one use of Scissors tool.
   - ☐ New color added from color wheel.
   - ☐ Minimum of one use of linked text box.
   - ☐ Minimum of one use of Freehand Line tool.
   - ☐ Minimum of one use of rule above or below paragraph.
   - ☐ Minimum of one use of runaround.
   - ☐ Minimum of one use of bullets.
   - ☐ Minimum of one use of table.
   - ☐ No errors on newsletter.

# ACTIVITY 4 • BUSINESS SETS

In this activity, you will become familiar with:

- Document Setup for Letterhead Templates
- Show Invisibles
- Color Wheel
- Grouping
- Fit to Print Area
- Document Setup for Fax Transmittal Templates
- All Caps

## Document Setup for Letterhead Templates

1. Create a new document with the following attributes: portrait orientation, one column, non-facing pages, and no automatic text box. All other elements in the New Document dialog box should not be changed.
2. Drag the Ruler Origin crosshairs to 0 inches.
3. Draw a rectangular text box from the left to the right margin and down vertically to 1 inch.
4. Draw a rectangular picture box in the left corner of the rectangular text box. It should be approximately 1-1/4 inches wide.
5. Go to the menu bar and choose File > Get Picture. Browse to your CD and double-click *MAC.gif*.
6. Resize the picture box to fit the logo.
7. While holding down the Ctrl key, resize the text box to fit the rectangular text box vertically and horizontally. It should be approximately 1-1/2 inches.
8. Go to the menu bar and choose Item > Frame.
9. In the Modify dialog box, on the Frame tab, change the width to 4 pt. and choose a frame color of Cyan.
10. Beginning at 1-1/2 inches horizontally, draw a rectangular text box almost to the right margin. Snap to the bottom margin.

## Show Invisibles

1. Go to the menu bar and choose View > Show Invisibles. It sometimes helps to see the hard returns and tab codes. In the figure below, can you identify the paragraph code? The tab code?
2. Input the information for the first three lines (company name; street address; city, state, and zip) into the rectangular text box from the figure below.

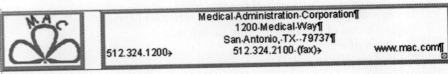

SOURCE: ©QUARKXPRESS

Invisibles

3. Select the three lines and go to the menu bar and choose Style > Alignment > Centered.
4. For the fourth line (telephone numbers and Web address), go to the menu bar and choose Style > Tabs.
5. On the tab ruler in the rectangular text box, set a center tab and a right tab. Determine the best place to set the center tab. Set the right tab as close to the right end of the ruler as possible.
6. Input the fourth line of the company information.
7. Select the four lines of text and change the font size to 12 and the color to Cyan.
8. With the rectangular text box selected, go to Item > Frame. Change the width to 4 pt. and choose Other for the color.

## Color Wheel

1. Use the color wheel to select a color that is close to the fuchsia color on the logo.
2. Drag the slider until you get a close color match to your document.

## Grouping

1. Click on the first text box, hold down the Shift key, and click on the picture box. Continue holding down the Shift key while selecting the other text box. When all three are selected, go to the menu bar and choose Item > Group.
2. Drag the entire group above the right margin. The top of the group should begin at approximately .75 on the vertical ruler.
3. Go to the bottom of the document.
4. Draw a rectangular text box at the bottom margin. It should go from the left to the right margin horizontally and about 1/2-inch on the vertical ruler.
5. Set a center tab and a right tab at the right margin.
6. Type the following names. Begin at the left margin but tab after each name.
     Madison Matilla, M.D.
     Ivan Abercrombie, Ph.D.
     Carlos Collier, M.D.
7. Select the three names. Change the color to cyan and italicize the font.
8. Use the Line Text-Path tool to draw a line from the left to the right margin above the names.
9. Change the line width to 4 pt. and the color to the new color you chose from the color wheel.
10. Group the text box and the line.
11. Drag the entire group down below the bottom margin. The line should snap to the bottom margin guide.

12. Go to the menu bar and chose File > Save As. In the Save as dialog box, click in the drop-down box for Save as type and choose Template (.qxt).

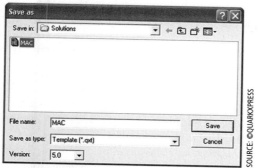

Save As Template

13. In the File name box, type "MAC."
14. Click on Save.

## Fit to Print Area

1. Go to the menu bar and choose File > Print.
2. In the Print dialog box, on the Setup tab, select the Fit in Print Area check box.

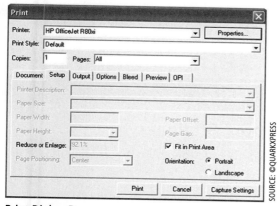

Print Dialog Box

3. Get printing instructions from your instructor.

## Document Setup for Fax Transmittal Templates

1. Open *MAC.qxt.*
2. Save it as *FAX.qxd.*
3. Draw a rectangular text box below the heading on the template. The text box should be approximately 1/4-inch from all margins.
4. Type "FAX" at the top left corner in the rectangular text box.
5. Select the word "FAX" and change the font to Berlin Sans, Size 60.
6. Immediately after the "X" in "FAX," change the font size to 14 and press Enter.
7. Type "To:" Use an underscore to type a line to approximately 3-1/2 inches on the ruler.
8. Tab so that there is at least one space between the underscore and the next word.
9. Type "From:" Type the underscore to the margin. Be sure it does not scroll to the next line. Erase any characters that scroll to the next line.

10. Repeat this process for the next line, typing the words "Fax:" and "Pages (including cover)."
11. Repeat this process on the third line, typing the words "Fax Number" and "Date."
12. Select the three lines. Go to the menu bar and choose Style > Formats.
13. On the Formats tab in the Paragraph dialog box, type ".1" in the Space Before and Space After blanks.
14. On the next line, type "Confidentiality Notice." Bold, italicize, and center the text.
15. Type the following paragraph in italic but not bold:

*The information contained in this fax may be confidential or privileged. This fax is intended to be reviewed initially only by the individual named above. If the reader of this transmittal page is not the intended recipient or a representative of the intended recipient, you are hereby notified that any review, dissemination, or copying of this fax or the information contained herein is prohibited. If you have received this fax in error, please immediately notify the sender by telephone and return this fax to the sender at the above address. Thank you.*

16. Type the word "Comments" a double space below the end of the preceding paragraph.
17. Select the rectangular text box and add a 2 pt. thick-thin-thick frame to it.
18. Go to the menu bar and choose Utilities > Check Spelling > Document. Replace any misspelled words. Verify all names.
19. Select the word "To:"

## All Caps

1. Go to the menu bar and choose Styles > Type Style > All Caps. Repeat this process for the next five captions.
2. Save the document as *FAX.qxt*.

## ACTIVITY 4 • MINI-PROJECT

## Create a Template for School Stationery

1. Visit with your instructor or principal to get the following information:
   a. Official school logo
   b. Mission statement or slogan
   c. Copy of official school letterhead and fax cover sheet
   d. Address, phone number, fax number, Web address, and email address for the school. Find out what the principal wants included on his or her business card.
2. Design a business card for the principal using the school logo and all other information necessary for a business card. Save as *Principal.qxd*.
3. Design school letterhead. Save as *SchoolLetter.qxt*. Notice that it is being saved as a template.
4. Design a fax cover sheet. Save as *SchoolFax.qxt*. Notice that it is being saved as a template.
5. The three designed pieces in a set should include the following criteria:
   ☐ Continuity of logo, slogan, and theme on all designs.
   ☐ No errors on any design.
   ☐ Images appropriate in type, size, and placement.
   ☐ Color appropriate to school colors.
   ☐ Fonts appropriate in size, type, and color.
   ☐ Creativity demonstrated in creation of letterhead.
   ☐ Fax cover sheet is realistic in terms of cost and expense of printing.
   ☐ White space balanced on all designed pieces.

# ACTIVITY 5 • CREATING A BOOK

In this activity, you will become familiar with:

- Setting Up a Document for a Book
- Page Numbering
- Find/Change
- New Book
- Add Chapter
- Book Palette
- Synchronizing Styles

## Setting Up a Document for a Book

1. Go to the menu bar and choose File > New > Document.
2. In the New Document dialog box, set up the document for portrait orientation, one column, facing pages, and automatic text box. Click OK.
3. Go to the status bar and click in the drop-down box. Choose the Master Document. You can also view the Master Document by going to the menu bar and choosing Page > Display > Master Document.
4. Create a rectangular text box in the top left corner. Type "Good Attitudes."
5. Go back to the document by going to the status bar and clicking on the drop-down arrow. Choose page 1.
6. Click inside the automatic text box on page 1. Use the shortcut Ctrl + Shift + C to center the line.
7. Type "Chapter 1."
8. Change the font to Size 16. Choose a sans serif font.
9. Before returning to the next line, change the font size to 14.
10. Press Enter twice. Type "Perseverance."
11. Press Enter twice. Use Ctrl + L to place your cursor at the left margin.
12. Go to the menu bar and choose File > Get Text.
13. Browse to your CD and double-click *Perseverance.doc.*

## Page Numbering

1. Go to the menu bar and choose Page > Section.
2. In the Section dialog box, accept the default. You can also change the numbering to start on each section by clicking on Section Start check box.
3. Click OK.

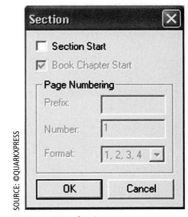

Page Numbering

## Find/Change

1. Go to the top of your document by pressing Ctrl + Home.
2. Go to the menu bar and choose Edit > Find/Change.
3. In the Find/Change dialog box, click in the Find What box and type "replace."

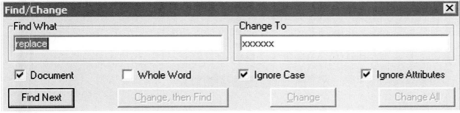

Find/Change

4. Click in the Change To box and type "xxxxxxx."
5. Click the Find Next button.

6. The cursor should stop on the first occurrence, allowing you to Change, then Find; Change, or Change All.
7. Choose Change then Find to check each occurrence.
8. When you have reached the end of the document, click on the document, then press Ctrl + Home to return to the top of the document.
9. In the Find What box, type "Find." Do not make a change in the Change To box.
10. Click on Find Next and change each occurrence as necessary in the document.
11. Save the document as *Chapter1.qxd*.

## New Book

1. Go to the menu bar and choose File > New > Book.
2. In the New Book dialog box, type "Good Attitudes." Click on Create.

**Add Chapter**

## Add Chapter

1. In the Good Attitudes dialog box, click on the Add Chapter icon.
2. Browse to your CD to find Chapter 1 and double-click on it. The first chapter always has an M beside it, as it is considered the Master Chapter.
3. Go to the menu bar and choose File > New > Document. Click OK to accept the defaults.
4. Click inside the automatic text box.
5. Type "Chapter 2" in Size 16 aligned at the center.
6. Press Enter twice. Type "Enjoy Life" in size 14 aligned at the center.
7. Press Enter twice. Go to the menu bar and choose File > Get Text.

## Book Palette

1. Browse to your CD and double-click *EnjoyLife.doc*.
2. At this point, the Book palette should still be floating in your document window. If it is not, it means the book is closed. Closing the Book palette will also close all open documents that have been added to the book.
3. Follow steps 3 through 7 in the "Add Chapter" section, and replace Chapter Numbers and Chapter Names with the following:

   Chapter3  *BeAccountable.doc*
   Chapter4  *HelpOthers.doc*
   Chapter5  Think of your own good attitude for this chapter.
             Insert the file *Think.doc*.
   Chapter6  Think of one more good attitude for this last chapter.
             Insert the file *OneMore.doc*.

   When you have finished, you should have six chapters added to the Book palette. See below.

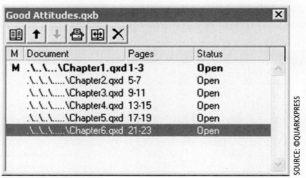

Book Palette

4. Once you have named the book, the book will automatically save changes.
5. Go to the menu bar and choose Edit > Style Sheets.
6. In the Style Sheets dialog box, click on New. Choose Paragraph Style Sheet on the pop-up menu.
7. In the Edit Paragraph Style Sheet dialog box, click on the General tab.
8. Name the style sheet Book, based on Normal.
9. In the Edit Paragraph Style Sheet dialog box, in the Character Attributes section, click on New.
10. In the Edit Character Style Sheet dialog box, name the style sheet "Book." Change the font to Times New Roman, 11 pt. See below.

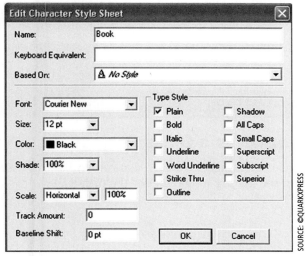

Style Sheet

11. Click OK.
12. In the Edit Paragraph Style Sheet dialog box, click on the Formats tab.

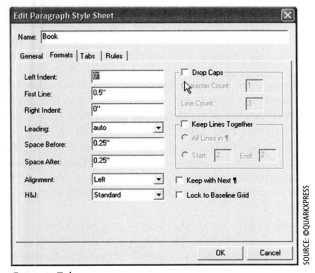

Formats Tab

13. Change the First Line indent to .5 inches.
14. Change the Space Before and Space After to .25 inches. Be sure the Alignment is on Left.
15. Click OK in the Edit Paragraph Style Sheet dialog box.
16. Click Save.

## Synchronizing Styles

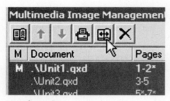

Synchronize

SOURCE: ©QUARKXPRESS

1. On your Book palette, click on Chapter 1. Hold down the Shift key and click on Chapter 6. This should highlight (select) all the units in the book.
2. Click on the Synchronize button on the Book palette. In the Synchronize Selected Chapters dialog box, click on Title and Subtitle.
3. Click on the right arrow for each of them to move them to the right pane.
4. Click OK.
5. Save the changes to your document by going to the menu bar and choosing File > Save.

# ACTIVITY 5 • MINI-PROJECT

## Create a Literary Magazine as a Class Project

1. Divide into four teams. If the class is larger than 20, you can add a fifth team. Decide on another section in the literary magazine for the fifth team.
   a. Poetry
   b. Short Stories
   c. Songs
   d. Art
2. In your team, brainstorm and submit a name to your instructor for the literary magazine. Submit the name with an appropriate font in a word processing program or image management software. Be creative! Save as *MagazineName* in the software you chose. The final name can be voted on by the class. As a class, decide on colors to use.
3. In your team, create a logo to use on the front cover of the literary magazine. Submit to your instructor. Create the logo in image management software and save as *MagazineLogo*. The logo can be evaluated by an advisory board, principals, or other group of school employees to determine which one will be used on the cover.
4. Within your team, each team member should be responsible for bringing to class five original pieces of art in the team's assigned area. For instance, the Poetry team will bring in five pieces of poetry. The poetry can be written by the student or a friend or relative. If students wish to, they can work with their English instructor to get some from an English class. It is recommended that the Short Story team bring in only two short stories each, depending on their length.
5. The team should create a division cover and save it as *DivisionCover.qxd*.
6. Each team will elect a leader from their team to report to the class and instructor on their progress and activities.
7. The team should create a Productivity Form that will keep a record of the date, assigned task, and team member completing the task. Each team should save their part of the book as the chapter number. Chapter 1 is Poetry; Chapter 2 is Short Stories; Chapter 3 is Songs; Chapter 4 is Art.
8. Each team will obtain the other chapters from the other teams. They will build the book with all four chapters in it and an index with a title page and cover pages for each chapter. Each team should be responsible for creating five copies of the book and binding it.

9. Save the final copy of the literary magazine as *ClassProject.qxd*.
10. The following criteria should be met:
    - ☐ Teams worked productively with all members contributing.
    - ☐ No errors on the copy of the magazine.
    - ☐ Work finished in a timely manner.
    - ☐ Appropriate colors used.
    - ☐ Appropriate fonts in style, size, and type used.
    - ☐ Images appropriate in size, color, and type.
    - ☐ Final product was put together correctly, organized, and bound.

# PART 3 • SIMULATION

## Using Quark to Market an Aquarium Business

1. John Wally is opening an aquarium business next month. It will be located at 3005 Aquarium Blvd., Corpus Christi, TX 78404. The phone number is 512/830-7708 and the fax number is 512/830-8077. They do not currently have a Web site, but there are plans for one in the immediate future. The Aquarium Center, Inc., will sell fish and tanks as well as all the accessories.
2. You decide to apply for a job as the marketing director and get the job. Your first assignment is to complete the following tasks:
   a. Create a flyer announcing the grand opening. It is the first Saturday in June. Mr. Wally has given you a $100 budget to offer door prizes or free give-aways. You need to decide on what you will do with the $100. Create a folder titled *Aquarium*. Save the grand opening flyer in the *Aquarium* folder as *GrandOpening.qxd*.
   b. Create a brochure to assist in marketing the new business. You may want to visit a fish store before beginning the brochure to get some prices and types of equipment and fish you will keep in your store. Some of the information you can get from the Internet by searching for goldfish, tropical fish, aquariums, and so on. Use a variety of sources for your information on the brochure. Interview or email someone who is in the business. Prepare a list of questions prior to the interview about how this person has marketed his or her business. Obtain a copy of anything he or she has used to develop a business image. Save the brochure in the *Aquarium* folder as *Brochure.qxd*.
   c. Create a business card, letterhead, and fax cover sheet. Design a logo to place on these business sets. Save in the *Aquarium* folder as *BusinessCard.qxd*, *Letterhead.qxt*, and *FaxCover.qxt*.
   d. Create a newsletter full of fun facts about fish. Research on the Internet, in an electronic encyclopedia, or at your library to obtain facts. You can also include some interesting fish stories. This newsletter should be geared toward the younger population as they will frequent the store. Include at least one word search puzzle created in a table with different names of fish. Save in the *Aquarium* folder as *FunFacts.qxd*.
   e. Build a book of at least four chapters and ten pages in length. The chapters can include Diseases of Fish, Types of Fish, Filtration Systems, and Tropical Fish Aquariums. You are not limited to these four; they are only sugges-tions for your chapters. You could also research four different types of fish and write a chapter on each type of fish you researched. Save the book in the *Aquarium* folder as *Book.qxd*.
   f. Create a tabloid-size poster to place on the door advertising some specials. Save in the *Aquarium* folder as *Specials.qxd*.

g.  Create an advertisement for the local newspaper announcing the grand opening as well as some specials. Save in the *Aquarium* folder as *Ad.qxd*.

3.  The following criteria should be met:

☐ All nine items saved correctly in the *Aquarium* folder.
☐ An effective business image created throughout the simulation.
☐ Colors appropriate and used throughout the simulation.
☐ Appropriate fonts in size, type, and style applied to all documents.
☐ Images creative and taken from a variety of sources.
☐ White space balanced and effectively used on all documents.
☐ Projects show some initiative and effective use of most tools learned in Quark.
☐ Documents are error-free.
☐ Information on aquariums is accurate and shows evidence of research.

# Glossary

**agenda**   a list of items to be discussed during a meeting, providing a reason for holding the meeting

**alignment**   the placement of text on a line either to the left, to the right, centered, or justified

**alpha channel**   a special channel used to store masks

**ambient sound**   noise that occurs naturally such as footsteps or phones ringing; it is generally not speech

**analogous colors**   colors that are near each other on a color wheel

**animate**   to make text or an image move in some way, such as flying onto the slide or blinking on and off

**animated character**   a person or figure that appears on a screen to interact with the audience by talking to them

**animated GIFs**   several bitmap graphics joined into a single file to give them the appearance of motion

**animation scheme**   a set of animation choices that includes the animation, timing, and response

**anti-aliasing**   an image function that smooths out edges by making them slightly fuzzy

**artifact**   "spare" pixels that scanners and digital cameras often include in an image, usually caused by lossy compression algorithms

**ascender**   the part of a lowercase letter that extends above the x-height, as in the letter *t*

**asynchronous** term indicating that information is not given and received at the same time

**axis** the vertical (*y*) or horizontal (*x*) value or category defining information on a chart

**background** the "paper" on which a presentation will be seen by the audience

**banner ads** Web ads that often contain a logo and additional business information designed to give corporate identity to a page

**bit depth** a measurement to indicate how much information is gathered about the red, green, and blue components of a pixel

**bitmap** a graphic created by using pixels

**bleed** a layout design that places an image or block of color so that it ends at the exact edge of the paper

**brick and mortar** describes the actual buildings where products are sold

**build** a term used in presentation software meaning to create a slide show with all its animation and slide transitions arranged in sequential order

**business geographics** maps used for business purposes

**cascading style sheets** style sheets that include typographical information on how the page should appear

**cell padding** the space within a cell that separates or pads the text or image within the cell

**cell spacing** the amount of space between cells

**channel** a graphics option that separates an image into its basic colors

**client-side access** dynamic HTML code that stores information on the user's (client's) computer

**clip art** a picture or drawing created with the intention that the artwork will be used by others; clip art is packaged with desktop publishing software or can be purchased separately

**CMYK** cyan-magenta-yellow-black; the basic colors that are the best choice for print documents

**color scheme** a series of choices that assigns to each slide the same color of background, title, and bulleted list

**color theory** the relationship between colors often based on location of colors on a color wheel

**colored stock** paper that may range from a pale off-white to a vivid color

**complementary colors** colors that appear directly across from each other on a color wheel

**compression** the process of reducing the size of a graphics image

**consensus building** the process used to reach agreement by a team of people

**cookie** computer code that stores information about a visitor to a Web site

**cropping** the cutting away of one or more "sides" of a picture to remove unwanted areas and to increase the focus

**curly quotes**   rounded marks used for quotations marks and apostrophes

**data mapping**   data displayed in a shade or pattern on a map

**descender**   the part of a lowercase letter that extends below the baseline, as in the letter *g*

**desktop publishing**   the process of adding both text and graphics to a page to enhance the message; the use of word processing software or specialized desktop publishing software on a personal computer to create a document in which graphics and text enhance the message

**dingbats**   graphic symbols or ornaments, rather than letters or numbers

**display fonts**   fonts designed to attract attention to the design of the font, as well as to the words

**distiller**   the software installed as part of Acrobat that converts documents into PDF files so that they can be read by Acrobat Reader

**domain name**   the generic term used to describe a Web site name

**dot matrix**   a means of printing by placing a series of dots close together so that they give the appearance of printed letters

**DPI**   dots per inch; a measurement used with printers and scanners to indicate how many points of ink or pixels are contained in an inch

**drawing**   a general term for graphics software that uses mathematically defined lines and curves to create an image

**drop cap**   a large, often ornate, first letter of a paragraph

**dynamic HTML**   any of numerous software functions that allow Web pages to be interactive

**e-commerce**   the selling of products via the Internet

**em dash**   a line the width of the capital letter *M* in the font and point size being used; indicates a break in thought

**em space**   a space the width of a capital letter *M* in the font and point size being used

**en dash**   a line the width of the capital letter *N* in the font and point size being used; it is used in ranges of numbers, letters, or dates

**en space**   half the size of an em space; a space the width of a capital letter *N* in the font and point size being used

**feathering**   a graphics technique that slightly blurs the edges of an image

**filter**   an image management technique that enables you to make an instant change to an image, such as making the image appear to be painted rather than photographed

**firewall**   blocking software that prevents certain actions from occurring within a server; a firewall often blocks access to files without a password

**FireWire**   also known as IEEE 1394 and originally developed by Apple Computer, a high-speed means of transfer between a computer and a peripheral such as a camera

**flash**   files that are vector animations created with Macromedia Flash or Adobe LiveMotion

**focus plan**   determines the path the eye will follow on a page

**font**   originally included typeface, style, and size, but now the term is interchangeable with *typeface*

**frames**   a means of joining two or more Web pages so that they appear on a single page

**FTP**   the means of transferring files from one computer to another over a network, it is often used to transfer files to a Web server

**gradient**   a graphics technique that stretches an array of values of one color from one side of an image to another

**greeking**   the use of placeholder words that have no meaning to show where text is to be placed in a layout; also, the use of gray bars in some desktop publishing software to represent text that is too small to be legible on the screen

**grunge type**   a modern typeface that appears "distressed," with letters oddly shaped and not completely formed

**gutter**   a vertical column of white space

**hacking a site**   the unauthorized modification of a Web site usually in ways that distort the original purpose of the site

**hanging punctuation**   punctuation such as quotation marks that needs to "hang" outside a paragraph rather than line up with the text below

**home page**   the first page of a Web site, but generally saved as *index*

**HTML**   hypertext markup language, the code used to create Web pages

**hyperlinks**   text and/or pictures that can be used to connect one page to another regardless of the sequence of pages

**image map**   a graphic divided into two or more parts, each part assigned a different link

**interlacing**   a process that displays an image on a Web page in stages until the image has reached its full resolution

**intranet**   a network designed for providing information within a company or an organization; functions much as the Internet does for the world

**jargon**   specialized words used within a particular industry, often incorporating acronyms as shortcuts; W3C (World Wide Web Consortium) is an example of an acronym used in the Web design community

**kerning**   spaces certain characters closely enough that the smaller character fits under the larger

**keyframe**   where on a timeline an action such as movement begins

**keywords**   terms used to identify and locate a particular Web site

**kiosk**   a term that, when used in conjunction with a computer, describes a freestanding computer used by visitors

**lag time**   the time between the moment a word is spoken by one person and the moment it is heard by another person

**layering**   the process of building an image that appears to be a single picture when it is actually a series of pictures stacked on top of each other

**layout**   the arrangement on a page of all the key parts without regard to the specific content

**leading**   the space between lines of text or between paragraphs

**legend**   a key, generally found in a box, used to identify the numerical data on a chart

**ligature**   two characters tied to each other in such a way that they appear to be one unit, such as *a* and *e* to form æ

**logo**   a graphical symbol that uses both text and graphics to convey the identity of a business

**lossless**   a compression formula that does not change any pixel data

**lossy**   a compression formula that reduces the size of a file by removing certain pixels

**masking**   a means of modifying an image without actually changing the original

**master slide**   a single slide that can be designed once and then applied to many slides

**media**   in PowerPoint, a term that includes sound, video, and movies

**meta name**   an HTML tag that stores information about a Web site

**monospace font**   a font that looks as if it were created with a typewriter because each character is given the same space

**motion path**   the track that an animated text or image will follow as it appears on a slide

**multimedia**   the combination of sound, animation, graphics, video, and color in a document

**native**   describes the file format in which a particular graphics program automatically saves an image

**navigation links**   the means of guiding a visitor to a Web site from one page in the site to other pages

**noninterlacing**   a process that displays an image on a Web page by rendering it from top to bottom until the image is complete

**OCR**   optical character recognition; the process of converting a scanned image of text into editable "live" text on the computer

**optimization**   a means of compressing animations to reduce the size of the file

**orphan**   a line of text that appears at the top of a column or page with the rest of the paragraph appearing at the bottom of the previous column or page.

**Pack and Go**   a feature of Microsoft PowerPoint that compresses a presentation for ease of transfer to another computer; it may also include a reader that lets you view the presentation even if you do not have PowerPoint on your computer

**painting**   a general term for graphics software that uses pixels to create an image

**panning**   the use of a "hand" to move small distances on a map

**parallelism**   a grammatical term indicating that the basic structure of two or more sentence or phrases is similar

**PDF**   the acronym for Portable Document Format; the file extension .pdf identifies a document encoded in this format; Adobe's Acrobat Reader enables you to read PDF files without having the original software installed on your computer

**photographic composition**   the selection and arrangement of subjects within a photograph

**pixel**   a data representation of a specific color at a specific location in a matrix or grid; a rectangular collection of pixels can produce an image on a computer screen or on a printed page

**plug-in**   a small software program that plugs into a larger application to provide more capabilities; often used to create dynamic HTML

**plug-ins**   additional computer instructions that add functionality to a program

**point**   a type measurement that equals 1/72 of an inch

**PostScript**   a programming language that describes the appearance of images or text on the printed page

**pre-press check**   verifies that all files and fonts needed to print a document by a printing service are present.

**pull quote**   a short text or article extract set off by rules or in a box

**resolution**   the density of pixels in an image

**reverse type**   white type on a dark background, designed to make the type stand out

**RGB**   red-green-blue; the basic colors that are the best choice for Web pages or computer screens

**rollover**   the changing of an image or text when a mouse clicks on it or "rolls over" it

**rule**   a horizontal or vertical line

**rule of thirds**   visually dividing a photograph into thirds (either horizontally or vertically) to provide a satisfying balance

**sans serif**   a typeface without serifs

**schwag**   a term used for promotional products such as fuzzy animals, calculators, and other items designed to carry a company logo

**scrolling marquee**   text that moves across a Web page

**search engines**   programs that search for keywords in documents or in a database; databases that store information about Web sites

**Section 508**   a law that requires federal agencies to make their Web sites accessible to all users regardless of abilities

**seminar notebook** a bound document, often in a binder, that contains all the printed information needed for a conference or meeting

**serif** a typeface with extensions at the ends of the main strokes that define each letter; these extensions are called serifs

**server-side access** dynamic HTML code that stores information on the server computer

**slide layout** the arrangement of design elements on a slide

**slide transition** movement from one slide to another that might include some kind of animation

**spider** a software program that roams the Internet, searching for information about Web sites that it then sends to a search engine database

**state of the art** a term used to indicate the most current hardware or software which is generally also the most expensive

**streaming audio** a technique that allows sound to be heard before the complete file has been loaded onto the user's computer

**streaming video** a technique that allows the viewing of a movie before it has completely loaded and without placing as many demands on the computer resources

**synchronous** means at the same time; synchronous communication is when two people are speaking either in the same room or perhaps via a telephone

**tag** a specific piece of HTML code used to tell a Web browser how information should be displayed

**talking head** a derogatory term for a video of someone who talks on and on to the point of boring the audience

**team charter** specifically identifies the team's goals, values, and approach to handling the task at hand

**template** document masters predesigned by professionals who have already chosen the background, font size and color, and bullets to be used

**text wrapping** moves text away from a graphic so that it flows around the image

**texture** a Paint Shop Pro option for painting backgrounds and figures

**thumbnails** miniature versions of larger images, they are generally used to allow quick browsing through multiple images or pages; they speed up the download process by allowing viewers to choose whether they want to see the larger image

**timecode** a means of tracking groups of frames within a video

**timeline** a means of recording when events occur in a flash file

**tombstone** a design in which two heads are "bumped" into each other across columns

**tracking** the amount of space between characters

**transforming** changing an image, such as making it larger or a different color

**transparency**   a GIF option that removes the background color of an image

**tube**   a Paint Shop Pro option that provides a series of images that can be dropped onto a page at random spots; each time you click on a new spot, a different version of the image appears

**TWAIN**   an acronym indicating that the software can work with a scanner

**tweening**   a Macromedia term used to describe the process of making a gradual change in an image

**typeface**   the design of the letters, numbers, and symbols that make up a font

**typography**   the study of all elements of type including the shape, size, and spacing of the characters

**vector**   an image created by using a series of mathematically defined lines and curves rather than pixels, making the image easier to rescale

**video conferencing**   a live meeting in which the participants are not physically present in the same room

**voice recognition**   the technology that allows the spoken word to be transferred to a computer

**W3C**   an organization that approves changes to HTML code

**watermark**   a pale image placed on the background of a page; often used for logos or other identification

**Web browser**   a software program that allows you to view Web pages created for the Internet

**Web editor**   software that creates HTML code automatically as part of the Web design process

**Web server**   a computer used to store and broadcast Web pages

**Web site**   one or more Web pages linked to form a single site

**Web-hosting server**   the computer on which a Web site is stored and that is accessed whenever someone keys the site's address in a browser

**Web-safe colors**   the 216 colors that all users can see regardless of their computer displays

**white space**   the area on a page in which text or graphics are absent

**widow**   a sentence at the bottom of the column or page that is separated from the rest of its paragraph

**WordArt**   a desktop publishing option that creates a graphic out of text by using curves, colors, and other effects

# Index

display fonts, 95
monospace, 97
in presentations, 161
print standards, 126
proportional fonts, 97
type fonts, 94–95
Web design, 204–206
foreground color, 24
forming stage, 281
frames, 200, 202
framing, 49
FTP, 195–196
Fulcher, Lisa, 278–279
Futty, Mari Ann Binder, 278–279
fuzziness, 37

**G**

GIF files, 16–17
animated, 177–178
compression, 14, 16
format, 14
licensing fees, 14
transparent background for, 32
globalism, 247, 248
governmental agencies, 220–223
gradients, 34
graphics, 105–108. *See also* print graphics
captions, 108
clip art, 106
defined, 5
development of, 8
download time, 16
file types and sizes, 106–107
floating graphics, 105
informational graphics, 68
inline graphics, 105
placement of images, 105
text wrap, 107
vector graphics, 17–18, 28, 178
graphics files, 106–107
Graphics Interchange Format. *See* GIF files
graphs. *See* charts and graphs
grayscale, 22
greeking, 117–118
GroupSystems, 286
grunge type, 95
gutters, 116

**H**

hacking, 195
handouts, 240
hanging punctuation, 128
hardware advancements, 9
hearing impairment, 220–223
Hewlett-Packard DeskJet, 8
Hewlett-Packard ScanJet, 9
hex number, 206
high-end paint programs, 22–23
highlights, 37
home page, 192

HSL (hue-saturation-luminescence), 22
HTML (Hypertext Markup Language), 10
dynamic HTML, 214–215
Web editing, 190–191
World Wide Web Consortium, 219–220
hue, 22
hue-saturation-luminescence (HSL), 22
hyperlinks, 149
Hypertext Markup Language. *See* HTML
hyphens, 100–101

**I**

IBM Selectric typewriter, 6
IBM ViaVoice, 241
image editing, 21–28
bitmap images, 27
color printing, 24–25
color selection, 24
colors, 22–23
image programs, 22
layering, 26–27
vector images, 28
image effects, 31–37
channels, 34–35
color adjustment, 37
feathering, 34
filters, 32–33
gradients, 34
masking, 35–36
textures, 33
transparency, 32
tubes, 33
unsharp mask, 37
image file types, 13–18
image formats, 14–15
image management
defined, 5
history and evolution, 4–10
introduction, 4–5
programs for, 14
timeline of, 10
image maps, 202–203
image programs, 22
images
copyright, 22
interlaced images, 17
modifying, 32, 48, 52–53
noninterlaced images, 17
placement of, 105
quality of, 58–59
saving, 15
thumbnails, 118–119, 207
TIFF format, 16
Web design, 207–208
impact printers, 7–8
indention, 127–128
Industrial Light & Magic, 8
information
census information, 81, 82
company information, 290–291

financial information, 290–291
print standards and, 126
Web content and, 293
information packets, 240
informational graphics, 68
initiative, 121
ink-jet printers, 8
inline graphics, 105
Inspiration software, 285
interactive CD-ROM, 259
interlaced images, 17
international business etiquette, 247
Internet, 9–10. *See also Web entries*
interviews, 25, 246–247
intranet, 211
Iomega Zip drive, 9
italic, 96

**J**

jaggies, 28
jargon, 248
Jasc Paint Shop Pro, 14, 15, 17, 24, 32, 33, 34, 57, 60, 177
Java applets, 214
JavaScript, 214
JAWS, 220
job search, 17
Joint Photographic Experts Group. *See* JPEG files
JPEG/JPG files, 16, 17
compression formula, 17
unsharp mask, 37

**K**

kerning, 98
keyboarding, 94, 146
keyboards, ergonomic, 194
keyframe, 179
keywords, 225
kiosks, 257–259

**L**

laser printers, 8
layering, 26–27
layout
print design, 117–120
slide layouts, 156–158
leadership, 213
leading, 98
legends, 70, 80
Lempel-Ziv-Welch (LZW) formula, 16
letterheads, 238
licensing, 14, 106
ligature, 98
line graphs, 69
links, 149, 200, 201–202
logos, 236, 238, 293
lossless compression, 16
lossy compression, 16
Lotus 1-2-3, 68
luminescence, 22